African American History

African American History

Volume 1

Editor

Kibibi Mack-Shelton, PhD

Claflin University

SALEM PRESS

A Division of EBSCO Information Services, Inc.

Ipswich, Massachusetts

GREY HOUSE PUBLISHING

Some of the updated and revised essays in this work originally appeared in the following titles from the *Great Lives from History series: The 17th Century* (2005), *The 18th Century* (2006), *The 19th Century* (2006), *The 20th Century* (2008), *African Americans* (2011).

Publisher's Cataloging-In-Publication Data
(Prepared by The Donohue Group, Inc.)

Names: Mack-Shelton, Kibibi, 1955- editor.
Title: Great events from history. African American history / editor, Kibibi V. Mack-Shelton, PhD, Clafin University.
Other Titles: African American history
Description: [First edition]. | Ipswich, Massachusetts : Salem Press, a division of EBSCO Information Services, Inc.; Amenia, NY : Grey House Publishing, [2017] | Includes bibliographical references and index.
Identifiers: ISBN 978-1-68217-152-3 (set) | ISBN 978-1-68217-154-7 (v.1) | ISBN 978-1-68217-155-4 (v.2) | ISBN 978-1-68217-156-1 (v.3)
Subjects: LCSH: African Americans—History.
Classification: LCC E185 .G74 2017 | DDC 973/.0496073—dc23

First Printing
Printed in the United States of America

CONTENTS

Volume 1

Publisher's Note

Great Events from History: African American History (3 volumes) is the latest set in the ongoing *Great Events from History* series, which was initiated in 2004 with the two-volume *Great Events from History: The Ancient World, Prehistory-476* and followed by *The Seventeenth Century*, *The Eighteenth Century*, *The Nineteenth Century*, and *The Twentieth Century*. This set addresses African American history from the arrival of the first slave ships in 1619 to the present day and Black Lives Matter

Expanded Coverage

These volumes incorporate revised and updated essays from the *Great Events from History: The 17th Century* (2005), *Great Events from History: The 18th Century* (2006), *Great Events from History: The 19th Century*, (2006), *Great Events from History: The 20th Century*, (2007 and 2008), *Great Lives from History: African Americans* (2011), and *African American History*, (2006) *Great Events from History: African American History* includes cross-references, appendices, indexes, sidebars, maps, and illustrations.

Each installment in the new series is being enlarged with a significant amount of new material—often more than half the original contents. *African American History* joins 80 completely new essays—commissioned especially for the new series and appearing for the first time—to over 500 previously published core entries. In addition, the new series features a new page design, expanded and updated bibliographies, internal and external cross-references, new appendices and indexes, plus numerous sidebars, maps, and illustrations throughout.

Scope of Coverage

The set begins with overview essays that address important aspects of African American history including African-American cultural impact on US culture, the Black Church, Sports, Science and Technology, Demographic Trends, Economic Trends, Education, Employment, Integration, Segregation, Slavery, and Politics and Government, to name a few. The remaining essays are arranged as a chronology. The beginning date of 1619 was selected because it represents the date that the first slave ships arrived in Point Comfort, Virginia, as part of the Middle Passage. The following decades' and centuries' events are marked by such pivotal moments as Nat Turner's Rebellion, the Selma-Montgomery March, the Tuskegee airmen as well as the Tuskegee experiment, Jackie Robinson's time as a major league baseball player, Spike Lee's impact on film, and emergence of Black Lives Matter.

Essay Length and Format

Each essay averages 1,600 words (2-3 pages) in length and follows a standard format. The thematic overviews present the topic in a clear manner, beginning with a summary paragraph, followed by a broad discussion of the theme or topic that typically covers a significant period of time, often brining the reader up to the present day. Articles that are arranged chronologically include the ready-reference top matter that prominently displays the most precise available information on the following:

- the most precise *date* (or date range)
- the *name of the event*

- a *summary paragraph* that encapsulates the event's significance
- the *locale*, or where the event occurred,
- the *Categories*, or the type of event covered, in forty-one different categories from Abolition to Women's Issues
- *Key Figures*, a list of the major individuals involved in the event, with birth and death dates, a brief descriptor

The text of each essay follows and is divided into standard sections:

- *Summary of Event*, devoted to a chronological description of the facts of the event
- *Significance*, assessing the event's historical impact
- *See also*, cross-references to other essays within the set

SPECIAL FEATURES

Accompanying the essays are sidebars—including quotations from primary source documents—as well as eighty-five additional illustrations including the people, and other icons of the period.

- The *Time Line* lists major events African American history; the Time Line is a chronological listing of events by subject area and lists both those events covered by the entries and also a substantial number of other events and developments during the period.
- The *Bibliography* cites more than 600 major sources on the period.
- *Category Index* lists essays by type of event (Agriculture, Architecture, Arts, and so on).
- *Notable Figures* lists major personages discussed throughout.
- *Subject Index* lists persons, concepts, terms, events, organizations, artworks, and many other topics of discussion,

THE CONTRIBUTORS

Salem Press would like to extend its appreciation to the contributors and to all who have been involved in the development and production of this work. The essays were written by academicians who specialize in the area of discussion, and without their expert contribution, a project of this nature would not be possible. A full list of contributors and their affiliations appears in the back matter of the final volume.

Editor's Introduction

From the publication of the first set of volumes in the *Great Events* series, up to and including this latest set, the *Great Events from History* series has continually expanded our understanding of the historical events that impact the way we live today. In addition to exploring the arc of European and American history, the series has examined a variety of themes including *Science and Technology* (1991); *Human Rights* (1992); *Arts and Culture* (1993); *Business and Commerce* (1994); *Ecology and the Environmental* (1994); as well as more provocative topics that are increasingly important in the twenty-first century, *Gay, Lesbian, Bisexual, Transgender Events* (2006) and *Modern Scandals* (2009). This set, appearing in 2017, *Great Events from History: African American History* marks the first one devoted to showcasing the significant historical events of a single, remarkable ethnic group—one that is woven tightly into the fabric of our national history.

It would be appropriate to argue that African American history actually got its start long before 1619 when the first indentured African servants arrived at Point Comfort in Virginia or suffered the horrors of the Middle Passage. These slaves from Africa, known as the *Dark Continent* by early European scholars, had a rich history that predated the great historical events of ancient Europe. Between 4000-1 BCE and 1500 CE, Africa peopled the earth following the birth of humankind 2.3 million years ago, according to the discovery by paleoanthropologists in 2012 of the oldest fossil remains to date. By 8000 BCE, still long before the settled societies existed in ancient Europe, indigenous Africans living along the Nile River had learned to control the waters by building sophisticated irrigation systems and had established cities with established governments, economic, religious, and cultural systems.

By 500 BCE, Africa had entered the Iron Age developing tools to cultivate the land and weapons for protection and expansion.

The rich legacy of Africa's great events included major migrations due to the gradual desiccation of the Sahara region between 2500-2000 BCE and the Bantu migrations between 1-2 CE. Both of these migrations meant that multitudes of ethnic groups relocated to other regions of the continent, spreading their cultures of trade and iron. These migrations led to the emergence of new city-states, states, villages, and kingdoms with highly developed civilizations: Egypt, Kush, Aksum, Kongo, or Zimbabwe. The Nok people of Western Africa, the region from which most African Americans descended, had a highly advanced culture, reflected in the huge terracotta clay structures that existed from 1000 BCE to 300 CE. Other major Western African states with high cultures emerged as well, including the empires of Ghana (700-1240 CE); Mali (1050-1500 CE); Songhai (1350-1600 CE); Ife/Oyo (1400-1850 CE); Benin (1400-1800 CE) and other smaller and larger states. One can point to several major achievements spanning the African continent over the span prior to the earliest slave ships and the Middle Passage: the establishment of transcontinental trade languages such as Hausa and Swahili; the smelting and use of iron, gold, and other metal resources; the development of written languages; the irrigation of land; the embalming of the dead; the practice of monotheism; the building of Timbuktu University; the building of the Coptic Church. Influences came from all corners of the earth as well: the Arabs conquered Egypt and the Romans defeated Carthage; the Portuguese settled in Angola and the Dutch in South Africa; and the British settled Sierra Leone with former African American slaves. By the time African Americans landed in the

New World, they had already been a major force in the great events of human history.

Great Events from History: African Americans is an important set that is able to highlight not only significant events but also the diverse themes that define African American history: inventions, social unrest, violence, cultural contributions, and achievements in music, dance, science, art, politics, business, and literature. The set fills an important need by bringing all of these topics and themes together with a chronological telling of events to bring African American to the fore, instead marginalizing these events by telling them through the lens of other ethnic or national groups. It confirms their validity and significance in United States history.

The final lists of topics selected for this set covers the span of this country's history, from before there even was a United States of America, travels through the geographical regions of the nation, looks at contributions from both men and women and represent as many aspects of African American experiences as possible, including those from varied economic backgrounds, sexual preferences, black or biracial mixes, religious beliefs, and political persuasions. Writing articles in "present-tense history" was particularly challenging, as significant events seemed to occur each and every day, changing our understanding of what it is to be an African American in the twenty-first century. Clearly, it seems important that we continue to plan for future revisions and updates of this important set.

The contributors and fact-checkers for this set spent brainstorming new topics, writing articles, gathering and documenting information from a wide array of print, electronic, audio-visual, and visual sources. Their professionalism and hard work built the strong foundation for this set. Whether the articles explore an ugly, checkered history of events or an inspired and illuminating one, *Great Events from History: African American History* is sure to provoke continued discussion and research into this rich story, so important to all Americans.

—Kibibi V. Mack-Shelton

Introduction to African American History

The techniques, approaches, themes, and theories that historians employ in their work are collectively known as historiography. Historiography recognizes that the discipline of history itself is a historical product. An African American historiography looks at how historians have thought and written about African American history. It also looks at the subjects and issues that have distinguished African American history from American history in general and at how African American history is connected to American history.

Most readers of this three-volume set are probably interested in specific topics in the history of African Americans. As they use this comprehensive work, however, they may want to remember that the topics covered in it are not here simply for their writers to set forth. They have emerged from more than a century of reflection on the past of African Americans by historians and the public. For this reason, I want to introduce these volumes with a brief discussion of how African American history has been studied and presented and the issues that have concerned those writing in this area. I will begin by examining how the discipline of African American history has developed, and then discuss the major issues that recur through this branch of history.

Generations of African American Historians

One of the most influential descriptions of the development of African American history comes from the work of the distinguished scholar John Hope Franklin. Franklin has argued that African American historians can be divided into four generations, from the late nineteenth century through the end of the twentieth century.

The first generation of historians consisted mainly of nonprofessional historians concerned with explaining how African Americans fit into American society. George Washington Williams (1849-1891) is often considered the first true scholar of African American history. Educated as a minister and with a background in politics, Williams trained himself in techniques of historical research. With an extensive investigation into primary sources, he published the two-volume *History of the Negro Race in America from 1619 to 1880* in 1882. An ardent advocate of integration, Williams was concerned with presenting African Americans as Americans.

Although there were arguably no other major scholars of African American history in Franklin's first generation, the study of African American history attracted a great deal of interest. In Philadelphia, a group founded the American Negro Historical Society in 1897. A little over a decade later, in 1911, African American New Yorkers founded the Negro Society for Historical Research. In these groups, readers and writers were driven by the desire to find a positive identity for members of the racial group, and to locate African Americans within American society. Franklin dates the second generation of African American historians from around 1915, with the publication of *The Negro*, by W. E. B. Du Bois, in that year, and with the founding of the *Journal of Negro History* the following year. The most important figure of this second generation was Carter G. Woodson, the new journal's first editor. Woodson is regarded by some historiographers as the true founder of African American history, since he brought together historians interested in the field and published their articles in his journal. He also encouraged them to write books and manuscripts, which he helped to publish through Associated Publishers, of which he was executive director. Woodson's own first major book was *The Negro in Our History* (1922).

His best-known book today is probably *The Mis-Education of the Negro*, first published in 1933, which criticized the inattention to black history and its misleading portrayal in American schools.

This second generation (which some scholars consider to have been the first generation) of historians was overwhelmingly concerned with the achievements of African Americans in politics, art, music, and other areas. To a large extent, its historians were reacting against the negative portrayals of African Americans in mainstream history and in educational institutions. Writing in a time when segregation and discrimination had been institutionalized and even legally prescribed in many parts of the nation, the second generation of historians attempted to bring to light parts of the past that most white scholars overlooked.

Franklin dates his third generation in African American history to around 1935. Its characteristic work was again published by Du Bois, whose long career spanned many changes and who was a sociologist and political activist as much as a historian. Du Bois's *Black Reconstruction*, first published in 1935, emphasized cooperation between black and white people during the Reconstruction era in the South. A primary area of interest to historians of this generation was how black and white Americans have interacted and dealt with one another. Accordingly, many white historians began working in African American history during this time and published their research in journals devoted to the field. Historians of this third generation were among those who laid the groundwork for the Civil Rights movement of the 1950's and 1960's, and participated in it.

Franklin's fourth generation began around 1970. Made up of well-trained and primarily academic historians, this late twentieth-century generation was distinguished by the range of topics it studied and by the fact that African American history was, by then, considered an integral part of mainstream history, even as it continued to criticize the mainstream. Popular demand for African American history, small at the beginning of the twentieth century, had become great by the century's end and this led to a deluge of books on the subject.

The fourth generation saw the rise of black, or African American, studies programs as an academic discipline, frequently with political implications, and African American history often became part of this new discipline. African American studies gave rise to calls for Afrocentric perspectives on the past and future. For many historians, this meant that the primary task was no longer to identify African American history within American history, but to work from the premise that African Americans were at the center of American history. Some scholars have suggested that a new generation is now emerging from Afrocentric historians, one that will deal with African Americans not simply as participants in the nation's history, but as creators of it.

Across these generations, a number of topics have frequently predominated. These topics are well covered within the three volumes of *African American History*. At least three major issues tend to cut across most discussions of African American history: slavery and its heritage, the rural and urban backgrounds of African Americans, and racism.

SLAVERY AND ITS HERITAGE

Slavery is one of the key topics across all generations of African American historians, and it intersects with most other topics. One of the issues in the writing on slavery has been its impact on African American culture. Many historians, from the beginning, have maintained that slavery basically destroyed African culture and left slaves psychologically isolated and demoralized. An early challenge to this point of view can be found in the work of the Jewish American anthropologist Melville Herskovits, who argued in *The Myth of the Negro Past* (1941), that African Americans had, in fact, preserved much of their African culture through slavery.

During the 1950's, historians Kenneth Stampp and Stanley Elkins published influential works arguing that slavery left such deep psychological scars on the slaves themselves that it damaged social institutions that the slaves passed on to their free black descendants. A long line of African American historians have concentrated on slave revolts and resistance to slavery to counter the view of slaves as damaged, helpless, and docile. Toward the end of the 1960's and into the 1970's, especially, historians reacted against claims that slavery had damaged African Americans culturally and psychologically. More recently, Ira Berlin, in works such as *Generations of Captivity: A History of African American Slaves* (2003), has offered evidence that slavery varied greatly from one region to another and that therefore the impact of slavery on African American culture varied by region. The influence of slavery on families has been an especially controversial issue for historians. The African American social scientist E. Franklin Frazier, in *The Negro Family in the United States* (1939), presented family instability and a tendency toward single-parent families as a consequence of slavery. This was later countered by Herbert Gutman's *Black Family in Slavery and Freedom: 1750-1925* (1976). Gutman offered evidence that slavery actually strengthened black families.

Relationships between slaves and masters have been another hotly debated subject in historical writing on slavery. In the early part of the twentieth century, mainstream white historians often presented slavemasters as largely paternalistic, almost benevolent. Reacting to this, African American historians tended to emphasize the horrors of slavery. Insights into the brutal nature of slavery came from interviews with former slaves conducted as part of the Federal Writers Project during the 1930's, and these interviews became essential primary sources for later historians. In 1974, Robert Fogel and Stanley Engerman published *Time on the Cross*, a statistical analysis of slavery that suggested it was actually a profitable and productive institution. Although Fogel and Engerman meant to emphasize black achievements through adversity, their work impressed some as an apology for slavery. *Time on the Cross* began a new round of historical investigations into how brutal master-slave relationships really were.

RURAL AND URBAN BACKGROUNDS

As the essay on demographic trends shows in the following pages, the African American experience in the years that followed slavery was one of a transformation from a mostly rural, agricultural population to a mostly urban one. Generally, the early second-generation historical works concerned with African Americans in urban settings concentrated on the movement from the countryside to the city. *Negro Migration During the Great War* (1920), by Emmett J. Scott, considered why African Americans had left the rural South for the cities during World War I and what that meant for their urban destinations. Many of the historical works that followed were concerned with the problems faced by African Americans in large cities, and they tended to concentrate on places such as Harlem and Chicago, which held the greatest black populations.

Toward the end of Franklin's third generation of historians, the development of ghettos became a topic of increased interest among scholars. Gilbert Osofsky's *Harlem: The Making of a Ghetto* (1966) and Allan H. Spear's *Black Chicago: The Making of a Negro Ghetto, 1890-1920* (1967) addressed concerns generated by the urban riots of the 1960's. In the years following, the development and maintenance of racial segregation in American cities became a central issue among historians and social scientists.

RACISM

Racism is intertwined with nearly all areas of study in African American history, from its origins during the slavery era to its continuing influence on American society in modern times. The enthusiasm of African American historians for promoting black achievements during Woodson's era stemmed from a conscious desire to counter the negative views of African Americans in mainstream history. For example, Du Bois's *Black Reconstruction* (1935) responded to portrayals of African Americans as passive and corrupt during the Reconstruction period. Du Bois ended *Black Reconstruction* with a chapter criticizing the distorted portrayal of African Americans in history books. Historian Robert W. Logan (1897-1982), an associate of both Woodson and Du Bois enjoyed a long career as a historian. The historical impact of white racism on African Americans was a central theme in all his writings.

One of the key questions among historians dealing with racism has been how racist attitudes have been connected to social structures. In *White Supremacy: A Comparative Study in American and South African History* (1981), George M. Fredrickson argued that the institution of slavery created racism. Historians dealing with urbanization have often studied how racial attitudes led to racially segregated cities, even in the North. Studies of family and class position among African Americans have emphasized that these cannot be understood without taking white supremacy and racial prejudice into consideration.

—*Carl L. Bankston III*

FURTHER READING

The best approach to African American historiography would be to read widely and deeply in the field. However, a good overview of the historiography can be found in *The State of Afro-American History: Past, Present, and Future* (Baton Rouge: Louisiana State University Press, 1986), edited by Darlene Clark Hine. That book's chapter "On the Evolution of Scholarship in Afro-American History" by John Hope Franklin is particularly recommended. *The African American*

Experience: An Historiographical and Bibliographical Guide (Westport, Conn.: Greenwood Press, 2001), edited by Arvarh E. Strickland and Robert E.Weems, Jr., looks at historical writing in twelve of the major topics in African American history. *Black History and the Historical Profession, 1915-1980* (Chicago: University of Illinois Press, 1986), by August Meier and Elliott Rudwick, offers five essays on the development of African American history. The essay on the career of Carter G.Woodson is especially useful for an understanding of the field.

Complete List of Contents

Appendixes

Indexes

OVERVIEWS

HARRIET TUBMAN.

AFRICAN-AMERICAN CULTURAL IMPACT ON US CULTURE

This entry highlights the multilayered influences of African Americans upon US culture by way of dance, music, dress, hair and language.

Culture is defined as the values, traditions, and beliefs which influence the behavior of social groups (Parsons). The struggle to find place and identities here in the United States has been intense; yet no other people have had greater influence upon American culture than African American via music, dress, language, hair and dance. These concepts share similar impact upon American culture in the attempt to increase Black cultural value, tolerance and cultural expressionism that has become a major demarcation in our democratic society.

DANCE

Although many scholars debate the exact dance forms brought to America through the slave trade due to the trauma of the Middle Passage, it is safe to assume there were various versions. Though forced to dance as a means of entertainment and exercise during their transport to America (Thompson), African slaves brought with them specific dance idioms from their varied homelands. However what cannot be disputed is the integral significance of African Drumming practice upon African Dance idioms. Western African dance traditions reached American shores during the early seventeenth century along with the introduction of the West African Drumming practice. Instruments like the *goje*, Shona *mbira*, Chopi *amadinda* xylophones, Mande *balo* and Dagare *gyile* all served as powerful instruments embodying black spirituality, speech and political power (Dor).

Along the shores of Virginia and North Carolina African influence infiltrated the cultural social dance creating "African American" dance (Malnig). Although distance served as a deterrent to socialization between plantations, dance masters would commune with particular families and rotated from plantation to plantation giving dance instructions (i.e. minuets, country dances, jigs, and quadrilles) while slaves, though prohibited to partake, watched, learned, and practiced them from afar. Particularly in the South during the Great Awakening (1730–1735), when slaves were prohibited from worshiping with their white masters; they began using modified dance forms in their worship that were an amalgamation of West African dance practice and European influence.

Jitterbugging at a juke joint, 1939. (Marion Post Walcott)

Following the Haitian slave revolt of the 1790s, Caribbean influence infiltrated New Orleans, bringing strong dance practices including advance shuffling of the feet, with the minimal play of the limbs, yet intense hip movement. Often these dance moves were misunderstood as expressing lasciviousness and immorality. Yet, duly noted is the reflection of physical, social, artistic, and communicative importance of African dance lodged in African American culture (Thompson, 2014). Even in today's society, the practice of stamping, clapping hands, and patting chest has given way to the urban phenomenon of "human beatboxing" that serve as a catalytic medium to many hip-hop dance forms (Waters). African American dance as evidenced in the 2000s, particularly in the Southern region of the United States, has dominated the image of black gender and masculinity as propagandized via mass media (Nichols, 2014).

MUSIC

The impact of African American music upon American culture is hard to quantify. Beginning with the Atlantic slave trade, African slaves brought musical styles that superseded the confines of European western tonal music. African music, with its heavily syncopated polyrhythms, particular instruments, religious and linguistic practices, became the impetus for the creation of many other sacred and secular American musical styles and traditions (Roach). From African slave utterances—chants, moans, and

Slaves on a Virginia plantation (The Old Plantation, c. 1790)

cries for deliverance—emerged sacred and secular African American genres: spirituals, black meter music, hymns, concert spirituals, ragtime, blues, gospel, rhythm-and-blues, jazz (in every idiom), hip-hop, and rap (in every idiom) (Walker). These African American-created music genres, and many more, have left an indelible impression upon American music.

Music traditions and practices such as "the Baptist-Hymn lining tradition" with its use of the pentatonic scale, highly syncopated rhythms, accent on the back beat, and the West African "call and response" practice all served as tools used to modify colonial European Christian hymns. The Fisk Jubilee singers gave rise to the concert spiritual with its fusion of the best of both Western tonal music practices and the Negro spiritual, which in turn fathered future sacred music genre that impacted American church history (Southern). With rise of blues and jazz in the post-antebellum period, the tentacles of music created by African American are irrefutably influential upon United States music and culture, even fashion.

DRESS

The sociological and cultural contributions of African American to *Dress* in America deserves great recognition. Historically, Africans established a body language which manifests itself in an acute display of "style" which created a distinct appearance (White and White). Beginning in the early eighteenth century, African American used *Dress* as means to express themselves, often in response to racial oppression. As a form of resistance to cultural norms, African Americans used *Dress* as a stark alternative to the European traditional dress—yet to the fascination of the majority culture. During the Antebellum period, slave women, though often forbidden to wear fine hats, would wear brightly colored head wraps

or distinguished looking turbans, while men might wear a cast-off jacket with slave work pants. African Americans often juxtaposed various colors and fabric textures that improved a unique style of their own.

During the height of the Harlem Renaissance in 1940's Black men wore Zoot Suits (a variation of a business suit with the coats worn with high waist pants, often cut wide at the knees and tapered at the ankle) as a statement of individuality and style. This was a mark of pride for African Americans, yet over time these suits became object of racially motivated bias by White military official who noticed a high influx of African American men flouting zoot suits during the time of war (Cosgrove). Despite many disturbing encounters, Black *Dress* took political dimensions with the introduction of the "Dashikis," brought to America via the return of Peace Corps volunteers in the 1960's. Dashikis became a symbol of black nationalism, identity and cultural pride particularly among student activism (Joseph). The sociological and cultural importance of African Americans to dress in the United States is well documented.

HAIR

In American history, *Hair* has represented beauty (Prince). African Americans have struggled to esteem themselves through a prism of beauty as defined by the majority culture. By defining beauty in a general sociological context can negatively affect the identities of the many people. The African American psyche has been haunted by feels of not measuring up to American standards of beauty—and *Hair* stands as a testament to this struggle (Patton; Tulloch). Yet, African Americans have influenced America thought by forcing the arbitrary parameters of beauty as ascribed by mainstream culture which belittled certain types of hair texture and grooming.

As early as the late seventeenth century, in an attempt to look presentable to the majority culture, African American women took particular interest in their hairstyles and headwear. Though forbidden to wear fashionable hats, Black women slaves sought to beautify themselves by wearing headwear and hairstyles that accentuated their beauty even under their slave master's criticisms (Foster). During the eighteenth century, it was fashionable for prominent white men to wear wigs; thus, many black slaves who worked in the "master's house" took up the practice of wearing wigs too. As a result fellow slaves began the practice of shaping their hairstyles to look like wigs (Thompson). It was clearly known that African hair was considered unattractive and inferior to European hair, leading to derogatory statement references to Black's hair being like, "wool" (Byrd). This evidenced the dominance of European influence upon African American definition of beauty and the racial division entrenched in American history.

In photographs taken post-Civil War, African American women wore long and straight hairstyles as complicit with the mainstream norm. Black entrepreneurs such as Madame C. J. Walker, the founder of African American hair and personal care products as early as 1906, was responsible for the creation a hair texturizer designed to straighten African American hair (Huber). This revolutionized African American hair care, yet nonetheless diminished the continual usage of fashionable hats in the Black Church.

LANGUAGE

The sweeping rhetorical impact of African Americans upon America is one of the greatest ever seen. Its impact goes beyond the known to the sublime, as preserved in the Black oral tradition of stories, sayings, songs, proverbs and other cultural linguistic phenomena. African slaves who spoke different languages from varied backgrounds discovered similar linguistic structural base despite their different languages, and were able to create a revolutionary form of communication that was distinctly African, yet part American (Hamlet, 2011). Replete with body gestures, metaphor, and imagery, African American speech became more than a means of communication, but "personal presentation, verbal artistry, and commentary on life's circumstance (Gay and Baber)."

Expressive forms such as "call and response" use extensively in African-American churches embodied the communicative and active listening traits shared between the speaker (i.e., preacher) and the listener (i.e., congregation). Semantic Inversion, the practice of reversing the meaning of a term (Jacobs), is another form of communication, as created and deployed by African American youth, as demonstrated in musical forms such as Hip Hop and Rap. Terms such as *fat*, *hot* and *bad* all have alternative means contrary its normal definition. Other dominate linguistic African American contributions such as: testifyin', signifyin' and trash talkin' have entered and saturated American culture (Hamlet).

—John Hill

BLACK CHURCH

Collective term for the many autonomous denominations of African American Christian churches. The black church evolved as a highly visible social institution in response to white racism in American society and racism in white-defined Christianity.

Although African American religious experience is diverse and social forms of religious life vary greatly, the black church has historically been the most visible religious institution in African American culture. As a visible institution controlled from within the black community, the black church has played a central role in African American social and political history. This history has evolved within the broader historical context of American racism and racial politics. The church, also evolving within that broader context, has been an important center for the development of African American Christian theology and for community identity.

The black church originated as a formal institution when African American religious leaders in Philadelphia were forcibly removed from worshiping on the main "whites only" floor of St. George's Methodist Episcopal Church. When Richard Allen and Absalom Jones were evicted from the church in 1787, they and their fellow black Christians concluded that the racism of white-defined Christianity precluded full Christian expression for African Americans in white-controlled congregations. Their formation of the Free African Society that year paved the way for the later creation of the fully autonomous African Methodist Episcopal (AME) Church, one of the earliest black churches in the United States. An institutionalized form of distinct African American Christian theology began to emerge.

LINCOLN/MAMIYA MODEL

In their expansive sociological study entitled *The Black Church in the African-American Experience* (1990), C. Eric Lincoln and Lawrence H. Mamiya propose a dynamic model for interpreting the sociology of black churches in their diversity and complexity. Lincoln and Mamiya identify the major black denominations as the AME Church, the AME Zion Church, the Christian Methodist Episcopal (CME) Church, the National

Baptist Convention, USA., Incorporated (NBCA), the Progressive National Baptist Convention (PNBC), and the Church of God in Christ (COGIC). These denominations, as well as many other smaller ones and local churches, provide institutional structure for the religious (and often political) life of millions of African American Christians.

Although sociologists and political historians debate the nature of the black church and its political role, Lincoln and Mamiya offer a "dialectical model of the black church" that encourages an open and ongoing analysis. The Lincoln/Mamiya model offers a way of analyzing the ongoing tensions, both theological and political, within African American Christianity as those tensions are embodied in the structure of the black church. The model proposes the following six "dialectically related" pairs, or opposites. With these pairs the focus is on the ways that human experience shifts back and forth between the two opposites, sometimes tending more toward one idea, sometimes tending more toward the other.

For example, the first dialectic is that between "priestly" and "prophetic" functions of the church. In other words, it concerns how the church balances its role as the center for worship (priestly) in relation to its role as an agent for social change in the community (prophetic). Second, there is a dialectic tension in the black church between the "other-worldly" and the "this-worldly." Does the church focus on individual spiritual salvation for the "life to come" or does it focus on social justice in the here-and-now? The third dialectic proposed by Lincoln and Mamiya is between "universalism" and "particularism": how the black church negotiates its role in Christianity, broadly speaking, and its very particular role in African American history. The black church is part of a universal religious institution but is also a very particular response to white racism in American Christianity. A fourth dialectic is between the "communal" and the "privatistic": How does the church address individual spiritual life in the context of the social realities of African American experience? The fifth dialectic is especially important politically; it is between the "charismatic" and the "bureaucratic." This involves how the church uses the power of personalized and local leadership in relation to developing larger-scale institutional structure and national leadership as well as how it handles the tensions inherent in doing both. Finally, Lincoln and Mamiya join many African American historians and cultural critics when they identify the dialectical tension between "accommodation"

and "resistance." Given the realities of white racism and African American history's origins in the experience of slavery, how has a primary social institution such as the black church moved between accommodating and resisting white mainstream culture in the United States?

POLITICS AND THE CHURCH

It is in this final dialectic that much of the debate over the role of the black church in the twentieth century Civil Rights movement evolved. It is debated, for example, whether the church served as an accommodationist spiritual escape that diluted the intensity of its members, whether the church served as a fundamental source of activism and militancy, or whether the black church did both.

During the 1950's and the 1960's, the Civil Rights movement accelerated and moved to the center of the national political stage. Beginning with efforts to integrate schools following the Supreme Court's *Brown v. Board of Education* decision in 1954 and continuing through the Montgomery bus boycott (1955–1956), the formation of the Southern Christian Leadership Conference (1957), the Freedom Rides summer (1961), and the March on Washington (1963), hundreds of thousands of African Americans confronted American racism and fought for fulfillment of the stated US commitment to freedom for all its people. The black church played a central role during these years, providing people and resources for grassroots organizing while cultivating leadership for the national movement.

During this period, tensions arose in the black community that illustrate the sociological complexity of the church as a social institution. From the perspective of the emerging Black Power movement, the church was suspect in its adherence to Christian principles of nonviolence in the face of white racial violence and was deluded in its emphasis on integration into mainstream American society. For black nationalists, this mainstream society remained white-dominated and white-controlled. Some nationalists argued that African American Christianity itself was flawed because of its origins as a religion of enslavement.

From another perspective, political and religious leaders such as Martin Luther King, Jr., proposed that African American Christianity provided both the spiritual and material bases for a militant liberation theology, one that posed a radical challenge to the white-supremacist status quo of the mid-twentieth century United States. King was a nationally recognized Christian leader, but with him were thousands of African American Christian women and men who argued that the black church provided the path of most, rather than least, resistance to white racism. As Lincoln and Mamiya point out, the fact that white racists bombed several hundred black churches during the civil rights period indicates that the threat posed to white supremacy by the black church was substantial.

A second debate that highlights some of the issues from the Lincoln/Mamiya model concerns the role of women in the black church. During the Civil Rights movement, women provided the "rank and file" of many organizing efforts, working together with men to form the core of the movement. In the church, however, men still maintained a monopoly in terms of formal congregational leadership. On the national level, this trend was even more pronounced; the nationally recognized black leadership of the Civil Rights movement was almost exclusively male. Women such as Rosa Parks, Fannie Lou Hamer, and Mamie Bradley (Emmett Till's mother) were recognized on a national level, but the political leadership of black women in many key political battles, especially on the local level, went unacknowledged

both in the national media and in the formal leadership structure of the church.

Gender politics are significant because they highlight tensions within the church when issues that are often expressed in secular political terms (such as women's oppression) are also engaged in theological and spiritual terms. This can result in significant structural change within a social institution such as the black church. In the case of women and the church, the political becomes religious and the religious becomes political, bringing into play the dynamic tensions between the "this-worldly" and the "other-worldly," between the "priestly" and the "prophetic."

—Sharon Carson

See also: African Methodist Episcopal Church; African Methodist Episcopal Zion Churches; Baptist Church; Black Christian Nationalist Movement; Black nationalism; Church bombings; Church burnings; Civil Rights movement; Free African Society

AGRICULTURE

Through most of American history, agriculture was the primary occupation of African Americans. It was only after World War II that African Americans joined the general shift of laborers away from agriculture.

African Americans have deep historical ties to agriculture. During the centuries of slavery, tending crops was the primary economic activity of enslaved African Americans. Along the South Atlantic Coast in colonial North America and in the young United States, tobacco depended heavily on slave labor. Later, rice, grown in parts of South Carolina and other states, and sugar cane, grown chiefly in Louisiana, became important cash crops grown by slaves. With the development of the cotton gin at the end of the eighteenth century, cotton became the most profitable agricultural export of the United States.

After the Civil War and emancipation, African Americans remained heavily involved in agriculture, particularly in the South. In the second half of the twentieth century, however, African American involvement in farmwork dropped dramatically, so that only a tiny proportion of African Americans were involved in agricultural labor as the twenty-first century began. While nearly two-thirds of African American workers were

engaged in agricultural labor in 1870, only about 1 percent worked in agriculture in 2000.

BLACK FARMERS AFTER SLAVERY
After slavery ended in 1865, most African Americans still lived in the rural South, where farming remained the most important occupation. In order to farm, however, workers needed land, tools, farm animals, and seeds and other supplies. As a result, most African Americans farmed on white-owned land through tenant, sharecropper, and crop-lien systems.

Tenant farmers rented their plots of land for fixed sums—in money or the equivalent in crops. Under the sharecropping system, the farmers borrowed fertilizer, tools, seeds, and other necessities from landowners. They then paid off their debts, with interest, by giving the landowners shares of their crops. Since the landowners often charged high rates of interest and were also the primary keepers of business records, sharecroppers frequently fell steadily deeper into debt with each harvest.

The crop-lien system gave merchants and landlords who provided supplies to farmers mortgages on the crops that the farmers promised to produce. Again, high interest rates gave the advantage to the lenders and contributed to keeping most black farmers in perpetual debt and poverty. At the same time, concentration on the planting of cotton, encouraged by white landowners, further hampered black farmers in the South. Overproduction of cotton led to a drastic drop in cotton prices during the second half of the nineteenth century.

Some scholars have estimated that by 1890, nine out of ten African American farmers were sharecroppers. Despite the many handicaps that African Americans face and widespread white southern opposition to their owning land, a substantial minority of African Americans did manage to acquire their own land in the late nineteenth and early twentieth centuries.

In 1886, African American farmers joined together to form a mutual-support organization, the Colored Farmers' Alliance, modeled on the white Farmers' Alliance founded two years earlier. This cooperative endeavor supported its members and aided in the progress of independent African American farms. Meanwhile, the founding of black-owned banks and other financial institutions helped in their efforts. About fifty black-owned lending institutions were founded between 1880 and 1911. By 1910, around 200,000 African American families had managed to obtain their own farmland. Their holdings totaled something over fifteen million acres—an average of about 75 acres per family.

THE GREAT MIGRATION NORTH

During World War I and the years immediately following it, African Americans continued to be concentrated regionally in the South and occupationally in agriculture. Two trends began to undermine these concentrations. First, US entry into the war in 1916 created thousands of new jobs in northern cities, and northern black leaders urged the oppressed populations of the rural South to move north. Second, cotton prices fell again, depressing the southern economy. Although black farmers were still more heavily involved in cotton growing than white farmers, government farm aid went primarily to the white farmers. The new black-owned lending institutions that had helped promote African American land ownership were hit hard, were unable to collect on their loans, and many went bankrupt. The troubles of black farmers were compounded by the spread of the boll weevil, an insect that destroyed cotton crops.

These new problems forced many black landowners to consider returning to sharecropping or working for white farmers as laborers at deplorable wages. Between 1910 and 1920, about 300,000 African Americans left the predominantly rural South, mostly for northern cities, in a movement that became known as the Great

Migration. During the 1920's, the exodus grew greater, as an estimated 1,500,000 African Americans left the South between 1920 and 1930.

THE DEPRESSION

The 1930's were hard years for many Americans but were even harder on African Americans—especially African Americans who worked in agriculture or had commercial ties to it. Black-owned banks, dependent on loans to African American farmers, had already started failing before the Depression. Of the fifty black-owned lending institutions in existence in 1911, only about twenty-five survived to 1930. Three years later, when President Franklin D. Roosevelt tried to stop investors from withdrawing all the money from banks by closing banks for three days, only eleven black-owned banks remained in the entire United States.

As northern jobs dried up during the Depression, the movement of African Americans to northern cities slowed. Surplus agricultural labor became plentiful in the South, and agricultural wages dropped. Black tenant farmers found it increasingly difficult to come up with rent for land and the sharecropping system took on renewed life.

According to the US Farm Security Administration, by the end of the 1930's, 47 percent of all African Americans in farming were sharecroppers, 32 percent were tenant farmers, and only 21 percent were landowners. In 1931, African American farmers, supported and encouraged by the Communist Party, joined together to found the Sharecroppers Union in Alabama. The union spread to other states and may have had as many as twelve thousand members by 1935. However, the union's connection with the Communist Party hindered its growth, as many black farmers were reluctant to become involved with an organization that had communist sponsorship.

Some government programs made the problems of African American farmers worse. For example, the federal Agricultural Adjustment Act (AAA), passed in 1933, paid farmers to cut back on their production of crops in order to stabilize crop prices. With an incentive to produce less, landowners frequently fired their farmworkers and evicted tenant farmers—workers who were predominantly black. Some funds paid by the Department of Agriculture were intended to go to workers or tenants, but the money went directly to landowners, who typically passed on little or none of it. In response, black and white tenant farmers in Arkansas formed the Southern Tenant Farmers Union in 1934. This organization spread to six other states and acquired an estimated 30,000 members. With little support from the federal government, however, the union gradually faded.

THE DECLINE OF AFRICAN AMERICAN AGRICULTURE

With the entry of the United States into World War II at the end of 1941, the African American movement to northern cities that had slowed during the Depression began once again. In the years that followed the war, African American movement out of rural areas and out of agriculture grew rapidly. In 1940, slightly fewer than one in three African American workers were in jobs in agriculture; this proportion dropped to less than one in four by 1950. By 1960, fewer than one in ten African Americans were in agriculture.

The decrease continued steadily, so that by the year 2000, only slightly more than one in one hundred African Americans were in agriculture. Meanwhile, the small farms owned by African Americans had become outdated, as large-scale agribusiness took over farming throughout the United States. Demand for farmworkers declined steadily over the second half of the twentieth century. By the 1960's, the sharecropper system had virtually disappeared in most of the South, where mechanization had reduced the need for human labor.

In 1967, the federal government included agricultural workers under its minimum wage law. As a result, farmworkers immediately became much more expensive for southern planters, who became even more reliant on machines and began controlling weeds with chemicals, instead of workers with hoes. After centuries of heavy African American concentration in agriculture, black agricultural workers had almost disappeared.

A decline in the numbers of black farmworkers was not the only change. The remaining farmworkers were growing much older. Few young African Americans were going into agricultural work by the end of the twentieth century. During the 1990's, the median age for black farmers was sixty years, one in every four was over seventy years old. These aging farmers held only a small percentage of America's farm land. Of the 960 million acres of agricultural land in the United States at the end of the twentieth century, only about 2.6 million acres—0.25 percent—were owned by African Americans.

SUING THE FEDERAL GOVERNMENT

Many African American farmers have argued that a long history of government discrimination against them has continued. In 1997, organizations representing them filed a class action lawsuit against the federal Department of Agriculture. The farmers maintained that the department had discriminated against them by denying them loans and other forms of aid. This discrimination, according to the farmers, contributed to the decline of African American agriculture.

In April, 1999, federal district court Judge Paul L. Friedman approved a settlement agreement on the case. African American farmers could file for compensation along two tracks. On the first track, they could file claims of past discrimination and receive automatic payments of fifty thousand dollars upon approval of their claims. The second track made possible greater compensation for farmers, but only after they went through hearings. The deadline for submitting claims was in September, 2000.

These settlements did not end legal action and did not end complaints about discrimination by the Department of Agriculture. Some farmers objected that the department had not sufficiently publicized the availability of compensation before the deadline passed. Others said that the department was slow in awarding compensation money and resisted paying out the money at every opportunity.

By July, 2002, the Department of Agriculture had awarded about $645 million in payments and forgiven loans. However, this was only a small portion of the amount that should have been paid, according to some observers. A report issued in the summer of 2004 by the Washington-based Environmental Working Group maintained that the Department of Agriculture had assigned Justice Department lawyers to fight claims. Among the 94,000 farmers who filed for compensation, according to the report, 81,000, or nearly 90 percent, were denied their claims.

—*Carl L. Bankston III*

See also: Demographic trends; Economic trends; Employment; Great Migration; Sharecropping; Slavery

SPORTS

Although sports are often prized by fans and participants alike as a refuge from mundane concerns, the sporting world has long provided a highly public forum for the debate and resolution of social issues. Matters of race and ethnicity have long been among the most contentious of these.

The rise of organized sports in the mid- to late nineteenth century coincided with the drawing of the "color line" and the institution of formalized, legally sanctioned modes of discrimination in virtually all walks of American life. In sports as in most other contexts, the most virulent discrimination has typically been directed against African Americans. Although relations between whites, Latinos, Native Americans, Jews, and members of other ethnic minorities would often be strained, both on the playing fields and in the stands, such tensions historically have been relatively minor in comparison to the intense feelings aroused by the participation of black athletes.

As one baseball historian has remarked, "With the breaking of the color barrier, other ethnic identities ceased to have much meaning. . . . where the Blacks were, everybody else was just White"—a statement that encapsulates the history of race relations not only in baseball but also in most other American sports. By the latter half of the twentieth century, the integration of most sports was an accomplished fact, but other issues of race and ethnicity continued to swirl around the world of sports.

BASEBALL AND DISCRIMINATION IN TEAM SPORTS

Baseball, the most popular and most widely played team sport of nineteenth century America, was also the first major sport to attain a secure organizational footing in North America, and in many respects, it long set the pattern for other American sports. In the early years of organized baseball, a certain degree of racial freedom prevailed on American playing fields; although African Americans, Native Americans, and members of other ethnic minorities did not commonly compete with white players, neither was their participation formally barred. All-black teams occasionally played all-white squads, and African Americans, Latinos, and Native Americans competed with whites in front of racially mixed audiences in the earliest professional leagues.

By the waning years of the nineteenth century, however, such tolerance was becoming increasingly rare. As white America grappled with the changed legal and

Lucy Diggs Slowe, tennis champion

social status of African Americans in the post-Civil War period, segregated facilities and institutions were established in virtually all walks of American life. In 1896, the US Supreme Court gave its blessing to such arrangements by endorsing the "separate but equal" doctrine in the landmark case *Plessy v. Ferguson*. Segregationists had their way in organized baseball as well, and by the century's close, African Americans had been effectively excluded from the sport's highest levels by means of an unwritten but nevertheless effective agreement among team owners and managers. (Sole responsibility for adoption of the ban is often assigned to Adrian "Cap" Anson, a star player and manager and a vocal proponent of segregation. Such an assessment, however, oversimplifies the reality; although Anson was one of the game's leading figures, he was only one among many who worked to exclude African Americans from the sport. African Americans were being systematically separated from whites in education, housing, and virtually every other arena, and the segregation of the country's most popular spectator sport was virtually inevitable.)

NATIVE AMERICANS AND LATINOS

No such restrictions, however, were placed on the participation of Native Americans and light-skinned Latinos in organized baseball. Louis "Jud" Castro, for example, an infielder, second baseman, and outfielder from Colombia, played in the inaugural season of the American League in 1902, and such Native Americans as Jim Thorpe and Albert "Chief" Bender had successful major league careers in the first decades of the twentieth century. As a consequence, white managers and owners made occasional attempts to pass off talented African American players as "Indians" or "Cubans"; legendary manager John McGraw, for example, tried unsuccessfully to play infielder Charlie Grant under the allegedly Cherokee name Charlie Tokohamo.

Although white teams sometimes played exhibitions against black teams, and although players of all races competed together in Latin America, the color line had been firmly drawn. For more than a half century, no openly African American players were permitted in the white professional leagues. Moreover, although light-skinned Latinos and Native Americans were not barred from the white leagues, they commonly experienced the same slights and racist treatments accorded members of ethnic minorities in all facets of American life—a fact perhaps reflected by the patronizing nicknames given even to star players; the nickname "Chief," for example, was routinely applied to Native American players, while Jewish players were often nicknamed "Moe."

In addition to Bender and Thorpe, Native American pioneers included John "Chief" Meyers, a star catcher for the New York Giants; the most successful Latino player of the early century was Adolfo "Dolf" Luque, a Cuban American pitcher also nicknamed "the Pride of Havana." (In the early part of the century, when many Americans were first- or second-generation European immigrants, ethnic identification was strong even among white players, and the achievements of athletes of Irish, Italian, German, Polish, or Jewish ancestry were celebrated by their respective communities to an extent unknown to later generations. Nicknames that called attention to a player's ethnicity were common; German American superstar Honus Wagner, for example, was known as "the Flying Dutchman.")

BREAKING THE COLOR LINE

Barred from the white leagues, African American professionals competed against one another in the Negro Leagues, a loose association of teams that flourished in the first half of the twentieth century. Negro League stars such as Oscar Charleston, Josh Gibson, Satchel Paige, and Buck Leonard were widely regarded as the equals of the best white players, but they were allowed to compete against them only in exhibitions, barnstorming tours, and foreign leagues.

In 1946, however, in a move that would have repercussions well beyond baseball or sports in general, baseball's color line was broken by Brooklyn Dodgers executive Branch Rickey, who signed Jackie Robinson, a rising star in the Negro Leagues, to a minor league contract. Robinson reached the majors the following season. Though he endured taunts and harassment both on and off the field, he quickly attained stardom (among

Robinson's notable supporters was Hank Greenberg, a Jewish superstar who had long crusaded against anti-Semitism). Robinson's on-field success was matched by the remarkable dignity and restraint with which he bore the torrents of abuse directed at him, and his shining example deprived baseball's powers of any further excuse for continuing to segregate the sport. A flood of talented black players entered the white leagues, and every major league team was integrated by 1958. As a consequence, the Negro Leagues, deprived of their reason for existing, soon shriveled and disappeared.

FOOTBALL

When the color line was drawn in baseball, football was in its infancy, and professional structures did not exist. In the early years of the sport's evolution, however, a number of black players excelled at the collegiate level, often while playing for such all black schools as Howard and Tuskegee Universities. Several black players, moreover, attained collegiate stardom at predominantly white schools; William Henry Lewis was named an All-American in 1892 and 1893 while playing for Harvard University, and Paul Robeson starred for Rutgers before becoming famous as a singer and actor. When the first professional leagues were formed in the 1920's, moreover, no color line existed, and Robeson, Brown University graduate Frederick Douglass "Fritz" Pollard, and University of Iowa product Fred "Duke" Slater, among others, were among the best of the early professionals. In the early 1930's, however, professional football followed baseball's lead and excluded black players. Notable early players of other ethnic backgrounds included Jewish stars Sid Luckman and Bennie Friedman and the multitalented Native American Thorpe, whose football achievements surpassed his baseball success.

At the same time that Robinson was integrating baseball to great publicity, the established National Football League (NFL) had to fend off a challenge from the upstart All-America Football Conference, which signed a number of black players in an effort to compete with the older league. Faced with these twin pressures, the NFL owners rescinded their ban on black players. As in baseball, African Americans soon came to play important roles on every professional team.

BASKETBALL

Basketball, like football, was slow to develop viable professional structures. As in football, therefore, the collegiate level of play was the highest level widely available; although black teams were generally unable to play white opponents, basketball flourished at black colleges. Before the formation of solid professional leagues, traveling professional teams played all comers; among the most successful of these teams were the all-black Harlem Renaissance (or "Rens") and the Harlem Globetrotters. Both teams enjoyed success against white competition; in order, in part, to deflect hostility from white crowds, the Globetrotters learned to supplement their play with minstrel-like antics, and the team eventually evolved into an entertainment vehicle rather than a competitive unit. Jewish players and teams were also important to the rise of the sport, and such stars as Moe Goldman, Red Holtzman, and Eddie Gottlieb endured anti-Semitic taunts from opposing teams and crowds while helping to establish the basis for the first successful professional leagues.

Prior to 1950, African Americans were excluded from the National Basketball Association (NBA) and its predecessor organizations. That year, three African Americans were signed by NBA teams; within two decades, African American players would come to dominate the sport. Segregation at the college level would persist for decades, as a number of southern schools refused to use black players or to play against integrated teams. In 1966, in a game sometimes referred to as "the *Brown v. Board of Education* of college basketball," an all-black Texas Western team defeated all-white, heavily favored Kentucky for the national collegiate championship.

INDIVIDUAL AND OLYMPIC SPORTS

Sports based on individual excellence rather than on team play have historically proven somewhat less amenable to overt racism than structured team and league sports; in addition, international competitions such as the Olympic Games have been relatively unaffected by parochial color lines. Nevertheless, issues of race have repeatedly reared their heads in international and individual sports. White boxing champions of the nineteenth and early twentieth centuries often refused to fight black competitors, and the 1908 capture of the world heavyweight championship by Jack Johnson, a flamboyant African American who flouted convention by consorting with white women, led to a prolonged search for a "Great White Hope" who could humble Johnson (who was concurrently persecuted by police).

In contrast, the midcentury heavyweight champion Joe Louis was applauded by many whites for his humility; when successors such as the irrepressible Muhammad Ali refused to defer to white sensibilities,

racial alarms again were sounded. Among his many celebrated and controversial actions, Ali in 1964 became the first of many prominent black athletes to change his birth name (Cassius Clay) to a name reflecting his African heritage.

Among other individual sports, the "elitist" games of tennis and golf have proven least amenable to widescale integration. In part, this state of affairs has reflected economic realities, as relatively few minority competitors have been able to afford the club memberships and private instruction that most successful players require. Yet the intractability of racist sentiment has played an undeniable part in limiting minority success in both sports.

Tennis stars of the 1950's and 1960's such as the Latino legend Pancho Gonzales and the African Americans Althea Gibson and Arthur Ashe often had to battle for permission to compete at race-restricted tournaments and clubs as did leading black golfers such as Lee Elder and Calvin Peete. Even after the resounding successes of golfing sensation Tiger Woods brought legions of new minority fans and players to the sport in the mid-1990's, country clubs across the United States—including some at which leading tournaments were held—refused to admit minority members.

International competitions such as the Olympic Games have traditionally been more open to minority participation. George Poage in 1904 became the first African American Olympic medalist, and Thorpe, generally acclaimed the world's greatest athlete, won two gold medals at the 1912 Games. In 1936, the African American track star Jesse Owens won four gold medals at the Berlin Olympics, to the chagrin of the Nazi hosts who hoped to use the Games to demonstrate Aryan supremacy. In 1968, many of the top African American athletes refused to participate in the Games, and two, sprinters John Carlos and Tommie Smith, engendered a worldwide controversy by giving a "black power salute" and refusing to acknowledge the US national anthem while receiving their medals (they were subsequently stripped of their medals and removed from the Olympic team).

OTHER CONTROVERSIES

As the integration of most sports at the playing level became an accomplished fact, questions of race and ethnicity in the sports world came increasingly to focus on other issues. Perhaps the most persistent of these was the fact that although members of minorities had made vital contributions as athletes in every major sport, only a handful had risen to fill managerial, administrative, and executive positions. In 1987, a furor erupted when Los Angeles Dodgers executive Al Campanis—who, ironically, had been a teammate and longtime friend of Jackie Robinson—told a television interviewer that African Americans were underrepresented in front-office sports jobs because they "lack the necessities" to fill such positions. Although many commentators dismissed Campanis's remarks as the confused, out-of-context ramblings of a tired old man, the incident touched off a round of recriminations and investigations.

Although baseball and other sports appointed panels to study the situation, more than a decade later, members of minorities had yet to achieve more than token representation in the power structures of most American sports. A similar reception greeted golfer Fuzzy Zoeller's indiscreet 1997 remarks that Tiger Woods, who is partly of African American heritage, might have a preference for stereotypically "black" foods such as watermelon and fried chicken. These and other such incidents served as ongoing reminders that racial and ethnic divisions persist in the world of sports to the same extent as they do elsewhere in American society.

—*Glenn Canyon*

See also: Baseball's integration; Segregation; Stereotypes

LITERATURE

In the eighteenth century, the African American presence in the United States added a new dimension to the cultural identity of American literature. African Americans first wrote about their experiences as slaves; later, they infused new perspectives into the literary canon through experimentation and revisions of existing conventions.

Personal accounts of slaves' journeys to and bondage in the United States produced a new genre, the slave narrative, in the eighteenth century. The genre borrows from the autobiography, travelogue, and captivity narratives that were already common forms of writing among the early settlers. While most Puritans and pilgrims expressed faith in their God and hope in their journey to a new land, the African American narratives convey extremes of alienation and suffering.

SLAVE NARRATIVES

Among the pioneer African American writers of slave narratives is Olaudah Equiano, also known as Gustavus Vassa, who narrates his experiences in the United States. His account, titled *The Interesting Narrative of the Life of Olaudah Equiano, or Gustavus Vassa, the African, Written by Himself* (1789), contains a description of the terrible journey by sea. Although African Americans came from diverse regions of Africa, slaves were perceived as members of a single ethnicity, so their diversity of heritage was overlooked and regional differences were ignored by slave owners, who defined them in terms of their functions.

From 1830 to 1865, with the exception of one poet, James Munroe Whitfield, some of the more popular genres among black authors were the autobiography and biography. *Scenes in the Life of Harriet Tubman* (1869, revised as *Harriet the Moses of Her People*, 1886) is the biography of a runaway slave who became a conductor on the Underground Railroad; at great risk to her life, she assisted slaves in fleeing to the northern states and freedom.

The most famous African American in the antislavery movement was Frederick Douglass. He wrote three autobiographies during various phases of his life. He reports his early interest in learning how to read and write, his confrontation with his inhumane owners, and his ultimate freedom. Dedicated to a vision of transforming the oppressed state of his race, Douglass shared his story to inspire others.

BIOGRAPHICAL NARRATIVES

After the Civil War (1861-1865), biographical narratives remained a popular genre among African American writers. These narratives integrate the art of storytelling and history telling and allow the authors to address the theme of racial discrimination within personalized contexts of economic and social challenges.

The autobiography of Booker T. Washington, *Up from Slavery: An Autobiography* (1901), is a personal testimony of success that is in many ways comparable to Benjamin Franklin's famous autobiography. As a native son of Virginia, Washington realized the importance of education. Washington became an advocate of the development of practical and technical skills; many of his African American opponents criticized him for his excessive loyalty to whites in a laboring capacity.

W. E. B. Du Bois is another black author who was concerned about the survival of African Americans in America; he advocated democratic rights for his race. He was conscious of the diversity among African American cultural experiences. Unlike Washington, who was born a slave, Du Bois was born free and grew up in the cosmopolitan culture of Massachusetts. He attended Fisk University in Nashville, Tennessee, then went to Harvard and was graduated magna cum laude. He recorded impressions of his complex experiences in *The Souls of Black Folk* (1903). In this work, he makes a case for a racial bond among African Americans despite their varied backgrounds. He explains that Washington's advice in *Up from Slavery* stems from his rural agrarian background. However, the future of the black race called for a more uniform approach to democratic rights.

Du Bois was aware of the psychological tensions linked to segregation, such as the double consciousness or the unique experience black people had of always looking at themselves through the eyes of whiteness. Therefore, he predicted the color line would be the problem of the twentieth century. He advocated that the talents and skills of African Americans must not be developed in contempt for other races, but rather in conformity to the greater ideals of the American republic. There was no need for African Americans to seek assimilation in America at the cost of their African heritage.

Some African Americans resorted to collaborative writing for biographical narrative. An example is *The Autobiography of Malcolm X* (1964), written in collaboration with *Roots* author Alex Haley. It blends the dramatic conventions of narration with first-person reporting. The book captures America's cultural landscape of the 1950's and 1960's, while highlighting the turning points in Malcolm X's life. The biography records his criminal activities, prison experiences, and conversion to the Nation of Islam. After his release from prison, Malcolm X's pilgrimage to Mecca led to the realization that the message of religion is to foster peaceful relations among all races. Therefore, upon his return to the United States, he renounced his allegiance to Elijah Muhammad, who was preaching hatred toward the white race. Malcolm X remained active in the struggle for equality of African Americans and became a popular black leader; he was assassinated in 1965.

POETRY

African American writers have used the genres of poetry and fiction to express their identity. Folk literature became a vehicle for blending the reality of their experiences in America with their nostalgia for the African past. Slaves were not allowed formal education and were generally perceived as unfit for intellectual activities.

Only a few slaves had their owners' permission to read and write, and their literacy centered on the reading and interpretation of the Bible. Among such privileged and literate slaves was the first published African American poet, Phillis Wheatley (1753?-1784), who was known as "a sable muse" among European educated circles. Wheatley faced the dual challenge of writing as an African American and as a woman. She blended the literary conventions of her time, such as heroic couplets, with innovative zeal. In many of her elegies, she addresses the subject of death in the metaphorical context of Christian hope for salvation, implying rescue from a state of bondage. It was her love of liberty that prompted her to write the poem "To His Excellency General Washington" for leading the forces of independence. Unfortunately, after being legally freed due to her master's death, Wheatley soon fell into poverty with her husband John Peters, a freed grocery. Living in destitute and—regardless of the past acclaim she gained through her writing—unsupported by the American public, Wheatley was unable to publish her next volume of poetry. She did publish a few pieces during the year of her death (1984). One of them was a 64-line poem in a pamphlet called *Liberty and Peaces*, published under the name Phillis Peters. Wheatley's literary work was primarily accepted as testimony of African American ability to participate in American literature.

The poetry of Paul Laurence Dunbar (1872-1906) captures the African American voice in American literature. Dunbar's mixed use of oral and written conventions was also practiced by realists such as Mark Twain. It is not surprising that a renowned realist writer, William Dean Howells, praised Dunbar for integrating the African American voice into literature.

HARLEM RENAISSANCE

The 1920's marked the beginning of the Harlem Renaissance, when African American writers transcended the constraints of the European tradition to infuse an independent perspective into American literature. The Harlem Renaissance produced powerful works of poetry by, among others, Langston Hughes, who claims ties to the grandeur of ancient civilization through his African heritage and depicts the ravages of social and economic disparity.

A recurrent theme to appear in the fiction of African American writers is the identity of the mulatto in relation to an environment of rejection. African American fiction treats such rejection as a lingering social phenomenon. Toward the end of the nineteenth century novelist Pauline E. Hopkins addressed racism in her serial novels, exposing the hypocrisy within race relationships. Hopkins's fiction is prophetic in the sense that, as did Du Bois, she saw that the problem of the color line would be the great problem of the twentieth century. Later, Jean Toomer's collection of short fiction, *Cane* (1923), embraced the tensions of segregation and victimization of the mulatto from the male perspective. He makes powerful use of folk sound, imagery, and symbol to portray racial barriers that signal that a claim to an interracial heritage is a social taboo.

NOVELS

The Harlem Renaissance allowed for novels that captured the reality of African American experience. Richard Wright's novel *Native Son* (1940) remains a masterpiece that portrays the fate of a black man who is overpowered by economic oppression. The protagonist accidentally kills the liberal daughter of his employer. Wright pursues the prevailing conventions of naturalism to depict restrictive conditions poverty and systematic racism creates for of African Americans. His novel resembles Theodore Dreiser's *An American Tragedy* (1925) in that both writers were inspired by real trials. In response to Wright's fiction, there were some black writers who were not interested in depicting merely the helpless condition of the black man; they were also interested in probing the challenges and complexities of African American experience to understand their own cultural identity in America. Among the leading male novelists who focus on the quest for identity is Ralph Ellison, who wrote *Invisible Man* (1952). This novel

combines realism with surrealism and draws upon black folklore and myth. James Baldwin was another African American novelist who investigated the archetypal theme of initiation and discovery of self in his novel *Go Tell It on the Mountain* (1953). This novel draws heavily upon the author's childhood experiences.

A contemporary leading black male novelist is Ishmael Reed. In his novel *Mumbo Jumbo* (1972), Reed experiments with the conventions of fiction to capture the complexity of African American identity as he integrates multiple layers of meaning in his prose. He parodies Western tradition and African American conventions. Reed decries any idealism that imposes unrealistic restrictions on the artist.

Among those African American writers whose style Reed parodies is Zora Neale Hurston, who grew up in the black community of Eatonville. Her work marks a major breakthrough for feminist literature. For example, in her novel *Their Eyes Were Watching God* (1937), she combines the voice of self-expression with the social challenges encountered by African American women. The Hurston legacy matures in Alice Walker's fiction. Walker uses a self-reflective voice in her epistolary novel *The Color Purple* (1982).

Probably the most memorable female African American voice in the twentieth century is that of Toni Morrison. In *Beloved* (1987, made into a film in 1998) she takes an innovative approach to a ghost story. She traces the historical context of slavery and exposes the hazards of allowing the past to override the present.

—*Mabel Khawaja*

See also: Film history; Harlem Renaissance; Music; *Roots*; Stereotypes

SCIENCE AND TECHNOLOGY

African Americans have made significant contributions to the fields of science and technology, despite the handicaps placed on their educational and research opportunities in the past, but the full extent of contributions made by African Americans during the slave era may never be known.

The documented history of African Americans in science and technology does not extend back as far as it might. African American slaves clearly played major roles in the planning and building of the great

plantations of the South during the slave era, but the scientific, architectural, and technological achievements of African Americans were ascribed to their masters. An example of this is the invention of a grain harvester, much of it based on technology devised by Joe Anderson, a slave owned by Cyrus McCormick. Credit for the McCormick reaper and the profits it produced accrued to the slaveowner. Under the United States Patent Act of 1790, free African Americans could be granted patents. However, slaves could neither receive patents nor assign their inventions to their masters to apply for patents. Because slaves were not United States citizens, they could not enter into contracts.

BENJAMIN BANNEKER

Given the conditions imposed by slavery, it is not surprising that only one African American in the eighteenth century has generally been widely recognized for scientific achievements. Benjamin Banneker was born in Baltimore in 1731, the son of a slave and a free African American mother, through whom his freedom was assured. Banneker's singular intelligence was apparent during his early attempts at self-education. He excelled in mathematics and studied astronomy independently. He accurately predicted a solar eclipse in 1782. He is credited with constructing, in 1754, the first clock made in the New World.

In 1790, after the site of the new nation's capital was selected, President George Washington appointed Pierre L'Enfant and Banneker to the District of Columbia Commission to design the new city. The distinction made Banneker the first African American to receive a presidential appointment. After L'Enfant was dismissed from the project, he left, taking his papers, including his plans for the proposed capital city, with him. Banneker reconstructed from memory L'Enfant's complicated plans for the new city. He also drew on his knowledge of astronomy and meteorology to publish an almanac that informed farmers of the optimal times for planting. This almanac continued periodic publication until Banneker's death in 1806.

NINETEENTH CENTURY INVENTORS

The documented history of inventions by African Americans before 1865 focuses on freemen. It is likely that many people held in slavery until after the Civil War were inventors; however, only anecdotal accounts of their inventions exist because they could not receive patents.

Patent records do not indicate the race of recipients, but it is thought that Thomas L. Jennings, who received a patent for a dry cleaning technology in 1821, was the first African American to receive one. James Forten, Jr., a free black, patented a unique sail-handling device that seamen clamored to buy. Forten became so prosperous that he opened his own sail company, which, by 1832, had forty employees. Henry Blair of Maryland received a patent in 1834 for a corn planter that planted seed in checkerboard patterns and greatly reduced the amount of time required to sow fields.

Among the most accomplished black scientists and inventors in pre-Civil-War America was Norbert Rillieux,

who studied mechanical engineering in Paris, where he also taught mathematics. Upon returning to his native New Orleans, he patented the technology for a multiple vacuum evaporation system to refine sugar, thereby revolutionizing the process by enabling one person to perform the work of several. This invention spawned significant changes in the worldwide production of food and made Rillieux rich, enabling him to settle permanently in France in 1854 to escape the racial discrimination that African Americans were subjected to in the South.

Lewis Temple devised a whaling harpoon that made it virtually impossible for hooked whales to break loose. Whalers accepted his harpoon enthusiastically, but Temple neglected to patent his invention, so his rewards from it were negligible. Like most early African American inventors, Temple, who lived in Massachusetts, was an ardent abolitionist.

Elijah McCoy's invention of a lubricating device for the wheels of steam locomotives, which he patented in 1872, was widely imitated. Before this technological advance, steam locomotives were forced to stop periodically to have their wheels lubricated, thereby wasting time. McCoy's invention permitted lubrication of the wheels while trains were moving. The term "the real McCoy" was coined to describe this invention by people making a distinction between McCoy's device and imitations of it. McCoy also patented a system of air brakes used extensively by railroads.

Another noteworthy inventor of the period, Lewis Henry Latimer, developed an important technology for producing the carbon filaments used in electric lights. He worked closely with Alexander Graham Bell, for whom he made the drawings that accompanied the patent applications Bell submitted for the telephone and other inventions.

W. B. Purvis obtained sixteen patents, nine of which involved technologies for manufacturing paper bags. In 1883, he also patented a hand stamp that is still in use today. Humphrey Reynolds patented a ventilation system for railroad cars that was widely used by the Pullman Company. Granville Woods, nicknamed "the black Edison," obtained twenty-two patents, many of them for devices concerned with railroad telegraphy.

Probably the most lucrative inventions by African Americans around the turn of the century were the hair products invented and marketed by Madame C. J. Walker and Annie Turnbo Malone, designed to control the kinky hair of black women. Both women became millionaires by 1910. They were the first African American women to achieve that level of wealth.

SCIENTISTS

The best-known African American scientist is George Washington Carver, a Tuskegee professor and researcher, who devoted himself to teaching and doing research in agriculture. He publicized the benefits of crop rotation at a time when many farmers were depleting their soil from constant replanting. Carver focused considerable attention on peanuts and soybeans as cash crops and as crops that add nitrogen to depleted soil. He explored ways to use peanuts and soybeans inventively as inexpensive sources of protein.

Born into slavery in 1864, Carver received a master's degree from Iowa Agricultural State College, while becoming the first African American graduate of that institution. Carver was inducted into Great Britain's Royal Society of Arts and Manufacturing and Commerce in 1916. In 1923, he received the Spingarn Medal of the National Association for the Advancement of Colored People (NAACP). In 1949, six years after his death, Carver was honored by having a postage stamp issued in recognition of his monumental contributions to American science.

Marine biologist Ernest Just conducted pioneering research into cell division in marine worms. After teaching at Howard University, he moved to Berlin's Kaiser Wilhelm Institute of Biology, where he remained until 1933, when the rise of Adolf Hitler drove him out. Unwilling to return to the United States, where his race would bar him from working in major science laboratories, he remained in Europe for the rest of his life.

One of eight African Americans who received doctorates in pure mathematics between 1875 and 1943, David Blackwell became the first person of his race to gain a tenured professorship at the University of California at Berkeley in 1955. Specializing in statistics and probability, he suffered the indignity of having his nomination for a Rosenwald Fellowship at the Institute for Advanced Studies at Princeton University rejected for racial reasons.

In 1918, Elmer Samuel Imes received a doctorate in physics from the University of Michigan, where his studies focused on quantum theory as applied to the rotational states of molecules. As space technology evolved, Imes's research proved highly significant for scientists in the United States' space program.

After chemist Percy Julian received a doctorate from the University of Vienna in 1931, he returned to the United States and, working out of the Julian Research Institute that he established in Illinois, developed technologies for creating synthetic substitutes for expensive drugs. His research greatly influenced the development of generic drugs in the United States.

As the fields of science and technology have grown increasingly complex, achievements in those fields have more often been team rather than individual efforts. Numerous African Americans have been members of teams that gained considerable recognition in subjects such as laser research, supersonic flight, particle science, and solid state technology. Marc Hannah captured an enviable place in the production of three-dimension special effects that are widely used in film. His work on *Terminator 2*, *Aladdin*, and *Jurassic Park* received many enthusiastic accolades.

One can list notable accomplishments by many other African Americans in the sciences. African American oncologist Isaac Powell has done pioneering research in prostate cancer. Jill Bargonetti, an African American biologist, has studied a specific gene that quells tumors and targets them for destruction. Geophysicist Waverly Person has engaged in innovative seismological research on earthquakes. His efforts gained him the directorship of the National Earthquake Information Center of the United States Geological Survey. Meredith Gourdine, an Olympic athlete with a doctorate from the California Institute of Technology, although blinded by diabetes, has devised technologies to produce electricity from chemical and thermal energy. He holds over seventy patents for his inventions.

Robert Lawrence was the first African American to become an astronaut but died in a training accident in 1967. In 1983, Guion Bluford became the first African American to orbit the earth; three years later, Ronald McNair became the second. Bernard Harris, a physician, served as a specialist on the STS-55 space mission of 1993 and in 1995 became the first African American to walk in space.

ENTICING AFRICAN AMERICANS INTO THE SCIENCES

During the days of segregation, black secondary school students were often counseled to avoid the hard sciences and mathematics. In the twenty-first century, emphasis is on enticing them into those fields. The ranks of African American college graduates with science and mathematics majors are growing steadily. The National Aeronautics and Space Administration (NASA) and private employers such as Bell Laboratories and the Howard Hughes Medical Institute employ many African American scientists.

17

Because enrollments of African Americans in medical school dropped precipitously during the 1960's and 1970's, the Association of American Medical Colleges in 1991 sponsored Project 3000 by 2000, aimed at graduating three thousand minority medical students, most of them African American, by the year 2000. This program was a notable success. The American Dental Association has launched a program that emphasizes the dental needs of African Americans.

The National Action Council for Minorities in Engineering sponsors a mentoring program to encourage minorities to study engineering. This program begins working with minority youth as early as fourth grade and has attracted nearly five thousand minority students, mostly African Americans, into engineering programs throughout the nation.

African American scientists have been instrumental in helping increase the emphasis on science in the secondary schools of the United States. Efforts such as Ruth Wright Hayre's "Tell Them We Are Rising" project makes it possible for impoverished African American youths finally to attend college and gain entry into the professions.

—*R. Baird Shuman*

See also: Agriculture; Black colleges and universities; Education; Talented Tenth; United Negro College Fund

COWBOYS

African Americans who worked as ranch hands on the Western frontier. The contribution of the African American cowboy to the westward movement and the settlement of the western United States is undeniable.

Despite the predominantly white images in television and film Westerns, many cowboys were African American. Attracted by the high wages and the pull of the open range, the cowboys were a diverse lot that included former Civil War soldiers, former African American slaves, Mexicans, and American Indians. Evidence suggests that perhaps as many as 25 percent of cowboys were African American. Most of these African Americans were unable to read or write, so few records of their daily life exist, but like their peers, they spent as many as four straight months in the saddle, working the long drives. The cowboy's job was dangerous, hard, and lonely.

Because cowboys had to work together to herd cattle on trails, segregation was impractical, but African American cowboys were constantly reminded of the inequalities of the time. Pay for African American cowboys was frequently less than for their white counterparts, and segregation was common in cattle towns along the trail. Despite the discrimination they faced, however, the contribution of the African American cowboy to the westward movement and the settlement of the western United States is indisputable.

—*Donald C. Simmons, Jr.*

See also: Film history; Segregation on the frontier; Stereotypes

CUBANS AND AFRICAN AMERICANS

The tension that arose between African Americans and post-1959 Cuban refugees in the Miami area of Florida (Dade County) represents an illuminating case study of the effects of immigration on urban racial and ethnic relations in the late twentieth century.

In the late twentieth century, the attitude of African Americans and their organizations to immigration was one of ambivalence. As a minority group, African Americans could not consistently oppose immigration as a threat to some imagined American cultural or ethnic purity. Yet many African Americans, struggling against discrimination and disadvantage, feared immigrants as competitors for scarce jobs and public services. In Dade County, Florida, unrestricted immigration from Cuba after Fidel Castro took power in 1959 fed the anxieties of black Miami residents about economic displacement and political disempowerment. The black riots that erupted in Miami in 1980, 1982, and 1989, although ostensibly sparked by police brutality, were widely ascribed by contemporary commentators to resentment against Cuban refugees.

CUBAN REFUGEES

Tensions between African Americans and black immigrants from Jamaica and Haiti have been mitigated somewhat by a shared African heritage; with the refugee flow from Cuba, however, this factor did not come into play as much. When Castro took power in Cuba in 1959, people of full or partial African descent constituted nearly 40 percent of the total population of Cuba; yet 90 percent or more of the Cuban refugees of the 1960's and early 1970's were white. It was not until the Mariel boatlift of May to September, 1980, that the proportion of Afro-Cubans in the refugee flow came to approximate that of the island's population.

By the beginning of 1980, many of the Cuban refugees of the 1960's and early 1970's, who had arrived nearly penniless, had grown prosperous. Such success was due to the relatively high proportion of professionals and entrepreneurs among the earliest refugees, the refugees' hard work, and the generous assistance (about $2.6 billion between 1972 and 1976) that the refugees, as defectors from a communist regime, received from the federal government to help defray the costs of vocational training and retraining, transportation, and resettlement. African Americans complained that the refugees received more assistance than either other immigrants or poor native-born Americans did. The Mariel boatlift refugees of May to September, 1980, and refugees who arrived after that year did not, however, receive as much government help as the earlier waves of immigrants.

African Americans also complained about the way refugees benefited from federal programs not specifically targeted at refugees. When affirmative action policies were implemented in the late 1960's to provide set-asides for minority businesses, Hispanics were considered to be a minority and Cubans were Hispanics; hence, refugee-owned businesses were judged to qualify as minority-owned businesses. Local African Americans resented what they saw as poaching by white newcomers on an entitlement originally intended for African Americans.

IMMIGRATION STATUS OF CUBANS AS BONE OF CONTENTION

From 1959 to 1980, hardly any Cuban reaching US shores was deported. The Cuban Adjustment Act of 1966 enabled all Cuban refugees to change their status to that of permanent resident after one year of living in the United States; other immigrants did not enjoy this privilege. After 1972, more and more Haitians, like Cubans, tried to reach the United States. Cubans fleeing by boat were always welcomed. In contrast, Haitians fleeing by boat were unceremoniously sent back to Haiti if intercepted at sea, detained in prison if they reached Florida, and often deported. Although the official justification for the disparity in treatment was ideological (Cuba was communist; Haiti was not), many Miami black activists perceived racism. Many Cuban escapees were white; almost all Haitian escapees were black. In May, 1995, US president Bill Clinton officially ended the privileged status of Cuban refugees. When the first Cuban escapees were sent back to Cuba, on May 10, Miami Cubans staged a four-day action of civil disobedience; Miami's native-born African Americans stayed away from the protest.

Between 1968 and 1989, there were several episodes of rioting by black Miamians, the bloodiest of which took place in 1980. The riots of 1980, 1982, and 1989 were widely attributed by journalists and scholars to the resentment of black Miami residents against Cuban refugees, although this was only one reason. All the riots stemmed from responses to alleged police misuse of force. In 1982 and 1989, the officers who used force were Hispanic, and Cubans did tend to rally around Hispanic police officers accused of brutality. Yet conflict between blacks and police officers had existed even before the mass arrival of Cuban refugees. Although one victim of black violence in the 1980 riot was a Cuban refugee, other victims were non-Hispanic whites: The mob was as much antiwhite as anti-Cuban. Nor were native-born African Americans the only ones to complain about police brutality. In 1992, an incident of police violence against a Haitian in a Cuban-owned store aroused protest; and in 1990, Miami's Puerto Ricans also rioted against an alleged police abuse of force.

JOB DISPLACEMENT AND CONFLICT IN LOCAL POLITICS

Whether Cuban refugees gained occupationally at the expense of Miami's African Americans is a controversial issue, although local black leaders lodged complaints about such displacement as early as the early 1960's. Allegations that Cubans ousted African Americans from service jobs in hotels and restaurants were met by counter-allegations that African Americans were themselves leaving such jobs voluntarily and that the percentage of Miami African Americans in white-collar jobs had increased by 1980. By founding many new businesses, Cuban refugees created jobs; many such jobs, however, went to fellow refugees rather than to African Americans. As the Hispanic population grew and trade links with Latin America expanded, native-born African Americans were hurt by the job requirement of fluency in Spanish. Although the Miami area economic pie grew during the 1960's and 1970's, the African American slice of that pie, scholars concede, was stagnant; compared with pre-1980 Cuban refugees, they suffered in 1980 from greater poverty and unemployment and had a lower rate of entrepreneurship.

From 1960 to 1990, the Hispanic percentage of Dade County's population (most, but not all of it, Cuban) rose from barely 10 percent to 49 percent; the black percentage of the county's population never rose above 20 percent. By the late 1970's, more and more Cuban refugees were becoming naturalized US citizens, gaining both the right to vote and a decisive weight in local politics. In 1983, the Puerto Rican-born mayor dismissed the black city manager, replacing him with a Cuban. Cuban American candidates defeated African American candidates for the posts of mayor of Miami in 1985, Dade County Schools superintendent in 1990, Dade County district attorney in 1993, and mayor of Dade County in 1996. The Cuban influx into elective politics prevented a black takeover of city hall (as had taken place in Atlanta, Georgia, and Detroit, Michigan), thereby reducing the chances for black businesspeople to benefit from municipal contracts. Yet African Americans' powerlessness was relative: They could vote and affect the outcome of elections.

THE NELSON MANDELA AFFAIR AND
THE MIAMI BOYCOTT

In spring of 1990, Mayor Xavier Suar persuaded the Miami city government to withdraw its official welcome to Nelson Mandela, the leader of the black liberation struggle in South Africa, who was then touring the United States. Mandela, in a television interview, had praised Castro. Partly in response to this slap at Mandela, a Miami black civil rights leader, H. T. Smith, called for a nationwide boycott by black organizations of Miami area hotels; this boycott was remarkably effective. It was ended in 1993 with an agreement promising

greater efforts to employ African Americans in Miami's hospitality industry.

Dade County's politics were not simply a Cuban-African American struggle. Sometimes African Americans saw non-Hispanic whites as allies against the Cubans: In his losing bid for Congress against a Cuban American in 1989, the non-Hispanic white candidate won most of the black votes. Sometimes African Americans saw both Cubans and non-Hispanic whites as oppressors of African Americans. In a lawsuit that met with success in 1992, African Americans and Cubans cooperated in an effort to make the Dade County Commission more representative of ethnic minorities.

African Americans did not always form a united front against the Cubans: In a 1980 referendum ending the provision of Spanish-language documents and services by the Dade County government, black voters split, 44 percent for the proposition and 56 percent against. (Bilingualism was restored in 1993.) Haitians and native-born African Americans did not agree on all issues; among non-Hispanic whites, white ethnic migrants from the North did not always agree with white Anglo-Saxon Protestants of southern background; and some of Miami's non-Cuban Hispanics resented Cuban predominance.

In other major US cities, Cubans were, if present at all, a smaller part of the larger Hispanic group. Only in Miami did Hispanics build up a powerful political machine; hence, black resentment of Hispanic political power played little role in race relations elsewhere. The police brutality issue also operated differently: in Compton, California, Washington, D.C., and Detroit, Michigan, for example, there were complaints, in the early 1990's, about alleged brutality by black police officers against Hispanics.

—Paul D. Mageli

See also: Haitians; Irish and African Americans; Jamaicans; Miami riots; West Indians

DEMOGRAPHIC TRENDS

Historical changes in the size, composition, characteristics, and geographical distribution of African Americans. During their long history in North America, African Americans have constituted one of the largest population groups in the Western Hemisphere, and their demographic history is a major part of American history. Since the first Africans arrived in North America during the early seventeenth century, the African American population has grown to reach a total of thirty-six million people—a number greater than the populations of about 158 members of the 191 countries in the United Nations in the year 2005.

The first African slaves arrived in Virginia in 1619. Through the following years, more people from Africa began appearing throughout the new colonies established by Europeans on the eastern coast of North America. The first slaves came to the Dutch lands in the northeast in 1626. The Dutch colonial city of New Amsterdam, later New York, had 100 African slaves in 1640, nearly one-third of the settlement's total population. By the time the English conquered the Dutch colony in 1664, an estimated 1,500 people were living in New Amsterdam, 300 of whom were slaves of African origin.

THE SLAVE POPULATION

With the growth of plantation economies in Virginia and surrounding areas from the late seventeenth century onward, the South became the main destination for people from Africa. During the 1680's, slave traders transported 2,000 Africans into Virginia, and this number increased to about 4,000 in the following decade. Arrivals from Africa doubled again, to an estimated 8,000 in the first decade of the eighteenth century.

In South Carolina and Georgia, the slave trade led to so rapid an increase in the African population in the early eighteenth century, that there were about twice as many people of African descent as whites in this part of the South by the 1720's, when arrivals from Africa had risen to 2,000 per year.

Spanish-held Florida also contained large numbers of free blacks, as well as slaves, at that time, and one-fourth of the 1,500 people in the Florida city of St. Augustine were of African ancestry in 1746. At the mouth of the Mississippi River, African slaves had arrived in Louisiana with French settlers in the early eighteenth century, but their numbers increased slowly until the Spanish took control of Louisiana in 1769.

AFRICAN AMERICAN POPULATION GROWTH, 1790-2000, WITH PROJECTIONS THROUGH 2050

Year	Total African Americans	Percentage of total population
1790	757,208	19.3
1800	1,002,037	18.9
1810	1,377,808	19.0
1820	1,771,656	18.4
1830	2,328,642	18.1
1840	2,873,648	16.8
1850	3,638,808	15.7
1860	4,441,830	14.1
1870	5,392,172	13.5
1880	6,580,973	13.1
1890	7,488,676	11.9
1900	8,833,994	11.6
1910	9,797,763	10.7
1920	10,463,131	9.9
1930	11,891,843	9.7
1940	12,865,518	9.8
1950	15,042,286	10.0
1960	18,871,831	10.5
1970	22,580,000	11.0
1980	26,945,025	11.7
1990	29,986,060	12.1
2000	35,818,000	12.7
2010	40,454,000	13.1
2020	45,365,000	13.5
2030	50,442,000	13.9
2040	55,876,000	14.3
2050	61,361,000	14.6

Source: U.S. Bureau of the Census, Census of Population and Housing, 2000; U.S. Interim Projections by Age, Race, and Hispanic Origin, 2004.

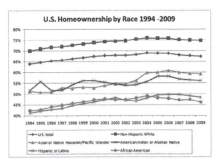

GEOGRAPHICAL DISTRIBUTION OF AFRICAN AMERICANS, 1870-2002

Year	Northeast	Midwest	South	West
1870	4.4	4.8	90.6	<0.1%
1880	3.4	5.4	91.2	<0.1%
1890	3.6	5.8	90.3	<0.1%
1900	5.1	5.7	88.8	0.3
1910	5.3	5.9	88.1	0.8
1920	6.9	7.2	85.2	0.6
1930	9.6	10.6	78.7	1.0
1940	10.3	11.3	76.9	1.5
1950	12.8	13.5	70.2	3.5
1960	16.1	18.2	60.6	5.1
1970	19.7	19.3	54.1	6.9
1980	18.0	20.4	53.4	8.2
1990	15.5	16.2	58.7	9.6
2000	17.6	18.8	54.8	8.9
2002	18.1	18.1	55.3	8.6

Source: Steven Ruggles et al., Integrated Public Use Microdata Series: Version 3.0 (Minneapolis: Minnesota Population Center, 2004); Jesse McKinnon, The Black Population in the United States (U.S. Census Bureau, Current Population Reports, March 2002).

PERCENTAGES OF AFRICAN AMERICANS AND WHITE AMERICANS LIVING IN CENTRAL CITIES, 1870-2002

Year	African American	White
1870	4.7	13.7
1880	5.8	15.8
1890	NA	NA
1900	11.0	23.9
1910	15.5	28.1
1920	21.3	31.9
1930	NA	NA
1940	27.5	28.6
1950	33.2	26.4
1960	47.1	26.2
1970	NA	NA
1980	57.2	23.9
1990	54.9	22.4
2000	52.7	21.3
2002	51.5	21.1

Source: Steven Ruggles et al., Integrated Public Use Microdata Series: Version 3.0 (Minneapolis: Minnesota Population Center, 2004); Jesse McKinnon, The Black Population in the United States (U.S. Census Bureau, Current Population Reports, March 2002).

Under the Spanish and then after the return to French possession, Louisiana rapidly developed an economy based on plantation slave labor.

POST-EIGHTEENTH CENTURY TRENDS

The numbers of African Americans have increased steadily over the course of American history. At the same time, the total American population has also grown. African Americans made up a much larger percentage of Americans at the beginning of the nation's history than at any time since. By the time of the first US Census in 1790, the African origin population had grown to a reported 757,208 people—a figure that represented nearly one-fifth of the new nation's entire population.

Before the mid-twentieth century, African Americans were highly concentrated in the South, where they made up an estimated one-third of the population from 1790 until the Civil War (1861–1865). Although the numbers of African Americans grew steadily through the first half of the nineteenth century, the European population—thanks to increased immigration—grew even more rapidly, so that the proportion of African Americans decreased through that period. By 1840, people of African descent made up slightly under 17 percent of the total population. This figure fell to slightly under 16 percent in 1850 and 14 percent in 1860.

Part of the slower growth of African Americans, compared to Europeans, was due to the fact that the US Constitution had officially ended the importation of slaves from Africa in 1808. Although some slaves continued to be smuggled into the country after that date, the end of the legal shipment of slaves from across the Atlantic did slow down African American population growth.

The United States has always had a free black population, but most African Americans were held in slavery until the end of the Civil War. Of the 757,208 people of African ancestry in the country in 1790, less than 8 percent (59,406) were free. In 1850, 434,495 "free colored" people (the term used by the census that year) lived in the United States. This meant that slightly under 89 percent of all African Americans remained slaves in the middle of the nineteenth century.

Immediately after the Civil War ended in 1865, the Thirteenth Amendment abolished slavery throughout the United States. Immigration from Europe then increased greatly, with virtually no immigration from

Africa. This disparity resulted in a steady decline in the African American proportion of the nation. By 1920, African Americans made up less than one-tenth of all Americans. After World War II ended in 1945, the African American proportion of the national population began to rise once again. By the beginning of the twenty-first century, slightly under 13 percent of Americans were of African ancestry, and that proportion was expected to continue to increase slowly until the middle of the new century.

GEOGRAPHICAL DISTRIBUTION

By the time of the American Revolution, slavery was concentrated in the plantation-farming regions of the South. Virginia, with an economy based on tobacco production, was one of the African American population centers. Rice and sugarcane in South Carolina and Louisiana were tended by slaves. With the invention of the cotton gin during the 1790's, cotton became a highly profitable plantation crop and its cultivation rapidly spread throughout the South. The concentration of slave labor in the South meant that African Americans were also concentrated there. In 1800, 92.7 percent of all people classified as "black" by the US Census in that year lived in southern states.

Some southern states had fairly large free black populations. In 1850, Maryland, which is considered a "border" southern state, had 74,723 free blacks—the largest number of any state at that time. Virginia, with a free black population of 54,333, had the second largest number. A few northern states also had significant numbers of free black residents. Pennsylvania's 53,626 free blacks in 1850 made it home to the third-largest free black population in the country. During that same year, New York, with 49,069 "free colored" people had the fourth-largest group.

After the Civil War, African Americans were no longer slaves, but they remained overwhelmingly concentrated in the South. In 1870, more than nine of every ten African Americans still lived in the South, and this continued to be true throughout the nineteenth century. The first "Great Migration" from the South to northern cities took place during the early twentieth century, particularly during and just after World War I.

One of the primary northern destinations of black southerners was the city of Chicago. In part, the popularity of Chicago was a result of the work of Robert S. Abbott, a businessman and publisher of the widely read newspaper the *Chicago Defender*. On May 15, 1917,

Abbott began promoting what he called "The Great Northern Drive," a campaign urging the oppressed people of the South to move north. Chicago's African American population more than doubled during the second decade of the twentieth century: from 44,000 in 1910 to 109,000 in 1920. Over the following ten years, it more than doubled again, to 234,000.

Movement to northern cities such as Chicago transformed the national distribution of African Americans. By 1930, few than 79 percent of African Americans were still living in the South. About one out of every ten lived in the Northeast, and one out of every ten lived in the Midwest. During the 1930's, the northward migration began to slow. Plantation owners resisted the loss of sharecroppers and other laborers. As northern jobs grew scarce during the Depression years, the attraction of Chicago and other northern cities diminished.

The next great shift in the distribution of African Americans occurred during World War II and the years following it. Between 1940 and 1970, an estimated 5,000,000 African Americans left the southern countryside for the cities of the North. In 1940, nearly 77 percent of all African Americans still lived in the South; by 1950, this figure had dropped slightly more than 70 percent and by 1960 to slightly more than 60 percent. By 1970, 1 in 5 African Americans lived in the Northeast and 1 in 5 lived in the Midwest. The West showed an even higher rate of increase. Before World War II, slightly fewer than 2 percent of the entire African American population lived in the West; by 1990, nearly 10 percent lived there.

Despite these changes, by the early years of the twenty-first century, a majority of African Americans still lived in the South. Even within the South, however, there had been a great change in where people lived. African Americans began the twentieth century living primarily in the southern countryside; they began the twenty-first century residing mostly in city centers.

FROM THE COUNTRY TO THE CITY

Before 1920, most Americans of all races lived in rural areas. African Americans, however, were even more likely than others to live in the countryside. In 1870, nearly 87 percent of African Americans were rural residents, compared to about 72 percent of white Americans. The 1920 census was the first to show a majority of Americans living in or around cities. In that year, close to two-thirds of African Americans still lived in rural areas, though.

Until World War II, African Americans remained more likely than whites to live in the country, and a majority of African Americans were rural residents. After the war, both tendencies began to change rapidly. From 1940 to 2000, the proportion of African Americans living in rural areas went steadily down, from just above 50 percent to only about 10 percent. The proportion of white rural residents were 38–39 percent in 1940 and 1950, and that proportion fluctuated around 25 percent from 1960 to 2000.

The disappearance of agricultural jobs encouraged the movement of African Americans to cities. By the 1960's, the sharecropper system, under which landless farmers paid landowners for the use of land with a large share of harvests, had virtually disappeared in most of the South. Mechanization had reduced the need for human labor. In 1967, the US government included agricultural workers under its minimum wage law. As a result, farmworkers immediately became much more expensive for southern planters, who became even more dependent on machines and used more chemical herbicides, instead of field workers, to combat weeds. After centuries of heavy African American concentration in agriculture, agricultural jobs were finally disappearing.

African Americans went through a dramatic demographic change, from an almost entirely rural group at the beginning of the twentieth century to an almost entirely urban group at the century's end. Moreover, African Americans became concentrated in the central areas of cities. In the late nineteenth century, about 1 in 20 African Americans lived in a central city. Until 1950, fewer African Americans than whites lived in central city areas. By the beginning of the twenty-first century, however, more than half of all African Americans not only lived in urban areas, but lived in the centers of urban areas. This contrasts with a figure of only about 20 percent for white urban residents. This concentration of African Americans in urban cores and the residences of whites in suburbs meant that white and black American residents of the same cities often lived in completely separate neighborhoods.

By the end of the twentieth century in 2000, African Americans constituted majorities in many large cities. With an 84-percent African American population, Gary, Indiana, led the nation. Other cities with black majorities included Detroit, Michigan (82 percent); Birmingham, Alabama (74 percent); Jackson, Mississippi (71 percent); New Orleans, Louisiana

(67 percent); Baltimore, Maryland (64 percent); Atlanta, Georgia (61 percent); Memphis, Tennessee (61 percent);Washington, D.C. (60 percent); and Richmond, Virginia (57 percent).

AGE, FAMILY SIZE, AND FAMILY STRUCTURE

During the twentieth century, the average age of all Americans rose. This was true for African Americans, as well as others, but African Americans have tended to be slightly younger than the majority white population. In the year 1900, the median age of African Americans was 19 years, meaning that the numbers of people above and below that age were equal. At that same time, the median age of whites was 23.

During the second half of the twentieth century, the aging of the population was briefly reversed by the so-called post-World War II "baby boom," which lasted until the early 1960's. As the baby boomers themselves aged, however, the average age of Americans again rose. In 1970, the median age of African Americans was 21 and that of whites was 28. By the year 2000, the median age of white Americans was 38 and that of African Americans was 30.

One reason that African Americans have tended to be somewhat younger than other Americans is that they have generally had somewhat larger family sizes. In 1900, the average African American family contained 5.41 members, while the average white family contained 5.13. By 2000, these figures had dropped to 3.32 for African Americans and 3.02 for whites.

Despite the fact that African Americans have continued to have larger families than the majority population, these families actually contained fewer adult members. In 1900, nearly 90 percent of white children and nearly 78 percent of African American children lived in families containing both mothers and fathers. During the 1960's, however, family structures in American society began to change rapidly, particularly among African Americans. By 2000, only 41 percent of African American children lived in two-parent families. The largest proportion, 47 percent, lived in families with only a mother. Another 6 percent lived in families with only a father and 6 percent (mostly older teenagers) lived in households with no parents present.

EDUCATIONAL ATTAINMENT AND INCOME

In 1870, five years after the end of slavery in the United States, only about 1 in 4 African Americans could read and write, and only about 1 of every 10 African American children between the ages of 6 and 12 was attending school. By 1920, 3 out of every 4 African Americans could both read and write, and nearly 80 percent of elementary school-age children were attending school.

Despite the rapid historical advancement in education, however, African Americans have continued to be at a disadvantage in educational attainment. In 2000, only 13 percent of African American men above age 25 had college degrees, while 15 percent of African American women over 25 had finished bachelors or advanced degrees. These figures indicate that large numbers of African Americans attained high levels of formal education; however, their proportions remained substantially below those of the white population. More than one-fourth (26 percent) of white men and nearly one-fourth (23 percent) of white women over 25 completed college educations.

A lower average level of education was one of the reasons African Americans received less income than other Americans, although some social scientists argue that continuing racial discrimination was a more important factor. In 2000, the median family income of all Americans exceeded $50,000, but the figure for African American families was only $33,255. African American family incomes represented about 62 percent of white family incomes. However, comparisons of only families containing two married partners narrowed the gap considerably, with African American families bringing home a median income of $50,690, compared to $59,199 for white families.

FUTURE TRENDS

In the year 2005, the size of the African American population was expected to continue to grow. However, other segments of the American population are also expected to grow, so that the African American proportion of the total population should not change dramatically. Projections by the US Bureau of the Census estimate that African Americans will number about 61 million, just under 15 percent of the total population in the year 2050. Much of the future population growth is expected to be the result of more rapid growth of other nonwhite groups, especially Latinos and Asians, who were the most numerous immigrants to the United States during the late twentieth and early twenty-first centuries.

Although some movement to the suburbs may be expected in years to come, especially as the size of the African American middle class grows, African Americans will probably continue to be more likely than the majority of the US population to live in the central parts of cities. Those in the central cities are likely to face continuing economic problems and difficulties in finding jobs.

—Carl L. Bankston III

See also: Agriculture; Black flight; Economic trends; Great Migration; One-drop rule; Slavery

ECONOMIC TRENDS

Burdened by being held in involuntary servitude throughout most of their long history in North America, African Americans have been at the bottom of the income scale; however, since the mid-twentieth century, their economic condition has steadily improved, helping them to close the gap with the rest of the population

In the year 1860—the last before the Civil War—the US Census counted a population of 4,441,830 African Americans in the United States. At that time, 9 of every 10 of those people were considered to be the property of others. Legally, they were slaves. Most people held in slavery worked in agriculture, but a small number in urban areas worked in trades or as laborers.

SLAVERY

Slaves tended many of the country's most important export crops. Tobacco, one of the earliest cash crops in Virginia and the surrounding regions, depended heavily on slave labor. Later, rice, grown in parts of South Carolina and other states, and sugarcane, grown chiefly in Louisiana, became important cash crops grown by slaves. With the development of the cotton gin at the end of the eighteenth century, cotton became the most profitable agricultural export of the entire United States. Even in the non-slaveholding North, much of the profit that made industrialization possible came from trade in crops produced by slaves.

The slave trade itself was a significant part of the early American economy. In 1807, the US Congress pass legislation banning the importation of slaves from abroad, beginning the following year. From that date, American involvement in the international slave trade dropped substantially. However, the internal trade in slaves continued. As the United States spread westward and as the cotton industry grew in the deeper South, the sale of slaves from older, upper South states to Deep South states became a major economic activity.

The relatively small number of African Americans who were not slaves—the so-called free blacks—occupied positions that were mostly at the bottom of the economic ladder. The 1860 census counted 488,070 "free colored" people in the United States, a little more than one-third of whom were of mixed race, according to census data. More than 70 percent of the free blacks worked in only four occupations: as laborers, domestic household and laundry workers, salaried farmworkers, and independent farmers. The most common category, accounting for 26 percent of all workers, was "laborer." Only about 7 percent of all free black workers in the United States were owners or tenant farmers, compared to one-third of all whites.

The small number of free African Americans also owned relatively little property just before the Civil War. Among free African American men over twenty-one years of age, 83 percent owned no real estate, such as a house or land, and 63 percent owned no personal property of recordable value. By comparison, just under 58 percent of adult white men owned no real estate and just under 37 percent had no personal property. The small number of free African Americans who did own possessions of substantial value had only a fraction of the wealth of whites. Among those the census referred to as "free colored" adult men who owned some real property, the median value of the property was $500, compared to $1,500 for white men. The median value of personal property of free men of color with property was just $100, compared to $370 for whites.

On the eve of the Civil War, then, slave labor was a key part of the developing American economy. Only about 10 of every 100 African Americans were part of the free labor force, though. Moreover, those who were free worked mostly in menial occupations and received little of the nation's wealth.

RECONSTRUCTION

Reconstruction was the period just after the Civil War when the southern states were occupied by northern military forces, as the US government attempted to bring about some political and social change in the South. After the US Congress took control of Reconstruction policies away from President Andrew Johnson in 1867, the federal government made efforts to include African Americans in public life. During the late 1860's and 1870's, African Americans were elected to public offices throughout the South. The Bureau of Refugees, Freedmen, and Abandoned Lands (known as the Freedmen's Bureau) tried to improve the economic situation of former slaves by negotiating labor contracts for them with plantation owners and by setting up schools. While Reconstruction did bring about some political participation for African Americans, it brought about little real economic change for them. Most African Americans remained at the bottom of the job market and worked on farms owned by other people.

In 1870, just over half of the working African Americans in the United States (52 percent) were farm laborers. The next most common occupation was in domestic service, as private household workers (13 percent), followed by unclassified laborers (12 percent). Another 11 percent were farm owners or tenants working farms belonging to others. By 1880, the percentage of farmers had almost doubled, to 19 percent. However, many of these farmers were sharecroppers, participants in a farming system that began to evolve in the wake of slavery. Sharecroppers worked lands belonging to others, generally white owners, handing over large portions of their crops to the owners after each harvest. The most common occupation for African Americans in 1880 was still that of farm laborer (36 percent), the percentage of general laborers had gone up to 20 percent. Another 14 percent of African Americans were in domestic service after the end of Reconstruction.

The United States was primarily an agricultural society during the years following the Civil War. During the 1870's and 1880's, about 43 percent of white Americans were in agriculture. However, African Americans were even more heavily concentrated in this industry, since 64 percent in 1870 and 65 percent in 1880 were in agriculture. The only other industry containing many African Americans was that of private household service, which contained about 14 percent of African American workers in 1870 and 19 percent in 1880. Well over three-quarters of the African American workers toiled in either low-level farmwork or domestic service during and after the years of Reconstruction

JIM CROW ERA

Reconstruction ended with the withdrawal of federal troops from the southern states in 1877. Afterward, the US economy began a period of rapid expansion and industrialization. The growth of the railroads, manufacturing, mining, and banking propelled the nation toward an urban, factory-based economy. Much of the new workforce for this industrializing nation came from immigration, though, not from African Americans, who continued to be concentrated in agriculture in the South. By 1910, nearly 90 percent of African Americans still lived in the South and a majority of all African Americans were still employed in agriculture, although only about one-third of all Americans and one-fourth to one-third of white Americans worked in agriculture. Most African Americans continued to work on land belonging to others. Of those who worked in agriculture in 1910, 70 percent were farm laborers and wage workers, working for land owners for pay or a share of the harvest. Many of these were sharecroppers, who had no money to rent land.

The sharecropping system emerged during and after Reconstruction. Most African Americans in the South were landless and had neither tools nor money. Landowners often could not afford to hire workers, or they found it more profitable to make use of workers they would not have to pay. Agricultural laborers moved onto land on which the owners provided small houses and tools. In return, the workers were obligated to turn over portions of their crops—usually from 20 to 50 percent—to the owners. Meanwhile, the owners extended credit for seed and living expenses until the harvests. Because the landowners kept the records of debts, sharecroppers were often overcharged when the harvest times arrived and lost even greater portions of the crops than originally agreed. Although there were also many white sharecroppers, African Americans were particularly concentrated in this kind of work.

Among the African American workers who were not in agriculture in 1910, over one-third (mostly women) were doing laundry in private homes or working as domestic servants. Another one-fourth of those outside agriculture were laborers. The concentration of African Americans in low-paying, manual labor was the economic side of the "Jim Crow" system in the United States. This was a name given to the system of maintaining racial inequality through laws requiring racial segregation, through limiting the rights of African Americans to vote and participate in government at all levels, and through occupational and housing discrimination.

THE FIRST GREAT MIGRATION

The movement of African Americans from the rural South to the industrial North is often called the Great Migration. That migration actually unfolded in two great waves. The first took place during and after World War I and the second during and after World War II. World War I began to break the hold of the rural South on African Americans and to offer economic opportunities in places where they would have greater freedom from the Jim Crow system.

As many men entered the military during the war and industries began hiring in greater numbers to meet the needs of the war-driven economy, new opportunities for employment for relatively unskilled workers opened up in the North. Although plantation owners in the South often resisted the loss of their workers, the lure of job opportunities and freedom from oppression drew many people northward.

One of the primary northern destinations of southern African Americans was the city of Chicago. In part, the popularity of Chicago was partly a result of the work of Robert S. Abbott, a businessman and publisher of the widely read newspaper the *Chicago Defender*. Abbott began "The Great Northern Drive" on May 15, 1917, urging the oppressed people of the South to move North. The African American population of Chicago more than doubled during the second decade of the twentieth century: from 44,000 in 1910 to 109,000 in 1920. Over the following ten years, it more than doubled again, to 234,000. By 1930, over 1 in 5 African Americans lived in the Northeast or Midwest.

Despite the Great Migration, most African Americans continued to live in the South, and agriculture continued to be a major economic activity for them. Nevertheless, by 1920 the majority of African Americans no longer worked in agriculture. However, even outside the South, they continued to hold positions at the bottom of the occupational ladder. One in 4 African Americans worked as laborers in 1920, compared to less than 1 of every 10 whites.

During this period, portering jobs in hotels, on trains, and in other places emerged as a major occupational opportunity for African Americans. In 1920, 3 percent of all African American men and about 10 percent of African American men outside the South worked as porters. Sleeping car porter positions on trains became prestigious and valued jobs for people who were shut out of most other jobs in American society, and they attracted some of the best-educated men in

African American society. The Brotherhood of Sleeping Car Porters became one of the most active and effective black labor unions, and it was an early leader in the struggle for civil rights.

THE SECOND GREAT MIGRATION

During the 1930's, the movement northward began to slow. Plantation owners in the South resisted the loss of sharecroppers and other laborers. As northern jobs grew scarce during the Depression years, the attraction of northern cities such as Chicago diminished. After World War II, though, the Great Migration began again, at a much greater level. Between 1940 and 1970, an estimated five million African Americans left the southern countryside for the cities of the North.

The northward migration led to a steady growth of African Americans living in the Northeast and the northern part of the Midwest. While over three-quarters of African Americans (77 percent) lived in the South in 1940, just over one-half (54 percent) lived in the South in 1970. At the same time, both the movement north and a movement to cities in the South transformed African Americans from a predominantly rural population to an urban population. This affected their positions in the American economy, since it placed them in cities at the moment when urban manufacturing jobs were beginning to decline as part of the American economy.

THE POSTINDUSTRIAL ECONOMY

By the 1960's, the sharecropper system had virtually disappeared in most of the South. Mechanization had reduced the need for human labor in agriculture. In 1967, the US government included agricultural workers under its minimum wage law. As a result, farmworkers immediately became much more expensive for southern planters, who relied even more on machines and began substituting chemicals for human laborers to eliminate weeds. After centuries of heavy concentration in agriculture, jobs as agricultural workers had finally become largely unavailable for African Americans. This did mean that they were no longer locked in to the kinds of rural labor that had held so many of their ancestors through the centuries of slavery and the decades of segregation following slavery. At the same time, however, the entire national economy was changing. After around 1970, factories located in cities became less important parts of American economic life, so that even factory jobs were becoming less available. As the old jobs in agriculture declined and African Americans were

becoming an urban population, jobs in the cities also declined.

One of the consequences of the postindustrial transformation of the American economy, in which jobs in manufacturing decreased, was that the gap between the unemployment rates of African Americans and whites grew even wider. In 1940, as the Depression of the 1930's drew to an end, African Americans had an unemployment rate of just over 10 percent, while the rate for white Americans was just under 10 percent. By 1970, the overall level of unemployment had gone down, but African Americans had a much higher unemployment rate than whites: over 7 percent for the former and under 3 percent for the latter. As unemployment rates increased through the rest of the twentieth century, unemployment among African Americans grew worse. Their unemployment rates were more than double those of whites through the rest of the century, and African American unemployment rates were consistently higher than they were in the difficult economy of 1940.

People are classified as "unemployed" if they are looking for work but do not have jobs. Those who give up looking for work are considered outside the labor force. During the postindustrial period of the American economy, African Americans were much more likely than others to give up looking for work completely. In 1970, 16 percent of African American men between the ages of 25 and 64 who were not in school were out of the labor force, compared to less than 8 percent of white men in the same age range. Rates of labor force nonparticipation went up steadily throughout the twentieth century, so that by the year 2000 one-third of African American men and 15 percent of white men who were not enrolled in school and between 25 years of age and retirement age were outside the labor force. Joblessness had become a serious problem for African Americans.

THE BLACK MIDDLE CLASS AND THE UNDERCLASS

Until the 1960's, widespread social and economic discrimination prevented the growth of a large black middle class. Although there were always black business owners and professionals, those people made up only a small part of the African American workforce, who tended to be heavily concentrated in low-income, low-status jobs. In 1960, for example, only 14.4 percent of all African Americans lived in households that enjoyed incomes two times higher than the poverty level, compared to 48 percent of whites. Using a slightly different definition of middle class, author Bart Landry, in his influential book *The New Black Middle Class* (1987) found that only 13.4 percent of African Americans could be found in middle-class jobs. Even those who were members of the black middle class often had difficulty passing their economic status on to their children.

From the early 1960's, the black middle class began to expand rapidly. By 2000, about half the people of African ancestry in the United States lived in households with incomes twice the poverty level. Although the proportion of whites at this income level had also increased rapidly over the previous four decades, to nearly three-fourths, the economic trend had been one of remarkable upward mobility for a minority group that had earlier had few economic opportunities.

A number of researchers have pointed out that government employment is particularly important to the black middle class. In 2000, more than 1 of every 5 employed African Americans worked for federal, state, or local governments, compared to only 14 percent of employed whites. This meant that middle-class African Americans were particularly vulnerable to government cutbacks, and that they had less access to private sector employment, which frequently offered better salaries than public sector jobs.

At the same time that the black middle class was growing, many African Americans continued to live in poverty. The percentage of African Americans with household incomes below the official poverty level declined steadily between 1960 and 2000. Nevertheless, nearly 1 African American of every 4 was living in poverty in the year 2000. Even more disturbing, more than 1 in 10 African Americans lived in extreme poverty, with household incomes that were one-half the poverty level or below, at the turn of the twenty-first century.

Low-income African Americans were heavily concentrated in cities, where employment was often either unavailable or offered few opportunities for advancement. With high rates of unemployment among men in these urban communities, single-parent households headed by women became a common pattern. The urban, economically disadvantaged segment of the African American population was described as the "underclass" by some scholars and journalists.

—*Carl L. Bankston III*

See also: Agriculture; Brotherhood of Sleeping Car Porters; Demographic trends; Education; Employment; Equal Employment Opportunity Act of 1972; Equal Employment Opportunity Commission; Fair Employment Practices Committee; Great Migration; Irish and African Americans; Poor People's March on Washington; Sharecropping

EDUCATION

Since the emancipation of the slaves in 1863, the debate has raged over the role of education and educational institutions in the African American community in the United States. After the Civil Rights movement of the 1950's and 1960's, the importance of an equal education and performance on standardized testing led the educational community to reevaluate the impact of education and its significance for African American students.

The Civil War (1861–1865), Reconstruction (1863–1877), and the Thirteenth Amendment (1865) ended slavery. Although free African Americans had attended schools in some northern states long before the Civil War, southern states had prohibited the teaching of either slave or free African American children. Emancipation in 1863 brought with it the challenge of providing educational opportunities for the freed men and women and their children, particularly in the former Confederate states.

THE LEGACY OF SLAVERY

In 1865, Congress created the Freedmen's Bureau to help former slaves adjust to freedom. The bureau continued to function until 1872 and, under the leadership of General O. O. Howard, established schools throughout the South. At their peak in 1869, these schools had about 114,000 students enrolled. The schools taught reading, writing, grammar, geography, arithmetic, and music through a curriculum based on the New England school model. A small number of African American teachers were trained in these schools, but the schools were usually staffed by northern schoolteachers, who brought with them their values, their educational ideas, and their methods. These white educators from northern states promoted the stereotypical idea of the kind of education African Americans should receive. Samuel C. Armstrong and many like-minded educators stressed industrial training and social control over self-determination. Many believe this philosophy was designed to keep African Americans in a subordinate position.

FROM WASHINGTON TO DU BOIS

Booker T. Washington was the leading educational spokesperson for African Americans after the Civil War. Washington, who was born a slave, experienced the hectic years of Reconstruction and, in a speech delivered at the Atlanta Exposition in 1895, articulated the outlines of a compromise with the white power structure, a policy later known as accommodationism. A student of Armstrong, Washington believed that industrial education was an important force in building character and economic competence for African Americans. He believed in moral "uplift" through hard work. At the Tuskegee Institute, which he helped establish in 1881, Washington shaped his ideas into a curriculum that focused on basic academic, agricultural, and occupational skills and emphasized the values of hard work and the dignity of labor. He encouraged his students to become elementary schoolteachers, farmers, and artisans, emphasizing these occupations over the professions of medicine, law, and politics.

Although revered initially, Washington has become an increasingly controversial figure. Some people say he made the best of a bad situation and that, although he compromised on racial issues, he can be viewed as a leader who preserved and slowly advanced the educational opportunities of African Americans. Critics of Washington see him as an opportunist whose compromises restricted African American progress.

W. E. B. Du Bois was a sociological and educational pioneer who challenged the established system of education. Du Bois, an opponent of Washington's educational philosophies, believed the African American community needed more determined and activist leadership. He helped organize the Niagara Movement in 1905, which led to the founding in 1909 of the National Association for the Advancement of Colored People (NAACP). Du Bois was a strong opponent of racial segregation in the schools. Unlike Washington, Du Bois did not believe in slow, evolutionary change; he instead demanded immediate change. Du Bois supported the NAACP position that all American children, including African American children, should be granted an equal educational opportunity. It was through the efforts of the NAACP that the monumental US Supreme Court case Brown v. Board of Education (1954) outlawed segregation in US public schools. Du Bois believed in

educated leadership for the African American community and developed the concept of the Talented Tenth, the notion that 10 percent of the African American population would receive a traditional college education in preparation for leadership.

POST-CIVIL RIGHTS ERA

Du Bois's educational and political philosophies had a significant influence on the Civil Rights movement of the 1950's and 1960's. Out of the effects of public school desegregation during the 1950's and 1960's and the Black Power movement of the 1970's grew a new perspective on the education of African Americans. Inspired by historians such as Cheikh Anta Diop and Basil Davidson, educational philosophers such as Molefi Kete Asante formed the Afrocentric school of education. Asante and his followers maintain that a curriculum centered on the perspective of African Americans is more effective in reaching African American youth than the Eurocentric curriculum to which most students are exposed. Low test scores and historically poor academic records could be the result, according to Afrocentrists, of a curriculum that does not apply to African American students.

STATISTICS

According to *The African American Education Data Book* (published in 1997 by the Research Institute of the College Fund/United Negro College Fund), in 1994, approximately 43.5 million students were enrolled in public elementary and secondary schools, and nearly 5 million students were enrolled in private elementary and secondary schools. African Americans represented 16.5 percent of all public school enrollments. African Americans were underrepresented at private elementary and secondary schools, where they constituted only 9.3 percent of all enrollments. The number of African Americans enrolled in public schools declined as grade level increased, a finding that supports the evidence that African Americans leave school at higher rates than children of the same age in other racial groups. African Americans represented only 12.5 percent of those who received regular high school diplomas in 1994.

In schools made up primarily of African American students and located mainly in economically depressed urban centers, nearly a quarter of all students participated in remedial reading programs, and 22 percent participated in remedial math. By comparison, schools with less than 50 percent African American students had

14.8 percent of students enrolled in remedial reading and 12 percent enrolled in remedial math. Furthermore, only 87 percent of African American high school seniors graduate on time compared with 93 percent of non-African American seniors.

TEST SCORES

African American students have historically scored far below whites in geography, writing, reading, and math. The National Educational Longitudinal Study of 1988 reported that the average seventeen-year-old African American student had a reading score only slightly higher than that of the average white thirteen-year-old. Compared with whites, African American Scholastic Aptitude Test (SAT) takers had lower high school grade-point averages, fewer years of academic study, and fewer honors courses. Data collected by the National Assessment of Educational Progress, however, reveal that African Americans had registered gains in reading, math, and other subjects between the 1970's and the 1990's. Despite these gains, African Americans are underrepresented among high school seniors applying for college and represented only 9 percent of the college population in the 1990's (a decrease from 10 percent in the 1970's).

It is not surprising that many African Americans see no value in postsecondary education. Regardless of socioeconomic status or whether they had received a high school diploma, a higher percentage of African Americans who were eighth-graders in 1988 were unemployed and not in college than their white counterparts in 1993, a year after their scheduled high school graduation. Despite affirmative action legislation, African Americans still are less likely to be hired for a job when competing against equally qualified white applicants.

SOCIOECONOMIC STATUS

In both 1980 and 1990, African American high school sophomores were concentrated in the lowest two socioeconomic status quartiles. The proportion of African Americans in the lowest socioeconomic status quartile declined from 48 percent in 1980 to 39 percent in 1990. In both 1980 and 1990, African Americans were underrepresented in the upper two socioeconomic status quartiles. In addition, African Americans often attend schools with fewer resources in poorer neighborhoods of large, urban areas. Fifteen percent of schools that have primarily African American students have no magnet or honors programming, as opposed to only 1.6 percent of schools with a majority of white students.

Also, a higher percentage of schools with a majority of African American students participated in the National School Lunch Program. The poverty level in the African American community is one of the factors believed to be responsible for consistently low scores on standardized testing. Along with poverty, the African American community has also experienced a greater amount of violence and delinquency among high-school-age youths. The homicide rate among African American men increased by more than two-thirds in the late 1980's, according to a study by Joe Schwartz and Thomas Exter (1990).

PARENTAL ATTITUDES

Although much of the effort of public policymakers goes into integrating schools and creating more diversity in inner-city schools, African American parents seem more interested in developing a stronger academic program in their children's schools. A survey taken in 1998 by Public Agenda, a nonpartisan public opinion research firm, showed that 80 percent of African American parents favored raising academic standards and achievement levels in primarily African American schools over emphasizing integration. Eleven percent of the parents polled said they would like to see the schools both integrated and improved. Of the white parents polled, 60 percent expressed a fear that discipline and safety problems, low reading scores, and social problems would result if African American students were transferred to a mostly white school. The Public Agenda survey demonstrates the differences in opinions on education based on racial background. For example, nearly 50 percent of African American parents felt that teachers demanded too little of their children because of the children's race. Despite the difference in opinion on these public issues, both African American and white parents expressed a great interest in their children's school success and the quality of their children's education.

—Jason Pasch

See also: Affirmative action; Afrocentrism; Ashmun Institute; Atlanta Compromise; *Bakke* case; Black colleges and universities; *Brown v. Board of Education*; Economic trends; Employment; Freedmen's Bureau; National Association for the Advancement of Colored People; Niagara Movement; School desegregation; Talented Tenth; United Negro College Fund

EMPLOYMENT

African Americans have historically been discriminated against in both hiring and promotion. Race relations will improve as African Americans become more prominent in positions of high responsibility.

African Americans continue to be confronted with the historical factors that produce racial discrimination in employment. Three salient factors contributing to racial discrimination in employment are trends in historical antecedents, educational level attainment, and employment and unemployment rates. Much excellent scholarly research provides data on these factors. In James Blackwell's *The Black Community: Diversity and Unity* (1975) and Talmadge Anderson's *Introduction to African American Studies* (1994), the authors provide historical and empirical data that more fully explain these areas.

HISTORICAL ANTECEDENTS

The first African American laborers were indentured servants who were brought to Jamestown, Virginia, in 1619. From the beginning, African Americans were not afforded a level playing field in employment. The seminal work by John Blassingame, *The Slave Community* (1972), offers a very good account of this period. Because the contemporary notion of rates of employment and unemployment is not relevant for slave labor, it is not possible to compare the work of African Americans and that of whites during the period of institutional slavery in America, which lasted from the mid-seventeenth century through 1865, more than two centuries.

Following slavery, most African Americans were involved in farm labor at very low wages. The majority lived in the South and often worked as sharecroppers or day laborers. In the first quarter of the twentieth century, in an effort to escape the rigid de jure (legal) segregation that restricted their opportunities for employment in the South, African Americans began moving to the North in search of better jobs in record numbers. Finding themselves in the midst of the rapidly growing Industrial Revolution, African Americans began to acquire jobs that paid wages that far exceeded those they could receive as farmhands in the South.

After World War II, more African Americans acquired skilled and professional jobs. Although in the 1990's, the wages earned by African Americans were still below those of white workers, they had slowly but steadily increased relative to those of whites. According to the US census, the African American median family income was 58 percent of that of whites in 1972. By 2001, that percentage had only increased to 66 percent. It is this trend that best reflects an important relationship between the races in the area of employment.

EDUCATIONAL ATTAINMENT LEVELS

The most pervasive trend in African American and white employment is that the former has always lagged behind the latter. In both percentage of employed and earnings, African Americans compare poorly with whites. Analysis of employment data from the 1960's into the 1990's shows that African American unemployment rates were double those of whites. As reported by Claudette E. Bennett in The Black Population in the United States, the unemployment rate for African American men in 1994 was 14 percent; the rate for white men was 6.7 percent. In that same year, African American women were unemployed at 12.1 percent while white women had an unemployment rate of 5.5 percent. Two factors substantially contribute to this disparity: educational differences and discrimination in hiring and promotions.

Educational attainment is perhaps the highest social goal among Americans. It is generally believed that success in life, especially employment, is directly correlated to the level of education a person obtains. Since 1940, the disparity between African Americans and whites in educational attainment for grades K-12 has narrowed greatly. By 1998, the median years of education among the two groups was about equal. By that year, the percentages of whites and African Americans having completed high school was 88 percent.

However, the percentage of whites with advanced degrees remained nearly three times that of African Americans. The educational inequality at the post-high-school level places African Americans at a disadvantage when attempting to qualify for professional jobs. Some of the proposed remedies include improving physical facilities in urban and rural schools, providing equivalent educational resources for all students, improving teacher quality and teacher training, enhancing school-community relations, and hiring and promoting substantially more African American faculty and administrators.

UNEMPLOYMENT RATES

Two factors stand out in any description of the African American experience in hiring and promotion in the United States. The unusually high rates of unemployment (official and hidden) and a modest presence in senior management positions point to major disparities between black and white people. Hidden unemployment refers to those persons discouraged in seeking employment and those who are involuntary part-time workers. The National Urban League estimates that the hidden unemployment rate for African Americans may be nearly double that of the official reported rate.

Independent of gender, the unemployment rate for African Americans has continued to be more than double that of whites. This reality has held despite affirmative action, set-asides, and minority hiring policy programs. Similarly, the median per capita income for African American households and families has remained greatly below that of whites. Wealth owned by African Americans is less than 1 percent of that owned by whites. In the area of median worth of household, the US Bureau of the Census reported in 1988 that African American worth was only 23 percent that of whites for families consisting of married couples. For female-headed families, African American families' worth was only 3 percent that of whites. Three times as many African American female-headed households live in poverty as those headed by white women.

Even within the corporate structure, African Americans have faired poorly. The federal Glass Ceiling Commission reported in 1995 that African Americans experienced disproportionately high resistance to advancement to high-level decision-making positions when compared with whites with similar education and training. Many of the experiences faced by African Americans in the corporate business environment are presented by George Davis and Glegg Watson in *Black Life in Corporate America: Swimming in the Mainstream* (1985). In a capitalist system in which employment and maximum fulfillment of human potential are vital to the accumulation of wealth, unfair employment practices have denied African Americans full opportunity to develop and maintain favorable conditions of wealth when compared with whites. With increasing national public policy that severely dampens affirmative efforts to level the playing field in hiring and promotion, the need for better education and employment seems less likely to be met.

Joe R. Feagin and Melvin P. Sikes argue in their book *Living with Racism: The Black Middle-Class Experience* (1994) that African Americans have been adversely affected by the racist hiring and promotion practices in the area of employment. However, most critical has been a failure of the nation to capitalize on an opportunity for a productive investment in African American human capital.

—*William M. Harris, Sr.*

See also: Affirmative action; Agriculture; Economic trends; Education; Equal Employment Opportunity Act of 1972; Equal Employment Opportunity Commission; Fair Employment Practices Committee; Great Migration; Sharecropping

FILM HISTORY

Cinematic representations of African Americans have been the subject of debate and contest since the inception of the film industry. Struggles over stereotypes within film and over who controls the production of images of African Americans are firmly linked to broad cultural understandings and conceptions of race.

The social and political stakes of film for African Americans were dramatically expressed early on, in the reception of D. W. Griffith's 1915 film *Birth of a Nation*. As the first full-length feature film, *Birth of a Nation* helped inaugurate the studio system, and Griffith's work as director supplied some of the basic elements of cinematic grammar. The film represented African Americans in purely stereotypical roles (as happy and loyal slaves, mammies, bucks, and brutes) while glorifying the Ku Klux Klan. Because the film was released while lynching was at its peak, the material it treated raised some concern, and the National Association for the Advancement of Colored People (NAACP) protested the film. As Ed Guerrero notes in *Framing Blackness* (1993), screenings of the film were often preceded by people dressed as members of the Klan riding through towns, and there was a march of twenty-five thousand Klansmen through Atlanta, Georgia, on opening night. Although the NAACP was not able to prevent the film from being shown, it did succeed in bringing enough political and economic pressure to make Hollywood executives think twice before producing a film that celebrated organizations like the Klan.

Although *Birth of a Nation* may have presented an unusually virulent form of racism, stereotypical cinematic representations of African Americans would predominate in mainstream films for decades to come. However, these films never existed without contest or debate. Some African Americans believed that the best way to counter stereotypical representations was to protest in the courtrooms and streets; others decided to produce their own images.

In the late 1920's and 1930's, a series of "race films" that were produced, written, and directed by African Americans attempted to present more realistic images of African Americans. Oscar Micheaux was the most famous of these filmmakers, releasing thirty-four films during a thirty-year period. Micheaux and the other independent black filmmakers who were his contemporaries had very limited resources, and it was not always clear that their representations were any less stereotypical than those of their mainstream counterparts. Nevertheless, they did manage to address black themes and to provide exposure for a large number of black actors while explicitly addressing a black audience.

HAITIANS

Haitians have immigrated to the United States, particularly New York and Florida, in significant numbers since the 1950's. US policy toward these immigrants has been generally unreceptive since the 1970's, treating them as economic migrants rather than as refugees.

During the 1980's and early 1990's, many Haitians seeking asylum in the United States were intercepted at sea and forced to return to Haiti. This treatment contrasts with that of Cuban asylum seekers, who have generally received a generous welcome to US shores as legitimate refugees. The US government's differential treatment of Cubans fleeing the Marxist-dominated Fidel Castro government and of Haitians fleeing a very poor country governed by right-wing repressive leaders caused many to question US refugee policy. In addition, Haitians speak Creole and are black, leading some to suggest latent racist motivations for the US government's actions.

THE HAITIAN IMMIGRATION EXPERIENCE
Haitians, like the peoples of most Caribbean islands, have for many decades participated in labor-based migration throughout the Caribbean region, including the United States. Haiti's economy is among the poorest in the Western Hemisphere, providing a significant reason for migration. However, authoritarian regimes also contributed to migration, as some people fled political repression. In the 1950's and 1960's, skilled

Haitian professionals legally entered the United States and Canada as permanent or temporary immigrants. Although many left Haiti in part because of political repression, they were treated as economic immigrants rather than refugees. Legal immigration continued throughout the 1970's and 1980's, but larger numbers of much poorer people also began to leave Haiti by boat.

For many years, Haiti was governed by the authoritarian regimes of François "Papa Doc" Duvalier and his son, Jean Claude "Baby Doc" Duvalier, who finally fled the country in 1986. A series of repressive regimes continued to rule the country until Haiti's first democratically elected government, that of Jean-Bertrand Aristide, was established in 1990. This government was overthrown by a military coup in 1991 and had to be reinstalled by the international community in 1994, after three years of devastating economic sanctions imposed by the United Nations that, coupled with domestic political repression, precipitated large flows of refugees. The refugee flows subsided once the military regime gave up power, the U.N. peacekeeping forces were deployed, the Aristide government was reestablished, and the economic sanctions were removed.

Thousands of Haitians have immigrated to the United States since the early 1970's. Many thousands more were deported because they were judged to be lacking legitimate asylum claims. Those who managed to stay in the United States concentrated around already existing Haitian communities in Florida, especially in the Miami area, and in New York City, where several hundred thousand Haitians make their home. Lacking significant public assistance, the Haitians who settled in the United States during the 1970's and 1980's were obliged to rely on aid from charitable organizations and the already established local Haitian communities.

REACTIONS TO THE IMMIGRANTS

Reactions to the Haitian migration varied considerably. Generally, the earlier and more skilled migration out of Haiti was noncontroversial. As larger numbers of poorer Haitians, especially the "boat people," sought entry into the United States, however, concern about the economic implications of these undocumented migrants arose. Local politicians—especially in southern Florida and under pressure from their constituents, including elite members of the Cuban exile group—along with others concerned about the potentially disruptive Haitian flow, put pressure on Congress and successive presidents to deter the Haitian migration.

However, steps by the federal government to staunch the Haitian migratory flows eventually prompted political opposition by second-generation Cuban Americans, voluntary agencies, human rights groups, and the Congressional Black Caucus. Many of these

groups charged that the discriminatory treatment of Haitians was based at least in part on race. Efforts to detain Haitians in the United States were successfully challenged in court, and advocates for Haitians won a number of court-related victories to ensure fairer treatment for Haitian asylum seekers. The interdiction programs instituted by President Ronald Reagan, however, continued under the presidencies of George Bush and Bill Clinton. Only with the return of democracy to Haiti in 1994 did the migration pressures from Haiti to the United States ease.

TWENTY-FIRST CENTURY PROSPECTS

The return of stability to the Haitian political system and the application of considerable international economic assistance holds out hope that Haiti will benefit from economic development, thus encouraging investment at home and further reducing pressures for migration abroad. The booming economy in the United States during the 1990's and the reduction in illegal and undocumented migration from Haiti helped to reduce the controversy surrounding Haitian migration.

—*Robert F. Gorman*

See also: Cubans and African Americans; Jamaicans; West Indians

INTEGRATION

Crucial changes in US public policy beginning in the 1940's helped promote the goal of racial integration. However, many social and economic factors acted to slow or prevent the complete intermingling of races.

A racially integrated society would be one in which African Americans and other racial or ethnic groups could participate in all aspects of national life without being handicapped by their color. In such a society, there should be no neighborhood where an African American could not reside simply because of being black; no hotel, restaurant, or other public facility that an African American could not use on equal terms with whites; no school that an African American child could not attend because of being black; no kind of vocational training, university education, or line of work from which an African American would be barred because of being black;

and no public office for which an African American could not contend.

In an integrated society, whites would see African Americans not as pariahs but as fellow Americans, fellow veterans, coworkers, and neighbors. This goal of a racially integrated society, despite much progress, is only half achieved; the role that public policy should play in creating a more racially integrated society remains a matter of lively debate.

Those who discuss the ethics of integration are dealing with the ethics of public policy rather than (as is the case, to some extent, with prejudice and racism) the morality of private behavior. The promotion of racial integration has been seen by its proponents as essential to the realization of an important value in public policy ethics: that of equality under the law regardless of race or color. This principle was publicly recognized in the United States by the Fourteenth

Amendment to the Constitution (ratified in 1868), which mandated that every state guarantee its citizens the equal protection of the laws. Nevertheless, de facto segregation reigned for nearly three-quarters of a century before significant steps were taken to break down racial barriers.

MILESTONES IN INTEGRATION, 1945-1968

Signposts of progress during these years (which witnessed the flowering of the Civil Rights movement) included the gradual desegregation of the American military, which began with President Harry S. Truman's Executive Order 9981 in 1948; the Supreme Court decision of 1954, that struck down the constitutionality of segregated schools; the admission of African Americans into southern state universities; the Civil Rights Act of 1964, which established the right of equal access to public accommodations and banned discrimination in employment; the Voting Rights Act of 1965; the Supreme Court decision of 1967 that overturned state laws against black-white intermarriage; and the federal Fair Housing Act of 1968. By 1990, many of these changes had achieved general acceptance; efforts to integrate employment, schools, and housing, however, continued to arouse controversy.

THE AFFIRMATIVE ACTION CONTROVERSY

By the late 1970's, affirmative action, in which the presence or absence of a fixed percentage of African Americans in a business, government department, or university is used to determine whether that institution discriminates, had become the chief tool by which the federal government tried to open up opportunities for African Americans. In 1975, in the book *Affirmative Discrimination*, the white sociologist Nathan Glazer condemned the application of this policy in both private businesses and government employment. Glazer argued that affirmative action undermines respect for merit and encourages ethnic and racial divisiveness; unlike many liberals, he denied that the underrepresentation of African Americans in a particular job or profession is necessarily evidence of discrimination. In the 1990's African American conservatives asserted that affirmative action stigmatizes as inferior those African Americans who do gain entrance to prestigious universities or get good jobs. Yet other thinkers—white as well as African American—argue that many employers would hire no African Americans at

all if they were not prodded to do so by the existence of a numerical goal.

RACIAL INTEGRATION OF PUBLIC SCHOOLS

In *Brown v. Board of Education*, in 1954, the Supreme Court declared that officially enforced school segregation by race (then found mostly in the southern states) violated the Fourteenth Amendment to the Constitution. In a 1968 decision, the Supreme Court exerted pressure on southern school boards to end segregation more quickly; in a 1971 decision, *Swann v. Charlotte-Mecklenberg Board of Education*, the Court held that school busing—the transportation of children out of their neighborhoods for schooling—might be an appropriate tool for achieving desegregation.

In the 1960's, the question arose of what to do about the de facto racial segregation of the schools, based on neighborhood racial patterns rather than on the law, found in many northern cities. In 1973, the Supreme Court ordered, for the first time, a northern school district (Denver, Colorado) to institute a desegregation plan. In 1974, however, the Court, in a sudden shift (in the decision *Milliken v. Bradley*) banned busing for integration purposes across city-suburban boundaries. In general, the Court has ordered steps toward ending de facto segregation only when evidence exists that local authorities have deliberately rigged school district boundaries to keep the races apart.

Ever since 1954, people have argued about how necessary integration of the races in the classroom is to providing equal educational opportunities for African American children. In the 1980's, some African American thinkers, such as Thomas Sowell and Robert Woodson, had their doubts. Woodson argued that a neighborhood school, even if it is exclusively African American, can become a valuable focus of neighborhood pride for low-income city dwellers; Sowell pointed nostalgically to a high quality African American secondary school of the pre-1954 era of segregation, Dunbar High School in Washington, D.C. (Critics stress how atypical Dunbar was.)

Integrationist scholars, however, argue that forcible exclusion from the company of white schoolchildren stigmatizes and psychically wounds African American children. The African American journalist Carl Rowan thinks that such exclusion is psychically wounding even if it results from white flight to the suburbs rather than government edict. White liberal political scientist Gary Orfield suggests that racial integration of the schools is necessary if African American children are to have greater access to information about jobs and other opportunities; white liberal education writer Jonathan Kozol contends, like many African American thinkers, that all African American public schools are more likely than integrated ones to be starved of money by legislatures that are beholden to white-majority electorates.

Although the compulsory busing of children into schools predominantly of the other race may be necessary to achieve racial integration in some cases, it does severely limit the rights of parents, thereby causing some resentment. However, the rights of parents over their children are, as the African American philosopher Bernard R. Boxill points out, by no means absolute. There is a societal interest in promoting interracial harmony, Boxill suggests, that perhaps should be allowed to prevail over the wish of bigoted white parents to preserve their children from all contact with African American children, and perhaps even over the wishes of parents who simply wish to spare their children the additional time spent traveling to a school across town and home again. Rejecting the notion (found in the writings of African American conservative Glenn Loury) of an irresolvable tension between integrationist goals and individual rights, Boxill also argues that government can use inducements as well as penalties to promote integration, in education and in other areas.

To promote integration of the schools while keeping busing to a minimum, some local school authorities have instituted so-called magnet schools. By placing elementary and secondary schools with above-average endowment in facilities and curricula in the middle of African American neighborhoods, authorities have sometimes persuaded, rather than forced, white parents to accept racial integration of the schools. Yet because funds are limited, the number of magnet schools that can be established is also limited; inevitably, some African American schoolchildren have often remained in primarily minority schools.

HOUSING INTEGRATION

By 1990, neither the federal Fair Housing Act of 1968 nor the many state and local laws banning discrimination in the sale or rental of housing had solved the problem of racially segregated neighborhoods. One troublesome issue that arises with respect to housing integration is the tension between individual rights and the goal of keeping a neighborhood integrated over time. Many whites are reluctant to live in a neighborhood or an apartment complex when the percentage of African American residents exceeds a certain number. To prevent wholesale evacuation by whites, so-called benign quotas have been introduced limiting the African American influx in the interest of stable integration. Benign quotas have been used by real estate agents in the Chicago suburb of Oak Park and by the management of the Starrett City apartment complex in New York City; in the latter case, the constitutionality of benign quotas was challenged in the 1980's.

Another difficult question is whether poor as well as middle or upper-income African Americans should be given the chance to live in the prosperous and mostly white suburbs. White suburbanites who might tolerate the occasional prosperous African American homeowner as a neighbor might also oppose the building of public housing projects in suburbia; yet it is the poorer African American who might benefit most from the greater employment opportunities found in the suburbs. In Chicago, the Gautreaux program attempted to circumvent the problem by settling small numbers of carefully selected poor African American families in prosperous white suburbs.

In a 1993 magazine essay, Nathan Glazer argued that only an extremely intrusive government could make racially integrated neighborhoods remain racially integrated over time. Bernard Boxill contends, however, that not every action that is beyond the penalties of law is necessarily moral, and that government, if it cannot force whites to stay in integrated neighborhoods, can at least offer inducements for them to do so.

—*Paul D. Mageli*

See also: Affirmative action; *Brown v. Board of Education*; Civil Rights Act of 1964; Civil Rights movement; Defense industry desegregation; Military desegregation; School desegregation; Segregation; Segregation on the frontier

IRISH AND AFRICAN AMERICANS

The concern of Irish Americans for their own survival and their view of African Americans as competition worked to sour relations between the two struggling groups.

Conflict has existed between Irish Americans and African Americans since the first great waves of Irish immigration in the 1840's. Before the Civil War, Irish Catholics were confronted with harsh discrimination by Anglo-Protestant Americans. When dangerous work needed to be done, many employers opted to hire cheap Irish labor instead of using slaves, preferring to risk the life of an Irishman over one of their slaves, the latter being valuable property. Struggling to survive at the bottom of the economic ladder, the Irish feared that if slaves were set free, they would face even more competition for scarce jobs. Many also believed that they should focus their energies on improving their own plight before expending any of their resources in helping African Americans. Irish Americans' concern for their own survival and their view of African Americans as competition worked to sour relations between the two struggling groups.

THE CIVIL WAR AND ITS AFTERMATH

During the Civil War, Irish Americans, who were loyal to the Union generally, had no interest in fighting a war to free the slaves. During the war, when disproportionate numbers of poor Irish were drafted to serve in the Union forces, riots broke out in cities throughout the North. On July 13, 1863, antidraft rioting broke out in New York City, lasting until July 15. Irish Americans, who viewed the conflict as a rich man's war fought by the poor, took out their anger at abolitionists and African Americans by burning, looting, and beating any African Americans in their path. New York militia were called out to stop the rioting.

After the Civil War, the economic struggle between African Americans and Irish Americans continued. Irish Americans and other white immigrants took jobs in the booming indus- trial sector, and African Americans found themselves once again relegated to southern fields. Many African Americans, seeing immigrants usurp jobs they felt rightly belonged to them, began to engage in nativist rhetoric. Many African Americans vociferously supported the anti-immigration legislation of the 1920's.

TWENTIETH CENTURY CHANGES

As Irish Americans gained greater political and economic power in the twentieth century, they continued to do so at the expense of African Americans. Although literacy tests and other racist laws denied the majority of African Americans the vote until the Voting Rights Act of 1965, the Irish used their access to the ballot to gain control of local political machines and city halls. As they lost their brogues and became established in the mainstream of white America, the Irish used their political influence to monopolize civil service positions while excluding African Americans and new immigrants.

By the twenty-first century, Irish Americans exceeded the national averages in education, income, and employment levels, while African Americans consistently lagged behind in all three areas. Although approximately one-third of African Americans could be considered at least middle class, poor African Americans outnumbered poor white Americans three to one.

—*Kathleen Odell Korgen*

See also: Cubans and African Americans; Economic trends; Employment; Jews and African Americans

JAMAICANS

Coming from a country with different patterns of race relations than those of the United States, Jamaican immigrants have had to adjust their expectations as they have dealt with native-born black and white Americans.

The movement of Jamaicans to the United States began in the early twentieth century and increased greatly after the 1965 relaxation of immigration restrictions. Jamaican immigrants clustered in metropolitan areas along the Eastern seaboard and in California, where many attained success as leaders in politics, religion, education, and business.

The Caribbean island of Jamaica was colonized by Spaniards in the sixteenth century. After most of the Arawak Indians died, the Spanish brought African slaves to work their sugar plantations. The British acquired Jamaica in 1670 and continued the practice of slavery. West Indian slavery did not encourage passivity, nor did it damage slaves' self-confidence to the extent that United States slavery did. Jamaican slavery ended in 1838, a generation before slavery's demise in the southern United States. Jamaica gained national independence in 1962.

Centuries of slavery left the island with a majority black population (many of whom were very poor), a smaller mixed-race segment, and a small, prosperous white population. Jamaica, unlike the United States, never developed Jim Crow laws, rigid color castes, or a tradition of lynching. Race is not a pressing issue in Jamaica, where black people occupy positions at all levels of society. Jamaican immigrants to the United States, most of whom are of African ancestry, often experience shock upon entering a society with a powerful white majority and a long history of blatant and rigid color prejudice and discrimination. They develop various strategies to deal with racism, such as confrontation, resignation, and development of heightened race consciousness.

TWENTIETH CENTURY IMMIGRATION

Immigration from Jamaica to the United States occurred throughout the twentieth century. Many propertied and educated Jamaicans had established themselves in New York City by the 1920's. Other Jamaicans entered the country as temporary migrant farmworkers under special visas. During the World War II labor shortage, Jamaicans were encouraged to work on farms and in factories in the United States. The 1952 Immigration and Nationality Act reduced West Indian immigration; however Jamaican immigration surged following passage of the Immigration and Nationality Act of 1965, which opened admission to nonwhite immigrants from Asia, Latin America, and the Caribbean. Jamaican newcomers settled mostly in the metropolitan areas of New York City and Miami. By 1990, 435,024 Jamaicans lived in the United States, about 80 percent of whom were foreign-born. The leading states of residence were New York, Florida, California, New Jersey, and Connecticut, according to 1990 US census figures. During the 1990's, Jamaican immigration into the United States averaged 18,000 people per year.

EDUCATION, BUSINESS, AND LEADERSHIP

Jamaicans arriving in the first decades of the twentieth century became black community leaders in the areas of business, politics, and the arts. In New York City, many were business owners and professionals. Some, such as Marcus Garvey, became government, civil rights, or labor union leaders. Others, including Claude McKay, a prominent writer who helped found the Harlem Renaissance of the 1920's, became cultural leaders.

The 1965 immigration act established a preference for skilled migrants. Accordingly, Jamaican immigrants in the latter part of the twentieth century tended to be well educated. The departure of many technical, managerial, and professional workers badly needed for the island's economic development has produced a "brain drain" in Jamaica. The value Jamaican immigrants place on education is reflected in the school performance of Jamaican American youth. Ruben Rumbaut's 1992 survey found that the children of Jamaican immigrants tended to have high grade point averages and to score high on standardized reading and math tests. The children reported spending a large amount of time doing homework (versus watching television) and had very high educational aspirations.

COMPARISONS WITH AFRICAN AMERICANS

Economic motivation underlies much Jamaican migration, and some transplanted islanders become business owners. Social scientists vary in their interpretations of West Indian entrepreneurship. Some, such as Thomas Sowell and Daniel Patrick Moynihan, credit West Indians with habits of thrift and hard work that cause them to be more successful economically than native-born African Americans. The implication is that African Americans should not blame race discrimination for their poverty.

Others, including Reynolds Farley and Stephen Steinberg, argue that Jamaican immigrants constitute a select group, skilled and highly motivated before they leave the island. Farley and Steinberg also argue that the differences in economic success between black immigrants and native-born African Americans have been exaggerated. Farley cites statistics showing that while West Indians are more often self-employed than US-born blacks, the self-employment rate for whites is much larger than for either nonwhite group. Statistics for unemployment and income also place Jamaican Americans well below whites. Most Jamaican Americans are not self-employed. Many obtain advanced education and become lawyers, doctors, and teachers; others work in construction. Women have high labor force participation and many work in domestic service and nursing.

QUESTIONS OF IDENTITY

As Jamaican Americans attempt to arrive at a sense of racial or ethnic identity, they encounter opposing forces. On one hand, they tend to retain their ethnic identity, thinking of themselves as Jamaican Americans, because of the constant influx of new immigrants who revitalize distinct cultural elements of folklore, food preferences, religion, and speech. This separateness is enforced by the attitudes of African Americans, who sometimes resent the islanders because of their foreignness, their entrepreneurial success, and because

some white employers apparently prefer foreign-born workers. On the other hand, Jamaican Americans may adopt an assimilated label, calling themselves black or African American, prompted by daily experiences with racism. Because of the conflicting pressures of living in the United States, second-generation islanders sometimes vacillate, at times identifying with African Americans and other times attempting to distance themselves from them.

—*Nancy Conn Terjesen*

See also: Cubans and African Americans; Haitians; Pan-Africanism; Universal Negro Improvement Association; West Indians

JEWS AND AFRICAN AMERICANS

Relationships between Jews and African Americans have varied over time, as economic, geographical, and other factors have changed. When relations between Jews and African Americans were good, both groups dramatically advanced the cause of civil rights. Their joint efforts helped bring about the end of legal segregation.

Although the leaders of the African American and Jewish communities enjoyed undeniably good relations in the thirty years after World War II, their friendship was not the historical norm. The periods before and after these years of closeness and cooperation were marked by ambivalence. The relationship between the two communities has varied across time, depending upon economic developments, geographical proximity, and the presence of other ethnic groups.

HISTORICAL BACKGROUND

Although both Africans and Jews came to North America early, their interaction was very limited. Most of the Africans were slaves on plantations; however, almost no Jews owned slaves or had reason to interact with them. Minimal contact began in the mid-nineteenth century in southern and border-state towns that had a population of freed slaves and a scattering of Jews from Central Europe. The Jews, many of whom opposed slavery, were among the few merchants willing to trade with the former slaves. Both groups shared a sense of being

outsiders, a strong attachment to the Hebrew Bible and its message of freedom for the slaves, and support for Abraham Lincoln and the liberal Republican Party during the Civil War (1861-1865).

Large-scale immigration of Eastern European Jews did not start until the mid-1880's. They came to the United States to escape legal discrimination, religious persecution, pogroms, and dire poverty. Very few of them had experienced any contact with African Americans; however, they firmly believed in equality and the rights of the workers, the oppressed, and the poor. Therefore, they were sympathetic to the plight of the African Americans, many of whom had moved from the rural South to northern cities in which Jews lived to escape problems very similar to those from which the Jews had fled.

DEPRESSION AND WORLD WAR II

During the Great Depression of the 1930's, the Jewish and African American communities came into contact in large industrial cities, but relations were mixed. Both groups shared poverty and persecution and liberal Democratic affiliation. However, as some of the Jews began to prosper, conflict ensued. Many Jews went into business for themselves, partly because of prejudice against them in the workforce. Because they had limited resources, they opened small stores and later bought small apartment buildings in their urban neighborhoods. Normal shopkeeper-customer and landlord-tenant conflicts developed, intensified by the racial and ethnic differences.

During World War II, the events in Germany provided a common enemy for Jews and African Americans, but that did not eliminate problems. Nazism was not a salient issue for most African Americans. One of the serious rifts between the two groups involved a charismatic member of the Nation of Islam, Sufi Ab dul Hamid, who built a reputation for himself partly by insulting Jews and their religion.

POST-WORLD WAR II

World War II and its aftermath provided opportunities for both groups. African Americans, still fleeing the South, moved into the neighborhoods evacuated by Jews. A decline in public anti-Semitism, combined with higher education, allowed Jews to move from blue-collar to white-collar jobs and to escape the inner-city ghettos. Many Jews who went to college were exposed to and apparently moved by the plight of African Americans.

Early in the twentieth century, Jews had formed a number of organizations, such as the Anti-Defamation League, to protect their rights. Several Jews worked with African American leaders to help them bolster parallel institutions to protect black people's rights, including the National Association for the Advancement of Colored People (NAACP), which had a significant Jewish presence both in funding and in legal staffing.

These civil rights organizations grew in number and in strength, especially after the sit-ins in the South during the early 1960's. The NAACP Legal Defense and Educational Fund, later headed by Jack Greenberg, took the lead in prosecuting the civil rights cases that broke down the legal support for segregation. In the most famous case, *Brown v. Board of Education* (1954), a number of Jewish defense organizations acted as supporting counsel and argued, along with Thurgood Marshall, before the US Supreme Court against the segregation laws. It was this cooperation at the top that led to the golden age of Jewish-African American relations.

Cooperation and support by Jews pervaded the Civil Rights movement. Jews offered much stronger support for racial equality than did other white Americans. Jews constituted more than one-third of all the northern Freedom Riders who went to the South to help organize and register African American citizens to vote. The

1964 murder of two Jewish civil rights activists, Michael Schwerner and Andrew Goodman, and of African American activist James Chaney, was one of the defining moments of the Civil Rights movement.

THE MID-1960'S AND BLACK POWER

The bond between the Jews and African Americans began to unglue with the increasingly antiwhite and anti-Semitic rhetoric of young black radicals such as Stokely Carmichael (later Kwame Toure) of the Student Nonviolent Coordinating Committee. Leaders of the nascent Black Power movement wanted complete control over their destiny; they wanted to run their own organizations and to live by their own cultural standards, not those of white Europeans. The role of Jews in these movements, therefore, began to diminish.

As the Black Power movement grew, several radical African Americans started attacking Israel, hastening the departure of most Jews. Many young secular Jews grew up with a strong affinity for civil rights but were ambivalent or had weak feelings toward Israel. However, because of the shrill anti-Israel rhetoric and the threat to Israel's existence in 1967 by numerically larger Arab forces, American Jews started to become more supportive of the Israelis. As the younger generation of Jews left the Civil Rights movement in response to the rise of black power, they turned their attention to issues involving Israeli and Russian Jews, and their sense of themselves as an ethnic group increased.

Although Carmichael was critical of the Jewish people, civil rights activist Martin Luther King, Jr., had many friends among Jewish leaders. King was a hero not just to African Americans but also to Jews, in part because of his intolerance for anti-Semitism and his support for Israel. King's death accelerated the split between African Americans and Jews. In the terrible riots following his assassination, a disproportionate amount of loss was sustained by Jewish shopkeepers and landlords who had stayed in the ghetto because they could not afford to relocate. The remaining Jews left quickly.

At the end of the 1960's, a series of hostile confrontations occurred, many in New York, where unionized Jewish teachers battled local African American leaders. Disputes also arose over a proposed housing project in a middle-class Jewish neighborhood and among white-collar municipal employees over jobs and promotions. After the 1970's, many of these inner-city conflicts subsided as Jews moved to the suburbs. For example, in the Los Angeles riots of 1992, friction arose between African Americans and Koreans, not Jews. In other cities, conflicts involved African Americans and Latinos rather than Jews.

1980's AND 1990's

Although friction between the two groups was more limited, it did not disappear. Black leader Jesse Jackson angered Jews during his 1984 bid for the presidency by referring to New York, which has a large Jewish population, as "Hymietown" ("hymie" is a derogatory term used to describe Jews) and courting Arab leader Yasser Arafat. On college campuses, a conflict of opinion arose over affirmative action. Jews, who had suffered from quotas that limited their enrollment in higher education, tended to oppose affirmative action, although perhaps less strongly than many white Americans. In 1991, in the racially mixed community of Crown Heights, Brooklyn, a car driven by a Hasidic Jew hit and killed an African American boy and injured his companion. In the rioting that followed, a Hasidic Jew was killed.

An ongoing source of tension in the 1980's and 1990's was Louis Farrakhan, a dynamic and media-sensitive member of the Nation of Islam with a passionate hatred of Jews and Judaism, which he called a "gutter religion." For many Jews, he was the devil incarnate; for many African Americans, he was an articulate spokesperson for black self-determinism and for self-respect and dignity.

The ties between the two groups were never completely severed, however. Both groups tended to be liberal and Democratic, so they had a common political predisposition. They typically lived in the same metropolitan areas and had a partial common history. Nonetheless, at the beginning of the twenty-first century, their political interests diverged. African Americans were focused on the large numbers of African Americans in what seemed like a permanent American underclass; Jews were worried about overseas Jews and their declining numbers due to widespread intermarriage and low birthrates. To many African Americans, Jews were just "white folks"; to many Jews, African Americans were ungrateful for the help that Jews had given to them in the past.

—Alan M. Fisher

See also: Black Jews; Black Power movement; Civil Rights movement; Crown Heights conflicts; Irish and African Americans; Nation of Islam; National Association for the Advancement of Colored People

KOREANS AND AFRICAN AMERICANS

Korean immigrants to the United States have tended to open small businesses, such as groceries, in central areas of American cities, where many of their customers have been African Americans. The cultural gap between African Americans and Korean Americans has resulted in a number of well-publicized clashes.

Ownership of small businesses is the most common occupation of people of Korean ancestry in the United States. Assisted by rotating credit associations (organizations that Koreans form to grant each other interest-free business loans requiring little collateral), Korean Americans have specialized in self-employment in small stores. The majority of Korean businesses in the United States are located in California and New York. In 1990, according to the US Bureau of the Census, 44 percent of all Korean business owners lived in California and 12 percent of Korean business owners lived in New York. Within these states, they were concentrated in the Los Angeles-Long Beach area and in New York City.

KOREAN BUSINESSES

Korean businesses are most often located in central areas of cities. During the 1970's and 1980's, owners of inner-city businesses began to leave, and Koreans, having access to business loans from their rotating loan associations but few job opportunities in established American businesses, began buying small urban shops. Although their businesses were in the city, the Koreans tended to settle in the suburbs. The people who do live in central urban areas and make up the majority of the customers of Korean businesses are African Americans. Korean shop owners are often looked upon by their inner-city customers as exploiters who come into neighborhoods to make a profit on the people and then take the money elsewhere. These customers complain about high prices, poor merchandise, and discourteous treatment. As new arrivals to the United States, Korean merchants sometimes have trouble with English and do not communicate well with those who come into their shops.

Korean businesspeople tend to hire other Koreans to work in their shops. Most of these shops are family enterprises, so family members frequently provide labor. Koreans not only live outside the communities where their stores are located but also hire few people who live in those communities. African Americans complain that Korean merchants do not hire black employees, do not buy from black suppliers of goods, and do not invest in the black neighborhoods in which they have located their businesses.

Although African American shoppers frequently view Koreans as outsiders and exploiters, the Koreans sometimes look with suspicion on those living in the neighborhoods where their businesses are located. Having little understanding of the history of US racial inequality, Korean business owners may see low-income urban residents as irresponsible and untrustworthy. The high crime rates in these neighborhoods can lead them to see all members of the communities, even the most honest, as potential shoplifters or robbers.

MISTRUST AND CULTURE CLASH

The cultural gap between African Americans and the Korean Americans who often own stores in black neighborhoods has resulted in a number of well-publicized clashes. In the spring of 1990, African Americans in Brooklyn began a nine-month boycott of Korean stores after a Korean greengrocer allegedly harassed an African American shopper. In 1992, trouble flared up again in the same neighborhood when an African American customer in a Korean grocery was allegedly harassed and struck by the owner and an employee. During 1995, an African American man was arrested while attempting to burn down a Korean-owned store, and both white and Korean store owners in Harlem received racial threats.

California, home to the nation's greatest number of Korean businesses, has seen some of the most serious conflicts between Koreans and African Americans. In April of 1992, a judge gave a sentence of probation to a Korean shopkeeper convicted in the shooting death of a fifteen-year-old African American girl,

Latasha Harlins. Two weeks after that, on April 29, riots broke out in South Central Los Angeles after the acquittal of police officers who had been videotaped beating an African American motorist, Rodney King. Although none of the police officers was Korean, Korean groceries and liquor stores in South Central Los Angeles became targets of the riots. The riots destroyed more than one thousand Korean businesses and an estimated twenty-three hundred Korean-owned businesses were looted.

Korean shop owners began leaving South Central Los Angeles in the years after the riots. Those who remained became even more wary of the local population than they were previously.

EFFORTS AT IMPROVING RELATIONS

Korean and African American leaders have made efforts to improve relations between the two groups. In the days following the riots in Los Angeles, some African American and Korean leaders formed the Black-Korean Alliance to improve communication and find common ground. In New York, the Korean-American Grocer's Association has tried to find ways of bringing African Americans and Koreans together. These have included sending African American community leaders on tours of South Korea and providing African American students with scholarships to Korean universities.

It may be difficult to resolve the problems between Korean merchants and their African American customers as long as American central cities continue to be places of concentrated unemployment and poverty. Investment in low-income communities and the creation of economic opportunities for their residents are probably necessary in order to overcome the suspicion and resentment between members of these two minority groups.

—*Carl L. Bankston III*

See also: Harlins murder; King beating case; Los Angeles riots

LYNCHING

Although lynching is often associated with hanging someone, lynching includes all types of brutal acts, including flogging, dismemberment, torture, burning, and shooting. It was a primary means used by white supremacists to intimidate and control African Americans in the South.

Lynching, the deadliest form of vigilantism, has a long history in America. At the time of the American Revolution, lynchings were used to punish Tories or British sympathizers. Until the 1850's, lynchings were associated with nonlethal forms of punishment such as beatings and tarring and feathering. In the years immediately before the Civil War, lynching took on its fatal connotation as it was used to suppress slave insurrections. Although lynching is often associated with hanging someone, lynching includes all sorts of violent acts, including flogging, dismemberment, torture, burning, and shooting.

HISTORY OF LYNCHING

After the Civil War, lynching became more widespread as former slaves came to be viewed as a threat by their former slavemasters. Accurate numbers on lynching are hard to come by, and it was not until 1872 that there was a systematic effort to obtain reliable data. Records kept by the Tuskegee Institute indicate that there were 4,743 lynchings in the United States between 1882 and 1968. Of those lynched, 3,446 (73 percent) were African Americans and 1,297 (27 percent) were whites. Even these numbers underestimate what most scholars believe to be the actual number of lynchings. A more accurate estimate would be close to 6,000 lynchings.

Lynchings were most prevalent from the 1880's to the 1920's. During the last two decades of the nineteenth century, there was an average of 150 lynchings per year, with a high of 230 in 1892. Between 1901 and 1910 there was an average of 85 lynchings per year, and from 1911 to 1920 there was an average of 61 per year. Lynchings declined to an average of 28 per year during the 1920's, to 11 per year during the 1930's, and to 3 per year during the 1940's. From 1951 to 1985 a total of 10 lynchings were reported in the United States. Although almost every state experienced lynchings, 82 percent occurred in the South. Mississippi ranks first with 581 lynchings, followed by Georgia with 530 and Texas with 493.

GROUNDS FOR LYNCHING

Although lynching was often justified as a method of protecting white women from black rapists, only 25 percent of lynching victims were suspected of rape or attempted rape. In most cases, lynching victims were summarily executed before receiving any trial. Their guilt was never established at all, let alone beyond a reasonable doubt. The justification for lynching in the cases of rape was to protect the white woman from the agony of testifying in court.

Approximately 40 percent of lynchings involved murder or attempted murder allegations. Nine percent involved assault or robbery charges, certainly not capital offenses, and 2 percent involved African Americans insulting whites, particularly white women. The most famous example of a black man who was lynched for insulting a white woman was Emmett Till.

Till, a fourteen-year-old Chicago native, was visiting relatives in Mississippi in 1955. Prodded by some friends, Till asked a white woman for a date. The woman immediately rejected Till and went to get a pistol. Till walked out of the store saying, "Bye, baby," and "wolf whistled" at her. Till's actions violated one of the major cultural taboos in the South, and he would pay with his life. That same day, the woman's husband and her half-brother abducted Till from the home he was visiting. Three days later, Till's decomposing body was found floating in the Tallahatchie River. Till had been beaten and shot before his weighted-down body was thrown into the river. The two white men who abducted Till were charged with his murder, but it took an all-white jury less than one hour to acquit them.

THE CAMPAIGN AGAINST LYNCHING

Few individuals who participated in lynchings were ever prosecuted. Coroners' juries repeatedly concluded that the death had come "at the hands of parties unknown." Seldom was anything further from the truth. Often lynchings took on a festive air, and local newspapers provided complete coverage, sometimes including photographs. In the event someone was arrested for the crime, such as the two white men accused of murdering Emmett Till, they would be found not guilty by all-white juries.

Leading the effort to abolish lynchings were the Commission on Interracial Cooperation, headed by

Will Alexander, and Southern Women for the Prevention of Lynching, led by Jessie Daniel Ames. Ames, one of the leading social reformers in the South, had forty thousand members in her organization within nine years of its establishment in 1930. When alerted about a possible lynching, Ames contacted women in the area who were members of her organization or sympathetic to its objectives.

One of the earliest objectives of the National Association for the Advancement of Colored People (NAACP), a civil rights organization established in 1909, was to pressure the US Congress to pass a federal antilynching bill. On several occasions, the House of Representatives passed such legislation, but it was always filibustered by southern senators when it reached the Senate. In the late 1940's President Harry S. Truman appointed a President's Committee on Civil Rights (PCCR). The PCCR urged Congress to pass a federal antilynching law, but without success.

The NAACP met with greater success in attempting to mobilize public opinion against lynching. The NAACP investigated lynchings and often sent special investigators into areas where a lynching had occurred. The NAACP prepared written narratives of the lynchings, including photographs if available, and distributed them to any media outlet that would publicize the lynching. The effort was to try to shame the South into stopping this despicable practice.

—Darryl Paulson

See also: Clinton massacre; Colfax massacre; Dyer antilynching bill; Film history; Jim Crow laws; Ku Klux Klan; National Association for the Advancement of Colored People; Scottsboro trials; *United States v. Cruikshank*

THE MEDIA

African Americans were long excluded from participation in publishing because of the restrictions placed on literacy among slaves. After emancipation, African Americans had to overcome discrimination and negative stereotyping before having their voices fully heard in print and broadcasting media.

Many African Americans throughout their history in the United States were largely isolated from society. During nearly two centuries of slavery, mandates prohibited slaves from being taught to read and write, although many slaves became literate despite such egregious restrictions. Slaves were discouraged from communicating with each other on any but the most superficial levels. The only places where they could communicate with a degree of freedom were their churches, where they were permitted to gather for religious services that sometimes evolved into forums in which they discussed their situations quite circumspectly. The early restrictions placed upon slaves and imposed by segregation encouraged the growth of print media among African Americans, which provided the best source of contact that most of them had with the free world.

With emancipation at the end of the Civil War in 1865, the legal status of African Americans changed drastically, yet many of the realities of their previous lives lingered. In the South—and in many northern states—segregation, legislated or de facto, was the rule.

In the early nineteenth century, not all African Americans were slaves. Some former slaves bought their freedom or achieved it when their masters died leaving directions to free their slaves. Many free African Americans gravitated to the northeast where they were more hospitably received than they would have been elsewhere in the country. Boston, New York City, and Philadelphia developed substantial enclaves of such freemen in the first half of the nineteenth century.

PRINT MEDIA

The earliest publishing by African Americans in the United States was undertaken by the AME Book Concern in Philadelphia, founded in 1817 by the African Methodist Episcopal Church. This company, the first such enterprise in the United States owned and operated solely by African Americans, published both religious and secular books. It continued to operate until 1952.

A second pre-Civil War African American publishing company, the AME Zion Book Concern, was founded in 1841 by members of the African Methodist Episcopal Zion Church in New York City. Still operating in Charlotte, North Carolina, it publishes only religious books. At least six other African American publishing companies were founded between the end of the Civil War in 1865 and 1956, the year in which the Nation of Islam sponsored Muhammad's Temple No. 2 Publications.

As African American colleges and universities were established, university presses were supported by at least five such institutions. Notable among these was Hampton Institute, which published a variety of books and pamphlets as well as *The Southern Workman*, an African American periodical published continuously between 1871 and 1939.

University presses also existed at Atlanta University, Tuskegee Institute, Fisk University, and Howard University. Atlanta University Press issued important monographs produced by the university's sociology department under the direction of its head, W. E. B. Du Bois. Beginning in 1912, *The Negro Yearbook* became a continuing annual publication of Tuskegee. Fisk University Press published important socioeconomic studies focusing on African Americans. Howard University Press, not officially organized until 1974, has published creative fiction and poetry as well as impressive critical studies in literature.

As early as 1913, the National Association for the Advancement of Colored People (NAACP) published books written for juvenile readers about prominent African Americans. Just So Publishers, a flourishing producer of children's books, was founded in 1988 and is owned and operated by African Americans. During the 1990's, a brisk trade in comic books aimed specifically at the African American market also developed.

The earliest African American newspaper, *Freedom's Journal*, which first appeared in 1827, was edited by Samuel Cornish and John B. Russwurm. The highly influential newspaper of abolitionist Frederick Douglass, *The North Star*, began publication in 1847 and greatly influenced white abolitionists in the Northeast.

During the 1880's, as African American populations in northern cities increased, more African American newspapers were founded. By 1890, Boston, New York City, Philadelphia, Baltimore, Chicago, Indianapolis, Washington, and Cleveland had African American newspapers. By 1900, African American daily newspapers were also being published in Norfolk, Virginia, and Kansas City, Missouri. The readership for such newspapers grew to the point that in 1940, over two hundred African American newspapers, most of them weeklies, were operating throughout the United States.

African American magazines appeared as early as the 1830's, but few survived for long before 1910, when the NAACP launched *The Crisis*, which gained a large and devoted readership. In 1945, John H. Johnson, who founded *The Negro Digest* in 1942, began publishing *Ebony*, which many people compared to *Life*. By the early twenty-first century, it was reaching more than two million subscribers.

Tan (retitled *Black Stars*), a woman's magazine that Johnson began in 1950, sold over 300,000 copies during its first year. Its success led to the launching of *Jet* in 1951. *Black Enterprise*, first published in 1970, attracted over 251,000 subscribers and was still the authoritative source of information about African American businesspeople and entrepreneurs in 2005.

RADIO BROADCASTING

By the 1920's, radio had found its way into many American homes. For African Americans, it was a medium for the dissemination of information that served a function similar to that served by churches during the days of slavery. Radio dramas of the 1920's represented African American characters more as buffoons than as rounded human beings deserving of serious attention. Such early radio shows as *Beulah* and *Amos and Andy* portrayed their title characters as undependable, unintelligent, and inept. Conversely, during the same period, radio performances by such talented musicians as Duke Ellington and Paul Robeson brought serious African American artists into mainstream American homes.

The first African American program aimed specifically at black audiences was *The All-Negro Hour* broadcast over Chicago's white-owned radio station WSBC beginning in 1929. The program offered music, serial drama, and comedy by African American performers. Despite the economic meltdown of the Great Depression during the 1930's, *The All-Negro Hour* survived until 1935, after which its host, Jack Cooper, continued to produce occasional black-oriented programs for WSBC.

Following World War II, African Americans made strides in radio broadcasting, although at the end of the war in 1945, every radio station in the United States was owned by whites. *Listen Chicago* became the first program in the news-discussion format directed to African American audiences.

Black disc jockeys played so-called "race music" and developed outrageous on-air personalities that began to attract listeners from a broad racial cross section. As these brash personalities came to dominate black radio broadcasting in the 1960's and 1970's, disc jockeys with "attitude" did much to encourage the Civil Rights movement of that period. In the segregated South, radio overcame some of the social and physical limitations that segregation imposed on black citizens.

It was not until 1949 that radio station WDIA in Memphis, Tennessee made history by employing an all-African-American on-air announcing staff. In the same period, Nashville's WLAC started broadcasting African American rhythm-and-blues music, first to largely black listeners but later to more racially diverse audiences, whose numbers justified sponsors' purchase of advertising time.

As African Americans became a strong economic and political force within many communities, they assumed ownership of many radio stations. By the early 1970's, two major black networks, the Mutual Black Network (now Sheridan Broadcasting), founded in 1972, and the National Black Network, founded in 1973, were in operation. In the 1980's, these networks had a combined audience estimated at more than ten million people. By 1990, radio stations in the United States that served African American audiences numbered over 600, of which 206 were owned by African Americans.

TELEVISION BROADCASTING

Lionel Monagas was an African American pioneer in television. In the 1950's, he directed such mainstream television programs as *Face the Nation* and Edward R. Murrow's *Person to Person*. Monagas also produced numerous children's programs for Philadelphia's WHYY-TV, including a ten-part series, *The History of the Negro*, narrated by Ossie Davis.

With the racial unrest that loomed in the late 1960's and early 1970's, television began to play a new and important role in the lives of Americans. Because it was able to bring the brutal realities of racial conflict into the living rooms of middle class Americans, television had a profound effect on the Civil Rights movement. Open conflicts in places such as Montgomery, Alabama, and Little Rock, Arkansas, were no longer abstractions but disturbing realities for those who watched them unfold on television.

In 1965, most African American journalists were still print journalists. In that year, Mal Goode was hired by the American Broadcasting Company (ABC) to read the news in two fifteen-minute weekly slots it had allocated to its African American audience. The network apparently interviewed thirty-eight African Americans when they sought to fill the job, but considered some of them "too light" to be recognized as African American on television screens. By contrast, other applicants were considered "too black"—presumably black enough to unnerve white viewers.

During the mid-1960's, Pat Connell anchored morning newscasts for the Columbia Broadcasting System (CBS), but WNEWTV, WOR-TV, and WPIX-TV had no African Americans on their staffs. In 1963, William C. Matney, Jr., became a television and radio reporter for Chicago's WMAQ-TV, which was owned and controlled by whites. Three years later, WNBC-TV news hired him. Eventually such luminaries as Bryant Gumbel, Ed Bradley, and Oprah Winfrey emerged as towering national personalities in mainstream network television.

Public television paid fleeting homage to African American viewers with Tony Brown's *Black Journal* (later renamed *Tony Brown's Journal*) in the 1970's. The show was well received by African American viewers, but conservative whites complained that it had an anti-presidential administration bias. The program was saved by a grant from Pepsi Cola. The only black commissioner on the Federal Communications Commission, Benjamin Hooks, joined the chorus of complaints against public television, condemning it for its arrogance and for its focus on topics of interest primarily to white viewers.

By the late 1980's, African Americans were beginning to enter positions in television management. Five became general managers of major television stations, including Philadelphia's influential WCAU-TV. When Jonathan Rodgers was named president of the CBS Television Stations Division in 1990, he became the nation's highest-ranking African American news executive.

Nevertheless, by the year 1990, African Americans constituted only 9.8 percent of television news staffs in the United States and 5 percent of the workforce in the nation's commercial radio stations. Most of the news stories on television continued to be the work of white men.

The course of television programming has reflected significant changes in American attitudes toward

African Americans. Shortly after World War II, there were few major roles for African Americans on mainstream television. They were often portrayed stereotypically. By 1970, however, network television featured African Americans in starring or co-starring roles in nineteen series, with a similar number of programs featuring African American characters in supporting roles. The popularity of some of these series is confirmed by the fact that a number of them, notably *The Fresh Prince of Bel-Air*, *Hanging with Mr. Cooper*, *Martin*, *Living Single*, *The Jeffersons*, *Sanford and Son*, and *The*

Cosby Show, endured for at least five seasons and some of them ranked among the most-watched programs on network television. By the early twenty-first century, African Americans had a pervasive presence throughout television broadcasting, but criticisms of the ways in which they were depicted continued.

—*R. Baird Shuman*

See also: Baseball's integration; Film history; Harlem Renaissance; Literature; Music; *Roots*; Sports

MILITARY

Racial and ethnic relations in the US military became the center of attention with the integration of the armed forces in 1948 and the shift to an all-volunteer service in 1973. Sociological, ethical, and political concerns revolve around recruitment, promotion, and official military policy regarding race.

The regular service of members of minorities, especially African Americans, in the US military is a relatively recent phenomenon. Before the Civil War (1861-1865), the US military tradition was one of erratic militia-based service and sanctioned prejudice. Therefore, minorities played very little role in US military life. The Civil War saw the first real attempt to incorporate African Americans into the service, strangely enough, on both sides of that conflict. However, they were largely used in noncombat roles, especially in the South, and their use, though playing a marginally important part in the Union's victory, was hotly debated and carefully segregated. This segregation continued well into the twentieth century through two world wars.

The years immediately after World War II saw the first impetus for change. Various segregated black units and a few individual black servicemen (such as Dorrie Miller, a Navy hero at Pearl Harbor) had distinguished themselves in battle, and this opened the debate on the desegregation of the armed forces. President Harry S. Truman initiated new policies on race relations in the military, and the services were mostly integrated by the start of the Korean War in 1950. The US Navy, previously the most conservative branch, actually took the early lead in promoting equality within the ranks. Gradually, African Americans began gaining some ground, a few even rising to officer status.

FROM CONSCRIPTION TO THE ALL-VOLUNTEER FORCE
Modern US wars, from the Civil War to the Vietnam War, were fought largely by conscripts or draftees. In the two world wars, conscription and segregation went hand in hand. The wars in Korea and Vietnam, especially the latter, were the first American experiences with draftees fighting in an integrated service.

Although conscription was designed to promote equitable social and ethnic representation in the services, it was often alleged that African Americans were overly represented and burdened with the risks of combat during the Vietnam War. Indeed, the poor and members of minorities appear to have suffered from the inequities of the draft, in large part because middle-class and more affluent people could more easily be excused from service or obtain deferments. This discrepancy was also caused by the war's increasing unpopularity. As the combat effectiveness of conscripts declined in the later years of the Vietnam War, the debate ensued as to the desirability of having an all-volunteer force (AVF).

Initially, opposition to ending the draft arose from many quarters. This opposition was based on notions that a large, all volunteer force would be mercenary, ineffective, socially unrepresentative, and costly. Nevertheless, in 1970, a presidential task force known as the Gates Commission forwarded recommendations that an AVF was possible if military pay and benefits were raised to meet civilian standards. By 1973, the AVF was in place as the last US troops left Vietnam. This AVF seemed to function well at first, but problems arose that led to a decline in quality of personnel for the next decade. The 1980's, however, saw two important changes occur: the onset of serious effort and spending to upgrade the AVF and the implementation of solid racial policies in the US military.

THE AVF AND RACE RELATIONS

The 1980's saw a marked improvement in the overall effectiveness of the AVF. Higher pay, better benefits, and more effective advertising have been cited as the cause. Enlistment eligibility requirements were raised considerably during this time. The number of African Americans enlisting in the service continued to rise, reaching 22 percent in 1989. The greatest increase in black recruits occurred in the US Navy, where enlistment doubled. Because of the higher eligibility standards, the educational and aptitude levels of all recruits, including members of minorities, continued to rise into the 1990's.

With this higher-quality recruit came a concerted effort at improving race relations and the advancement prospects of members of minorities in the services. In some respects, an outward attempt was made to make the AVF not only combat effective but also an ideal model in the areas of cost-efficiency, team effort, and race relations. Efforts to improve recruits' sensitivity to race began as early as 1973, but the US military consistently added policies throughout the years that have achieved a remarkable level of color-blind professionalism. Racial incidents underwent a steady decline and

have been dealt with sternly. The military maintains a complex system of grievance procedures and racial protocol. Indeed, the US military's record on race is, by most accounts, far better than its record on gender and other issues.

The issue of race and social representation is also a factor in both vocational placement and promotion through the ranks. For active-duty personnel, there appears to be equal representation in combat roles, while African Americans occupy larger numbers of clerical, administrative, and logistical positions. A few experts have even suggested capping minority recruitment in some areas, although this would revive the issue of discrimination. The US military boasts the largest percentage of members of minorities in command roles in its entire history, and an African American officer, General Colin Powell, served as chairman of the Joint Chiefs of Staff during the critical period of the Gulf War. When that conflict erupted in early 1991, it was seen as a major test of the effectiveness of the AVF. Smart bombs and other high-tech weaponry may have garnered the attention of most viewers, but professional military men were quick to point out the readiness and steady professionalism of the men and women of the all volunteer force that handily won the Gulf War.

—*Gene Redding Wynne, Jr.*

MUSIC

Throughout the course of North American history, black musicians have drawn from their African heritage and borrowed from outside sources to create a variety of musical genres that have generated interest from multiracial audiences, weakening interracial barriers while reinforcing negative or simplistic stereotypes of African Americans.

The history of African American music illustrates an ongoing cultural interaction between African Americans and European Americans from the colonial period through the twentieth century. Through a constant exchange of material, styles, and instrumentation, black and white Americans forged a pluralistic and distinctly American musical culture that survived despite prevailing institutional racism that discouraged cultural interaction. The advent of mass media in the twentieth century resulted in a general breakdown of social, cultural, and regional barriers, thus exposing

diverse audiences to black musical styles and catapulting African American music into the cultural mainstream.

EARLY AFRICAN AMERICAN MUSIC

Africans transported to North America as slaves brought with them a rich musical heritage that included professional and common folk stylings. From the beginning, slaves from various tribal and linguistic backgrounds relied on music as a vehicle for communication and expression and as a means of coping with the physical discomfort and psychological despair of bondage. Distinctively African musical traits such as blue notes and call-and-response patterns persevered in the music of plantation slaves. The scarcity of African instruments on southern plantations encouraged the development of a cappella vocal music exemplified by the field song and the spiritual, which developed as increasing numbers of slaves became Christians. Both field songs and

Matilda Sissieretta Joyner Jones in an 1889 poster

spirituals used rich imagery and emotional intensity to impart themes of joy, suffering, and longing, often employing double meanings and subtle metaphors as a means of "signifying" the Africans' true desires and poking fun at their white masters. Slave music often contained hidden social connotations; the cakewalk, an elaborate slave pageant with musical accompaniment held during plantation holiday celebrations, clandestinely ridiculed white mannerisms to the bemusement of both the slaves and unwitting whites.

POPULAR GENRES OF NINETEENTH CENTURY BLACK MUSIC

By the 1820's, white entertainers were performing parodies of slave songs and dances for white American audiences. Blackening their faces with burnt cork and affecting exaggerated "darky" behavior, these performers laid the foundation for the minstrel show, which peaked in popularity just before the Civil War (1861-1865). The minstrel show exposed white audiences to a diluted form of African American music and produced lasting works by composers such as Daniel Decatur

Emmett (author of "Dixie") and Stephen Foster. Nevertheless, the vitality and poignancy of the best minstrel compositions were eclipsed by the negative images of childish, shiftless black people that defined minstrelsy. The blackface minstrel show declined in popularity following the Civil War as the minstrel style became increasingly associated with black performers seeking to enter show business; as late as the 1920's, many black performers still called themselves minstrels.

Following the Civil War, black musicians made inroads into American popular culture, aided by increased attention from patrons of high art and the migration of black musicians into new geographical regions. Northern missionaries traveling south to minister to freed blacks sparked white interest in African American spirituals through publication in 1867 of a collection entitled *Slave Songs of the United States* and the organization of the Fisk Jubilee Chorus, a group of nine black youths who in 1871 embarked on a seven-year tour of the United States and Europe that would raise $150,000 to found Fisk University in Nashville, Tennessee. The Jubilee chorus was widely imitated throughout the South as black and white educators sought to raise money for black schools, establishing the place of spirituals in the American mainstream and further eclipsing the minstrel show as a cultural phenomenon.

The popularization of African American vocal music through spirituals coincided with the development of various styles of black instrumental music, the most influential of which was ragtime, a multiethnic mixture of folk stylings that rose to popularity in the 1890's. Although conceived by African Americans, ragtime was from its inception a multiethnic art form influenced by black interaction with urban immigrants. Early manifestations of ragtime combined modified Latin rhythms with a European march cadence. Black musicians, with a few notable exceptions such as Scott Joplin, dissociated themselves with ragtime before the turn of the century; nevertheless, ragtime continued to be associated with African Americans, partly because of the readiness of white music publishers and promoters to exploit popular interest in black American culture. By the time Joplin's "Maple Leaf Rag" was published in 1899, popular white composers were exploiting the ragtime style, and more often the name, for commercial gain. This trend culminated in the production of "coon songs" written by Broadway and Tin Pan Alley composers in a ragtime style with humorous lyrics about "negro life" that perpetuated the mythical stereotype of black people as carefree, childlike, and rhythmic.

JAZZ AND BLUES

In the late nineteenth century, as ragtime and spirituals defined high black culture and cultivated white audiences, new strains of music reflecting various degrees of African influence developed in the South. Emancipation of slaves after the Civil War created a new mobility among black musicians, who traveled throughout the United States playing in saloons, brothels, juke joints, medicine shows, and minstrel shows, often to white or mixed audiences. From this polyglot of styles emerged two distinct genres that would shape popular music through the twentieth century: jazz and blues. Blues, which flourished in areas with a high black population density such as the Mississippi Delta, set the field song to musical accompaniment by incorporating European and Hawaiian influences into a distinctly African musical framework; jazz, rooted in cosmopolitan New Orleans, resembled ragtime in its multiethnic nature and its emphasis on the African musical devices of syncopation, polyrhythm, and call-and-response.

Jazz and blues emerged in the midst of a growing white fascination with African American culture in the early twentieth century. Although jazz was conceived in an interracial environment, the first jazz recordings in 1917 featured the all-white Dixieland Jazz Band (the first popular all-black jazz band, the King Oliver Band, first recorded in 1923). By the mid-1920's, the United States and Europe had become obsessed with jazz. Blues, while less popular among whites than jazz, exerted considerable influence upon white folk musicians (such as Jimmy Rodgers) and attracted the attention of progressive whites through its association with the Harlem Renaissance.

THE RISE OF "RACE" MUSIC

The commercialization of American music through radio and records in the 1920's exposed black and white audiences to a wide range of African influenced musical styles, and promoters and performers of this music often sought to enhance their appeal by embracing racial stereotypes. Record companies marketed various black folk styles under the category of "race" music, and radio stations catering to black audiences (but attracting white ones as well) proliferated throughout the South and in urban areas in the North. Black migration to northern cities skyrocketed during World War II, resulting in a mixing of musical styles in urban ghettoes that produced a diverse body of music ranging from the gospel of Malhalia

Nat King Cole and his wife, Maria, in 1951

Jackson to the electric blues of Muddy Waters and John Lee Hooker.

THE COMMERCIAL ERA

The ongoing American obsession with jazz through World War II nurtured an ongoing white fascination with African American culture. In the late 1940's and early 1950's, black rhythm and blues enjoyed increasing popularity among white teenagers economically empowered by postwar prosperity. Less cerebral than bebop jazz and less "ethnic" than electric blues, this hybridized, dance-oriented music provided a sound track for the emerging youth culture of mobility and independence. From this culture emerged rock and roll, a culmination of generations of exchange between black and white southern folk music. The arrival of rock and roll in the American mainstream both symbolized and influenced the changing course of race relations in the United States of the 1950's: Many popular early rock-and-roll performers were African American, and white rockabilly artists such as Elvis Presley openly affected black speech and mannerisms; early rock-and-roll package tours were interracial and played to interracial audiences. White middle-class objections to the racial liberalism and overt sexuality of rock and roll created a backlash against the music in the late 1950's that coincided with a white backlash against school desegregation. Yet rock and roll had already broken down barriers that had been weakening for generations.

The explosion of rock and roll in the 1960's catapulted African American music and artists into the mainstream of American culture. By mid-decade, Quincy Jones had become the first African American record label executive, and the distinctive sound of a black-owned record label, Motown, permeated the airwaves of AM radio. The atmosphere of experimentation that defined late-1960's popular culture encouraged a multicultural creative environment in which various styles clashed and merged and interracial groups such as the Jimi Hendrix Experience, Sly and the Family Stone, and Santana symbolized the openness and youth-oriented solidarity of the counterculture.

The experimental mind-set of the 1960's combined with a new black consciousness brought new black musical genres to prominence in the 1970's, from rock-influenced fusion and funk to Afro-Caribbean styles such as dub (a precursor of rap), ska, and reggae, a mixture of calypso and New Orleans rhythm and blues that evoked millennialist religion and black separatism in its lyrics. Meanwhile, the mainstream of black music was dominated by vocal rhythm and blues, which retained much of its early style while incorporating contemporary musical and social themes. From the lighter side of funk and rhythm and blues emerged disco, a predominantly white cultural phenomenon that nevertheless reflected the social diversity of the urban club scene, garnering special appeal among Latino and gay American communities.

LATE TWENTIETH CENTURY

During the last two decades of the twentieth century, African American music continued to demonstrate an eclecticism and image consciousness reflected in its history and exacerbated by the ever-increasing power of mass media. The 1980's and 1990's witnessed greater financial and creative empowerment of African Americans in the American music industry, as music videos brought increased exposure for African American music and artists. Nevertheless, the marketing of black music retained its historical penchant for stereotyping: Despite the professed realism of hardcore rap, its images of violence and misogyny exploited white apprehension of and fascination with inner-city African Americans; the enormous popularity of hip-hop—itself a multiplicity of styles—encouraged commercial stereotyping that at times echoed past images of carefree, rhythmic black people.

The history of African American music is one of increased popular acceptance and exposure accompanied by a decreased sense of identity. Black musical expression, once regarded as an exotic but exploitable raw material, gradually became yet another entry in the diverse lexicon of American music. Black music at the beginning of the twenty-first century reflected the general eclecticism of the age as well as the obsession with formulas characteristic of the popular music industry; nevertheless, it remained significant as both a reflection and a determinant of American popular culture.

—*Michael H. Burchett*

See also: Anderson's Lincoln Memorial concert; Film history; Great Migration; Harlem Renaissance; Literature; Stereotypes

See also: Brownsville incident; Buffalo soldiers; Civil War; Defense industry desegregation; Military desegregation; Tuskegee Airmen; Vietnam War; World War II

NATIVE AMERICANS AND AFRICAN AMERICANS

Traditional American racial history, by focusing on American Indian white or black-white relations, has ignored the important cultural contributions of interactions among Native Americans and African Americans.

Since the 1960's, revisionist historians have shown great interest in the histories of American Indians and African Americans. The study of the history of the contact between these two groups has been a logical development, and much new evidence has emerged. For example, significant contact between American Indians and Africans occurred in Europe at the time of Portuguese encounters with Africans. In the sixteenth century, American Indians were traded for West African slaves, who were needed to work on Brazilian plantations.

EARLY EXPLORERS AND THE COLONIAL ERA

The Spanish first made major use of African slaves in the New World. An initial function of Africans, because of their knowledge of Indian culture, was to aid in exploration as guides and interpreters. The first African in the New World known by name was Estevanico Dorantes, a Muslim from North Africa. He accompanied the expedition of Pánfilo de Narváez, which was shipwrecked off the coast of Florida in 1529. Francisco Vásquez de Coronado was also accompanied by Africans as he explored central Kansas in 1541.

Indigenous forms of servitude were modified by the Spanish to serve the labor needs of their mines and plantations. Beginning with Hernando de Soto in 1538, the Spanish transported thousands of Indians from the Southeast to the West Indies. By 1540, however, Indian slavery was deemed unsuitable because of the Indians' susceptibility to disease; thereafter African labor began to be used. The mixing of Native American and African slave populations in sixteenth century Spanish America created a solidarity between the two groups, as seen in numerous revolts and insurrections.

Contacts among the races in the age of exploration were minor compared with those that occurred in the period of colonization. The main areas of interaction can be divided geographically into, first, New England, the Middle Colonies, and the Chesapeake, and second, the Southeast and Indian Territory. Except for the case of the Seminole Wars in Spanish Florida, the relations between African Americans and Indians were not as amicable in English North America as they were in Spanish America. This was attributable in large part to demographics. The numbers of Indian and African slaves in the area from New England to the Chesapeake were small in the early seventeenth century.

Over time the Indian population diminished, and the black population increased. Although the two groups were initially few in number and spread over a large geographical area, there was extensive intermingling, which served to modify the physical appearance of both in Massachusetts, Connecticut, New York, New Jersey, Delaware, Maryland, and Virginia. The main form of relationship during this time was intermarriage between free blacks and reservation Indians. Reservations, in fact, were centers of racial fusion all the way from Cape Cod to the Chesapeake. Crispus Attucks, Paul Cuffe, and Frederick Douglass were among the famous men of mixed African and Native American heritage.

A mulatto named York, the first black to cross the continent, was critical to the success of the Lewis and Clark expedition of 1804-1806. The explorers would have turned back at the Rocky Mountains had not York befriended the Shoshone, who provided needed supplies and horses. The son of slaves, York was known as "Big Medicine" by the Indians. He spoke several Indian languages as well as French. The Indian guide Sacagawea was his constant companion during the expedition.

INDIAN SLAVE OWNERS

The most massive contact between Indians and African Americans arose within the system of slavery developed by the so-called Five Civilized Tribes of the Southeast—the Cherokee, Chickasaw, Choctaw, Creek, and Seminole. Predominant among the Five Tribes were the Cherokee, whose 12,395-member nation held 583 slaves in 1809. By 1824, the numbers had grown to 15,560 and 1,277 respectively. Although it seems that the Cherokee were not unduly harsh masters, they refused to allow intermixture with blacks. The Chickasaw and Choctaw tribes together counted 25,000 members, with 5,000 slaves. Believing, like the Cherokee, in racial separation, these two tribes were harsh masters. The Chickasaw, who on occasion murdered the slaves of other owners, were especially harsh.

The Creek and Seminole were considered the least "civilized" of the Five Tribes, partly because they had the least prejudice toward African Americans. This was especially true of the Seminole, who allowed their "slaves" to live in separate farming communities while paying a small annual tribute. The Creek, a patriarchal society, had children by slave women. The Creek reared these children as equals to their full-blooded progeny. A famous Creek chief, Tustennuggee Emartha, or Jim Boy, was of such mixed ancestry. The Seminole, who numbered about 3,900 in 1822, owned 800 slaves. These slaves were "maroons"—they had escaped the plantations of Georgia and the Carolinas. It was the presence of the maroons that initiated the Florida Wars.

WAR AND POLITICS

Native American and African American military cooperation occurred in two campaigns closely related in time, geography, and cause. The second decade of the nineteenth century saw, in the Southeast, the outbreak of the Creek War and the First Seminole War. Both were precipitated by the anger of white slave owners who sought the return of their runaways from neighboring reservations. Andrew Jackson led the assault that crushed the Creek Red Stick Revolt in 1814, and he ended the First Seminole War in 1818 by capturing a Seminole stronghold in Florida.

African Americans figured prominently in both of these wars, since they had the most to lose in the event of a defeat. In numerous battles, Indians and African Americans fought and died together. Jim Bowlegs, who was a slave of Chief Billy Bowlegs and served as his interpreter and adviser, later became a Seminole maroon leader, organizing a resettlement for his group in Mexico in 1850. The Indians and African Americans continued to fight for their independence in two successive wars until the Civil War broke out.

The participation of slave-holding Indians in the Civil War (1861-1865) was determined by their respective views on slavery. The Chickasaw and Choctaw tribes, who were the most prejudiced against African Americans, supported the Confederacy; the Creek and Seminole opposed it. The Cherokee held a divided position; mixed-bloods (part Indian, part white) generally supported the South, while full-bloods tended to sympathize with the North. In the confusion of war, the slaves were left largely on their own, attacking both Unionists and Confederates.

After the war some African Americans sought incorporation into the various tribes. This action was resisted by the Choctaw and Chickasaw. After the

tribes' removal to Indian Territory, the legacy of Indian slave-holding was clearly evident. By 1907, no Seminole family was free of black intermixing, and almost no Creek families were pure-blooded. The other three tribes, however, had practically no mixture.

Since the 1960's a new alliance has developed between Native Americans and African Americans in the arena of political activity. The Black Power and Civil Rights movements inspired Red Power organizations such as the American Indian Movement (AIM). Black theology has been the model for the development of what has been called "red theology." Such political actions have spread to international bodies such as the United Nations and the Organization of Indigenous Peoples, in which African and indigenous New World peoples sustain positive contact.

—William H. Green

See also: Civil War; Slavery

POLITICS AND GOVERNMENT

African Americans have occupied a central place in American politics since the founding of the United States, when the issue of how slaves should be counted for purposes of political representation influenced the writing of the US Constitution.

Throughout the first half of the nineteenth century, slavery was one of the most bitter and divisive political questions in the nation. Most historians agree that the enslavement of African Americans was the fundamental cause of the American Civil War. Throughout the twentieth century, race shaped American politics.

Despite the importance of African Americans to political life in the United States, throughout much of the nation's existence, African Americans were allowed to participate very little in elections or other types of formal political activities. During the nineteenth century, widespread African American political activity largely began and ended with the brief historical period known as Reconstruction. After that, black involvement in electoral politics only began to flourish again in the late twentieth century.

POLITICAL REPRESENTATION

When representatives of the new independent United States held a Constitutional Convention in 1787 to devise

a basic framework for American government, nearly one-fifth of the people living in the new nation were held in slavery. Their status was one of the fundamental political issues at the convention. A number of the signers of the Constitution were opposed to slavery. However, many representatives, especially from the South, would not have accepted a Constitution that did not tacitly accept the institution of slavery. Therefore, in order to gain acceptance for this political charter, even the Framers of the Constitution who were against holding humans in bondage agreed to compromise and recognize the institution.

Northerners and southerners, whether they opposed or favored the continuation of slavery, tended to disagree on how slaves should be counted for purposes of political representation in the House of Representatives, who were to be apportioned according to the numbers of people living in each state. If slaves in the southern states were counted as part of those states' populations, white voters in those states would be able to elect more representatives than similar numbers of voters in other states. Northerners at the Convention therefore argued that slaves should not be counted for purposes of representation, but should be regarded in the same way as any other form of property.

The enumeration clause of the Constitution was a compromise between these two conflicting sets of interests. The members of the Constitutional Convention agreed that every five slaves—referred to as "other persons" in the Constitution—would be counted as three persons for purposes of calculating political representation. This agreement became known as the three-fifths compromise. Thus, during the remaining years of slavery, the slaves who made up the overwhelming majority of African Americans were counted in political representation, even though they were unable to elect their own representatives. Active participation in US politics on the part of African Americans only began in earnest after the abolition of slavery, during the Reconstruction era.

RECONSTRUCTION

At the end of the Civil War in 1865, the Republican Party controlled both the US Senate and the House of Representatives. Members of the party were divided between moderates and radicals. Moderates supported the abolition of slavery but opposed bringing African Americans in the South into full participation in the political system. Radicals favored full citizenship and political rights for all African Americans.

Andrew Johnson became president of the United States after the assassination of Abraham Lincoln in April, 1865. As president, he appointed provisional governors for each of the states of the defeated Confederacy. These governors held constitutional conventions that would outlaw slavery and bring their states back into the Union. The new state governments in the South accepted Johnson's plan. They also acted to limit the political and personal freedom of newly freed African Americans. White residents of the southern states attempted to control their freed slaves and force them to continue doing plantation-type labor through laws known as black codes.

Many people in the victorious North were angry with President Johnson, who seemed to be giving too many concessions to the defeated South and too little support to the former slaves. The US Congress responded by refusing to recognize the new governments of the southern states and by rejecting elected representatives to Congress from those states. Congress created a Joint Committee on Reconstruction, replacing presidential Reconstruction with Radical Reconstruction. To help the freed slaves, Congress established the Freedmen's Bureau in 1865. The following year, Congress passed the first federal civil rights act, which was designed to protect the rights of African Americans in the South by outlawing the black codes. Under Reconstruction,

African Americans began to win election to offices in the new southern state governments and, for the first time, to take part in representative politics.

The Military Reconstruction Acts of 1867 required that all of the southern states adopt constitutions guaranteeing African American men the right to vote. After the ratification of the Fifteenth Amendment to the US Constitution, Congress passed the Enforcement Act in 1870, guaranteeing the right to vote to all male citizens, regardless of whether they had previously been slaves, and imposing penalties for interfering with the right to vote. In many parts of the South, branches of the Union League helped to bring African Americans into the political process. Originally founded in Ohio in 1862 to counter pro-Confederate groups in the North, Union League associations moved south in the wake of the Union army to register African American voters and mobilize their support for the Republican Party.

Black political participation grew rapidly during the late 1860's and the 1870's. After passage of the Military Reconstruction Acts, an estimated 700,000 African Americans registered to vote. By 1872, 324 African American representatives were serving in state legislatures and Congress in the eleven former Confederate states. During the first half of the 1870's, South Carolina had eighty-seven African Americans in its legislature, and only forty whites. The state of Louisiana elected 133 African Americans to its state legislature during the years following the Civil War. Six black lieutenant governors served in southern states during these years. One of these, P. B. S. Pinchback, briefly served as governor of Louisiana, from December, 1872, to January, 1873, after the successful impeachment of Louisiana's northern-born white governor, Henry Clay Warmoth.

The Reconstruction period saw the election of the first African Americans to serve in the US Senate. Hiram R. Revels was born free in North Carolina, served in a black regiment in the Union army, and arrived in Mississippi in 1865. He was chosen by the Mississippi legislature to finish that state's term in the Senate, from February, 1870, to March, 1871. Blanche K. Bruce, who spent his childhood as a slave in Virginia, held a variety of local offices in Mississippi before being elected as that state's senator. Holding office from 1875 to 1881, Bruce was the first African American to serve a full term in the US Senate.

During the early 1870's, white southerners who were opposed to Reconstruction governments and to black political participation joined together to support the Democratic Party. Terrorist organizations, such as the Ku Klux Klan, helped to keep African Americans away from the polls. Lacking land or means to support themselves, African Americans in the South were economically dependent on white employers and landowners. With support from the North weakening, African Americans were unable to maintain their political power in the South.

THE END OF RECONSTRUCTION

In 1877, newly elected President Rutherford B. Hayes withdrew all remaining federal troops from the southern states, thereby ending Reconstruction. Throughout the South, "redeemer" governments, which sought to return white control, took power. The Ku Klux Klan and other terrorist organizations helped by keeping black voters away from the polls. South Carolina elected Wade Hampton as its "redeemer" governor, and Hampton's government became an example for other southern states. Hampton was committed to the idea of paternalism, of restricting political participation to "qualified" African Americans who would accept the position of their race in southern society.

This type of paternalism was followed by state voting laws that attempted to remove African Americans from voting lists altogether. In the late nineteenth and early twentieth centuries, literacy tests were established as means of denying the vote to African Americans in Mississippi (1890), South Carolina (1895), Louisiana (1898), North Carolina (1900), Arkansas (1901), Virginia (1902), and Georgia (1908).

Poll taxes were enacted in all the former Confederate states. This type of legislation also often had the effect of limiting participation by poorer whites. Mississippi, for example, cut back the total number of voters in the state by about 70 percent between the end of Reconstruction and the early 1890's. In 1897, Louisiana had 130,000 registered black voters and 164,000 registered white voters. By 1904, just over 1,000 registered Louisianian voters were black, and 92,000 were white.

THE TWENTIETH CENTURY

Throughout the first half of the twentieth century, African Americans were generally shut out of electoral politics, especially in the South, where the majority of African Americans lived. As African Americans began to move out of the South in the early part of the century, they did achieve some representation. In Chicago, a large African American residential area emerged. Working with the city's Republican political machine, Oscar De Priest won election to the Chicago city council in 1915, and then to the US House of Representatives in 1928. Able to build their own political organization

during the 1930's, Chicago's African Americans sent Arthur W. Mitchell to the House of Representatives in 1934 and William L. Dawson in 1942.

During the 1920's and 1930's, those African Americans who could participate in politics began to shift their allegiance from the Republican to the Democratic Party. Northern Democrats sought to compete against the dominant Republicans by actively seeking African American votes. When the 1924 Democratic presidential candidate John Davis stated that he would not make distinctions among Americans on the basis of race, creed, or color, this made the national Democratic Party appear to be the party of racial equality, even though southern Democrats still promoted segregation and discrimination.

The election of President Franklin D. Roosevelt in 1932 solidified African American support for the Democratic Party. Even though Roosevelt's New Deal primarily benefited whites, African Americans gained from it. In addition, President Roosevelt appointed African Americans as federal officials, particularly in positions relating to racial matters. By the end of Roosevelt's first term, most African Americans with party identifications had become Democrats. In 1936, when Roosevelt was nominated by his party for a second time, African American delegates attended the Democratic National Convention for the first time. The first African American congressman from the Democratic Party, Arthur Mitchell, gave the convention's welcoming address.

CIVIL RIGHTS AND THE "DIXIECRATS"

During World War II, African Americans began to call for new attention to civil rights. In 1941, civil rights

Elected African American Officials, 1970-2001	
Year Officials	
1970	1,469
1980	4,890
1990	7,335
1995	8,385
1998	8,830
1999	8,896
2000	9,001
2001	9,061
Source: Statistical Abstract of the United States, 2004.	

leader A. Philip Randolph called for a March on Washington to demand jobs and an end to segregation and discrimination in government programs. President Roosevelt responded by issuing Executive Order 8802, providing for some attempts at lessening discrimination in employment in defense industries.

After World War II, limited governmental support for civil rights led to the rise of a new political party based in the South. President Harry S. Truman showed some support for racial equality, and the Truman administration allowed the Justice Department to provide support for school desegregation in important court cases. In 1947, Truman appointed the President's Committee for Civil Rights to study ways of improving the lives of African Americans. The following year, under pressure from civil rights activists, Truman issued Executive Order 9981, which substantially desegregated the military.

President Truman's mild advocacy of civil rights angered many white southern voters and southern politicians. Three days after the Democratic Party nominated Truman for another term in 1948, delegates from the southern states met in Birmingham, Alabama, to organize the States' Rights Party, which is better known as the Dixiecrat Party. Racial segregation was a basic part of its platform. The Dixiecrats nominated Governor (later Senator) Strom Thurmond of South Carolina as their presidential candidate and Governor Fielding Wright of Mississippi as their candidate for vice president. Although Truman won the national election, Thurmond won four states, illustrating the continuing role of race as a central issue in American politics.

THE CIVIL RIGHTS MOVEMENT AND AMERICAN POLITICS

Protection for the right to vote was one of the fundamental demands of the Civil Rights movement in the 1950's and 1960's. In a number of states, particularly in the South, African Americans were still being prevented from voting at the middle of the century. Under the administration of President Dwight D. Eisenhower, the US Congress passed the Civil Rights Act of 1957, its first civil rights legislation since Reconstruction. The new legislation enabled the federal government to sue whenever an individual was denied the right to vote. It also created the US Commission on Civil Rights, which investigated the situation of African American voters.

During the 1960's, federal government support for the political rights of African Americans grew. In southern states, civil rights organizations were organizing African American voters and the publicity generated by their efforts spurred President John F. Kennedy to propose a new civil rights bill in 1963. The following year, the Civil Rights Act of 1964 passed under the administration of President Lyndon B. Johnson. This was followed by the Voting Rights Act of 1965, which abolished poll taxes and other strategies for discrimination in voting. It also gave the federal government the power to send federal registrars into any counties where there had been evidence of voting discrimination. Together, the two acts of 1964 and 1965 helped to bring African Americans throughout the nation into electoral politics.

THE RISE OF BLACK ELECTED OFFICIALS

In the late 1960's and early 1970's, the numbers of African American voters increased rapidly. The Civil Rights movement had drawn attention to the importance of political activity, and the acts of 1964 and 1965 had removed many of the barriers these voters faced in earlier decades. The growth of African American voters led to a rapid increase in African American elected officials. In 1970, there were fewer than 1,500 African Americans in elected public offices throughout the United States. Just ten years later, this figure had grown to close to 5,000 officials. By 1990, the number had grown to exceed 7,000.

As African Americans began taking a greater part in the electoral politics of the United States, they created new political associations. Thirteen African American members of the House of Representatives joined together to form the Congressional Black Caucus in 1969. They believed that the organization would help them achieve the unity needed to affect national policy. In 1971, the members of the Black Caucus met with President Richard M. Nixon and presented him with a list of sixty recommendations on domestic and foreign policy issues. In the same year that the congressional Black Caucus was founded, Shirley Chisholm, a former New York state legislator, became the first black woman to enter the House of Representatives. Chisholm went on to campaign for the Democratic presidential nomination in 1972.

Most of the increase in African American elected officials occurred at local and state levels. A number of cities with large African American populations elected African American mayors. Carl B. Stokes, an Ohio state legislator, was elected mayor of Cleveland in 1967 and 1969. In 1972, thirteen recently elected black mayors met in Fayette, Mississippi, and formed the National Council of Black Mayors. The following year, fifteen mayors met in Tuskegee, Alabama, and created the Southern Conference of Black Mayors. In 1976, at its second annual meeting in Atlanta, Georgia, that body changed its name to National Conference of Black

Mayors. In 1977, African American officials at the state level throughout the United States formed the National Black Caucus of State Legislators, with headquarters in Washington, D.C., to offer support to black officials and to help them communicate with each other.

TWENTY-FIRST CENTURY AFRICAN AMERICAN POLITICS

By the year 2001, 24.1 million African Americans were part of the voting-age population of the United States; they represented 11.9 percent of the total voting-age population. However, African Americans were still vastly underrepresented in the political system. A December, 2000, study conducted by the Joint Center for Political and Economic Studies showed that at the end of the twentieth century, African Americans held only 1.7 percent of all public elected offices. Nevertheless, the number of African Americans who did hold public offices was six times greater than it had been in 1970. States with the most elected African American elected officials in 2001 were Mississippi (892 officials), Alabama (756), Louisiana (705), Illinois (624), and Georgia (611). Only Hawaii, Montana, North Dakota, and South Dakota had no elected officials who were identified as African American in 2001.

The link between African Americans and the Democratic Party, first forged during the 1920's and 1930's, continued into the twenty first century. The connection between race and political affiliation became an especially heated question in the 2000 presidential election, when Democratic nominee Al Gore narrowly lost the election to Republican George W. Bush as a result of the delayed vote count in Florida. Problems with ballots led some observers to maintain that many African American votes had not been counted, possibly costing the Democrats the national election.

In the 2002 General Social Survey conducted by the National Opinion Research Center, 71 percent of African American potential voters identified themselves as Democrats and 21 percent as independents, with only 8 percent as Republicans. By comparison, 41 percent of whites identified themselves as Republicans, 38 percent as Democrats, 19 percent as independents, and 2 percent as members of other parties.

—*Carl L. Bankston III*

See also: Black cabinet; Chisholm's election to Congress; Compromise of 1877;Congressional Black Caucus; Gerrymandering; Grandfather clauses; Jackson's run for the presidency; *Lassiter v. Northampton County Board of Elections*; President's Committee on Civil Rights; Thomas-Hill hearings; Three-fifths compromise; Twenty-fourth Amendment; Voting Rights Act of 1965; Voting Rights Act of 1975; White primaries; Wilder's election to Virginia governorship

SEGREGATION

Segregation of members of minorities in the United States was a negative social and economic practice that kept the country from achieving "liberty, freedom, and equality," promises upon which the nation was founded; the practice consigned millions of people to second-class citizenship.

American segregation was born in the colonial era, when the "majority" practiced de facto segregation. When most African Americans were slaves, free blacks suffered de facto segregation in housing and social segregation based on custom and folkways. As the northern colonies abolished slavery, de facto segregation sometimes became de jure separation supported by local ordinances and/or state law.

As long as the South maintained slavery, that institution regulated race relations, and de jure segregation was not needed. In 1865, however, the southern slaves were set free and legal segregation made its appearance. After the Civil War, most southern states passed legislation known as black codes, which resembled the old slave codes. Under the new codes, social segregation was often spelled out. For example, most states moved immediately to segregate public transportation lines. By the end of Reconstruction (1866–1877), race lines had hardened, and social segregation was the rule rather than the exception.

UNSUCCESSFUL CHALLENGES

Some African Americans challenged segregationist laws. In 1896, blacks from Louisiana sued a public transportation company (railroad) that operated segregated passenger cars, as stipulated by Louisiana's state laws. Black leaders argued that the state laws and the railroad's actions

An African-American man goes into the "colored" entrance of a movie theater in Belzoni, Mississippi, 1939

violated the Thirteenth and Fourteenth Amendments to the Constitution. The case, *Plessy v. Ferguson,* reached the US Supreme Court, which ruled that segregation was legal as long as "separate but equal" facilities were made available for members of minorities. A lone dissenter, Justice John M. Harlan, who happened to be a white southerner, rejected the majority opinion, saying that the Constitution should be "colorblind" and that it should not tolerate "classes" among the citizens, who were all equal.

Despite Harlan's dissent, the *Plessy* decision gave absolute legal sanction to a practice that many states, including some in the North, were already practicing by custom and tradition—*Plessy* froze segregation into the highest law of the land. Thereafter, segregationists, especially those in the South, used their legislatures to pass a host of new laws that extended the supposed "separate but equal" doctrine to all areas of life. For example, restaurants, hotels, and theaters became segregated by law, not only by custom. Railroad cars and railroad stations divided the races; hospitals, doctors'

offices, and even cemeteries became segregated. Some southern state laws called for segregated prisons, while prisons in other states took criminals from both races but separated them within the facility. At least one state passed a law that forbade a white and a black prisoner to look out the same prison window at the same time. If the prisoners were physically close enough to look out at the same time, they were too close to please segregationists.

As the United States matured during the twentieth century, segregation was extended to whenever technology made it seem necessary. For example, in 1915, Oklahoma became the first state in the Union to require segregated public pay telephone booths. When motor cars were first used as a taxi service, taxi companies were segregated—a "white" taxi serving whites only and a "black" taxi serving African Americans only. Public water fountains became segregated, as did public restroom facilities.

Another problem became associated with segregation. Often, there was no separate facility for blacks, who were denied service altogether. For example, as late as the 1960's, President Lyndon B. Johnson's personal maid and butler-handyman experienced difficulty traveling by car from Washington, D.C., back to Johnson's Texas home. There were few if any motels along the way that would rent rooms to African Americans.

SUCCESSFUL CHALLENGES
Eventually, the National Association for the Advancement of Colored People (NAACP) launched new attacks against segregationist laws—especially in circumstances in which no separate facilities existed for African Americans.

For example, in *Gaines v. Missouri* (1938) and *Sweatt v. Painter* (1949; a Texas case), the Supreme Court ruled that blacks could attend white law schools because no separate school was available in state for African Americans. In 1950, in *McLaurin v. Oklahoma,* the NAACP tested the same concept and won another court battle. As *McLaurin* showed, the University of Oklahoma had admitted a black student to its graduate program but then had segregated him on campus. After the Supreme Court ruled that such segregation was unfair and illegal because it denied equal education, Thurgood Marshall of the NAACP became even more determined to challenge segregation. He did so successfully when, in *Brown v. Board of Education* (1954), the Court declared segregated public education illegal.

If segregation was unjust and unconstitutional in education, it seemed clear that it was also unjust in other areas of life. In 1955, under the leadership of Martin Luther King, Jr., and others, a nonviolent protest movement took to the streets and eventually won victories that included new laws such as the Civil Rights Act of 1964 and the Voter Registration Act of 1965. Ultimately, a limited social and economic revolution occurred that condemned segregation and, in part, created a new American society.

—James Smallwood

See also: *Alexander v. Holmes County Board of Education*; Baseball's integration; Black codes; *Bolling v. Sharpe*; *Brown v. Board of Education*; Civil Rights movement and children; *Cooper v. Aaron*; *Evans v. Abney*; *Green v. County School Board of New Kent County*; *Heart of Atlanta Motel v. United States*; Integration; Jim Crow laws; *Jones v. Alfred H. Mayer Company*; *Keyes v. Denver School District No. 1*; *McLaurin v. Oklahoma State Regents for Higher Education*; *Milliken v. Bradley*; *Missouri ex rel. Gaines v. Canada*; Orangeburg massacre; *Palmer v. Thompson*; *Plessy v. Ferguson*; Restrictive covenants; Segregation; Segregation on the frontier; Separate but equal doctrine; *Shelley v. Kraemer*; Slavery; Sports; *Sweatt v. Painter*

SEGREGATION ON THE FRONTIER
Several thousand African Americans moved to the American West in the late nineteenth and early twentieth centuries in an effort to escape the racism that existed in the eastern United States. Once on the frontier, African Americans established segregated communities that allowed them to live apart from whites who would discriminate against them.

Most people who have studied the western frontier have found that racial discrimination existed there, but that it was different from that found in the former slave states in the southeastern United States. For example, some western territories and states passed statutes requiring segregation of the races in schools and other public facilities, but these laws were not enforced as vigorously as in the South. Incidents of racial violence (such as white mobs lynching African Americans) were less numerous on the frontier than they were east of the Mississippi River.

Still, racism did exist on the frontier, and African Americans sought to avoid it. Even before the Civil War (1861–1865), free blacks established segregated communities in isolated areas of Arkansas, Louisiana, and Texas. After the war, African Americans who had been slaves to Native Americans created several all-black towns and agricultural colonies in Indian Territory. Other African Americans availed themselves of the provisions of the Homestead Act (1862), which allowed them to claim 160-acre parcels of public land on the frontier. Many of these black homesteaders created segregated communities where they could live by their own rules rather than those imposed upon them by white Americans.

ALL-BLACK COMMUNITIES
Several of the all-black settlements were towns in which all of the businesses were owned by African Americans. Others were agricultural colonies whose residents

expected to earn their living primarily by farming. In reality, however, the distinction between the two types of communities often became blurred. The farmers needed businesses to supply some of their needs, and the business owners often farmed to make extra money. Consequently, many of the segregated frontier communities were small urban areas surrounded by farms.

Perhaps the most famous all-black frontier settlement was Nicodemus, Kansas. A few promoters of an all-black settlement chose a spot on the western Kansas prairie to establish Nicodemus. They filed homestead claims and mapped out town lots on part of their land. They then went back east to make speeches and distribute brochures encouraging people to move to the proposed town. The promoters then charged the recruits fees for helping them move to Kansas and for filing their homestead papers.

The Nicodemus settlers established churches, schools, and various social organizations to improve their quality of life. This attempt to create a sense of community was essential in making the colonists feel content in strange surroundings. As the people became friends with their neighbors and worked to help one another succeed, the sense of community began to grow and to become stronger. This sense of community was one of the main reasons that African Americans chose to live in segregated settlements on the frontier. However, while the sense of community was strong in Nicodemus and other all-black frontier colonies, other factors caused most of them to fail.

The frontier environment was such that droughts often led to crop failures, which sometimes caused residents to grow disillusioned and move elsewhere to farm. A second problem was that many of the settlers lacked the capital to obtain enough animals, supplies, and equipment to make farming successful. This, of course, had an adverse effect on the businesses that relied on the farmers' patronage. Many businesses

went broke, and African American farmers often had to work for nearby whites in order to eke out a living from the harsh frontier land. Eventually, many inhabitants of all-black communities abandoned their claims and moved into or near towns where whites also lived.

BLACK NEIGHBORHOODS IN WHITE COMMUNITIES

Even in these larger, predominantly white settlements, African Americans usually segregated themselves. Many frontier towns had a neighborhood where African Americans lived and socialized, creating a black community within the larger, white-controlled community. In these situations, African Americans experienced social segregation while participating in an integrated business environment that allowed them to benefit from their more prosperous white neighbors. Some African Americans worked as hired hands and domestic servants for white families, and others ran restaurants, hotels, barbershops, laundries, repair shops, and other businesses that catered to customers of all races.

Laws and customs of the late nineteenth and early twentieth centuries dictated that the social contact between black and white people be limited. This was true in the American West just as it was in the older eastern sections of the country. However, a relatively low level of prejudice on the western frontier allowed for much business activity between the races. Thus, although African Americans on the western frontier usually lived in segregated communities, their lives were more prosperous and successful when they engaged in commerce with their white neighbors.

—*Roger D. Hardaway*

See also: Cowboys; Segregation

SHARECROPPING

A system in which Freedmen - newly freed Africans, mulattos, and negros-farmed on white-owned land and paying for the privilege to work and live on the land with shares of their crops. During the half century following the abolition of slavery in the South, sharecropping provided landless former slaves with meager incomes, while helping to keep the South's ruined economy going.

In the aftermath of the American Civil War (1861–1865), the South faced many difficulties. Its cities, factories, and railroads had been shattered, and its valuable agricultural industry had been turned upside down. Many large planters lost their entire workforce when the Thirteenth Amendment to the US Constitution freed southern slaves. Newly freed slaves, most of whom were farm workers, had no land to cultivate.

A FSA photo of a cropper family near White Plains, in Georgia, USA (1941)

Landowners, former slaves, and small farmers negotiated a compromise: sharecropping. The system they created would eventually lead to a steady decline in southern agriculture during the twentieth century.

Deeply in debt after the war, many southern landowners were forced to give up all or fragments of their property to local merchants, banks, and corporations. By the end of Reconstruction (1863–1877), large portions of southern farmland were controlled by absentee landlords who neither lived on nor worked their land but managed it from afar. Southern landowners had a large number of acres to be planted and not enough money to hire farm laborers. At the same time, thousands of Africans, Mulattos, and Negros were free from enslavement, but without the homes, land, or tools they needed to support themselves.

To earn a living, agricultural laborers agreed to become tenants on farmland. Landlords provided tenants with land, a small house, and tools to grow a crop.

Tenants worked the land and promised a percentage of their annual crop yield, usually between 20 percent and 50 percent, to the landlord. Landlords frequently arranged credit for tenants with local merchants to help them establish a household and buy seed. Storekeepers and landowners, who sometimes were the same person, placed liens on the farmers' crops to protect their interests. Tenants hoped to yield enough profit from their labor not only to pay off their liens but also to eventually purchase the land they worked.

A bad year or depressed cotton prices could easily leave many farmers in debt at the end of the season. Sharecroppers frequently promised an additional percentage of their crop to local merchants to purchase the next year's seed and feed their families through the winter. Year after year, sharecroppers became more indebted. Forced to work until liens were paid, tenants became bound to their land, continually impoverished and with little hope of becoming property owners.

Sharecropping in the South increased steadily in the latter half of the nineteenth century until approximately 75 percent of all southern farmers were sharecroppers. Cotton prices began to drop after the turn of the century and then fell drastically during the Great Depression of the 1930's. These conditions forced thousands of tenants to leave the land and move to northern cities in search of employment. Others were forced to leave when landlords decided farming was no longer profitable. As a result of this loss of labor and increases in technology, sharecropping represented only a small percentage of farming in the South by the end of the twentieth century.

—Leslie Stricker (original article author)
—Patrica A. McDaniel (2016 article reviewer)

See also: Agriculture; Employment; Great Migration; Reconstruction

SLAVERY

Slavery has historically constituted a significant denial of human rights and, as practiced in the United States, laid the foundations for conflict between whites and African Americans for generations to come.

Slavery is one of the oldest institutions of human society. Slavery was present in the earliest human civilizations, those of ancient Mesopotamia and Egypt, and continued to exist in several parts of the world through the late twentieth century.

Despite the near universality of slavery, there is no consensus regarding what distinctive practices constitute slavery. In Western society, a slave typically was a person who was owned as property by another person and forced to perform labor for the owner. This definition, however, breaks down when applied to non-Western forms of slavery. In some African societies, slaves were not owned as property by an individual but were thought of as belonging to a kinship group. The slave could be sold, but so too could nonslave members of the kinship group. In certain African societies, slaves were exempted from labor and were used solely to bring honor to the master by demonstrating his absolute power over another person.

Sociologist Orlando Patterson suggested that slavery is best understood as an institution designed to increase the power of the master or the ruling group. Slaves can fulfill this role by laboring to make the master rich, but they can also do so by bringing honor to the master. One of the defining, universal characteristics of slavery is that the slave ceases to exist as a socially meaningful person. The slave relates to society only through the master. Slavery includes many mechanisms to remove the slave from membership in any groups, such as the family, through which the slave might derive an independent sense of identity. By placing the master in a dominant position over another individual, slavery is believed to increase the honor and power of the master. The slave's status is permanent and it is typically passed down to the slave's children.

SLAVERY IN WORLD HISTORY

The use of slavery was widespread in the ancient world, especially in Greece and Italy. During the classical ages of Greek and Roman society, slaves constituted about one-third of the population.

Following the collapse of the Roman Empire in Western Europe during the fifth and sixth centuries, declining economic conditions destroyed the profitability of slavery and provided employers with large numbers of impoverished peasants who could be employed more cheaply than slaves. Over the next seven hundred years, slavery slowly gave way to serfdom. Although serfs, like slaves, were unfree laborers, serfs generally had more legal rights and a higher social standing than slaves.

Familiarity with the institution of slavery did not, however, disappear in Western Europe. A trickle of slaves from Eastern Europe and even from Africa continued to flow into England, France, and Germany. Western Europeans retained their familiarity with large-scale slave systems through contacts with southern Italy, Spain, and Portugal, and with the Byzantine Empire and the Muslim world, where slavery flourished. Western Europeans also inherited from their Roman forebears the corpus of Roman law, with its elaborate slave code. During the later Middle Ages, Europeans who were familiar with Muslim sugar plantations in the Near East sought to begin sugar production with slave labor on the islands of the Mediterranean.

Thus, as Western Europe entered the age of exploration and colonization, Europeans had an intimate knowledge of slavery and a ready-made code of laws to govern slaves. During the sixteenth century, as European nations sought to establish silver mines and sugar plantations in their new colonies in the Western Hemisphere, heavy labor demands led to efforts to enslave Native Americans. This supply of laborers was inadequate because of the rapid decline of the Indian population following the introduction of European diseases into the Western Hemisphere. The Spanish and Portuguese then turned to Africa, next most readily available source of slave laborers.

Between 1500 and 1900, European slave traders imported 9.7 million African laborers into the Western Hemisphere. Every European colony eventually used slave labor, which became the principal form of labor in the Western Hemisphere. Because the wealth of several modern nations was created by slave labor, some contemporary African Americans have claimed the right to receive reparations payments from nations such as the United States, which continue to enjoy the wealth accumulated originally by the use of slave laborers.

SLAVERY AND RACE

The large-scale use of African slaves by European masters raised new moral issues regarding race. There is no necessary connection between slavery and race. A massive survey by Orlando Patterson of slave societies throughout history found that in three-quarters of slave societies, masters and slaves were of the same race. Slavery in the Western Hemisphere was unusual in human history because slaves were drawn almost exclusively from the black race.

In most colonies of the Western Hemisphere, the use of African slaves was accompanied by the rise of racism, which some scholars claim was a new, unprecedented phenomenon caused by slavery. Scholars seeking to understand contemporary race relations in the United States have been intrigued by the rise of prejudice in new slave societies. Did Europeans enslave Africans merely because they needed slaves and Africa was the most accessible source of slaves? If so, then prejudice probably originated as a learned association between race and subservience.

Modern prejudice might be broken down through integration and affirmative action programs aimed at helping whites to witness the success of African Americans in positions of authority.

Did Europeans enslave Africans because they saw Africans as inferior persons ideally suited for slavery? If so, then contemporary racism is a deeply rooted cultural phenomenon that is not likely to disappear for generations to come. African Americans will receive justice only if the government establishes permanent compensatory programs aimed at equalizing power between the races.

Historical research has not resolved these issues. Sixteenth century Europeans apparently did view Africans as inferior beings, even before the colonization of the Western Hemisphere.

These racial antipathies were minor, however, in comparison to modern racism. Emancipated slaves in recently settled colonies experienced little racial discrimination. The experience of slavery apparently increased the European settlers' sense of racial superiority over Africans.

After the slave systems of the Western Hemisphere became fully developed, racial arguments became the foundation of the proslavery argument. Supporters of slavery claimed that persons of African descent were so degraded and inferior to whites that it would be dangerous for society to release the slaves from the control of a master. In the United States, some proslavery theorists pushed the racial argument to extreme levels. In explaining the contradiction between slavery and the American ideal that all persons should be free, writers such as Josiah Nott and Samuel Cartwright claimed that African Americans were not fully human and, therefore, did not deserve all the rights belonging to humanity.

A minority of proslavery writers rejected the racial argument and the effort to reconcile slavery and American egalitarian ideals. Writers such as George Fitzhugh claimed that all societies were organized hierarchically by classes and that slavery was the most benevolent system for organizing an unequal class structure.

Slavery bound together masters and slaves through a system of mutual rights and obligations. Unlike the "wage slaves" of industrial society, chattel slaves had certain access to food, clothing, shelter, and medical care, all because the master's ownership of the slaves' bodies made him diligent in caring for his property.

Slavery was depicted by some proslavery theorists as the ideal condition for the white working class.

THE ANTISLAVERY MOVEMENT

From the dawning of human history until the middle of the eighteenth century, few persons appear to have questioned the morality of slavery as an institution. Although some persons had earlier raised moral objections to certain features of slavery, almost no one appears to have questioned the overall morality of slavery as a system before the middle of the eighteenth century.

Around 1750, however, an antislavery movement began to appear in Britain, France, and America.

The sudden rise of antislavery opinion appears to be related to the rise of a humanitarian ethos during the Enlightenment that encouraged people to consider the welfare of humans beyond their kin groups. The rise of the antislavery movement was also related to the growing popularity of new forms of evangelical and pietistic religious sects such as the Baptists, Methodists, and Quakers, which tended to view slaveholding as sinful materialism and slaves as persons worthy of God's love. The rise of the antislavery movement was encouraged by the American and French Revolutions, whose democratic political philosophies promoted a belief in the equality of individuals. The rise of antislavery opinion also coincided in time with the rise of industrial capitalism. The historian Eric Williams argued in *Capitalism and Slavery* (1944) that the economic and class interests of industrial capitalists rather than the moral scruples of humanitarians gave rise to the antislavery movement.

Antislavery activism initially focused on the abolition of the Atlantic slave trade. Reformers succeeded in prompting Britain and the United States to abolish the slave trade in 1807. Other nations followed this lead over the next half century until the Atlantic slave trade was virtually eliminated.

The campaign to abolish the slave trade achieved early success because it joined together moral concerns and self-interest. Many persons in the late eighteenth and early nineteenth centuries were prepared to accept the end of the slave trade while opposing the end of slavery itself. Even slaveholders were angered by the living conditions endured by slaves on crowded, disease-infested slave ships. Some masters, in fact, attempted to justify their ownership of slaves by claiming that the conditions on their plantations were more humane than the conditions on slave-trading ships or in allegedly primitive Africa.

Some slaveholders supported the abolition of the slave trade because they realized that limiting the supply of new slaves from Africa would increase the value of the existing slave population.

Finally, many persons believed that it was wrong for slave traders to deny liberty to freeborn Africans, but that it was not wrong for slave masters to exercise control over persons who were born into the status of slavery. Indeed, supporters of slavery argued that the well-being of society required masters to exercise control over persons who had no preparation for freedom and might be a threat to society if emancipated.

The campaign to eradicate slavery itself was more difficult and was accompanied by significant political upheavals and, in the case of Haiti and the United States, revolution and warfare.

British reformers such as William Wilberforce, Thomas Clarkson, and Granville Sharp made, perhaps, the most significant contributions to the organization of a worldwide antislavery movement.

In 1823, British activists formed the London Antislavery Committee, soon to be renamed the British and Foreign Antislavery Society. The society spearheaded a successful campaign to abolish slavery in the British Empire and, eventually, worldwide.

It remained in existence in the 1990's. Known by the name Antislavery International, the society had the distinction of being the world's oldest human rights organization. Antislavery reformers were also active in the United States. From the 1830's through the 1860's, abolitionists such as William Lloyd Garrison, Wendell Phillips, and Frederick Douglass sought to arouse the moral anger of Americans against slavery. More effective, however, were politicians such as Abraham Lincoln, Charles Sumner, and Salmon P. Chase, whose antislavery message was a mixture of idealism, self-interest, and expedience.

EMANCIPATION OF SLAVES

Beginning in the late eighteenth century and accelerating through the nineteenth century, slavery was abolished throughout the Western Hemisphere. This was followed in the late nineteenth and twentieth centuries by the legal abolition of slavery in Africa and Asia.

In evaluating the success of abolition in any society, it is necessary to distinguish between legal and de facto emancipation.

Changing the legal status of a slave to that of a free person is not the same thing as freeing the slave from the control of a master.

Legal emancipation often has little impact on persons held as slaves if governments fail to enforce the abolition of slavery. For example, Britain in the nineteenth century outlawed slavery in its colonies in India, the Gold Coast, Kenya, and Zanzibar. Yet, fearing a disruption of economic production in these colonies, the British government simply abstained from enforcing its own abolition laws until pressure from reformers put an end to slavery.

A similar situation existed in Mauritania, where slavery was prohibited by law three separate times, in 1905, 1960, and 1980, yet the government of Mauritania enacted no penalties against masters who kept slaves in violation of the emancipation law, and the government waged no campaign to inform the slaves of their freedom. As a result, journalists and investigators for the International Labor Organisation found slavery still flourishing in Mauritania in the 1990's.

Even in societies that vigorously enforced their acts of abolition, legal emancipation was usually followed by a period of transition in which former slaves were held in a state resembling that of slavery. The Abolition of Slavery Act of 1833, which outlawed slavery in most colonies of the British Empire, provided that slaves would serve as apprentices to their former masters for a period of four to six years. In the American South after the Civil War, former slaves were subject for a time to black codes that greatly reduced the freedom of movement of African Americans and required them to work on the plantations of former slave masters. After the Civil Rights Act of 1866 and the Fourteenth Amendment outlawed such practices, southerners created the sharecropping and crop-lien systems, which allowed planters to control the labor of many African Americans through a form of debt bondage.

—*Harold D. Tallant*

See also: Abolition; Abolitionist movement and women; Agriculture; *Amistad* slave revolt; Antislavery laws of 1777 and 1807; Baptist Church; Civil War; *Clotilde* capture; Confiscation Acts of 1861 and 1862; Demographic trends; Emancipation Proclamation; Free blacks; *Groves v. Slaughter*; National Coalition of Blacks for Reparations in America; Native Americans and African Americans; New York City slave revolt; Northwest Ordinance; *Roots*; *Scott v. Sandford*; Segregation; Slavery and families; Slavery and race relations; Slavery and women; Slavery in Massachusetts; Slavery in Virginia; Stono Rebellion; Three-fifths compromise; Underground Railroad

SLAVERY AND FAMILIES

Despite immense obstacles, African American slaves forged strong family bonds and created communities that valued marriage, nurtured children, cared for the aged, and preserved commitment to nuclear family groups.

Although conditions under slavery varied widely and included many humane and even loving master-slave relationships, the laws governing slavery made it impossible for slaves to enjoy secure family lives. Not only could slaveholders sell any of their slaves, regardless of family ties, but slaves could not legally marry. Moreover, any child born to a slave woman was legally a slave, even if the father was a free black or a white man. None of these deterrents to stable family life, however, kept slaves from valuing and trying to maintain family groups and kinship ties, and slaves were able, even in the face of immense obstacles, to shape a family-oriented culture that provided them emotional support, self-esteem, and a measure of autonomy from the white culture that controlled so much of their lives.

MARRIAGE
Although slave marriage vows were not legally binding, slaves themselves—and most masters—recognized the commitments of those who claimed to be married. Most owners encouraged marriages: Marriage was regarded as the foundation of moral society; Moreover, family ties and responsibilities increased owners' hold on their slaves, since masters could determine whether to allow relationships to continue and could dictate the conditions under which they survived. Being able to separate spouses or family members was a powerful threat that slave owners held over their workers.

Some slaveholders arranged marriages, but most allowed their slaves to choose their own mates. Although most owners preferred that their slaves select spouses from their own holdings, they usually allowed marriages with slaves owned by others.

Despite their positions of authority, owners probably worried about the ill effects of having workers discontented by thwarted love. Hence, the majority of slave marriages were marriages of love, not arrangement.

Most slaves marked their commitment by a ceremony of some sort, ranging from elaborate weddings that imitated those of whites (and were sometimes even arranged and attended by white families) to simply moving in together. Often weddings were accompanied by the folk custom of "jumping the broomstick" to see who would have the most authority in the relationship.

In wedding ceremonies, couples usually refrained from pledging to be together "till death do us part," as there was little assurance that they would have the final say in the matter. "What God has brought together, let no man put asunder" was not a realistic pronouncement at slave weddings, since owners could legally sunder couples at any time. Instead, some slaves vowed to stay married "till death or distance do us part." If slave couples were separated by the sale of one spouse, more often than not the sale was considered, realistically, tantamount to the spouse's death.

Remarriage was the norm after such breakups, and children from former unions were assimilated into the new households. Nevertheless, a majority of slave marriages lasted for many years.

Most married slaves lived in single-family cabins. If husbands or wives were lucky (and, usually, light-skinned), they were perhaps assigned to work in the "big house" of the master or engage in a special craft, such as blacksmithing or carpentry. But most slaves, male and female, were field hands. Field workers usually spent from dawn to dusk, six days a week, plowing, planting, weeding, or harvesting. Some owners gave their hands Saturday afternoons off to take care of their own chores—washing clothes, hunting, making and mending clothes, making candles, repairing their cabins, or tending their own gardens. Even then, slave couples had little time to spend together. Slaves who had married "abroad"—that is, to someone not owned by the same master—might or might not have been allowed to spend weekday evenings with their spouses.

CHILDREN AND CHILDHOOD

On average, slave women had around seven children. Pregnant women were often not given adequate prenatal care. Infant mortality among African Americans was greater than among whites, probably because of the lack of care and poor diets during pregnancy and early childhood. Pregnant women were typically expected to perform their normal duties to within a month of giving birth and to be back on the job a few weeks following birth.

Generally, nursing mothers could leave their work long enough to feed their infants only three or four times a day, and they were expected to wean their babies at what for the time was an early age. Slave women too elderly to do field work often tended infants and young children, while older children were frequently left unsupervised.

Most slave children were allowed to have real childhoods of carefree play. They did not, however, get to spend a great deal of time with their parents, who would be away from them from dawn to dusk. Youngsters were not usually expected to work until they were eight to twelve years old, and then they were gradually assimilated into the workforce. They would, over several years, begin to be assigned duties. At first they performed light chores and spent fewer hours working than adults, but in the course of adolescence they came to take on the full workload of adults. Many children did not realize their condition of bondage until they were close to working age. Their realization sometimes came when their white playmates would go off to school without them or when the masters' children began to assume authority over them.

PARENTS AND PARENTING

Slaves, like nineteenth century Americans in general, considered fathers to be the head of the household. Even though parents could be subjected to various humiliations at the hand of their owners and had to be deferential in public, African American families tried to preserve the dignity of parents, especially fathers, within the household. Since white owners provided slave families with food staples, clothing, and housing, many of the roles traditionally assigned to fathers were preempted by slave masters. Moreover, white masters and mistresses could discipline any slave; parents were often helpless in protecting themselves and their families from verbal and physical abuse. Some female slaves had to submit to being raped by their white masters or were even forced to live the lives of concubines. Husbands, parents, and siblings were helpless to defend their loved ones from this fate. Children were often shielded from knowledge of the worst abuses of slavery, such as rapes or whippings, but they ultimately learned of the full implications of bondage. Many slave narratives describe how youngsters were traumatized when they first witnessed a lashing or other event that made them fully cognizant of their own condition.

Although slave parents tried to shield their children from the effects of slavery, they also had to teach their children survival skills. Harsh punishments were meted out to children who violated racial codes of conduct. Children had to learn early on to be deferential in the presence of whites and to submit to the authority of even young white children. They also had to learn to protect the community in the slave quarters. Discretion and not repeating conversations they heard were of great importance. Parents whose children violated survival codes of conduct usually responded with severe punishments, including slaps, shakings, and hard spankings, for children who did not learn these survival behaviors endangered themselves, their families, and communities.

Despite the many ways slavery undermined traditional parental roles, African American parents remained providers for their families. There was enough food on most plantations, but it was not plentiful and lacked variety. Diets often lacked protein unless they were supplemented by game. Male slaves were sometimes allowed to supplement their families' food allotments by hunting, fishing, and trapping. Parents of both sexes sometimes tended personal gardens. Mothers cooked, cleaned, and sewed.

Although most masters provided male slaves with blankets and clothes, women were usually given cloth and expected to make their own dresses and children's clothes. Generally, boys as well as girls wore baggy, dress-like garments until they reached the age of ten or twelve. When young boys reached this age, they were given their own chores to do and also graduated into wearing pants. With these changes, they came of age.

Parents' roles in family life revolved around the satisfaction of families' daily needs. Slave narratives reveal strong bonds of love between parents and children, especially between children and mothers. Loving home lives offered slaves a psychological buffer that offset the damages of slavery and provided a sanctuary where they could be themselves away from the scrutiny of whites.

Moreover, the culture that flourished in the slave quarters fostered strong family and community values and practices that differed significantly from those of white Americans.

AFRICAN HERITAGE

By the mid-nineteenth century, African Americans were usually several generations removed from their African heritage, yet some Africanisms remained central to their lives. Their music retained African rhythms; their games were often adaptations of African games. Many slaves preferred folk remedies to the medicines prescribed by white practitioners.

Although most slaves became Christians, their Christianity was generally of a more exuberant kind than that of whites, and it often existed side by side with beliefs in conjuring and voodoo.

Moreover, the values of the slave community did not always mirror those of the white culture that shaped so much of their lives. For example, in an era when white America demanded chastity of unmarried women, African American communities often followed the practice of many African tribes, accepting as normal some premarital sexual experimentation while expecting fidelity

after marriage. Marriage to blood cousins was also usually taboo in African American communities, although it was fairly common in white society. Extended kinship networks were maintained, and the elderly were valued as they had been in Africa.

ATTITUDES AND ASSUMPTIONS

Common assumptions about the family life of African Americans have been rooted in misperceptions that arose both during the era of slavery and in modern times. In the nineteenth century, slavery apologists and antislavery proponents alike often maintained that African Americans did not possess the same capacity for familial love as did whites, were by nature promiscuous, and were too childlike to take seriously the responsibilities of family life. These assumptions were held despite massive evidence to the contrary. Of course, such beliefs made it easier to condone slavery, especially the practice of selling individuals away from their families.

Slave owners, however, often acknowledged in practice their slaves' family feelings. As the law allowed owners to sell slaves without regard to family and kinship ties, many did so, but others took pains to keep families together—at least until economic factors outweighed their good intentions. Most owners sold slaves, even removing them from their families, if they got into serious financial trouble. In such cases, owners often arranged family breakups while parents or spouses were away to avoid emotional scenes as much as possible. Such precautions are evidence of their anticipation of heartfelt responses to their actions; records by persons who witnessed children being sold away from their parents, spouses being separated from each other, and brothers being taken away from their sisters bear testimony to the heartbreak such separations caused.

In the mid-twentieth century it was commonly believed that slavery had fostered a matriarchal structure in many modern black families, with mothers providing economic stability and fathers either emasculated or absent. By the 1970's, however, studies refuted assumptions that modern manifestations of African American family life or current dysfunctions in black families could be accounted for by slavery. Studies of the family life of slaves showed that they valued nuclear families and kinship ties.

Most slave families were two-parent families, and in the years following emancipation thousands of African Americans tried desperately to reunite families forcibly separated during slavery, creating new communities with strong kinship and friendship ties that provided support networks. Such evidence suggests that the matriarchal family structures and dysfunctions found in some twentieth-century African American families have more recent origins than slavery.

GENEALOGY

Family trees show that slaves often used naming patterns that emphasized kinship ties, especially in the nineteenth century. In the first two centuries of slavery in America, masters commonly assigned names to slaves they purchased and to children born as their property. Slaves, however, resisted this co-opting of their identity. Many had private names used only in the slave quarters, and when allowed to name their children, slaves often followed African customs, naming offspring after events or seasons. Males were commonly named after their fathers, grandfathers, or other family members but almost never after a master, although sometimes female slaves might be given the name of a particularly favored mistress. Genealogy also reveals many slave families with racially mixed lineages. Children of slave women raped by white men were usually assimilated into their mothers' homes and raised without any acknowledgment of kinship from their white fathers.

African Americans who try to trace their family roots often have a difficult time finding records before 1870, the first year the United States census named most African Americans, since slaves were listed as numbers only. Plantation records sometimes list births, deaths, and sales; letters and diaries might shed light on family histories. Nonetheless, tracing family lines during slavery is quite difficult; tracing lineages back to African origins is usually impossible. In this respect, slavery has had an ongoing effect on African Americans' sense of family.

—Grace McEntee

See also: Slave codes; Slavery; Slavery and race relations; Slavery and the justice system; Slavery and women; Slavery in Massachusetts; Slavery in Virginia

SLAVERY AND WOMEN

Although black and white women frequently found themselves at odds regarding slavery, women from both races transcended prevailing stereotypes and played an important role in the demise of this "peculiar institution."

The first known African slaves to arrive in North America were brought to Jamestown, Virginia, in 1619. Initially, British colonists were reluctant to embrace slavery, choosing rather to use white indentured servants. As late as 1680, only about seven thousand black people could be found in all the colonies combined. In time, however, labor demands, as well as the profitability of tobacco and cotton, made slave labor an increasingly attractive economic investment for white landowners.

Not everyone, however, was happy with slavery. By the mid-eighteenth century, Pennsylvania's Quakers were denouncing slavery as immoral. By the nineteenth century, the sentiment to free the slave population was growing nationwide. The American Colonization Society was organized in 1817 with the aim of recolonizing freed slaves in Africa. Their efforts, however, were largely unsuccessful: Most freed slaves considered North America to be their home and were unwilling to go to Africa. Additionally, most masters were unwilling to free their slaves without financial compensation, and no adequate plan was ever formulated to that end.

In 1831, a Virginia slave named Nat Turner led an uprising that left some sixty white people dead. Fear of massive uprisings had been prevalent (although largely unsubstantiated) since the late eighteenth century, and Turner fulfilled the worst nightmare of slaveholders. Subsequently, many white people became more determined to control the South's slave population. To free the slaves would cost a fortune, and most white southerners feared reprisal from the black community. As a group, white women in the South were as determined as their male counterparts to keep African Americans legally subjugated.

It is important to note, however, that most southerners did not own slaves. In 1860, only about 25 percent of all southerners owned slaves. About one-half of this group owned five or fewer slaves. These figures were partially the result of the high cost of purchasing them; in the 1850's, field hands were usually sold for at least $1,500. Consequently, slave ownership served as both a gauge of personal wealth and as a social status symbol. The more slaves one possessed, the more wealth one commanded. Even those white southerners who did not own slaves had a vested interest in the South's upper class. Poorer white people could always look to the slaveholding gentry for inspiration to gain more wealth.

GENDER AND PLANTATION SOCIETY

Throughout the early nineteenth century, American society, particularly in the South, was typically patriarchal. Most men and women lived their lives under the assumption that each gender had a distinctive "sphere." Men assumed roles of leadership and power, while women were expected to live according to the tenets of what scholars call the Cult of True Womanhood. As such, women were to be sexually chaste and pure. They were to be religiously pious, guarding society's morality by keeping their households in good order. Likewise, they were to be keepers of the home for their husbands. Finally, they were to be submissive to established authority structures.

These expectations bore especially heavy on southern women.

Contrary to prevalent mythology, southern women rarely conformed to the "southern belle" stereotype, and the plantation did not shield them from a hard life. Since plantations emphasized large-scale agriculture, plantation women usually suffered from social and cultural isolation. In order to compensate for their loneliness, some wealthy women hosted extravagant social functions for which guests sometimes stayed for days. Despite their loneliness, however, plantation wives did not seek friendship from their female slaves.

In addition to rural isolation, southern women also had specific jobs to perform. Plantation wives usually supervised the slaves who worked in "the great house." Moreover, the nature of plantation agriculture demanded frequent business trips, and, in their husbands' absence, plantation wives were responsible for maintaining the entire plantation, including supervising field labor and managing the financial ledgers.

Middle-class and lower-class southern white women left few detailed accounts of their lives. Nevertheless, several things are clear. Most poor white women lived a much harder life than their plantation sisters. In addition to their family duties, such as cooking, cleaning, making clothes, and rearing children, most women worked in the fields with their husbands whenever possible. These women tended to be fiercely independent and generally refused to do certain menial tasks they deemed "servant work."

Life for slave women in the antebellum South was substantially different from life for white women. In slavery's earliest phases, black men outnumbered black women by an overwhelming margin. Sex ratios stabilized over time, however, and black women were expected to labor in the fields side by side with black men. Those who did not perform fieldwork had other chores. For example, if they were too old to perform manual labor or were specifically chosen for the task, some women supervised the young children of other slaves. In some cases, they might even watch their masters' children. Thus, unlike white women, many slave mothers were frequently denied the opportunity to rear their own children. Still others worked in the plantation home as a house servant. Such opportunities were a mixed blessing.

On one hand, house servants had a higher status on the plantation than field hands. Some house servants, especially on large plantations, considered themselves to have a higher social status than poor white people. On the other hand, they generally labored under closer supervision than the other slaves, and the slightest offense could invite harsh discipline.

Most masters realized that they had an interest in promoting slave marriages, believing that married slaves were less likely to run away. The masters also valued female slaves for their ability to bear children. Slave children were likewise valuable both as part of the plantation's labor force and as a measure of control over their parents. Among slaves, it was understood that those who seemed loyal and docile were less likely to be sold, and few slaves would cause dissention on the plantation if they thought their children would be punished as a result of their actions.

Family life also added a measure of stability to the slave quarters, from the slaves' perspective. However bad plantation conditions might be, family members could always look to one another for solace. The family was one of the few places where slaves were free to be themselves, and mothers and fathers taught their children how to survive the rigors of plantation life.

Unfortunately, slave marriages had no official legal standing in white courts. Even so, both men and women sought companionship.

Sometimes, men tried to marry women from neighboring plantations to avoid seeing their wives and children mistreated. The masters had the final say in such matters, however, and they generally encouraged male slaves to marry on the plantation; otherwise, determining who owned the resulting children might be problematic. Yet, it does appear that a female slave had some role in choosing who would become her husband.

Despite the benefits that marriage and family life afforded, slaves lived in constant fear. Women lived in a special kind of fear that is difficult to describe. In addition to the fear of seeing their husbands and children sold, female slaves had no protection from their masters' unwanted sexual advances. White men some-times fathered children by their female slaves, thus creating tension between black and white women. As Mary Boykin Chesnut, a plantation mistress in South Carolina, wryly observed, "Any lady is ready to tell you who is the father of all the mulatto children in everybody's household but her own."

WOMEN AND ABOLITION

As slavery became more ensconced in the social and economic fabric of early nineteenth century America, critics, many of whom were women, began calling for its demise. Among white women, Angelina and Sarah Grimké were particularly outspoken critics of "the peculiar institution." Reared in a slaveholding household in Charleston, South Carolina, the Grimké sisters came to abhor slavery in their early adulthood because of their belief that slavery was in moral opposition to God's purposes. Angelina published two forceful indictments against slavery entitled *An Appeal to the Christian Women of the South* (1836) and *An Appeal to the Women of the Nominally Free States* (1837). Both sisters earned a reputation for their public lectures against slavery.

In addition to lecturing, some female abolitionists committed their sentiments to verse. Julia Ward Howe was an American poet who co-edited *Commonwealth*, an abolitionist newspaper in Boston, with her husband, Samuel Gridley Howe. In 1861, she visited military camps near Washington, D.C., and received the inspiration for her most famous work, "The Battle Hymn of the Republic." It was an instant success, and Union forces soon whistled and sang the tune as they marched into battle. This song so pointedly expressed the abolitionists' righteous indignation against slavery that it was widely published in church hymnals.

Among the white women who championed abolition, however, Harriet Beecher Stowe is without peer. Her novel *Uncle Tom's Cabin* (1852) has been hailed by some as the most influential fictional work in American literary history. Stowe depicted slavery, at its worst, as a monstrous institution that would victimize even the best, most loyal slaves such as Uncle Tom by allowing them to fall into the clutches of sadistic ogres such as Simon Legree. She infuriated many southerners by implying that their form of Christianity had sinned in failing to respond to slavery's cruelty. Stowe also struck a chord with many northerners who had never considered the many negative aspects of slavery.

White women were not alone in the campaign against slavery.

Several black women gained notoriety as abolitionists, particularly Harriet Tubman and Sojourner Truth. Tubman became famous as a "conductor" in the Underground Railroad, a system of individuals who helped fugitive slaves flee the South prior to the Civil War. Tubman herself had escaped from slavery in 1849, and she returned to the South nineteen times to help an estimated three hundred slaves, including her parents, secure safe passage to the North.

Likewise, Sojourner Truth became a popular antislavery lecturer in the North. Born in Hurley, New York, in 1797 as Isabella Baumtree, she ran away from her master when he refused to acknowledge New York's emancipation law of 1827. In 1843, after a series of visions, she adopted the name "Sojourner Truth" because she believed that it reflected her divine mission. Truth believed that God had ordained her to speak out against slavery.

While she may not have convinced every person in her audiences of slavery's evils, few could listen to her and not be impressed by her resonant voice and oratorical skills.

LEGACY OF THE ABOLITIONIST MOVEMENT

Assessing the antislavery movement can be difficult, partly because many reform efforts had overlapping objectives. Such is the case with women and abolition. Many women who favored abolition also favored equal rights for women, creating one reform movement within another. These white women tended to see the plight of black slave women in the light of their own social and political powerlessness. Consequently, they sincerely wanted to see slavery abolished, but they also wanted to better their own state.

Some male critics, notably William Lloyd Garrison, editor of the abolitionist newspaper *The Liberator*, agreed that women should have full social and political equality with men. Garrison also called for the immediate freedom of all slaves without compensation to their masters, as well as full social and political equality for freed African Americans. Many people saw Garrison as a radical, but it was his attitude toward women's rights that separated him from some of his earliest backers, particularly Arthur and Lewis Tappan. Equality for women was an issue that some abolitionists refused to address.

Ironically, as women called for equality and slave liberation, they may have been stifled most by a feminine influence. Abolitionists constituted a minority in nineteenth century America, and most women tended to stay within their own sphere. Catharine Beecher was perhaps the most outspoken proponent of distinct spheres for men and women. As she saw it, women had considerable power to shape society's morality by shaping the home.

Many women chose to remain keepers of their homes rather than to fight for either abolition or women's rights.

By the end of the nineteenth century, the idea of dual spheres had assumed a new cast. Many women demanded the right to vote precisely because society needed their perceived moral influence.

The experience and organizational skills learned by an earlier generation of female abolitionists, both black and white, was without doubt extremely useful to subsequent reformers.

—Keith Harper

See also: Abolitionist movement and women; Slave codes; Slavery; Slavery and families; Slavery and race relations; Slavery in Massachusetts; Slavery in Virginia

SLAVERY AND RACE RELATIONS

The enslavement of people of African ancestry was closely connected to the development of both racial prejudice and racial inequality in the United States. The heritage of slavery prevented African Americans from entering into the mainstream of American life even after slavery was abolished. Debates over responsibility for slavery and the legacy of slavery have complicated relations between African Americans and whites.

One of the theoretical points debated by historians is whether Europeans and Euro-Americans imposed slavery on people from Africa because they viewed Africans as inferior or whether racism came into existence as a justification for slavery. Some historians have suggested that as Europeans expanded their control over much of the world, they came into contact with many who were unlike themselves in appearance and in culture. Ethnocentrism, the tendency to see one's own group as the standard by which all others are to be judged, may have led Europeans to see the people of Asia and Africa as inferior to themselves. Thus, people from China, as well as people from Africa, were brought to the Americas as forced labor at various times.

Historians such as George Frederickson, however, have maintained that racism was a consequence rather than a cause of slavery.

From this point of view, the growth of plantation economies in North and South America encouraged the importation of slave labor because these economies required large numbers of workers.

Native Americans did not make good slaves because they were in their homeland and could easily escape.

Slave owners needed to justify holding other humans in bondage, according to this theory, so they

argued that their slaves were childlike and needed the protection of their masters. Thus, the influential apologist for slavery Henry Hughes argued in his *Treatise on Sociology* (1854) that the simple slaves as well as the masters benefited from the arrangement.

To some extent, the relationship between slavery and racism is similar to the ancient question of whether the chicken or the egg came first. The European enslavement of Africans was probably encouraged by feelings of European superiority. Once slavery became established, though, it was necessary to justify it, and the American descendants of Europeans could comfort themselves with claims that their slaves were inferior beings.

Many of the stereotypes of African Americans developed during slavery continued to flourish well into the twentieth century.

The racism of slavery outlived slavery itself; films, radio programs, and books before the Civil Rights era often portrayed black Americans as childlike, comic, servile, or dangerously unable to control themselves. The sociologist Stanford M. Lyman has observed that popular American films ranging from *Birth of a Nation* (1915) to *Gone with the Wind* (1939) drew on the racial images of slavery to portray "good" blacks as humorous, loyal, obedient family servants and "bad" blacks as rebellious and violent.

CONSEQUENCES OF MASTER-SLAVE RELATIONS

Economist Raymond S. Franklin has noted that one of the debates regarding consequences of master-slave relations concerns whether slaves and their descendants were in some way damaged by being owned and controlled. A number of historians, including Kenneth Stampp, Stanley Elkins, and William Styron, have held that being slaves left psychological scars on the slaves and damaged social institutions that slaves passed on to free black Americans. Along these lines, in 1966, Daniel Patrick Moynihan published a controversial report on the black family, in which he maintained that the experience of slavery contributed to the weakness of the black family. More recently, Harvard sociologist Orlando Patterson has claimed that the slave status undermined the roles of husband and father for black men and reinforced the central role of women in families.

Franklin observes that some historians and social thinkers have argued that the master-slave relationship actually strengthened many black social institutions by promoting the need to resist slavery. Historian Herbert Gutman, for example, offered evidence that slavery had actually strengthened black families. The historian Eric Foner has traced the origins of the black church, a central institution in African American history, to the religious activities of slaves who organized themselves into churches after emancipation.

GEOGRAPHICAL CONSEQUENCES OF SLAVERY

Slaves were heavily concentrated in the southern part of the United States. Even after the end of slavery, African Americans continued to be a southern population. In 1860, on the eve of the Civil War, 94 percent of the people of African ancestry in the United States were concentrated in the slave-owning states of the South. This percentage did decline notably in the years following World War I, and the descendants of slaves did move to other regions over the course of the twentieth century. Nevertheless, at the end of the century, the geographical legacy of slavery was still evident; the 1990 US census showed a majority of the American black population residing in the South.

In many areas of the South, working as sharecroppers or low paid wage laborers during the years following slavery, African Americans continued to do much the same sort of agricultural labor that they had performed as slaves. In order to maintain white domination, in regions with large black populations, southern whites sought to replace slavery with segregation, which placed African Americans in a separate and disadvantaged position.

This kept African Americans dependent on whites and subservient to whites in a manner that was similar in many ways to the old master-slave relationship. These patterns may have even survived the years following the Civil Rights movement. As recently as the 1990's, sociologist Ruth Kornfield, looking at a rural community in Tennessee, found that patron-client relationships

between white employers and black employees continued to mirror master-slave relationships.

The continuing concentration of African Americans in the South was one of the reasons that early actions of the Civil Rights movement concentrated primarily on this region. Despite the stubborn survival of many old patterns of racial inequality in this region, numbers have given African Americans in this part of the country some measure of power. In 1993, two-thirds of the black elected officials in the United States were from the southern states. Furthermore, the major southern cities of Atlanta, Georgia; New Orleans, Louisiana; Birmingham, Alabama; and Richmond, Virginia, all had black mayors.

THE LEGACY OF SLAVERY AND URBANIZATION

Although the South did not cease to be home to the largest proportion of African Americans, the group did shift from being heavily rural to being heavily urban. Over the course of the twentieth century, the agricultural jobs that black Americans continued to perform after slavery became increasingly unavailable as farms mechanized. In the years following World War II, African Americans moved to cities. They tended to settle in central urban areas because the US government built housing projects reserved for the poor in these urban areas, and the heritage of slavery and of the system of segregation that had emerged from slavery left African Americans disproportionately poor. During the same years, whites were moving from cities to suburbs. Racism, an ideology with roots in America's centuries of slavery, contributed to the unwillingness of homeowners, real estate companies, and mortgage lenders to allow African Americans to move into homes in the suburbs.

As a result of the movement of whites to suburbs and African Americans to cities, the two groups came to live in separate places. Although schools and other public facilities ceased to be legally segregated after the 1960's, many urban neighborhoods and schools contained virtually no whites. This not only limited contact between members of the different races, but it also separated African Americans from the jobs and opportunities that became much more abundant in the suburbs. Further, even after it became easier for middle-class African Americans to move into suburban neighborhoods, the poorest were left isolated in inner cities.

QUESTIONS OF RESPONSIBILITY

Professor and social commentator Shelby Steele has observed that the question of innocence is central to race relations in the United States. Many African Americans maintain that they are innocent victims of the aftermath of slavery. The problem of race relations, from this perspective, is one of achieving equality of condition for people who suffer disadvantages as a group through no fault of their own.

White Americans also frequently put forward claims of innocence.

They maintain that white people alive at the end of the twentieth century, well more than a century after the end of slavery, cannot be held responsible for the legacy of slavery. Therefore, programs such as affirmative action that aim at increasing African Americans' share of positions in employment and education seek to benefit the descendants of slaves at the expense of whites who are innocent of responsibility for slavery. In discussing issues of historical responsibility, whites will often become defensive, and any assertions of black disadvantage will sometimes be seen by whites as moral accusations.

REPARATIONS

The issue of reparations is one of the most controversial consequences of the thorny ethical issue of historical responsibility. The term "reparations" refers to compensation paid by one nation or group of people to another for damages or losses. The United States government, for example, has made some payments to Japanese Americans for violating their civil rights by imprisoning them during World War II.

Advocates of reparation payments for African Americans, such as the scholar Manning Marable, have argued that slavery was a massive denial of civil rights to this group. These advocates point out that slave labor built up much of the nation's wealth, allowing it to industrialize and therefore making it possible for the United States to achieve its current level of development. They point out that the descendants of slaves continue to suffer damages from slavery because African Americans have lower incomes, on average, than other Americans and tend to hold much less of the country's wealth.

Opponents of reparations maintain that while slavery is a historical source of contemporary disadvantages of African Americans, reparations would attempt to right a past injustice by penalizing present-day whites. Further, if reparations were paid to all African Americans, some rich African Americans would be receiving tax money taken from middle-class or even poor whites.

Finally, opponents of reparations suggest that payments of this sort would be enormously unpopular politically and might increase racial hatred and conflict.

—*Carl L. Bankston III*

See also: Abolition; Great Migration; Jim Crow laws; Moynihan Report; National Coalition of Blacks for Reparations in America; *Roots*; Slavery; Slavery and families; Slavery and the justice system; Slavery and women; Slavery in Massachusetts; Slavery in Virginia; Stereotypes; Stono Rebellion

SLAVERY AND THE JUSTICE SYSTEM

Slavery defined the legal treatment of African Americans for two and one-half centuries, and the crusade against slavery gave rise to modern concepts of citizenship and civil rights.

The first African laborers in the English colonies of North America arrived in Virginia in 1619. By the 1770's, slaves made up one fifth of the population of the English colonies. At this time, slave labor was used in every colony, including those in the North.

Only in the South, however, did slavery dominate economic life.

Slaves were used primarily to grow staple crops such as tobacco and rice for exportation to Europe and the Caribbean.

SLAVERY AND THE TERRITORIES

As Americans moved westward, the issue of whether slavery should expand into the new territories became increasingly important.

Americans realized that new western states would determine the balance of political power between North and South.

Congress initially divided the new territories between North and South. In the Northwest Ordinance (1787), Congress banned slavery in the lands north of the Ohio River while implicitly accepting slavery south of the Ohio. In regard to the Louisiana Purchase, the Missouri Compromise of 1820 banned slavery north of the line at 36° north latitude while allowing slavery to exist south of the line.

The Missouri Compromise resolved the issue of slavery in the territories until the Mexican War of 1846–1848 added new western lands to the United States. Subsequently, four positions emerged regarding the issue. Many northerners favored the Wilmot Proviso, a proposal to ban slavery in the territories. Other Americans favored popular sovereignty, which would allow the people of the territories to decide the issue for themselves. Some Americans favored extending the Missouri Compromise line to the Pacific coast. Many southerners believed the federal government should protect slavery in the territories.

In the 1850's, the popular sovereignty approach gained ascendancy.

The Compromise of 1850 applied popular sovereignty to California, New Mexico, and Utah. The Kansas-Nebraska Act (1854) repealed the old Missouri Compromise boundary and enacted popular sovereignty for the Louisiana Purchase. The Kansas-Nebraska Act created such great controversy that the existing political alignment was shattered. Opponents of the act created a new antislavery political party, the Republican Party, while supporters of the act reconstructed the Democratic Party as a proslavery party.

Disagreements regarding slavery-related issues and sectional competition for political power led ultimately to the outbreak of the Civil War in 1861. During the war, northern military officials increasingly believed that freeing the South's slaves would severely injure the Confederacy. President Abraham Lincoln issued the Emancipation Proclamation in 1863, proclaiming that the Union army would henceforth liberate the Confederacy's slaves.

In 1865, the Thirteenth Amendment to the US Constitution freed all remaining slaves belonging to American citizens.

SLAVERY AND THE US CONSTITUTION

Slavery significantly influenced the writing of the US Constitution. The Constitutional Convention of 1787 nearly broke up because of disagreements regarding sectional issues. Ultimately the sectional impasse was resolved with the Compromise of 1787.

Direct taxes and representation in the House of Representatives were to be apportioned according to the three-fifths rule: All free people and three-fifths of the slaves were to be counted in determining a state's tax burden and congressional representation.

Congress could prohibit the importation of slaves into the United States after the lapse of twenty years. States were prohibited from freeing fugitive slaves, and slaveholders were given the right to cross state boundaries to recapture fugitives. Congress was prevented from taxing exports so that slavery would not be injured by excessive taxes on the products of slave labor. Finally, to ensure that the compromise would not be abrogated, the clauses regarding the international slave trade and the three-fifths rule were declared by the Constitution to be unamendable.

As the Civil War approached, Americans debated the significance of these actions. What was the relationship between the US Constitution and slavery? Before 1860, most Americans believed that the Constitution did not establish a federal right to own slaves. Slavery was thought to exist as a result of state laws, and the federal government was thought to have few constitutional powers regarding slavery. Northerners and southerners disagreed regarding the practical application of this idea.

Southerners believed the federal government was increasingly intruding into matters related to slavery. They called for an end to federal interference with slavery. Northerners argued that the federal government had been indirectly providing protection to slavery for years. They called for the withdrawal of this protection.

In the 1840's and 1850's, militants on both sides developed new constitutional theories regarding slavery. Some southerners claimed that there was a federal right to own slaves, established in the fugitive slave clause and the privileges and immunities clause of the US Constitution. The federal government, they said, must protect the right of citizens to own slaves in the territories. Some southern extremists argued that the federal right to own slaves was so comprehensive that even northern states could not outlaw slavery within their own boundaries. Ironically, the branch of the abolitionist movement led by William Lloyd Garrison agreed with this argument, claiming that the Constitution protected slavery and arguing that northern states should abandon this corrupt document by withdrawing from the Union.

Another branch of the abolitionist movement, led by Gerrit Smith and William Goodell, argued to the contrary that the Constitution was best read as an antislavery document. They claimed that citizenship was based on residence in the United States and that slaves therefore were citizens. The privileges and immunities clause of the Constitution, they claimed, prevented both the states and the federal government from giving unequal treatment to citizens. The due process clause of the Fifth Amendment prevented citizens from losing their liberty without due process of law. Slavery violated these principles, and judges therefore ought to declare slavery unconstitutional. While this interpretation of the Constitution seemed extreme and utopian at the time, after the Civil War, the abolitionists' constitutional ideas were incorporated into the Fourteenth Amendment.

FUGITIVE SLAVE LAWS

One of the most significant controversies regarding slavery involved fugitive slave laws. In 1793, Congress adopted legislation to enforce the fugitive slave clause of the US Constitution. The Fugitive Slave Act of 1793 allowed slaveholders to obtain warrants from either state or federal courts for the rendition of fugitive slaves. In the 1820's and 1830's, several states passed personal liberty laws to prevent state officials from assisting in the recapture process. In *Prigg v. Pennsylvania* (1842), the US Supreme Court upheld the constitutionality of personal liberty laws by ruling that the enforcement of fugitive slave laws rested entirely in the hands of the federal government.

Without the assistance of state officials, slaveholders found that it was difficult to recapture their slaves. Southerners clamored for federal assistance. Congress responded by passing a new Fugitive Slave Act as a part of the Compromise of 1850. A new group of federal officials was created for the sole purpose of assisting slaveholders recapture slaves. State officials were forbidden to resist the rendition of fugitives. Even ordinary citizens could be compelled to serve in posses for the purpose of capturing fugitives. To prevent black people who were seized as fugitives from challenging their seizure, their legal rights, including the right of *habeas corpus*, were abolished.

The Fugitive Slave Act of 1850 was met with strong opposition in the North. Hundreds of fugitives, and even some free blacks, migrated to Canada to avoid seizure under the new law. Many northern communities formed vigilance committees to assist fugitives, and in a few cases northern mobs tried to rescue fugitives from the hands of government officials.

One rescue in 1854 led to a conflict between Wisconsin and the federal government. This case is notable because Wisconsin, a northern state, used states' rights arguments to challenge federal authority, a ploy normally used by southerners to defend slavery.

Sherman M. Booth, an abolitionist, was arrested by federal marshals for participating in the rescue of a fugitive slave. The Wisconsin State Supreme Court twice issued writs of *habeas corpus* to free Booth from federal imprisonment and declared the federal Fugitive Slave Act to be unconstitutional. The US Supreme Court in *Abelman v. Booth* (1859) reasserted the primacy of federal over state law and the right of the federal government to enforce its own laws through its own courts. The Wisconsin court accepted this decision, now believing that it did not help the antislavery cause to promote the idea of states' rights and nullification of federal law.

LEGAL TREATMENT OF SLAVES

African laborers occupied an ambiguous status in the American colonies before 1660 because English law did not recognize the status of slavery. Some Africans were held as slaves; others were held as indentured servants, persons whose term of labor expired after several years. Indentured servants enjoyed certain additional legal protections since, unlike slaves, their physical bodies were not owned by their masters. After 1660, Virginia and Maryland constructed elaborate slave codes to establish the legal status of slavery. For the next two centuries, the vast majority of African Americans were slaves.

In making and enforcing slave codes, Americans recognized slaves as both people and property. As property, slaves generally had few legal rights as independent beings. Slaves could not own property, enter into contracts, sue or be sued, or marry legally.

Slaves had no freedom of movement. Masters could sell their slaves without restriction, and there was no legal protection for slave families against forced separation through sale. The status of slave children was inherited from their mothers, a departure from the traditional common-law doctrine that children inherited the status of their fathers.

In some ways, the masters' property rights in slaves were limited by compelling public interest. Most southern states made it difficult for masters to free their slaves on the theory that free blacks were a nuisance to society. Most southern states also tried to prevent slaves from becoming a threat to society. State laws often required slaves to carry passes when traveling away from their masters' homes. Laws in several states prohibited slaves from living alone without the supervision of whites. In all but two states, it was illegal for anyone to teach slaves to read or write. Some states banned the use of alcohol and firearms by slaves; others outlawed trading and gambling by slaves. Although these laws were primarily a burden to the slave population, they also restricted the manner in which masters could manage and use their property.

Southern law codes occasionally recognized slaves as people as well as property. By the mid-nineteenth century, most states provided slaves with a minimal degree of protection against physical assaults by whites, although these laws were generally poorly enforced. All states outlawed the murder and harsh treatment of slaves. Although masters were occasionally put on trial for murder of their slaves, evidence suggests that most homicidal masters either received light sentences or were not punished.

Laws protecting slaves against other forms of inhumane treatment (such as excessive beatings or starvation diets) were almost never enforced. In practice, masters could beat or starve their slaves with impunity. Battery of slaves by strangers was illegal and was often punished by southern courts. Rape of slaves by whites, however, was not illegal. Masters had the full legal right to rape their own slaves, although masters could charge other whites with criminal trespass for an act of rape without the master's permission.

Under the law, black people were assumed to be slaves unless they could prove otherwise, meaning that free blacks were forced always to carry legal documents certifying their freedom. Many actions, including the use of alcohol and firearms, were illegal for slaves but not for whites. Penalties for crimes were generally more severe for slaves than for whites. For slaves, capital crimes—those for which death was the penalty—included not only murder but also manslaughter, rape, arson, insurrection, and robbery. Even attempted murders, insurrections, and rapes were subject to the death penalty.

PUNISHMENTS

Despite the harshness of the law, actual executions of slaves were rare because even slave criminals were valuable property.

State laws generally required governments to pay compensation to the masters of executed slaves. The fact that the labor of slaves was valuable meant that, in all states except Louisiana, imprisonment was rarely used as punishment for slave criminals. Instead, most penalties involved physical punishments such as whipping, branding, or ear-cropping, punishments which were rarely used against whites after the early nineteenth century.

While southern courts did not give black and white people equal treatment, the courts made some effort to be fair to slaves, probably because of the influence of wealthy slaveholders with an economic interest in the acquittal of their property. The proportion of slaves among those people accused of crime was about equal to the proportion of slaves in the population. Slaves appear to have been convicted at nearly the same rate as whites. Southern law codes also reflected the slaveholders' interests. Many states required that slaves have access to counsel and protected them against self-incrimination and double jeopardy. Slaves, however, could not testify in court against whites, meaning that it was nearly impossible to prosecute crimes against slaves when other slaves were the only available witnesses.

—*Harold D. Tallant*

See also: Abolition; Emancipation Proclamation; Fugitive Slave Law of 1793; Fugitive Slave Law of 1850; Kansas-Nebraska Act; Missouri Compromise; Reconstruction; *Scott v. Sandford*; Slave codes; Slavery and families; Slavery and race relations; Slavery in Massachusetts; Slavery in Virginia; Stono Rebellion

STEREOTYPES

A number of stereotypes regarding African Americans, positive and negative, impair intergroup relations because they cause people to view all African Americans as being the same rather than possessing individual traits and characteristics.

Over the years, a number of stereotypes have developed concerning African Americans. Some of these stereotypes—earth mother/mammy, natural musician, and super athlete—have basically positive connotations; however, others—Sambo, Uncle Tom, sexual predator, smart-mouthed but clever adolescent, welfare

queen—have primarily negative connotations. Negative stereotypes are obviously detrimental, but even their positive counterparts are destructive and dangerous because they create the expectation that all members of a group will be able to achieve certain feats or will act in certain ways. These sorts of expectations place excessive pressure on those who cannot or do not want to live up to the stereotype.

EARLY STEREOTYPES

During slavery, African Americans were often viewed as "Sambos," or mentally inferior, lazy people, usually

Black "Brute" and "Buck" Stereotypes

To help counter growing African American political power and freedoms after Reconstruction, some white southerners justified a wave of terrorism and lynching by creating new stereotypes of black male brutality. The black "brute" stereotype was a figure who was inhumanly brutal, and the "buck" was a figure who combined brutality and sexual monstrosity and who desired nothing more than to rape white women. These stereotypes found their clearest early expression in the novels of Thomas Dixon and in D. W. Griffith's 1915 film *Birth of a Nation*, which was based on Dixon's novel *The Clansman* (1905).

Although only a minority of male lynching victims were charged with rape—and many of even those allegations were false—the stereotypes were important to lynching's public defenders, who insisted that lynching was necessary to defend the supposed purity of white womanhood. One of the most important strategies for antilynching activists and organizations, such as the National Association for the Advancement of Colored People, was to attempt to undermine public support for lynching by debunking the stereotype of the black rapist. Controversy surrounding the use of black "brute" and "buck" stereotypes in a variety of modern arenas (including media and national politics) remains an important area of racial discourse in the twenty-first century.

Jonathan Markovitz

cheerful and childlike, a characterization that made slavery more palatable to its practitioners. Three other early stereotypes cast African American men as sexual predators ("bucks") or Uncle Toms and women as mammies, or nurturing earth mothers. Both whites and African Americans used the term "Uncle Tom" to refer to an African American man (occasionally a woman) who gives in readily to demands made by members of the dominant white group. This term is often said to have originated with Harriet Beecher Stowe's 1852 novel *Uncle Tom's Cabin;* however, the term probably entered popular culture as a result of George L. Aiken's *Tom Shows* (1852), a crude and violent traveling show that presented caricatures of both slaves and slave owners.

The stereotypical depiction of an African American woman as a mammy, a sort of earth mother selflessly caring for children, probably originated because so many African American women cared for the children of white plantation owners. The mammy figure was popularized by Margaret Mitchell's 1936 novel *Gone with the Wind*, which was made into an Academy Award-winning movie.

Another early stereotype was the portrayal of African American men as sexual predators, or black "bucks," who would attack any white woman they encountered. This stereotype, born of white fears about the mixing of races, forced many African American men in the Deep South to be very careful in their attitude toward and dealings with white women from shortly after emancipation through the second half of the twentieth century. The slightest suspicion of sexual relations between a black man and a white woman could mean legal problems and even physical danger (lynching) for an African American man.

MODERN STEREOTYPES

In the second half of the twentieth century, some of the early stereotypes diminished in intensity and others persisted in a somewhat altered form. For example, although the Sambo image faded, African Americans were still commonly believed to be mentally inferior to whites. These old stereotypes were, however, joined by new ones that were adopted and popularized by the media. Typically, the African Americans who appeared in films and television programs in the 1950's and early 1960's portrayed one-dimensional characters who embodied common stereotypes.

One stereotype that developed in this period was of the African American as a super athlete. The success of African American athletes such as baseball player Willie Mays, football star Jim Brown, and boxers such as Joe Louis and Muhammad Ali (Cassius Clay) led many Americans to believe that all African Americans possessed super athletic abilities.

Another common stereotype viewed all African Americans as having a superior sense of rhythm that produced excellent music and made them skillful dancers. Although much of the music regarded as American—jazz, blues, gospel, and rock—has its origins in African American culture and thus can be regarded as a product of African Americans, it is a mistake to project this level of musical talent onto all members of the group. Also, the stereotype ignores the historical and cultural reasons behind the creation of these musical genres. Likewise, although some African Americans possess an excellent sense of rhythm and are extremely skilled dancers, not all members of the group are similarly talented.

A common stereotype often exploited by the media is that of the street-smart, wisecracking, slightly goofy male adolescent (or young adult) African American. This cynical, know-it-all attitude is common among teenage boys or young men, but the stereotype turns it into an African American characteristic, often depicting the young black adolescent as a gang member. Of course some African American adolescents belong to gangs, but adolescents from numerous other racial and ethnic groups also join gangs.

The welfare queen—a woman who refuses to work and maintains an "upscale" lifestyle through unfair use of welfare—is a new twist on the stereotype that African Americans are slothful, childlike people. Welfare queens, usually single mothers, are depicted as lazy, perhaps immoral women who are having babies to increase the amount of their welfare check and to avoid working. In fact, in 1993, more white women were receiving welfare benefits than were African American women.

—*Annita Marie Ward*

See also: Black Is Beautiful movement; Cowboys; Film history; Literature; Music; Slavery and race relations; Sports; Tuskegee experiment

WEST INDIANS

The success of black West Indian Americans in the United States has drawn the attention of sociologists and other scholars and created some conflict with other African Americans.

Black West Indian immigrants from the former British West Indian Islands, Belize and Guyana, and their US-born descendants, a small group among the African American population, have achieved considerable economic, educational, and political success in the United States relative to other African Americans. Notable conservatives such as economist Thomas Sowell of Stanford's Hoover Institution and author Dinesh D'Souza contend that this group's relative success in part demonstrates the error in attributing the economic and social plight of some African Americans exclusively to racism. The group's exceptionalism has also been noted by sociologists such as Stephen Steinberg in *The Ethnic Myth: Race, Ethnicity, and Class in America* (1981) and Reynolds Farley and Walter Allen in *The Color Line and the Quality of Life in America* (1989).

The portrayal of exceptionalism is only part of this group's profile. Structural shifts in the US economy mean that segments of this community will face severe sociopsychological adjustments to migration, coupled with constricted assimilation into American society. Pressures against full assimilation are greater for lower-class West Indians. Typically, middle- and upper-class professionals alternate between a more inclusive West Indian American or particularistic African American identity, and the lower/working class chooses a more ethnically focused, West Indian identity.

Most of the West Indian immigrants arrived in the United States in the late nineteenth and early twentieth centuries. In 1924, restrictive immigration legislation effectively halted immigration from the islands. Most of the immigrants settled in the Northeast, creating urban ethnic communities in Miami, Boston, Newark (New Jersey), Hartford (Connecticut), and New York City; they settled in Brooklyn and formed ethnic enclaves in East Flatbush, Flatbush, Crown Heights, Canarsie, and Midwood districts.

WEST INDIAN EXCEPTIONALISM

Generally, West Indian immigrants have been perceived as models of achievement for their frugality, emphasis on education, and ownership of homes and small businesses. Economist Sowell argued that the group's successes, including those of famous members such as General Colin Powell, derived from a distinctive cultural capital source and an aggressive migrant ideology, legacies of their native lands. Home ownership and economic entrepreneurship were financed partly by using a cultural source of capital, an association called *susu* (known in West Africa as *esusu*), that first reached the West Indian societies during slavery. A *susu* facilitates savings, small-scale capital formation, and micro lending. These traditional associations have been incorporated into mainstream financial organizations such as credit unions and mortgage and commercial banks as they adapt to serve the needs of West Indian Americans.

Demographer Albert Murphy, in a report for Medgar Evers College's Caribbean Research Center in New York, found that in 1990, 29.1 percent of West Indian Americans had a bachelor's degree or higher degree, compared with the US average of 20.3 percent. In addition, their median household income in 1989 was $28,000, compared with $19,750 for African Americans overall and $31,435 for whites.

POLITICAL AND SOCIAL INCORPORATION

Early immigrants such as Pan-Africanists Edward Blyden and Marcus Garvey and poet activist Claude McKay were among the first West Indian Americans to become well-known and well respected figures. Other famous West Indian Americans are Congresswoman Shirley Chisholm; Franklin Thomas, former head of the Ford Foundation; federal judge Constance Baker Motley; Nobel laureate Derek Walcott; and actor Sidney Poitier. Activist Stokely Carmichael, Deputy US Attorney General Eric Holder, and Earl Graves, businessman and publisher of *Black Enterprise,* have made impressive efforts on behalf of African Americans.

From the 1930's to the 1960's, West Indian American politicians were elected with the help of the African American vote; many of the West Indians, believing their stay in the United States to be temporary, did not become citizens and were thus ineligible to vote. In the 1970's, this trend changed, and two congressional districts in New York with heavy concentrations of West Indians became represented by African Americans. However, West Indians Americans, becoming increasingly dissatisfied with African American representation, have been fielding their own candidates in state and local elections in New York, Connecticut, and New Jersey. These efforts have been aided by the fact that since 1993, when legislation less favorable to the immigrant population was passed, West Indian Americans have been acquiring US citizenship in greater numbers.

DIFFERENTIAL ASSIMILATION

At the beginning of the twentieth century, West Indian Americans and African Americans held negative stereotypes of each other and rarely interacted socially. In the 1930's, 1940's, and 1950's, the children of some West Indian immigrants downplayed their ethnicity and attempted to integrate into the African American community, but both groups' images of each other changed slowly. Powell, in his autobiography, *My American Journey (*1995), recalls his African American father-in-law's reaction when he proposed marriage to his daughter Alma: "All my life I've tried to stay away from those damn West Indians and now my daughter's going to marry one!"

The late 1960's, with its emphasis on racial solidarity and group identity, eroded much of the conflict between African Americans and West Indian Americans and supplanted it with black nationalist sentiments and identity. In the late twentieth century, many West Indian Americans were caught in an identity crisis, unsure of whether they should be West Indians with a strong ethnic orientation, African Americans with a focus on their racial identity, or "West Indian Americans" with a more hybrid identity. Class pressures play influential roles in this identity dilemma. Lower- and working-class West Indian Americans have strong affiliations with their ethnicity and its cultural symbols, using the ethnic community as a "structural shield" in their coping repertoire. However, a growing segment of West Indian American professionals regard themselves as West Indian Americans because this identity unites the more desirable choices by eliminating obstacles to their ultimate assimilation as Americans. In addition, this community is not monolithic, and class divisions segment the group as well as influence its responses to racism and other societal challenges.

—*Aubrey W. Bonnett*

See also: Cubans and African Americans; Haitians; Jamaicans; Pan-Africanism

CHRONOLOGY OF EVENTS

THE MIDDLE PASSAGE TO AMERICAN SLAVERY

1619-c. 1700

In the British North American colonies, slavery arrived late, and then only after a significant transitional period, during which chattel slavery gradually supplanted the system of indentured servitude that had supplied the main source for manual plantation labor. By 1700, chattel slavery had become legally institutionalized throughout British North America, but it flourished primarily in the Chesapeake region and the Carolina Low Country.

Locale: West Africa, Atlantic Ocean, and colonial North America

Categories: Social issues and reform; trade and commerce; economics; agriculture; colonization

KEY FIGURES

John Punch (d. after 1640), first documented African in Virginia to be enslaved for life

Sir John Yeamans (1611-1674), British planter and colonial governor of Carolina, 1672-1674, who imported the first African slaves into the Carolina Low Country

Anthony Johnson (Antonio, a Negro; d. after 1660), African-born indentured servant who became a prominent Virginia landowner

Sir George Yeardley (1587?-1627), Virginia's acting governor, 1616-1617, and governor, 1619-1621, 1626-1627

SUMMARY OF EVENT

The Middle Passage long predated the year 1619, which is traditionally denoted as the occasion of the arrival of the first African slaves in the British North American colonies. In point of fact, the two phenomena—the Middle Passage and chattel slavery—would never truly coincide until much later, though by the end of the seventeenth century, chattel slavery would indeed be established as the pattern for British North America.

The Middle Passage may be defined as the second "leg" of the Atlantic world's Triangular Trade which, briefly stated, consisted of European articles being shipped to and exchanged for African trade items, including slaves; African items (mainly slaves) being transported across the Atlantic to the New World; and American-produced or refined items, such as rum, tobacco, and molasses, then being carried back to Europe and sold. This is, of course, a more simplified overview of an extremely complex process, but slavery became such an integral part of the

transatlantic socioeconomic system and so affected the movement of so many millions of people that it has become synonymous with the term Middle Passage.

As it developed from the time of initial contact between West Africans and Portuguese mariners around the late fifteenth century, the Middle Passage began with the actual capture of individuals within Africa itself and their immediate transformation into marketable chattel labor. Though some Africans (mainly those who dwelled closest to the coast) were kidnapped by Europeans, many were taken by other Africans, either as the traditional spoils of warfare between tribal and national units or as captives to be transported to the trading posts and fortresses on the coast and sold to Europeans. It was in the course of the actual abduction, and the often long, always arduous trek to the coast, that the first fatalities

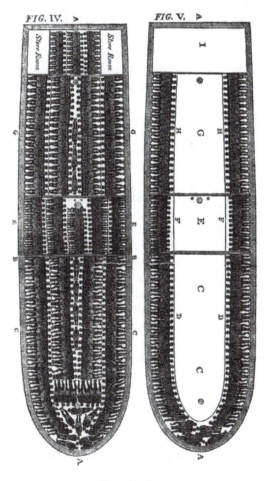

Slave ship diagram

83

(some sources assert as many as half the numbers involved) occurred.

Some died resisting or were killed attempting to escape; others might be chained together and forced to march—some were even strapped to poles and carried along—and these latter captives might succumb to the beatings they received to keep them moving or to the exhaustion of the forced march itself.

Once on the coast, some captives were sold right then and there to be immediately loaded into waiting slave ships, although it was more often the case that European-controlled redoubts would open their gates and the slaves would be hustled into semi-underground prisons to await loading and transport aboard the next available ship. The cannons of these fortresses were invariably pointed seaward so as to provide defense from other Europeans rather than to counter any threat from the Africans—which was considered negligible.

To avoid disputes over ownership at busy ports where several slave ships might be harbored at the same time, all simultaneously loading their human cargo, slaves were branded with hot irons, receiving the mark of their ship's captain or of the company that owned the sailing vessel. The slaves were then placed below deck, in holds where they were chained lying on their backs to the planks. In order to increase their profits, some ship captains advocated "tight" packing, that is, cramming as many individuals in as small a space as possible so as to assure that, by sheer weight of numbers, more Africans would complete the journey alive.

Those who favored "loose" packing, for their part, argued that a higher survival rate would exist when the captives were placed into less cramped and, theoretically, less unhealthy conditions.

With at most five feet from floor to ceiling, minimal lighting, stagnant air, and very basic, haphazard facilities for the disposal of human waste, the slave ships were prime for the spread of diseases on these voyages. Many captives died from dysentery, smallpox, scurvy, measles, malaria, yellow fever, suicide, and in slave mutinies, which were occasionally successful. The diet was usually minimal and most often consisted of water served with yams or rice.

With lack of sanitation, whippings, and malnutrition, and despite the captives being occasionally taken on deck for air and forced to do "exercises," the death rates on the Middle Passage were high. Anywhere from 10 percent to 50 percent of the captives perished en route. Bodies were tossed overboard, and it became the norm for a slave ship to be so identified on the high

seas by the sighting of scavenging sharks following in its wake.

The actual numbers involved have always been a source of controversy from the moment that W. E. B. Du Bois put forward a figure of fifteen million individuals who were transported to the Americas (this did not account for fatalities along the way). Though initially the tendency was to reduce this figure, the estimate began to increase over the course of the late twentieth century. By the beginning of the twenty-first century, commonly accepted estimates ranged between twenty million and thirty million people transported from Africa to the Americas. Basil Davidson has speculated that the Middle Passage cost Africa fifty million people, including fatalities en route. With smooth sailing, the Atlantic crossing might take less than a month, though it might also last sixty to ninety days. Those who survived would be disembarked and auctioned to the highest bidder in the New World.

In 1619, when the first "twenty and odd" Africans were recorded to have been sold in Virginia, and for years thereafter, chattel slavery as practiced in the Iberian-settled colonies was not established in the British colonies. Initially, the Africans brought to these colonies were indentured servants, on a par with white indentured servants and with at least the nominal, legal right to freedom when their terms of indenture (the "contract periods" during which they were required to labor under the direction of their masters) expired. The "contract period" generally lasted seven years. Most of these indentured Africans had been purchased under these terms from a Dutch ship by then-governor of Virginia Sir George Yeardley and some of his associates. The best known of these African servants, Anthony Johnson, who was originally documented in 1625 as "Antonio, a Negro," had arrived in Virginia in 1621, and, having served his indenture, had by 1651 acquired a 250-acre (100-hectare) farmstead on the Eastern Shore of Virginia at the Pungoteague River.

Even during Johnson's lifetime, however, attitudes were shifting toward discontinuing the indentured labor system and supplanting it with chattel slavery based on race. In 1640, John Punch, the only black man among three indentured servants who had attempted to escape from their master, was sentenced to servitude for life by the court at Jamestown, while his two white accomplices received lesser sentences. Indentured servitude could provide only a temporary, increasingly restive and unreliable, source of labor, while chattel slavery placed at the plantation owner's beck and call a racially and legally distinct population that could be more readily controlled.

During the course of the seventeenth century, nine colonies endorsed and codified slavery into law, Massachusetts (1641), Connecticut (1650), Virginia (1661), Maryland (1663), New York (1664), New Jersey (1664), South Carolina (1682), Pennsylvania (1700), and Rhode Island (1700). Anti-miscegenation laws were also enacted by most colonies, and a Virginia statute of 1669 dictated that henceforth a master might under certain circumstances hold the power of life or death over his slaves. During the last quarter of the century, large numbers of Africans were imported via the Middle Passage into the colonies, particularly into the South Carolina Low Country, where in 1671 the future Carolina governor Sir John Yeamans established a plantation into which he introduced African slaves.

Except for certain rare instances, newly arrived slaves were displayed for auction, inspected, and sold after bidding.

They were then taken to wherever they were to dwell and work. Conditions and circumstances varied from master to master and from region to region. In the two main areas of southern colonization, the Chesapeake and the South Carolina Low Country, slaves were engaged almost exclusively in the plantation economy, mainly in tobacco or rice and indigo, respectively. For the "field slaves," who were certainly in the majority, housing was provided but in simple wooden structures with beaten-earth floors, and work went on from morning to dark (if the moon were shining, it was not unheard of to labor well into the night). Clothing was rough, practical, and basic; shoes might be distributed once a year, if at all.

The "house slaves," who had the fortune of living near the plantation house and usually working indoors, sheltered from the elements, were nevertheless subject to constant supervision by the master and his family. Life as a slave, then and later, was a life punctuated by constant labor, tight restriction, and the ever-present possibility of physical and emotional abuse. Attempts to achieve literacy were certainly discouraged and in many instances subject to severe, exemplary punishment. While its application varied from master to master, use of the whip, either to punish offenses or to discourage slacking on the job, was standard procedure.

Though pains were usually taken to see that not too many Africans from the same nation were placed together on the same plantation (the rationale was that a common language would make it easier for them to plot revolts and escapes), the influx of slaves was so massive and sudden in Carolina that this proved an impossible goal, and it was there that African cultural remnants (language such as Gullah, steep-roofed structures for slave quarters, foodways, music) endured most tenaciously.

The fact that the African population of the Carolina Low Country was so culturally integrated within itself and far outnumbered the white population led of necessity to a much stricter and more oppressive system there than in the Chesapeake region. Everywhere, however, the threat of slave uprisings and the presence of African or African-Native American (so-called maroon) communities, formed by escaped slaves and existing in remote areas, were facts of life in the South that lasted into the years of the American Civil War (1861-1865).

SIGNIFICANCE

The Middle Passage was a crucial part of the greatest mass movement of humanity in history, the molding of the Atlantic world. The displacement of millions of African people depleted that continent of much of its human resources and made possible its later vulnerability to colonial domination and "underdevelopment." On the other side of the Atlantic, the institutionalized slave trade arguably determined the course of history in the Americas.

Certainly, without the labor supplied by enslaved Africans, the southern North American, Caribbean, and Latin American plantation system could not have existed as it did, and the economic development and subsequent history of the Americas would have been much altered. However, the legacy and issues of racism and exploitation that the trade in human bondage brought in its wake have not been resolved to this day.

—*Raymond Pierre Hylton*

See also: Africans Arrive in Virginia; Massachusetts Recognizes Slavery; Virginia Slave Codes; Settlement of the Carolinas; Beginning 1671: American Indian Slave Trade.

Related articles in *Great Lives from History: The Seventeenth Century, 1601-1700:* Nathaniel Bacon; Aphra Behn; Jacob Leisler; Njinga; John Smith; António Vieira.

AFRICANS ARRIVE IN VIRGINIA

August 20, 1619

The arrival of between twenty and thirty African indentured servants in Virginia marked the beginnings of what would ultimately become a firmly entrenched institution of slavery in the British North American colonies and a plantation economy dependent upon slave labor for its existence.

Locale: Point Comfort, Virginia
Categories: Social issues and reform; colonization

KEY FIGURES

Anthony Johnson (Antonio, a Negro; d. after 1660), African-born indentured servant who became a prominent Virginia landowner
John Punch (d. after 1640), first documented African in Virginia to be enslaved for life

SUMMARY OF EVENT

In August of 1619, a Dutch warship carrying "20 and odd" Africans landed at Point Comfort, Virginia. These Africans, the first to arrive in the British colonies, most likely were put to work not as slaves but as indentured servants. Neither the laws of the mother country nor the charter of the colony established the institution of slavery, although the system was developing in the British West Indies at the same time and was almost one hundred years old in the Spanish and Portuguese colonies.

To be sure, African indentured servants were discriminated against early on—their terms of service were usually longer than those of white servants, and they were the object of certain prohibitions that were not imposed on white servants—but in the early seventeenth century, at least some black indentured servants, like their white counterparts, gained their freedom and even acquired some property. Anthony Johnson, who labored on Richard Bennett's Virginia plantation for almost twenty years after he arrived in Virginia in 1621, imported five servants of his own in his first decade of freedom, receiving 250 acres (100 hectares) on their headrights. Another former servant, Richard Johnson, obtained one hundred acres for importing two white servants in 1654. These two men were part of the small class of free blacks that existed in Virginia throughout the colonial period. Such cases as the two Johnsons were rare by midcentury.

As early as the 1640's, some African Americans were in servitude for life, and their numbers increased throughout the decade. In 1640, in a court decision involving three runaway servants, the two who were white were sentenced to an additional four years of service, while the other, an African named John Punch, was ordered to serve his master "for the time of his natural Life." Punch is the earliest African enslaved in Virginia for whom documents still exist. In the 1650's, some African servants were being sold for life, and the bills of sale indicated that their offspring would inherit slave status. Thus, slavery developed according to custom before it was legally established in Virginia.

Not until 1661 was chattel slavery recognized by statute in Virginia and then only indirectly. The House of Burgesses (or General Assembly) passed a law declaring that children followed the status of their mothers, thereby rendering the system of slavery self-perpetuating. In 1667, the assembly strengthened the system by declaring that, in the case of children that enslaved at birth, "the conferring of baptisme doth not alter the condition of a person as to his bondage or freedome; that divers masters, freed from this doubt, may more carefully endeavor the propagation of christianity." Until this time, Americans had justified enslavement of Africans on the grounds that they were "heathen" and had recognized conversion as a way to freedom. This act closed the last avenue to freedom, apart from formal emancipation, available to African American slaves.

In 1705, Virginia would establish a comprehensive slave code, completing the gradual process by which most African Americans were reduced to the status of chattel. Slaves could not bear arms or own property, nor could they leave their plantation without written permission from their master. Capital punishment was provided for murder and rape; lesser crimes were to be punished by maiming, whipping, or branding. Special courts were established for the trials of slaves, who were barred from serving as witnesses, except in the cases in which slaves were being tried for capital offenses.

In the other British colonies, the pattern was similar to that of Virginia. African racial slavery existed early in both Maryland and the Carolinas. Georgia attempted to exclude slavery at the time of settlement, but yielding to the protests of the colonists and the pressure of South Carolinians, the trustees eventually repealed the prohibition in 1750. The Dutch brought slavery to the Middle Colonies early in the seventeenth century. The advent of British rule in 1664 proved to be a stimulus to the system in New York and New Jersey, but in Pennsylvania and Delaware, the religious objections of the Quakers delayed its growth somewhat and postponed legal recognition of slavery until the early eighteenth century.

In seventeenth century New England, the status of Africans was ambiguous, as it was in Virginia. There were slaves in Massachusetts as early as 1638, possibly before, although slavery was not recognized by statute until 1641, the first enactment legalizing slavery anywhere in the British colonies. New England became heavily involved in the African slave trade, particularly after the monopoly of the Royal African Company was revoked in 1698. Like Virginia, all the colonies enacted slave codes in the late seventeenth or early eighteenth century, although the New England codes were less harsh than those of the Middle or Southern colonies. In all the colonies, a small class of free blacks developed alongside the institution of slavery, despite the fact that formal emancipation was restricted.

SIGNIFICANCE

Slavery in Virginia grew slowly in the first half of the seventeenth century. In 1625, there were twenty-three Africans in Virginia, most of whom were probably servants, not slaves. By mid-century, a decade before the statutory recognition of slavery, the black population was only three hundred, or 2 percent of the overall population of fifteen thousand. In 1708, there were twelve thousand African Americans and sixty-eight thousand whites. In a little more than fifty years, the black population had jumped from 2 percent to 15 percent of the total Virginia population. In the Carolinas, blacks initially made up 30 percent of the population but within one generation outnumbered whites, making South Carolina the only mainland colony characterized by a black majority.

In New England, blacks numbered only about one thousand out of a total population of ninety thousand.

Although slavery developed haphazardly, as it developed, it became more and more entrenched. Plantation owners and others who used slaves developed ideologies justifying the institution of slavery at the same time that economic structures developed that depended upon slavery for their success. Moreover, as the Virginia colony developed its own distinctive culture, separate from the British culture that had been left behind, slavery came to be an integral part of that culture. Thus, by the time of the American Civil War (1861-1865), the end of slavery would become synonymous in the minds of many Southerners with the demise of a way of life.

—Anne C. Loveland and Laura A. Croghan

See also: The Middle Passage to American Slavery; Massachusetts Recognizes Slavery; Virginia Slave Codes.

Related articles in *Great Lives from History: The Seventeenth Century, 1601-1700:* Nathaniel Bacon; John Smith.

VIRGINIA SLAVE CODES

March, 1661-1705

The first laws recognizing and institutionalizing slavery in Virginia were passed by the General Assembly. Based on the laws regulating white indentured servitude, the laws created vast differences between the status of black and white forced laborers, instituting a de jure, rather than merely de facto, system of racial segregation.

Locale: Virginia
Categories: Laws, acts, and legal history; social issues and reform

SUMMARY OF EVENT

In March, 1661, the Virginia General Assembly declared that "all children borne in this country shal be held bond or free only according to the condition of the mother." Enacted to alleviate confusion about the status of children with English fathers and African mothers, this law was the first in a series of laws recognizing perpetual slavery in Virginia and equating "freedom" with "white" and "enslaved" with "black." This law is especially indicative of the hardening of race relations in mid-seventeenth century Virginia society, as status in the patriarchal society of England traditionally was inherited from the father. By reversing this legal concept, perpetuation of enslavement for blacks was ensured for their children, whether of black or white ancestry.

Despite the extent to which the 1661 law narrowed the options for defining Africans' status, this act did not in itself establish slavery as permanent and inescapable. Africans had two available windows through which they could obtain freedom—conversion to Christianity and manumission (formal emancipation). In 1655, mulatto Elizabeth Key had brought a successful suit for her freedom, using as her main argument the fact that she had been baptized.

In 1667, a slave named Fernando failed in a similar suit when he contended that he ought to be freed because he was a Christian and had lived in England for several years.

Not only did the court deny Fernando's appeal, but also that same year the General Assembly took another step toward more clearly defining blacks' status, by declaring "that the conferring of baptisme doth not alter the condition of the person as to his bondage or freedome." Planters felt that if baptism led to freedom, they would be without any assurance that they could retain their slave property.

The 1667 law built on the earlier one to define who would be a slave and was clarified in 1670 and again in 1682, when the Assembly declared that any non-Christian brought into the colony, either by land or by sea, would be a slave for life, even if he or she later converted.

In 1691, colonial leaders provided a negative incentive to masters wishing to free their slaves by declaring that anyone who set free any "negro or mulatto" would be required to pay the costs of transporting the freedmen out of the colony within six months. Although manumissions still occurred and some free blacks managed to remain in the colony, the primary status for African Americans in Virginia was that of chattel.

Although who was to be a slave in Virginia had now been defined, it had yet to be determined precisely what being a slave meant on a daily basis for Africans and their descendants. Between 1661 and 1705, nearly twenty separate laws were passed limiting, defining, and prescribing the rights, status, and treatment of blacks. In general, these laws were designed to protect planters' slave property and to protect the order and stability of white society from an "alien and savage race."

The greater the proportion of black slaves in the overall Virginia population, the more restrictive and oppressive the laws became. Whereas Africans were only 2 percent of the total population of Virginia in 1648, they were 15 percent in 1708. In certain coastal counties, such as York, the demographic picture was even more threatening. In 1663, blacks already made up 14 percent of York's population; by 1701, they counted for 31 percent of the county's inhabitants. In large part, the slave codes were motivated by the growth of the black population and whites' fears of slave uprisings.

The piecemeal establishment of slavery in these separate laws culminated in 1705 in a comprehensive slave code in Virginia. This code reenacted and strengthened a number of earlier slave laws, added further restrictions and harsher punishments, and permanently drew the color line that placed blacks at the bottom of Virginia society. Whites were prohibited from trading with, having sexual relations with, or marrying blacks. Blacks were forbidden to own Christian servants "except of their own complexion," leave their home plantation without a pass, own a gun or other weapon, or resist whites in any way.

In Virginia society, in which private property was a basic legal tenet, a slave's property was not protected: "[B]e it enacted . . . that all horses, cattle or hoggs marked of any negro . . . shall be forfeited to the use of the poore of the parish . . . seizable by the church warden thereof." Neither was slave life or limb protected by the codes. It was legal both to kill slaves accidentally while punishing them and to dismember slaves guilty of running away as a means of dissuading other slaves from also trying to escape.

Slaves were not allowed to assemble for prayer, for entertainment, or to bury their dead. They could not testify against white people in court and were not given the right of trial by jury. The only protection mandated in the slave code was that masters must provide adequate food, clothing, and shelter for their slaves, and that they "not give immoderate correction," the latter provision being essentially meaningless, given that accidentally killing slaves while "correcting" them was officially sanctioned.

Many of these enactments lacked any means of enforcement, including the sole protection, and remained as almost dead letters in the statutes. Many of the harsher penalties for slave crimes—for example, the death penalty and maiming—were not carried out nearly as frequently as the laws suggest, because doing so would harm or destroy the master's property. Laws prohibiting slaves from trading or hiring themselves out were disregarded almost routinely. The disadvantage for slaves of this lack of enforcement was that laws prohibiting cruel treatment or defining acceptable levels of correction often were ignored as well. Where abuse was noticeably blatant, action against white offenders was taken only reluctantly, and punishments were insignificant and rare. Generally, laws in the economic and political interest of the white planter elite were enforced and respected; laws that restrained planters' pursuits were not.

SIGNIFICANCE

To a large extent, the laws regulating and defining slavery in Virginia grew out of the early to mid-seventeenth century laws regulating indentured servitude. Servants had also been prohibited from having sexual relations with or marrying their masters; indentured women who became pregnant through such liaisons were fined, made to serve extra time, and had their children bound out to labor.

Like slaves, servants were punished for attempting to run away or for resisting their masters. Servants also were treated harshly and exploited by ruthless masters eager to get every penny's worth of effort from their laborers. Unlike African slaves, however, white indentured servants had legal rights and were protected by the laws and courts of the colony. This distinction is crucial in understanding the Significance of the slave laws, which codified, not a difference between those forced to labor and those who were free, but rather a difference between a race inherently unworthy of being free and one whose members might be temporarily bound to service. White servants ultimately served out their time, became freemen and full citizens, acquired land and servants of their own, and became respected members of the community, regardless of their earlier status. Indentured servants had rights and opportunities, but African and African American slaves, by the turn of the eighteenth century, virtually had neither.

—*Laura A. Croghan*

See also: The Middle Passage to American Slavery; Africans Arrive in Virginia; Massachusetts Recognizes Slavery.

Related articles in *Great Lives from History: The Seventeenth Century, 1601-1700:* Aphra Behn; John Smith.

CHARLES TOWN IS FOUNDED

April, 1670

The English founded the first permanent European settlement in South Carolina, eventually displacing Spanish claims. With immigrants coming from British Barbados, France, Scotland, and Ireland, and with the arrival of African slaves, Charles Town became one of the most racially and religiously diverse colonies in the New World.

Locale: Charles Town, South Carolina
Categories: Colonization; expansion and land acquisition

KEY FIGURES

Charles II (1630-1685), king of England, r. 1660-1685
Henry Woodward (c. 1646-c. 1686), liaison between Europeans and the Kiawah Indians

SUMMARY OF EVENT

In 1562, Huguenots (French Protestants) escaping from the Catholic-Protestant wars in France settled in Port Royal, South Carolina, under the leadership of Jean Ribaut, but this settlement quickly failed. In 1629, King Charles I of England gave a grant to Sir Robert Heath to resettle Huguenot refugees from England to South Carolina, but this plan also failed. In 1669, the Spanish were still the major European power in the Carolina area. Although the Spanish claimed Carolina, however, their closest settlement was 200 miles (320 kilometers) away in Saint Augustine, Florida. England also made claim to Carolina, and the English challenged Spain's claim. The Stuart monarchy was restored in 1660, when Charles II became king of England, and in 1662-1663 he gave Carolina as a grant to the eight lords proprietors who had helped him regain the throne.

In 1669, one of the proprietors, the earl of Shaftesbury, Anthony Ashley Cooper, took charge of the project and began to develop the area for economic reasons. Three ships, the *Carolina*, the *Port Royal*, and the *Albemarle*, left England for the seven-month voyage to America. The *Albemarle* wrecked and was replaced in Barbados by the *Three Brothers*, and the *Port Royal* wrecked and was not replaced, but in April, 1670, the *Carolina* entered what is now called Charleston harbor, followed by the *Three Brothers* on May 23. The two ships brought approximately 148 people.

The immigrants had planned to settle at Port Royal, about 60 miles (100 kilometers) from present-day Charleston, but landed by mistake a little north of Charleston. They still planned to go to Port Royal, but the cacique (chief) of the local Kiawah tribe persuaded them to settle in the Charleston area instead, partly to help protect the Kiawahs from the Spanish and Spanish-allied Native Americans, such as the Westoes. Contrary to the "wild savage" image held by the English, the Kiawahs lived in semi-permanent homes in villages, practiced some diversified agriculture, and had a fairly developed political system. Henry Woodward, an Englishman, had lived with the Kiawahs for several years and had good relations with them, which in turn helped develop good relations between the Kiawahs and the settlers.

The English went five miles northwest up the Ashley River and then west a short distance up Old Towne Creek, to the first high land that afforded a view of the river, so Spanish ships could be seen before they reached the settlement. Marshlands and a short palisade also helped the defense. Because of the threat of attack by the Spanish or by Spanish-allied Native Americans, Charles Town (briefly called Albemarle Point) was developed as a fort, with people sleeping inside and working outside during the day. Later in 1670, Spaniards from Saint Augustine attempted to attack but were defeated, because Native Americans friendly to the English warned them of the planned attack. In the 1670's, there were battles with the Westoe and Stono tribes. In 1686, another attempted attack by the Spanish and their Indian allies was stopped by a hurricane.

The settlers traded with the Indians, largely for animal furs and skins, and obtained lumber, tar, and pitch from the forests. About fifteen different crops were experimented with, but corn was the main food raised. Cattle were raised, and fish and wild animals were plentiful. There were problems (for example, malaria), but fewer than in most other settlements.

Charles Town became very popular among Barbadians, who needed a place to move to escape from overcrowding and a lack of land on Barbados. In 1671, more than one hundred Barbadians (mostly of English heritage) had joined the settlement. Industrious and business-oriented, the Barbadians soon exercised a powerful economic and political influence. By 1672, there were thirty houses and about two hundred people at Charles Town. By 1680, the settlers had moved

the settlement back down the Ashley River to where it joined the Cooper River to form the bay or harbor area, a few miles west of the Atlantic Ocean.

One of the unique features of Charles Town at its new location was that it was a planned city, following the checkerboard plan proposed for London after the Great Fire of 1666. At the time, only in Philadelphia and Charles Town were the streets laid out before the city was built. By 1680, approximately one thousand people lived in Charles Town. By 1690, with one thousand to twelve hundred residents, Charles Town was the fifth largest city among the North American colonies that would become the United States, after Boston, Philadelphia, New York, and Newport. By 1700, Charles Town still was an 80-acre (32-hectare) fortified city-state, four squares long by three squares wide, surrounded by a wall. Six bastions helped protect the city. Many farms and plantations existed outside the city, and the city had become a trading center for the farms, plantations, and native villages, with rivers and original Indian trails becoming the avenues of commerce into the city. Deerskins and beaver skins remained important, but rice had become the major economic crop by the early 1700's.

By 1717, the Spanish threat had waned, unfriendly local tribes had been defeated in the Yamasee War, and friendly local tribes had settled primarily as farmers and hunters along local river areas in South Carolina. In 1717, the wall was removed from around the city to allow growth. Pirates remained a problem until 1718.

SIGNIFICANCE

Charles Town was unique in its early ethnic mixture. Some scholars think that one African slave was on the *Carolina* in 1670, but even if this were not the case, African slaves were brought in soon afterward. Some of the Africans were free, and many, whether slave or free, were skilled craftsmen. There was a relatively small white middle class, because the large white wealthy class stymied middle-class growth, and an even smaller white craftsman class, because of the predominance of free Africans and African slaves as expert craftsmen. Against strong opposition from the lords proprietors, some Native Americans were enslaved. Huguenot refugees from England, France, and other places began moving to the city in the mid-1680's. The Barbadians and Huguenots soon formed the largest part of the cultural and political elite of the area. Close contact was maintained with Barbados, and these ties also helped the Barbadians and the city to prosper.

Barbadian architecture, Huguenot wrought iron, and formal gardens became hallmarks of Charles Town. The proprietors encouraged Dissenters (Protestants who were not members of the Church of England) to move to Charles Town in order to limit the power of the Barbadians. Immigrants, mostly Calvinist Presbyterians, came from Scotland and Ireland, and they engaged in political conflict with the Barbadians and Huguenots. Quakers, and by 1695 Spanish and Portuguese Jews, also settled in Charles Town.

Charles Town remained unique in its tolerance of religious and ethnic diversity. It was the only major city in the colonial era that did not exclude undesirable strangers and probably was the least religious of the early major cities. In fact, Charles Town developed a well-deserved reputation as a cultured, wealthy, and pleasure-oriented city, a place of theaters, gambling, horse racing, dancing, and drinking.

Much of this was possible only through exploitation of African slaves to provide most of the manual labor.

In 1970, Charles Town Landing was developed as a state park and major tourist attraction on the site of the original Charles Town settlement, celebrating the tricentennial of the 1670 settlement, which is also considered the tricentennial of South Carolina. A reconstruction of a village of the 1600's; a forest with animals found in Charles Town in 1670—such as black bears, bison, bobcats, alligators, snakes, and puma—a crop garden with tobacco, rice, indigo, cotton, sugar cane, and other crops grown in season; a reproduction of a seventeenth century trading vessel docked at the original landing area; a museum; a theater; and other re-creations showed many facets of the 1670 settlement.

—Abraham D. Lavender

See also: The Middle Passage to American Slavery.

Related articles in *Great Lives from History: The Seventeenth Century, 1601-1700:* Charles I; Charles II (of England).

EXPANSION OF THE ATLANTIC SLAVE TRADE 18TH CENTURY

Benefiting from the complicity of European nations, the Atlantic slave trade expanded dramatically during the eighteenth century. This development set the stage for the mass transportation of Africans to the Americas, with more than 70 percent of all slaves arriving in the New World after 1700. Although an antislavery movement emerged in the late eighteenth century, economic influences obstructed its effectiveness.

Locale: West Africa; New World colonies
Categories: Trade and commerce; economics; social issues and reform; colonization

KEY FIGURES
John Hawkins (1532-1595), the first Englishman to trade in slaves between West Africa and the West Indies
Charles Pinckney (1757-1824), adviser to George Washington and a powerful political figure who argued that slavery was necessary in the colonies
William Wilberforce (1759-1833), leader of the Society for the Abolition of the Slave Trade

SUMMARY OF EVENT
Portugal, which established the Atlantic slave trade in the mid-fifteenth century and remained its dominant force until the beginning of the eighteenth century, enslaved thousands of Africans for work on sugar plantations in Brazil. Operating on a limited scale initially, the trade increased after Christopher Columbus made his voyage in 1492 and opened the New World to Europeans. Beginning in the 1550's, the Spanish transported Africans into their Central American and South American colonies. The French and the Dutch entered the trade in the 1650's to provide workers for their holdings in the Caribbean.

In 1562, British admiral John Hawkins inaugurated the British slave trade by profitably transporting African captives during a three-year period (through 1565) to Caribbean colonies claimed and ruled by the Spanish. Because of Spain's objections to this encroachment on its territory, England remained on the sidelines for another century. In the mid-1600's the demand for labor in Britain's Caribbean and North American colonies prompted British investors to enter the trade. By the beginning of the eighteenth century, England ruled the slave market, with both British seamen and those from the New England colonies pursuing the lucrative business. Great Britain and other European countries transported approximately three million Africans to the New World during the 1600's.

The next century saw that number double. It is estimated that eleven million Africans were enslaved and transported to the Americas and the Caribbean during the entire course of the slave trade.

The leaders of the various nations considered slaves essential to the expansion of their far-flung colonies, which produced profitable and popular commodities such as sugar, coffee, and tobacco. Charles Pinckney, a prominent politician, slaveholder, and close associate of George Washington, summed up his belief in the economic necessity of slavery by calling African slaves raw materials that were essential for planters to cultivate their land. Others involved in the trade justified the practice by arguing that slavery figured in the divine plan. By "rescuing" Africans from savagery and converting them to Christianity, they believed they were doing God's work. Considering the competitive nature of the trade, an endless series of disputes and clashes took place on the high seas and at various ports when one nation would accuse another of infringing on its territory. By winning the Seven Years' War (1756-1763) they fought against France, the British gained several French colonies in the Caribbean. Earlier, Great Britain faced the brutal First Maroon War in Jamaica when the British attempted to take the colony from Spain in 1730. The *asiento de negros*, established by the Spanish in the 1600's, added to the complications. The *asiento* was essentially a license issued for a fee to supply slaves to a specific colony, but it was not always a guarantee against disputes. Slave uprisings and rebellions in Saint Vincent, Grenada, and Saint Domingue (which became Haiti in 1804) caused additional problems. Africa, too, faced upheavals brought by the slave trade. The unceasing demand for captives led to skirmishes between the coastal Africans who profited from the trade and those who lived in central Africa, the area from which most of the slaves were drawn.

Much has been recorded about the horrific conditions on what is known as the Middle Passage—the lengthy sea journey between Africa's west coast and the Americas. Even though the human "cargo" was extremely valuable, the captives faced poor sanitary conditions, little if any medical attention, and inadequate types and amounts of food. As a result, many died during the first phase of their bondage. In some instances, the slave traders threw the sick overboard to prevent the spread of disease. One ship's physician described how the deck, where hundreds of

slaves were chained, was covered with blood, mucus, and excrement—a scene he found so repugnant that it lay beyond human imagination. After arriving in a foreign port, the dejected and frightened survivors faced humiliating auctions, where prospective buyers judged the survivors as if they were livestock. Although England captured the market in the 1700's, it would also lead the movement to end slave trading. Initial efforts concentrated on ending the trade, not slavery itself, even though that remained the ultimate goal of the Society for the Abolition of the Slave Trade (formed in 1787). Two years later, William Wilberforce joined the society. He was influenced by John Newton, a former slave trader who had experienced a dramatic conversion that led him into the ministry and into the abolition movement.

After years of urging the British parliament to abolish the trade, Wilberforce finally succeeded: In 1807 both houses passed a law ending the transportation of slaves from Africa to the Caribbean and North American colonies. This act, which was influenced in part by economic circumstances, caused ripples throughout the European community, and one by one other nations followed suit. In the next few years most European nations abolished slavery as well, and, in 1833, the British parliament halted the practice throughout its global empire. The slave trade continued on a limited scale until Brazil and Cuba were pressured during the 1860's into banning the importation of slaves.

SIGNIFICANCE

The expansion of the slave trade marked a significant point in world history, but the stain it left did not miraculously vanish with its demise beginning in the early nineteenth century. The practice had long-lasting effects on both the slaves and their "masters." The immediate impact was economic. Because the wealth Great Britain and other European nations gained through their colonial ventures relied on slave labor, abolition deprived plantation owners of their most vital resource. As a result, various forms of slavery and slave trading continued not only in the United States, where it was not abolished until 1863, but in other regions as well.

From the outset, African slaves had not been docile in their captivity. Uprisings took place in the 1700's, and the resistance continued into the nineteenth century, with bands of runaway and freed slaves sabotaging plantations. At the same time, the freed slaves who wanted to settle and take advantage of the prosperity they had helped create found themselves outcasts and lived in conditions little different from enslavement. Although slavery had faded into the past, it was replaced by racism— a new form of bondage that was to have lasting consequences.

Africa's role in the slave trade helped to determine the continent's destiny. Through alliance with Great Britain and European countries, the coastal slave traders inadvertently opened up Africa to colonial exploitation. Once the overseas scramble for the continent succeeded, the empire builders no longer transported Africans into bondage but enslaved them on their own land.

—*Robert Ross*

See also: Stono Rebellion; Pennsylvania Society for the Abolition of Slavery Is Founded; Northeast States Abolish Slavery; Free African Society Is Founded; First Fugitive Slave Law; Second Maroon War.

Related articles in *Great Lives from History: The Eighteenth Century, 1701-1800*: Benjamin Banneker; Joseph Boulogne; Olaudah Equiano; Benjamin Franklin; First Earl of Mansfield; Nanny; Guillaume-Thomas Raynal; Benjamin Rush; Samuel Sewall; Granville Sharp; Toussaint Louverture; George Washington; Phillis Wheatley; William Wilberforce.

Dealing in Slaves

Dutch West India Company employee William Bosman, the company's chief factor, or European agent, at Elmina along the Guinea Coast in West Africa in the late seventeenth and early eighteenth century, documented slave dealing. Slave dealing and trading included the cooperation of local African chiefs, who would receive customs duty in exchange for giving the Europeans the right to buy slaves. The language here clearly evokes the "commodity" status of the African captives.

When these slaves come to Fida [in present-day Dahomey], they are put in Prison all together, and when we treat concerning buying them, they are all brought together in a large Plain; where by our Chirurgeons [surgeons], whose Providence it is, they are thoroughly examined, even to the smallest Member, and that naked too bothMenand Women, without the least Distinction orModesty. Those which are approved as good are set on one side; and the lame or faulty are set by as *Invalides*, which are here called *Mackrons*. . . .

The *Invalides* and the Maimed being thrown out . . . the remainder are numbered, and it is entered who delivered them. In the meanwhile, a burning Iron with the Arms or Name of the Companies, lyes in the Fire; with which ours are marked on the Breast. . . .but we yet take all possible care that they are not burned too hard, especially the Women who are more tender then the Men. We are seldom long detained in the buying of these Slaves, because their price is established, the Women being . . . cheaper than the Men. . . . When we have agreed with the Owners of the Slaves, they are returned to their Prison.

Source: William Bosman, "A New and Accurate Description of Guinea" (1705), excerpted in *The Horizon History of Africa*, edited by Alvin M. Josephy, Jr. (New York: American Heritage, 1971), p. 335.

NEW YORK CITY SLAVE REVOLT

April 6, 1712

A small group of black and American Indian slaves rebelled against mistreatment and restrictive laws, leading to further legal restrictions on slaves, freed or not, including the weakening of due process rights and the prohibition against owning or inheriting property. Also, slave owners, before they could free a slave, had to pay a bond to the government as well as an annual allowance for life to each freed slave.

Locale: Manhattan Island (now New York City)
Categories: Wars, uprisings, and civil unrest; social issues and reform

KEY FIGURES
May Bickley (d. 1724), an attorney general who led the prosecution of those indicted in the conspiracy and revolt

Cuffee (fl. early eighteenth century) and *Dick* (fl. early eighteenth century), two slaves who presumably were promised immunity to testify against others implicated in the rebellion

Robert Hunter (1666-1734), royal governor of New York, 1709-1719

Elias Neau (1662-1722), a Huguenot merchant who ministered to New York City slaves

John Sharpe (fl. early eighteenth century), an Anglican chaplain to the British garrison at Fort Anne

SUMMARY OF EVENT

The New York City slave revolt of 1712 calls attention to slavery having become more firmly established in colonial New York than in any other British province north of Chesapeake Bay. Slaves were already an integral part of the labor force when England conquered Dutch New Netherland in 1664. As European immigration lagged, slave labor became increasingly important. Between 1703 and 1723, New York's total population almost doubled, increasing from 20,540 to 40,564; but its black population (slaves and free blacks were lumped together statistically and listed in the census as "Negroes") almost tripled, jumping from 2,253 to 6,171.

As the number of bondsmen increased, so did the anxiety level of white New Yorkers. In 1708, following the grisly murder of a Long Island planter and his family, four slaves were tried, convicted, and executed "with all the torment possible for a terror to others." Shortly thereafter, the provincial assembly passed the Act for Preventing the Conspiracy of Slaves, which defined the judicial proceedings and made death the penalty for any slave found guilty of murder or attempted murder. Fear of slave conspiracy led whites to look with ambivalence upon Anglican catechist Elias Neau's teaching among New York City blacks and American Indians.

Small-scale slave owning prevailed in New York. Few white families owned more than a slave or two, so slave husbands, wives, and children might be scattered among several households. Regulations restricting their freedom of movement were bitterly resented by slaves, because they interfered with their domestic life. Such restrictions often were more apparent than real, because slavery in New York City and surrounding villages, where slaves were most heavily concentrated, was tied to a developing urban economy that demanded a flexible, if not free, labor supply. Slaves in New York City and Albany often hired themselves out, splitting the pay with their respective owners, but otherwise lived separately from their masters. The hustle and bustle of the urban economic scene afforded slaves considerable opportunity to meet, socialize, and discuss common grievances, despite the best efforts of whites to keep them under surveillance.

The slave uprising of April 6, 1712, apparently began as a conspiracy on March 25, the day that was formerly celebrated as New Year's Day. The ringleaders reportedly were of the Cormantine and Pawpaw peoples, Africans who had not been long in New York; a few Spanish Indian slaves; and at least one free black, a practitioner of African medicine and magic who reportedly supplied special powder to protect the rebels from the weapons of the whites. Their motivation, according to both Governor Robert Hunter and Chaplain John Sharpe, was revenge for ill treatment at the hands of their respective masters. Their goal was freedom, which, claimed Hunter and Sharpe, was to be achieved by burning New York City and killing the white people on Manhattan.

During the early morning hours of Sunday, April 6, 1712, about two dozen conspirators, armed with guns, swords, knives, and clubs, gathered in an orchard in the East Ward on the northeast edge of New York City. They set fire to several outbuildings and waited in ambush for the whites who came to put out the blaze, killing nine and wounding seven. Soldiers were dispatched from the fort, but when they arrived, the rebels had dispersed, taking refuge in the woods surrounding the town. The next day, local militiamen systematically searched Manhattan Island for the rebellious blacks. Rather than surrender, six slaves killed themselves, with several cutting their own throats.

White New Yorkers were in full panic. "We have about 70 Negro's in Custody," read a dispatch from New York, dated April 14 but published in the *Boston News-Letter* on April 21, but it was "fear'd that most of the Negro's here (who are very numerous) knew of the Late Conspiracy to murder the Christians." Fear of another uprising drove the judicial proceedings. On April 9, a coroner's jury implicated thirty-eight slaves, identifying fourteen of them as murderers. In accordance with the 1708 conspiracy act, the coroner's findings were turned over to the Court of Quarter Sessions of the Peace, which convened on April 11. Attorney General May Bickley handled the prosecution, moving the trials from the Quarter Sessions to the State Supreme Court on June 3.

Forty-two slaves and one free black were indicted and tried. Crucial to both the indictments and trials was the testimony of two slaves: Cuffee, who belonged to baker Peter Vantilborough, and Dick, a boy slave owned by Harmanus Burger, a blacksmith. The coroner's jury had found Cuffee and Dick guilty of at least two murders, but Bickley apparently promised them immunity, and they became the Crown's prime witnesses. Some whites, including such substantial citizens as former mayor David Provost, coroner Henry Wileman, and lawyers Jacob Regnier and David Jamison, testified for a few of the defendants.

However, the general adequacy of defense counsel may well be doubted. Many of the convictions hinged upon the dubious testimony of Cuffee and young Dick, both of whom were manipulated by Bickley, described by Governor Hunter as "a busy waspish man." Bickley also demonstrated considerable bias against certain slave defendants, depending upon who owned them. For example, Mars, belonging to Jacob Regnier, a rival attorney with whom Bickley had a private quarrel, was tried twice and acquitted before being found guilty in the third trial and sentenced to be hanged.

Most of the trials were over by early June. Twenty-three slaves were convicted of murder; fifteen slaves were acquitted, along with one free black. Two slaves were found guilty of assault with intent to kill, and two were acquitted of that charge. The twenty-five who were convicted were sentenced to death. Twenty were to be hanged; three were burned alive, one in a slow fire for eight to ten hours until consumed to ashes. Another was broken upon the wheel and left to die, and one was hung in chains and "so to continue without sustenance until death." Eleven were "executed at once," including those burned, broken at the wheel, and chained without food or water. These barbaric executions were defended by Governor Hunter as "the most exemplary that could be possibly thought of."

Yet even Hunter doubted the justice of it all. He postponed the execution of six slaves, including two Spanish American Indians taken and sold as slaves despite their claim of being free men, a pregnant slave woman, and the much tried and finally convicted Mars. At Hunter's request, Queen Anne pardoned several of them, and perhaps all of those he had reprieved (the record is rather vague), despite the efforts of Bickley in New York and of Lord Cornbury, a former governor of New York, in London to obstruct the pardons.

SIGNIFICANCE

There were other ramifications of the slave uprising. The provincial government passed laws making it impossible to free slaves without putting up a £200 bond and paying the freed slave £20 per year for life. Africans, American Indians, and mulattoes were prohibited from inheriting or otherwise owning property. Finally, due process rights were weakened for slaves accused of murder or conspiracy.

In the wake of the revolt, Elias Neau, the preacher and catechist of Trinity Church, found it difficult to continue his school for blacks and American Indians. Only two of his many pupils were implicated in the conspiracy, and Chaplain John Sharpe doubted that either was involved in the violence.

After the rebellion, New Yorkers were reluctant to import slaves directly from Africa or to purchase Spanish Indians as slaves. Black slaves from the West Indies were preferred over the other two groups. Yet slavery remained a primary source of labor for both the province and city of New York, slaves constituting about 15 percent of the population. In 1730, other regulations were added to the slave code because "many Mischiefs had been Occasioned by the too great Liberty allowed to Negro and other Slaves." In 1741, white paranoia and slave discontent provoked a so-called slave conspiracy in which 150 slaves and 25 whites were jailed. Of that number, 18 slaves and 4 whites were hanged, 13 blacks were burned alive, and 70 were sold and sent to the West Indies.

—*Ronald W. Howard*

See also: Stono Rebellion; Caribbean Slave Rebellions; Free African Society Is Founded.

Related articles in *Great Lives from History: The Eighteenth Century, 1701-1800*: Benjamin Banneker; Benjamin Franklin; John Jay; Nanny; Guillaume-Thomas Raynal; Paul Revere; Benjamin Rush; Samuel Sewall; Granville Sharp; Toussaint Louverture; Phillis Wheatley.

SETTLEMENT OF THE CAROLINAS

The Carolinas became the seat of the South in British North America, central to the tobacco and sugar plantation culture that the colonists developed and to the slave trade necessary to support that culture.

Locale: Eastern Carolinas
Categories: Expansion and land acquisition; colonization

KEY FIGURES

Sir William Berkeley (1606-1677), governor of Virginia, 1641-1649, 1660-1677, and an original Carolina proprietor

John Colleton (fl. 1663), wealthy Barbadian planter who took the initiative in acquiring the proprietary charter for the Carolinas

John Culpeper (1644-1691/1694), leader of a rebellion against Albemarle's proprietary government

William Drummond (d. 1677), first governor of Albemarle County, 1664-1667, which became North Carolina

Edward Hyde (c. 1650-1712), first governor of North Carolina independent of South Carolina, 1711-1712

John Locke (1632-1704), English political philosopher, who helped to prepare the Fundamental Constitutions

Philip Ludwell (c. 1637-after 1710), first governor of both Carolinas

First Earl of Shaftesbury (Anthony Ashley Cooper; 1621-1683), proprietor and architect of the Carolina proprietary system

Sir John Yeamans (1611-1674), leader of South Carolina's Goose Creek faction

SUMMARY OF EVENT

The origins of English settlement of TheCarolinas can be traced to 1629, when Charles I of England granted all land between 31° and 36° north latitude to Sir Robert Heath, who called the area "New Carolina." Heath planned to open the territory to French Protestants, or Huguenots, who were under siege in the latest of French religious conflicts. Agents of The Carolina settlers attempted to obtain supplies in Virginia to the north but were largely unsuccessful, and no settlements were established. Heath shortly thereafter gave up on the enterprise, and nothing further was attempted during Charles I's reign.

The introduction of large-scale sugar production during the early 1660's to Barbados, in the West Indies, among the wealthiest of the English colonies, had forced many small English planters to consider emigration from

the island. When Sir John Colleton, a wealthy Barbadian, returned to England and gained a seat on the Council for Foreign Plantations, he conceived the idea of establishing a proprietary colony and recruiting Barbadians to settle it. For fellow proprietors, Colleton turned to powerful Englishmen who had already been associated with colonial expansion, the first earl of Shaftesbury, Sir William Berkeley, John Lord Berkeley, George Monck, the first earl of Clarendon, the earl of Craven, and Sir George Carteret. On March 24, 1663, King Charles II granted to the proprietors a charter similar to that granted by his father, redefined as all land between 29° and 36°30″ north latitude and extending west to the "South Seas"; they called the area Carolina after King Charles.

Required only to pay a nominal annual sum to the king, the proprietors possessed vast powers. They were empowered to fill offices, erect a government, establish courts, collect customs and taxes, grant land, confer titles, and determine military matters. They were obliged to guarantee the rights of Englishmen to their settlers, however, and could enact laws only with the consent of the freemen. The proprietors in England also constituted a Palatine Court, which, in addition to appointing the governor of the colonies, was empowered to disallow laws and hear appeals from the colony.

Having devised plans for the creation of three counties and having begun negotiations with two groups of prospective settlers in Barbados and New England, the proprietors drafted the "Declaration and Proposals to All That Will Plant in Carolina," which outlined a headright system of land distribution and a framework for participatory government. Sir William Berkeley received authorization to appoint a governor and council for Albemarle County (later North Carolina), and in October, 1664, he named William Drummond of Virginia as its governor. A few months later, Sir John Yeamans was commissioned governor of Clarendon County. As a further inducement to settlement, in January, 1665, the proprietors drew up the Concessions and Agreements, which provided for a unicameral legislature that included representatives of the freemen and ensured religious toleration. However, friction between new arrivals and original settlers in combination with hostility from Native American tribes and the news of better land to the south, led to the abandonment of Clarendon County in 1667.

Settlement of The Carolina during this period was focused primarily on the estuaries of the southern regions rather than the large bays and dangerous banks of the north. Settlers in the region were a varied lot, consisting of a mixture of English Dissenters, French Huguenots, and Presbyterian Scots. The largest contingent, however, consisted of emigrants from Barbados; by 1671, they constituted half the population in the region.

As a system of laws, the Concessions and Agreements had proven unsatisfactory, so in 1669, the earl of Shaftesbury collaborated with his protégé, John Locke, to write the Fundamental Constitutions of Carolina. Essentially, the program called for development of a landed aristocracy for the region, in the form of 12,000-acre (4,850-hectare) baronies. Two-thirds of the land would be held by a colonial nobility. Although a "parliament" consisting of the nobility and popular representatives would sit in the colony, the proprietors in England, functioning as a Palatine Court, could veto the legislature's decisions. Some of these provisions were implemented, but the proprietors never succeeded in winning approval of the system as a whole. Few baronies were ever surveyed, and no manorial system was ever established. Reflecting the exigencies of a governing body in England removed from the day-to-day running of a colony, the actual government consisted of a governor and council appointed by the proprietors and representatives elected by the freemen. Until a Supreme Court was established in 1700, the governor and council would constitute the colony's highest court.

Despite the abandonment of the Clarendon region, The Carolina's proprietors continued to develop plans for settlement of the region. Shaftesbury was able to convince the proprietors that a larger investment was essential for success. Drawing upon earlier experience and the expertise and resources of investors from Barbados, it was decided to attempt to establish a settlement at Port Royal. More than one hundred settlers, led by Joseph West, left England in August, 1669. However, after landing at Port Royal, already an important anchorage, they were persuaded by the local tribes to travel to another estuary some sixty miles up the coast. There, in April, 1670, they established Charles Town (modern Charleston).

Because the settlers were predominantly tradesmen ignorant of farming methods, many went into debt and deserted the colony. Recruitment efforts proved successful, however, and a rapid influx of settlers from Barbados and elsewhere continued to populate the colony. Many along the estuaries. They quickly learned the ways of agriculture. Disparate ethnic enclaves began to form, such as French Huguenots settled along the Santee and a Scottish settlement at the anchorage of Port Royal. Despite religious contention, prosperity within the colony increased. In 1674, Dr. Henry Woodward was commissioned Indian agent to establish trade with local Native American tribes; the colonists developed a thriving trade in furs and naval stores with England and in meat, lumber, and Indian slaves—a practice frowned upon by the proprietors—with the West Indies.

A large proportion of the colonists having emigrated from Barbados, this particularly significant group soon gained control of the government. Known as the "Goose Creek men," from the site of their settlement just outside of Charles Town, this faction was to determine the colony's politics for the next fifty years. Despite success in the areas of trade and farming, conflict between the proprietors and settlers over debts, land distribution, and the slave trade nearly brought an end to the colony in the 1670's. Attracted by the proprietors' promise of toleration, many Dissenters also came, only to encounter the resentment of the conservative Anglican Barbadians, who resisted the proprietors' efforts at reform; both pro and anti-proprietary factions were formed.

During the 1670's, dissension culminated in what became known as Culpeper's Rebellion. In 1677, Thomas Miller, governor and leader of the proprietary faction, attempted to combine his position with the duties of customs collector. In December, an anti-proprietary faction established a revolutionary government and imprisoned Miller. Miller escaped to England and pleaded his case before the Privy Council; John Culpeper, a leader of the dissident group, represented the rebels. The council decided that Miller had indeed exceeded his authority. Culpeper was tried for treason but through the influence of Shaftesbury was acquitted.

When Governor James Colleton declared martial law in February, 1690, in an attempt to halt the abuses of the Native American trade and collect the quitrents, the Goose Creek men ousted him and replaced him with Seth Sothel. In 1691, Sothel was suspended by the Palatine Court and charged with treason, though Sothel's death in 1694 ended the controversy. Meanwhile, Philip Ludwell was appointed governor by the proprietors (1691), and the popular freemen's branch of the legislature was allowed to meet separately and to exercise parliamentary privileges.

Unlike the turmoil of earlier decades, the 1690's would be a decade of relative peace and prosperity. Ludwell and his successors were to reside in Charles Town, while Albemarle County, governed by Ludwell's deputy, was to retain a separate legislature. Trade with Native American tribes prospered. Perhaps even more important, during this period it became apparent that a new crop, rice, was perfectly suited for the swampy lowlands of The Carolinas.

Rice quickly became a staple export. Critical to the development of rice farming was the large influx of African slaves into the region, bringing with them knowledge of rice cultivation. By the beginning of the eighteenth century, the Black population equaled that of the white: There were approximately four thousand of each race. The region of Albemarle, known as North Carolina after 1691, was repeatedly torn by religious strife in the first decade of the new century. Huguenots from Virginia had settled the area south of Albemarle Sound; German Palatines and Swiss had settled in the region of what would be founded as New Bern (1710). Although toleration had prevailed in the earlier years and many Dissenters held positions of power, Anglicans were determined to establish the Church of England in the colony.

With the passage of the Vestry Act of 1704, Assembly members were required to take an oath of loyalty to the Church of England. The act aroused such intense opposition that deputy governor Thomas Cary was removed for attempting to enforce the law. In 1712, North Carolina was established as a separate colony; the proprietors appointed Edward Hyde deputy governor, the first governor of North Carolina to be independent of the royal governor of Carolina. The new legislature nullified the laws of the previous administrations.

SIGNIFICANCE

The Carolinas were thus a crucible for many of the controversies shaping the evolution of both the colonists' home countries and the other English colonies. Religious strife, disagreements over the proper form of colonial government and over the role of government as such, and interrelations between Europeans, Native Americas, and African slaves, all came to a head in the Carolina colonies.

The crisis in North Carolina was exacerbated by the war with the Tuscaroras, the worst Indian war in the colony's history. In September, 1711, the Tuscaroras, seeking revenge for encroachment by the settlers on their land, enslavement of their people, and unfair trading practices, attacked New Bern and other settlements from the Neuse to the Pamlico Rivers. Before the raids were over, hundreds of settlers had been massacred and their farms destroyed. Two expeditions, led by Colonel Jack Barnwell and Colonel James More in 1712 and 1713 and aided by men from South Carolina, finally defeated the Tuscaroras. Although the war had placed the colony in dire financial straits, it drew the people together, and they entered a new period of peace.

The choice of rice as a staple crop had its greatest impact in the south. Unlike the tobacco crop, grown in the region of the Chesapeake to the north, rice growing required special water facilities to maintain an annual flooding of the fields. However, once the facilities were established, the rice crop could be grown in the same fields year after year. It was unnecessary to plant new fields or to continue shifting the settlements themselves. Thus, the settlements, once established, could maintain a semblance of stability, except for the frequent internal rivalries. Consequently, settlement followed the river systems as extensions from the city of Charles Town. By 1708, the population of the district (and in essence the entire colony) consisted of four thousand whites, forty-one hundred African Americans, and fourteen hundred Native Americans; most of the African Americans and Native Americans in the settlements were slaves.

Factional rivalries were revived at the beginning of the eighteenth century. The selection of an Anglican governor for The Carolinas in 1700 aroused the opposition of the Dissenters to the establishment of the Church of England in the colony; indeed, in 1704, the parish vestries had become the seats of power. The popular division over religion was superseded by a division over the issue of paper currency in 1712. As early as 1703, the colony had emitted its first bills of credit to pay for an expedition against the Spanish in Florida. Other emissions followed.

The planters and tradesmen who did business solely within the colony favored the use of paper money, but the Charles Town merchants who had to pay their English creditors in specie bitterly opposed its use. The proprietors had never moved decisively to control the long-standing abuses of trade with Native American tribes. As a result, in 1715, the Yamasee War, the longest and costliest war with Native Americans in South Carolina's history, erupted. During the conflict, people were driven from their homes to seek refuge in Charles Town. To end the abuses of trade, the Commons House of Assembly created a monopoly of the Native American trade under its own direction.

In 1718, the proprietors launched a strong attack upon some of the colony's most popular laws, disallowing measures providing for bills of credit and import duties, removing the monopoly on trade, and weakening the power of the legislature; consequently, antiproprietary sentiment crystallized in favor of royal government. All that lacked for rebellion was a catalyst.

The catalyst came in November, 1719, in the form of the rumor of an imminent invasion of the colony by the Spanish. When the assembly convened in December, it declared itself a convention and petitioned the Board of Trade to be made a royal colony. Because the region represented a major line of defense against both the French and the Spanish, King George I accepted the removal of the proprietary government, and South Carolina became a royal colony in 1719. The "royalizing" process also had its counterpart in North Carolina. The Crown bought out the proprietors on July 25, 1729, and North Carolina also became a royal colony.

—*Richard Adler, updated by Patricia A. McDaniel*

See also: The Middle Passage to American Slavery; Charles Town Is Founded.

Related articles in *Great Lives from History: The Seventeenth Century, 1601-1700:* Charles I; Charles II (of England); First Earl of Clarendon; John Locke; George Monck; First Earl of Shaftesbury.

SETTLEMENT OF GEORGIA
June 20, 1732

Georgia became the last of the original thirteen British colonies when it was settled in 1732 by philanthropists who hoped the new colony would relieve the plight of thousands of destitute debtors and provide a haven for persecuted Protestants from other European countries. The British Empire also saw economic and militaristic benefits from the region: It occupied the area to protect its colonies from not only the encroaching Spaniards established in Florida but also indigenous peoples, who naturally resented European settlers in their homeland.

Locale: Southern United States
Category: Expansion and land acquisition

KEY FIGURES
John Martin Bolzius (1703-1765), leader of the German Salzburger settlers
Mary Musgrove (c. 1700-c. 1763), an American Indian interpreter and trader who, with her husband John, assisted the Georgia settlers
James Edward Oglethorpe (1696-1785), a British parliament member who proposed the founding of Georgia and was its first civil and military leader
John Perceval (First Earl of Egmont; 1683-1748), a promoter and recorder of the Georgia venture
Tomochichi (c. 1650-1739), chief of the Yamacraw Indians who resided in the Savannah area
James Wright (1716-1785), the most successful of the royal governors

SUMMARY OF EVENT
The founding of Georgia attracted more attention in England than that of any other colony. Because the project suited both philanthropic and imperial interests, it drew support from all segments of society and government, including philanthropists, such as James Edward Oglethorpe, a member of Parliament, and Thomas Bray, founder of the Society of the Gospel in Foreign Parts. The Crown was concerned with the Spaniards who had gradually expanded northward from their Florida settlement, establishing presidios and missions, first on the Sea Islands and then on the mainland of Georgia.

In addition to protecting their frontier against the Spanish, the British government had to contend with the Yamasee Indians, who were resentful of the encroaching European settlers.

The Crown also perceived economic advantages from a new colony that could contribute raw materials for English manufacturers, provide a market for their goods, and ease the mother country's unemployment problem.

Therefore, when John Perceval (later the earl of Egmont), an associate of the late Dr. Bray, acted upon the suggestion of Oglethorpe and petitioned the Crown for a tract of land south and west of Carolina between the Savannah and Altamaha Rivers, the request was approved.

On June 20, 1732, the Crown conferred upon the twenty-one members of the board of trustees for Georgia a charter empowering them to found and to manage for twenty-one years the land between the Savannah and Altamaha Rivers, stretching as far westward as what had been called the South Sea (the Gulf of Mexico). Although the government took a calculated view of their enterprise, the trustees considered it the greatest philanthropic and social experiment of their age. Numerous churches, organizations, and individuals responded to their promotional campaign with contributions.

Because the settlers were to participate in a social experiment, they were individually selected from among applicants who included imprisoned debtors, the poor, and the downtrodden. Each received free passage to Georgia, tools, seeds, provisions until their first harvest, and fifty acres of land. Slaves, hard liquor, Catholics, and lawyers were prohibited in early Georgia.

In November, 1732, 114 settlers set sail on the ship *Anne*, with Oglethorpe leading the expedition to America. Disembarking in the Carolinas at Charleston in January, 1733, Oglethorpe soon chose a settlement site. With Mary Musgrove, an American Indian, serving as interpreter, Oglethorpe reached an agreement with Tomochichi, chief of the Yamacraws, a Creek group who lived in the area. On February 12, 1733 (Georgia's founder's day), the colonists arrived. With the aid of Colonel William Bull, a Carolinian, Oglethorpe laid out the city of Savannah, where settlement began. The communal arrangement provided that each family own a town lot with a garden and a piece of farmland nearby. Settlers held their land through "tail male," meaning that tenure was for life and only eldest sons could inherit land. The prohibition against the sale or rental of property eliminated the possibility of unselected immigrants becoming part of the community. Hoping once again to make silk production a profitable colonial enterprise, the Crown required each settler to clear ten acres and plant one hundred mulberry trees within ten years. Moreover, Georgia's colonial settlers were to produce wine, grow tropical plants, and provide other raw materials that would benefit the British mercantile system.

In addition to the "charity settlers," the trustees admitted approved adventurers, persons who paid their own passage to the colony. Persecuted Protestants, such as the Lutheran Salzburgers from Germany, also came. The Salzburgers, under the dynamic leadership of John Martin Bolzius, settled outside Savannah in the town of Ebenezer and quickly became the most prosperous group in early Georgia. Their church, New Jerusalem, is the oldest brick structure in the state.

Authority over Georgia's affairs was officially shared by the board of trustees and the British government, although in practice a smaller body known as the

common council did most of the work. Among the most active trustees were Oglethorpe, Perceval, James Vernon, the earl of Shaftesbury (Anthony Ashley-Cooper), and Benjamin Martyn, the secretary. Although all laws passed by the trustees had to be reviewed by the king, the trustees neglected the political side of the Georgia colony.

While the trustees held the philanthropic and social goals to be of primary importance, the government was concerned chiefly with the economic and defensive advantages that Georgia might contribute to the British Empire. The trustees came to distrust Sir Robert Walpole, the chancellor of the exchequer, and in order to evade the authority of the government, tried, as far as possible, to govern by regulations rather than laws. In the absence of local governmental institutions, Oglethorpe acted as Georgia's unofficial leader.

SIGNIFICANCE

Georgia's most serious problems in the early years were caused by the conflicting purposes it was expected to fulfill. Times were hard, rewards few. Inevitably, Georgia assumed a military character, and the colonists were distracted from the business of building a stable society. Oglethorpe focused much of his time on negotiating with the American Indians and leading his regiment into a series of skirmishes against the Spanish, for which he was rewarded military rank. When the fighting ended in 1743, General Oglethorpe left Georgia, never to return.

In the absence of a leader, hard times increased for the Georgia settlers; they ignored the liquor and slave prohibitions; and many resettled in other colonies. Furthermore, the trustees abandoned the colony a year before their charter ended. Consequently, Georgia became a royal colony under the auspices of King George II, for whom the colony was named. The royal colony was under the leadership of three governors from 1754 to 1776: Captain John Reynolds, an unpopular leader who was forced back to England after serving two years; Henry Ellis, who was in poor health and did not last; and, finally, Sir James Wright, who was appointed in 1760. Under Governor Wright, colonial Georgia began to stabilize as its population grew. Among the new colonists were more than fifteen thousand African slaves who contributed much to colonial development. Wright remained governor of Georgia until the changes wrought by the American Revolution forced him from power. In 1777, under a new constitution, John Truetlen, a Salzburger, was elected the state's first governor as colonial Georgia theoretically ended.

—*Warren M. Billings, updated by Linda Rochell Lane*

See also: Stono Rebellion; African American Baptist Church Is Founded.

Related articles in *Great Lives from History: The Eighteenth Century, 1701-1800*: George II; Alexander McGillivray; James Edward Oglethorpe; Robert Walpole; Charles Wesley; John Wesley.

STONO REBELLION

September 9, 1739

African slaves in South Carolina staged a rebellion that was quickly and brutally suppressed. The revolt demonstrated to white settlers, who were in the minority, the precariousness of their situation in the colonies, and it led them to pass laws designed both to increase their control over their slaves and to decrease discontent among slaves that might lead to future uprisings.

Locale: St. Paul's Parish, near the Stono River, South Carolina (now in the United States)
Categories: Wars, uprisings, and civil unrest; social issues and reform

KEY FIGURES

Jemmy (fl. 1739), enslaved African rebel leader
William Bull (1683-1755), lieutenant governor of South Carolina

SUMMARY OF EVENT

Conditions in South Carolina in the 1730's led to white fear of slave uprisings. The high numbers of Africans imported through Charles Town port led to legislation against Africans congregating, holding meetings, or appearing in public after nightfall. Charles Town had a watch committee to guard the port city, and the rest of the colony had a white patrol system to police Africans in militia districts. South Carolina used public punishment as a deterrent. Contrary to their intent, these white controls increasingly led to greater resistance from newly imported Africans.

Cases of verbal insolence joined arson as a recurring feature of colonial life. Whites blamed illnesses and deaths on African knowledge of plants and their poisonous powers. In the 1730's, massive importations from the Congo-Angola region meant that more than half of the colony's slaves had been there fewer than ten years.

Slave unrest was blamed on outside agitators—Native Americans with assistance from both the Spanish and

French. Rumors of a Spanish invasion increased after the Spanish king granted liberty to African fugitive slaves in 1733. Tension thus was high in 1739. Then, a smallpox epidemic, coupled with the escape of slaves to Spanish Florida, led to massive loss of investments. A yellow fever epidemic hit during the summer months. In the fall, deaths decreased with the return of cool weather, but the situation was ripe for insurrection. Since Sundays afforded slaves their best opportunity for meeting in communal activities, the legislature passed the Security Act in August, 1739, requiring all white men to carry firearms to churches beginning September 29 or pay a stiff fine. News of conflict between England and Spain reached Charles Town the weekend before the uprising began, explaining why the Stono Rebellion began immediately without betrayal, caught white masters in church unarmed, and had slaves marching toward Spanish St. Augustine.

The insurrection included elements typical of early rebellions in South Carolina: total surprise, brutal killings, extensive property damage, armed fighting, and extended consequences. On the morning of September 9, 1739, twenty slaves, mostly Angolans, gathered in St. Paul's Parish near Stono River, 20 miles from Charles Town. Led by a slave named Jemmy, the group broke into Hutchenson's store near the Stono Bridge to gather guns and ammunition. Storekeepers Robert Bathurst and Mr. Gibbs were beheaded. The slave band moved on to the Godfrey house, killing the family, gathering supplies, and burning the building. The slaves took the main road to Georgia, stopping at Wallace's Tavern but sparing the innkeeper, who was known to be a kind master. His white neighbor, however, lost his life, along with his wife and child. The band continued, sacking and burning houses on Pons Pons Road and killing all the white occupants.

Slave owner Thomas Rose was successfully hidden by his slaves as the band moved through. The group's numbers grew as reluctant slaves were forced to join.

101

Increased numbers led to diminished discipline. The group took up a banner, beat on two drums, and shouted, "Liberty!" They pursued and killed any whites they encountered.

Lieutenant Governor William Bull and four other white men were traveling to Charles Town for legislative session when they encountered the rebel slaves. They escaped to warn others. By late Sunday afternoon, the band of nearly one hundred rebel slaves stopped in an open field, showing their confidence and hoping to be joined by other slaves by morning.

Nearby, white colonists had been alerted by Sunday afternoon and had organized an armed and mounted resistance of somewhere between twenty and one hundred men. Moving to the field, the white forces caught the slaves off guard, killing or wounding at least fourteen rebels. They surrounded other rebels, who were briefly questioned before being shot to death. They released the slaves who had been forced to participate. Almost one third of the rebelling slaves escaped the fighting. Some returned to their plantations, hoping not to be missed. Upon their return, planters cut off their heads and placed them on posts to serve as a reminder for other slaves seeking freedom.

The white colony engaged in an intensive manhunt to recapture those participants who remained at large. Whites armed themselves, and guards were posted at ferry posts. By some accounts, twenty to forty rebels were captured, hanged, disemboweled, or beaten within the two following days. Another account, a month later, reported the rebels had been stopped from doing further mischief by having been "put to the most cruel Death." The Georgia general James Edward Oglethorpe called out rangers and American Indians, garrisoned soldiers at Palachicolas—a fort guarding the only point on the Savannah River where fugitives could cross—and issued a proclamation for whites to keep a watchful eye on any Africans.

Despite these acts of retribution and retaliation against both free blacks and slaves, white fears did not subside. Most whites thought persons of African descent were dangerous and possessed of a rebellious nature. By the fall of 1739, many planters near Stono had moved their wives and children in with other families for greater security. The assembly placed a special patrol along the Stono River. Outlying fugitives were still being brought in for execution by early 1740. Finally, two fugitive slaves seeking a large reward captured the last remaining leader, who had been at large for three years following the insurrection.

SIGNIFICANCE

The white minority responded to the Stono Rebellion in several ways. First, the colony tightened restrictions on all blacks, giving South Carolina the harshest penalties of any mainland colony. The colony also sought to improve conditions that provoked rebellion. Finally, the colony sought to lessen the influence of the Spanish settlement in St. Augustine as a constant source of incitement. The war against the Spanish curbed that stimulant.

The white minority also tried to correct the numerical racial imbalance. A prohibitive duty on new slave imports cut the rate of importation from one thousand per year in 1730 to one hundred per year by 1740. Collected duties went to recruit white immigrants. The legislature required one white man present for every ten Africans on a plantation. Fines from this infraction went to fund additional patrols.

The government intensified efforts to control the behavior of slaves. Through the Negro Act of 1740, the legislators shaped the core of the South Carolina slave codes for more than a century. Masters who failed to retain control of slaves received fines. The right to manumit slaves was taken out of the hands of owners and turned over to the legislature. No longer could slaves have such personal liberties as freedom of movement, of education, of assembly, to raise food, and to earn money. Surveillance of African American activity increased. Slaves received rewards for informing on the actions of other slaves. The legislature discouraged the presence of free blacks in the colony. The white minority developed several strategies of calculated benevolence. The government assessed penalties on masters known for excessive labor requirements or brutality of punishments for their slaves. A school was founded in Charles Town to train slaves to teach other slaves about selective Christian principles requiring submission and obedience.

These efforts did not lessen white dependency on African labor. Machines did not supplant their labor until after the American Revolution. White immigration did not increase substantially, despite offers of free land on the frontier. High duties reduced the importation of slaves, but the racial proportions varied slightly from those prior to insurrection.

The suppression of the Stono Rebellion was a significant turning point for the white minority. White factions had to cooperate to maintain the English colony. Techniques used to maintain white control shaped the race relations and history of South Carolina. The heightened degree of white repression and the reduction in

African autonomy created a new social equilibrium in the generation before the American Revolution.

—*Dorothy C. Salem*

See also: Expansion of the Atlantic Slave Trade; Apr. 6, 1712: New York City Slave Revolt; Caribbean Slave Rebellions; Pennsylvania Society for the Abolition of Slavery Is Founded; Northeast States Abolish Slavery; First Fugitive Slave Law.

Related articles in *Great Lives from History: The Eighteenth Century, 1701-1800*: Benjamin Banneker; Olaudah Equiano.

CARIBBEAN SLAVE REBELLIONS

1760-1776

The ambiguous position of the Maroons—runaway slaves—continued to affect, but not stop, slave rebellions and plots in British Jamaica, as Maroons often worked in alliance with the British. This alliance made clear that the sugar plantations could not function without the help of the Maroons. Also, colonies newly acquired from the French were rocked with their own maroonage and slave revolts.

Locale: Jamaica; Saint Vincent; Tobago; Dominica; GrenadaCategories: Wars, uprisings, and civil unrest; social issues and reform

KEY FIGURES

Tacky (d. 1760), an Akan leader of a 1760 revolt in Jamaica

Joseph Chatoyer (d. 1795), the elected leader of the Black Carib between the 1760's and 1770's

Pontiac (fl. 1776), a Jamaican slave who claimed an alliance between Maroons and slaves in Hanover Parish

SUMMARY OF EVENT

Sugar and slavery in the West Indies generated such unprecedented profits that they continued to spread during the eighteenth century, despite not only a constant threat but also actual outbreaks of collective slave revolts. As plantations moved to newly established colonies, the pattern of resistance that had rocked the older British colonies of Barbados and Antigua was repeated in Jamaica, Dominica, Grenada, Saint Vincent, and Tobago between 1760 and 1776.

Maroons were enslaved Africans who, after escaping their slaveholders, created their own societies in the interiors of islands far away from the sugar estates. They remained a threat to the planters, especially those planters who had been on the frontiers of European settlement. In Jamaica, where groups of Maroons had earlier fought the British Empire to a draw in the 1730's, Maroons had signed treaties with the British in 1739, guaranteeing a degree of autonomy. Yet Maroons allied themselves with their former "owners" to keep their own tenuous grip on freedom. While the planters' hold on power was based upon the pragmatic rule of "divide and conquer," slaves took advantage (as they had earlier) of wars between whites to gain their liberty. As the Middle Passage pumped hundreds of thousands of slaves into the Caribbean, Britain and France fought each other over control in the Caribbean, sparking many slave plots and escapes.

Occurring during the Seven Years' War (1756-1763) between Britain and France, Tacky's Rebellion (1760) in Jamaica exposed the planters' dependence upon Maroon support for putting down further slave revolts. The ongoing global conflict spread British forces thin and also interfered with food and other necessities getting to the islands, which then accelerated the inherent discontent among bondsmen being worked to death. Erupting in an area known as St. Mary's Parish, which had very few resident whites, Tacky's Rebellion took advantage of the Easter holiday to catch off guard the local planters, who were worried more about a French invasion. Led by an Akan warrior named Tacky, the insurgents planned to create their own, more ambitious version of maroonage, during which they would eventually kill all whites remaining on the island, and create their own "kingdom" rather than settle for Maroon reservations deep in the forests and hills as earlier Maroon leaders, such as Kojo and Nanny, had done a generation before after the First Maroon War (1730-1739).

Tacky's Rebellion spread from St. Mary's to points throughout western Jamaica, with the majority of conflicts in Westmoreland. There, captured slaves from the French island of Guadeloupe, who were apparently seasoned in battle, confidently dispatched of the local militia; only the bravery of Maroon mercenaries and armed slaves defending their masters saved the English. Ironically, however, the same ethnic unities forged by earlier groups of Maroons who were now on the British side shaped the outlooks and strategies of this uprising. As with his predecessors, Tacky emerged as a leader whose legitimacy was built on Akan, Asanti, and Fanti traditions.

Maroons, particularly in the western part of the island, drew their strength from relative ethnic homogeneity and identity as Kromanti (the anglicized Coromantine or Koromantyne) people. This identity stemmed from the fact that many of the enslaved transported to Jamaica came through or had relatives pass through the English slave factory at the Fanti town of Kromantine on the African Gold Coast. Tacky was one of many physically strong bondsmen from the Gold Coast preferred by planters, slaves who then carried on the martial and militant reputation of Kromanti and, more specifically, Akan men. Yet that common and adopted identity was not enough to prevent a Maroon lieutenant from killing Tacky, which quickly extinguished the revolt in St. Mary's and helped the British erode resistance elsewhere as well.

Britain's victory over the Bourbon Dynasty's powers in the Seven Years' War with the Peace of Paris (1763) gave Britain four more islands in the Caribbean—Dominica, Grenada, Saint Vincent, and Tobago, called the Ceded Islands—to develop as sugar and slavery moneymakers, a prospect that disrupted cultures already there and that portended revolt and resistance in every place it was carried out. In Dominica, for example, rough terrain and thick rain forests provided shelter for many escapees from the new estates. The incoming British tried to use indigenous American Indians, the Caribs, as slave catchers of a sort, giving them their own informal autonomy on the eastern side of the island in return for refusing to take in fugitives. Yet, there were so many other locations in which to hide that Maroons improvised and found their own plots of covert sugar and other fields. The French used the Maroons and the Caribs to recapture the island during the American Revolution, a temporary reoccupation that served to bolster the Maroons' confidence when they rebelled against the reimposition of British rule in the 1780's.

On Grenada, the French influence and presence were even greater, as both French settlers—whites and free blacks—and their Francophone slaves resented the British takeover and actively sabotaged the new order at every opportunity. Yet it was in Saint Vincent that a combination of French, indigenous, and African cultures most successfully resisted the British Empire during the 1760's and 1770's. The black Caribs, an alloy of shipwrecked slaves, a stray Frenchman or two, and indigenous peoples refused to allow the British to take away their lands without a fight. Fighting a successful guerrilla war at home and gaining a few parliamentary supporters in Britain, the black Caribs, led by their elected chief, Joseph Chatoyer, were able to hang on to almost the whole northern half of the island, as outlined in a 1773 treaty. In return, the black Caribs proclaimed their loyalty to English king George III, and collusion with the French was not permitted. The Caribs also were not to give asylum to fugitives from the newly established sugar estates.

Planters were not satisfied with the fugitive provision, however, because they felt that the soils and topography of the northern areas were the most conducive for sugar cultivation. Consequently, they schemed with the imperial authorities in the 1790's to defeat and to deport the black Caribs once and for all.

In contrast to Grenada and Saint Vincent, Tobago had far fewer inhabitants when the British arrived there in 1763. The Caribs and the French were not factors in Tobago, but only a year after the first land grants were distributed in 1769, a major uprising was beaten back by soldiers coming from Barbados by warship. The rebels fled to the wooded highlands, where they became Maroons.

Rebellions continued throughout the 1770's; a lull in collective resistance in the 1780's and 1790's in Tobago was quickly brought to an end with the elaborate Christmas plot of 1801. While the Ceded Islands seethed with discontent and intrigue, in Jamaica, the Hanover Parish plot of July, 1776, tried to once again exploit the notion of an empire divided and stretched too thin. With the distracting backdrop of the American Revolution and the faint echoes of patriotic sentiments among the West Indian grandees, wide racial imbalances in favor of Africans, as well as newly established plantations and forbidding geography, allowed both Kromanti and, for the first time on a wide scale, Creole in a northwestern pocket of the island to plan the end of slavery, at least locally. Before the plan could be implemented, however, one master interrogated a domestic who had been caught with the master's gun and who then told of the wider conspiracy.

The parvenu sugar magnates in Hanover were extremely lucky, in part because the rebellion had apparently been scheduled for the following week. Most dangerous to colonial authorities was furtive evidence of an alliance between the slaves of Hanover Parish and the Maroons in Trelawney Town, who were the ostensible allies of the British. These allegations, made from an inside source named Pontiac, proved to be unfounded, but the very possibility of an African popular front against slavery put local planters on edge and made them more likely to embrace deportation as the final solution to the question of the Maroons and their lands in the 1790's. In the eighteenth century, despite the colonists' suspicions about the loyalty of the Maroons, the Maroons in Jamaica remained the gendarmes of the regime, coming to the aid of the colonists in the uprisings of 1831-1832 on the eve of emancipation in 1834 as well as in the Morant's Bay rebellion of 1865, after slavery in the West Indies had long ended.

SIGNIFICANCE

Tacky's Rebellion and the Caribbean rebellions of 1760-1776 marked a beginning of a new, continuing round of slave uprisings, but these rebellions also underscored the British Empire's tenuous alliance with Maroons, particularly in Jamaica, in putting down such disturbances. Imperial ambitions and rivalries, as dramatically revealed during the Seven Years' War and its aftermath,

allowed slaves to resist and to flee British rule, which, in turn, led to suppression and deportation, especially where uncultivated Maroon lands were involved, such as there were in Saint Vincent. However, the slave revolts in the Caribbean in the 1760's and 1770's paralleled similar revolts in North America, prompting at least a few individuals in the Atlantic world, including an American patriot, Colonel James Otis, to finally come out against the slave trade and slavery.

—Charles H. Ford (original article author)

Patricia A McDaniel (2016 article reviewer)

See also: New York City Slave Revolt; Stono Rebellion.

Related articles in *Great Lives from History: The Eighteenth Century, 1701-1800*: Joseph Boulogne; George III; Nanny; Guillaume-Thomas Raynal; Granville Sharp; Toussaint Louverture; Tupac Amaru II.

AFRICAN AMERICAN BAPTIST CHURCH IS FOUNDED

1773-1788

An amalgamation of African and European forms of religious worship developed into the African American Baptist Church. The cosmologies and churches fashioned by blacks in the United States helped them survive and transcend the harsh realities of slavery in the South.

Locale: Savannah River Valley, Georgia
Categories: Religion and theology; organizations and institutions

KEY FIGURES

Andrew Bryan (1737-1812), a slave who was converted, purchased his freedom, and founded the Savannah Church
David George (b. 1742?) and
George Liele (1750?-1825?), slaves who became preachers and founded churches for African Americans

SUMMARY OF EVENT

The religious revivals collectively known as the First Great Awakening transformed the spiritual climate of

British North America in the mid-eighteenth century. Church membership grew, and evangelical religious ideas, which emphasized a person's own relationship with God, began to acquire hegemony over the religious values propagated by the established churches. Among those people who embraced evangelical ideals were African American slaves, who found attractive the notion of a personal God, the hope for salvation, and the less formal style of evangelical worship. This was especially true in the South, where African Americans benefited from a practice among some white evangelicals of allowing blacks to preach to other blacks and where African Americans were the targets of white missionary activity.

African Americans were particularly drawn to the Baptist faith, especially in the latter part of the eighteenth century. White Baptists, themselves often among the poorest in Southern society, actively recruited African Americans. Furthermore, Baptists did not require formal education as part of ministerial training, and what learning they did encourage centered on mastering the contents of the Bible. Even

African Americans held in bondage and denied opportunities for formal education could fulfill these expectations, and more than a few became ministers. African American slaves not only joined biracial Baptist churches but also fashioned their own fellowships, where they blended the traditional folk religions they brought from Africa with the evangelical nostrums of the Europeans, thus creating a hybrid African American religion.

One area where African American Baptists flourished was the Savannah River Valley, which connected the hinterlands around Augusta, Georgia, with the port city of Savannah. Here, evangelical revivals among whites and blacks bore organizational fruit among African Americans. Indeed, African Americans formed their own Baptist church at Silver Bluff, near Augusta, in 1783, following one such revival.

About that time, a slave named George Liele heard a sermon preached by Reverend Matthew Moore, a white minister, and became convinced that he needed to respond to the gospel. "I was sure I should be found in hell, as sure as God was in heaven," Liele recalled. Baptized by Moore, Liele became a preacher and began to exhort other slaves in the vicinity of Augusta to become Christians.

Liele's master, who was loyal to the British during the American Revolution, temporarily had to flee Georgia for his life and freed Liele. For the next several years, Liele and a colleague, David George, preached regularly at Silver Bluff, South Carolina, at the first black Baptist church in the Savannah River Valley region. George had been born a slave in Virginia and had run away from his cruel master to South Carolina. to South Carolina. He was a servant to Creek chief Blue Salt then Natchez chief King Jack before the latter sold him to Silver Bluff plantation owner George Galphin. Becoming convinced of his own iniquity and borrowing from whites an evangelical vocabulary and worldview, he was converted after hearing sermons in the mid-1770's by several African American preachers, including Liele.

Both George and Liele initially had become Baptists because of their own desire to go to heaven, but quickly they took it upon themselves to preach to their fellow slaves. Having found a sense of inner peace because of his religion, Liele wanted others to experience in themselves "the work which God had done for my soul." Liele and George organized other churches, including the congregation at Yamacraw, outside Savannah, in 1777.

Among those who heard Liele preach at Yamacraw was Andrew Bryan. Bryan had been born in Goose Creek, South Carolina, and was baptized by Liele in 1782. Bryan eventually purchased his freedom and devoted himself to his ministry. It was a decision not without consequences, as whites who feared an unshackled black man whipped Bryan twice and imprisoned him once. Undeterred, he continued to preach to ever-larger congregations, which often contained both blacks and whites. In 1788, his congregation constituted itself into First Bryan Baptist Church. At the time, it boasted 575 members and would grow to more than 800 at the time of Bryan's death.

Liele, George, and Bryan stood at the forefront of an important movement among African Americans in the South. Their religious teachings fused the African concepts of a unitary universe where the sacred and profane are not segregated; the European mythologies of Heaven, Hell, and redemption; and their present reality of slavery. God would help Africans through their travail of slavery and would one day lead them out of bondage.

In this melding process, certain African religious practices were proscribed. The church covenant of Liele's Yamacraw Baptist Church specifically banned the consumption of blood and strangled meat of animals offered to idols, which had been a part of some West African religious rituals. Other African practices were given an important place, such as moaning as part of religious singing.

This practice originated in ecstatic African religious rituals, and moaning and wailing have been preserved in Southern gospel singing. This hybrid religious ritual did not confine itself to African American communities. The emotional shouts and ritual cadences of African worship affected the rhythms of white discourse as well, especially the sermon form, in which the preacher and congregation engage in something of a dialogue.

Liele, George, and Bryan founded churches and baptized ministers who started other churches. One man converted by George and Liele was Jesse Peter. A slave, he was allowed uncommon liberties and preached around Savannah and Augusta. He helped constitute the Springfield Baptist Church in Augusta in 1793, which was later recognized by white Baptists for its excellent church music. Until the American Civil War, the churches started by these men existed, sometimes tenuously. Often, they had to accept direct white oversight to avoid being shut down, but they clung tenaciously to as much independence as local custom and law would allow.

SIGNIFICANCE

The careers of George Liele, David George, and Andrew Bryan also illustrate the protean political nature of evangelicalism. The formation of churches operated by African Americans reflects the capacity of blacks to avoid complete organizational enslavement as surely as the forming of a black theology kept African Americans from psychic enslavement. From these organizational and intellectual bases, African Americans could confront slavery in various ways. Both Liele and George fled the South for the British Empire, seeking to continue their ministerial work without the specter of slavery hanging over them. Liele went to Jamaica, establishing the first Baptist churches there.

George went to Canada, where he worked with both blacks and whites before organizing a back-to-Africa movement, in which one thousand Canadian blacks went with George to Sierra Leone in 1792. Bryan, however, remained in the South, calling upon African Americans to lead better lives and, sometimes stealthily,

urging whites to live out the Golden Rule in dealing with blacks. At his death, he was lauded by blacks and whites alike. By establishing churches that counseled patience while teaching a theology of ultimate deliverance, African American leaders like Liele, George, and Bryan helped African Americans survive slavery by encouraging them to expect freedom soon.

—*Edward R. Crowther*

See also: Settlement of Georgia; First Great Awakening; Second Great Awakening.

Related articles in *Great Lives from History: The Eighteenth Century, 1701-1800*: Francis Asbury; Isaac Backus; Charles Carroll; Jonathan Edwards; Ann Lee; Cotton Mather; Increase Mather; Samuel Sewall; Granville Sharp; Charles Wesley; John Wesley; George Whitefield; William Wilberforce.

PENNSYLVANIA SOCIETY FOR THE ABOLITION OF SLAVERY IS FOUNDED

April 14, 1775

The first antislavery society in America was formed by, mostly, members of the Society of Friends, or Quakers. The Quakers had formed an abolitionist philosophy that was in line with the religion's belief in equality for all individuals.

Locale: Philadelphia, Pennsylvania
Categories: Organizations and institutions; social issues and reform

KEY FIGURES
Anthony Benezet (1713-1784), a teacher and philanthropist who converted to the Quaker religion
John Woolman (1720-1772), a teacher and Quaker leader

SUMMARY OF EVENT

On April 14, 1775, a group of men gathered at the Sun Tavern on Second Street in Philadelphia to establish the first antislavery society in America. After electing John Baldwin their president and adopting a constitution, they named their organization the Society for the Relief of Free Negroes Unlawfully Held in Bondage. Sixteen of the twenty-four founders were members of the Society

of Friends, or Quakers. The creation of this antislavery society was instigated when Philadelphia Quakers Israel Pemberton and Thomas Harrison aided American Indian Dinah Neville and her children, who were being detained in Philadelphia waiting to be taken to the West Indies to be sold as slaves. Harrison was fined in a Philadelphia court for giving protection to the Neville family. When this incident gained notoriety, members of the Quaker Philadelphia Meeting came together to form the antislavery society. At its first meeting, the antislavery society enlisted legal counsel to help the Nevilles and five other victims illegally held in bondage and to form a standing committee to investigate any conditions of slavery in the Philadelphia area.

The Revolutionary War interrupted regular meetings until 1784. At this time, Quaker abolitionist Anthony Benezet revived the antislavery society as members learned that two African Americans had committed suicide rather than be illegally enslaved. Benezet increased the membership to forty, including Benjamin Franklin, James Pemberton, and Benjamin Rush. The society renamed itself the Pennsylvania Society for Promoting the Abolition of Slavery, for the Relief of Free Negroes Unlawfully Held in Bondage, and for Improving the Condition of the African Race.

Since the majority of the members were Friends, the group developed directly from Quaker religious beliefs and within the Quaker social structure. To explore the founding of the Pennsylvania Society for the Abolition of Slavery, it is critical to trace events and movements within the Society of Friends in seventeenth century colonial Pennsylvania.

One of the basic principles espoused by Quaker founder George Fox was that all people are created equal. On a visit to the colonies in 1671, Fox spoke at Friends' meetings and encouraged Quaker slaveholders to free their slaves after a specified period of service. In 1676, Quaker William Edmundson, an associate of Fox, published the first antislavery literature in Rhode Island.

While Quakers were formulating an antislavery position early in their movement, German Mennonites migrating to America had vowed that they would not own slaves. Several members of the Mennonite community and Dutch Pietists adopted Quakerism and became members of the Friends' Germantown Meeting. These Quakers, their minister Pastorius, and other Friends of the Germantown Meeting delivered a petition to the Philadelphia Meeting in 1688 demanding that slavery and the slave trade be abolished. The protest addressed to slave owners of the Philadelphia Monthly Meeting challenged these Friends to explain why they had slaves and how such a practice could exist in a colony founded on the principles of liberty and equality. Representing the radical leadership of Philadelphia Friends, George Keith published a tract entitled *An Exhortation and Caution to Friends Concerning Buying or Keeping of Negroes*. He gave several directives: that Friends should not purchase African slaves except for the express purpose of setting them free, that those already purchased should be set free after a time of reasonable service, and that, while in service, slaves should be given a Christian education and taught how to read.

During the early eighteenth century, the conservative, wealthy membership of the Philadelphia Meeting took a somewhat confusing position on slavery. Their inconsistent policies included a separate meeting for African Americans, a request that Quakers in the West Indies stop sending slaves to Philadelphia, and disciplinary measures for members of the meeting who were engaged in antislavery activity. Many prominent Quakers, such as James Logan, Jonathan Dickinson, and Isaac Norris, continued to purchase and own slaves. The customary procedure of resolving issues at Friends' meetings was to achieve a consensus

by gaining a sense of the meeting. Thus, the Quaker drift toward an antislavery sentiment gained momentum with the efforts of a few radicals but achieved success only when the majority bowed to the principles of Quaker conscience.

Unpopular radical member Benjamin Lay was unwelcome at the Philadelphia Meeting because of his unorthodox promotion of the antislavery cause. For example, Lay once had kidnapped a Quaker youth in order to illustrate the tragedy of abduction of African children for the slave trade. In 1738, he outdid himself at the Philadelphia Yearly Meeting, wearing a military uniform to emphasize the connection between slavery and war and concealing under his cloak an animal bladder that he had filled with red juice. Delivering an inflamed speech on the evils of slavery, he concluded by saying that slavery took the very lifeblood out of the slave, simultaneously piercing the bladder and splashing the horrified audience with simulated blood.

By the 1730's, the effects of the antislavery movement were evident among Quakers as more Friends provided for the manumission of their slaves in their wills. In addition, the increased immigration of Germans in need of work eliminated the demand for slave labor in the Middle Colonies.

Much of the credit for the success of the antislavery movement among Quakers must be given to New Jersey Quaker John Woolman. Known for his gentle, persuasive approach as a Quaker minister, he began a series of visitations to Quaker slaveholders in New England, the Middle Colonies, and the South in 1743. In 1754, he published *Some Considerations on the Keeping of Negroes*, which proclaimed the evils of slavery and the absolute necessity for Friends to free their slaves. Meetings throughout the colonies and England effectively used his visitations to pressure Quakers to free their slaves. By 1774, Quaker meetings in England, New England, and Pennsylvania had adopted sanctions to disown any member for buying slaves or for serving as executor of an estate that included slaves. It also required slaveholders to treat their slaves humanely and to emancipate them as soon as possible.

SIGNIFICANCE

Some have argued that Quakers were willing to emancipate their slaves because slavery was not profitable in Pennsylvania in the absence of labor-intensive agriculture.

Others claim that Quaker sensitivity to antislavery was aroused not by their own religious ideals but rather by eighteenth century Enlightenment philosophy, which held that liberty is a natural human right. These may be considered arguments; nevertheless, it was the Quakers who first championed the antislavery cause and who organized the first antislavery group in America. The Pennsylvania Society for the Abolition of Slavery served as a model for other antislavery groups. As early as 1794, other states that had formed antislavery societies were asked to send representatives to Philadelphia for annual meetings.

As new associations were formed, Friends constituted a majority of the membership. Statesmen such as Franklin, Rush, Alexander Hamilton, John Jay, and Thomas Paine believed that the institution of slavery contradicted the ideals of the Declaration of Independence and joined in support of the Friends' antislavery campaign.

—*Emily Teipe*

See also: Stono Rebellion; Caribbean Slave Rebellions; African American Baptist Church Is Founded; Free African Society Is Founded.

NORTHEAST STATES ABOLISH SLAVERY

July 2, 1777-1804

Eight northeastern states emancipated their slaves and ended slavery during and in the wake of the American Revolution. Most of the states chose to phase out slavery gradually, and the slave population of the North decreased during the next few decades until abolition was accomplished.

Locale: Northeastern United States
Categories: Laws, acts, and legal history; social issues and reform

KEY FIGURES
Moses Brown (1738-1836), Rhode Island abolitionist
Aaron Burr (1756-1836), United States senator, 1791-1797, and leader of the fight against slavery in New York
Caleb Cushing (1800-1879), Massachusetts judge who ruled that slavery was illegal
Quork Walker (fl. 1781-1783), Massachusetts slave who successfully sued for freedom

SUMMARY OF EVENT
In 1775, Pennsylvania's Provincial Congress called for an end to the importation of slaves and the gradual emancipation of all slaves in the colony. Two years later, on July 2, 1777, Vermont became the first state to abolish slavery fully. Its 1777 Constitution outlawed a "male person, born in this country, or brought in by sea...to serve any person" as a servant, slave, or apprentice after he or she reached twenty-one years of age.

Despite the earlier call of its Provincial Congress, Pennsylvania waited until 1780 to pass a law gradually ending the slave system, because some leaders argued that abolishing slavery during the Revolutionary War would divide the colonies and hamper the war effort: Any radical attack against human bondage would antagonize the South, where slavery was a deeply embedded institution.

Pennsylvania, like the other Northern states, had allowed slavery since its beginning as a colony, but slaves had never become an important part of the workforce there. In 1780, only 3,761 of Pennsylvania's 435,150 inhabitants were slaves, and most of them were household servants. White workers argued successfully that free labor cost less than slavery, because slave masters had to take care of their slaves even if they were not working.

Pennsylvania's 1780 "Act for Gradual Abolition of Slavery" law called for a gradual end to slavery. Property rights were respected, and children born slaves in 1780 would remain in service to their owners until they were twenty-eight years of age. This length of service was to compensate masters for the cost of raising slave children. The law required owners to register their slaves by the end of the year. Any African Americans not registered would be freed immediately. The law also resulted in the decrease legalized discrimination against black people: They could now testify against Caucasians in courts, the separate courts established for them were abolished, and interracial marriage became legal. Pennsylvania became the only Northern state to provide for this kind of equality. Conservatives, who could not accept the idea of equality for African Americans, resisted all these measures and successfully defeated a proposal granting freed slaves the right to vote.

Massachusetts acted slowly on the slavery question. In 1777, opponents defeated a gradual emancipation bill, arguing as they had in Pennsylvania that such a bill would divide the new nation by antagonizing the South. Three years later, voters turned down a new constitution that declared all men free and equal and provided voting rights for free blacks. In 1781, however, a slave named Quock Walker sued for his freedom in a state court because his owner had severely abused him. The trial judge, William Cushing, instructed the jury that the idea of slavery conflicted with state law, so Walker was ordered freed. Although the legislature refused to act, by 1790, as a result of similar court actions in dozens of other cases, slavery no longer existed in Massachusetts.

More than six hundred slaves lived in New Hampshire prior to the American Revolution. During the war, the state legislature granted freedom to any slave who volunteered for the militia. Other slaves gained their liberty by running away and joining the British military, which also promised freedom to slaves who fought with them. Thus, when the state's 1783 constitution declared all men equal and independent from birth, only fifty slaves remained the property of masters in New Hampshire. Although slavery was never abolished legally, slave property was removed from tax rolls in 1789, and eleven years later only eight slaves remained in the state.

Rhode Island acted in 1784, after Moses Brown and five other Quakers petitioned its assembly for the immediate liberation of all human beings kept as property. The cautious legislators passed a gradual emancipation bill instead. Under its provisions, all slave children born after March 1, 1784 would be apprentices. Girls became free at the age of eighteen years, while boys could be kept until they reached twenty-one years of age. Until then, the apprentices would get food and economic support from the towns in which they lived. After slaves were freed, their masters were required to post bonds with the state guaranteeing that the former slaves would never require public assistance.

Connecticut, the New England state with the largest population of African Americans, granted freedom to slaves who fought against England, but three times—in 1777, 1779, and 1780—the legislature rejected gradual emancipation. Some lawmakers feared a race riot if blacks were freed. In 1784, however, the legislature finally declared an end to slavery. The law declared that male African American and mulatto (mixed-race) children would become free at twenty-five years of age and women at the age of 21. Persons being held as slaves at the time would be freed by the end of the year. At the same time, discriminatory colonial laws similar to those found in Massachusetts became part of the state legal code. Free people of color could not vote, could not serve on juries, and could not marry Caucasians. African Americans were free but not equal.

New York and New Jersey were the last Northern states to act on the slavery question. Both of these states freed African Americans who served in the army, but opponents of emancipation warned against doing anything more, so as to respect property rights. Some opponents used openly racist arguments, saying that free blacks would not work unless forced to do so. They argued that blacks were lazy, ignorant, and criminal, and that slavery protected whites from an onslaught of savagery. New York's legislature rejected gradual emancipation in 1777. Eight years later, a freedom bill supported by the New York Manumission Society, whose membership included Alexander Hamilton, John Jay, and Aaron Burr, went down to defeat. Although proposals to discriminate legally against blacks failed, the legislature did agree to deny African Americans the right to vote.

In 1785, New York prohibited the sale and importation of slaves and allowed masters to manumit (free) their slaves, but only if they guaranteed that they would not require public assistance. The next year, New Jersey passed similar laws. In 1788, New York declared that slaves would no longer be judged or punished under standards different from those used to judge whites. Still, freedom did not come. In the 1790's, the New York Manumission Society fought a constant war against the slave system. It sent petitions with thousands of signatures to the state legislature.

The Society for Promoting the Abolition of Slavery in New Jersey conducted a similar campaign. In both states, antislavery groups organized boycotts of businesses that had any connection with slavery, such as newspapers that advertised slave auctions and companies that built slave ships. Auctions of slaves ended in both states by 1790. Only in 1799, however, did New York pass an emancipation bill. Owners could free their slaves regardless of age or condition, although children could still be kept as property—boys until twenty-eight years of age and girls until the age of twenty-five. In 1804, New Jersey became the last of the original Northern states to end slavery legally.

Neither New York nor New Jersey allowed free African Americans to vote.

SIGNIFICANCE

The 1810 census found that the five New England states—Vermont, New Hampshire, Massachusetts, Connecticut, and Rhode Island—had 418 slaves out of an African American population totaling more than 20,000. New York and New Jersey, on the other hand, had nearly 18,000 slaves, because their laws provided longer time periods for emancipating children and were passed much later. Pennsylvania, the first state to provide for gradual emancipation, had fewer than 50 slaves.

Thus, despite racist attitudes and the desire of many legislators to protect property rights, slavery was close to an end in the North by the second decade of the nineteenth century. It would take a bloody civil war to end slavery in the South fifty years later. Emancipation in the North did not mean equality for African Americans, however. Laws discriminating against free black people were passed, usually alongside or shortly after bills calling for the end of slavery. Prejudice remained high in Northern states, although they had very small African American populations—less than 1 percent in most cities and towns. Efforts to end slavery did not eliminate racism and belief in white supremacy.

—*Leslie V. Tischauser*

See also: Expansion of the Atlantic Slave Trade; New York City Slave Revolt; Stono Rebellion; Caribbean Slave Rebellions; Pennsylvania Society for the Abolition of Slavery Is Founded; First Fugitive Slave Law.

Related articles in *Great Lives from History: The Eighteenth Century, 1701-1800*: Olaudah Equiano; Alexander Hamilton; John Jay.

FREEMASONS IN BOSTON

September 29, 1784

Since its founding, Boston's Prince Hall Masonic Lodge has provided moral teachings, aid to members in need, and even business contacts for the millions of African American men who passed through the ranks of the order.

Identification: First African American Masonic lodge
Place: Boston, Massachusetts

Prince Hall, a former slave living in Boston, perceived the many benefits of belonging to the fraternal group called the Freemasons. In the thirteen colonies, many of the most prominent and respected citizens were Masons, including George Washington, Samuel Adams, and Benjamin Franklin. As in the mother country, Masonic lodges in America stressed religion, morality, and charity to members in need and to all humankind. Many members developed business ties with their Masonic associates.

Prince Hall was born a slave in 1748. When he was twenty-one years of age, he was granted his freedom by his master. Hall entered into the trade of leather work. He pursued this calling for the rest of his life, although later, his Masonic leadership and his catering business occupied increasing amounts of his time. Tradition holds that Prince Hall fought against the British in the American Revolution. This is almost certainly true, but since several Massachusetts soldiers were named Prince Hall, details of this Prince Hall's army career are not clear.

In 1775, just before the outbreak of the American Revolution, a white Mason named John Batt initiated Hall and fourteen other free black Bostonians into the Masonic order. The fifteen initiates soon organized the first black Masonic lodge in America, calling it African Lodge. They continued to meet, but under the strict hierarchy of Masonry, a local group such as the African Lodge must be subordinate to a Grand Lodge, making regular reports as well as payments into the Grand Lodge charity fund. The American Masonic hierarchy was still evolving, and Prince Hall and his associates knew that many white Masons in the new country did not approve of black lodges or even black members.

CHARTERING THE LODGE

On March 2, 1784, and again on June 30 of that year, Prince Hall wrote to the Grand Lodge of England asking for an official charter. This charter would confer added legitimacy on African Lodge and would give it a powerful ally. Difficulties in getting letters and money between Boston and England slowed the process of obtaining the charter, but Hall's group finally got the requisite fees to the Grand Lodge of England, and in 1787 African Lodge received its charter. The document, dated September 29, 1784, gave African Lodge the right to initiate new members and the duty of reporting regularly to the English Grand Lodge.

Some of the activities of African Lodge related directly to race. In 1787, three free African Americans from Boston were kidnapped by men who took them to the Caribbean island of St. Bartholomew and prepared to sell them into bondage. One of the three was a member of African Lodge. Prince Hall and the other black Masons of Boston agitated actively for release of their brother Mason, and for law enforcement officers to protect free African Americans from kidnapping. The petition circulated by Prince Hall helped goad the Massachusetts legislature into passing a law to punish slave traders and kidnappers. The three men won their release when the one who was a member of African Lodge gave a Masonic sign that was recognized by a white Mason living on St. Bartholomew, and the white Mason had the captors arrested and the three men returned to Boston.

ACTIVITIES OF THE LODGE

Although the records of the early meetings of African Lodge are scarce, copies of two addresses by Prince Hall and one sermon by the lodge chaplain have survived. All three documents exhibit a strong degree of racial pride and solidarity. In his first charge to the African Lodge, delivered and published in 1792, Hall chided white Masons who claimed that the existence of black Masons would somehow make the order too common. He pointed out that that had not been the feeling during the recent Revolutionary War, when white and black soldiers had fought shoulder to shoulder. Prince Hall concluded by saying that any man who rebuked an African American man because of his skin color actually was rebuking God, who had made all people in his own image.

Hall's second charge to his lodge was delivered and published in 1797. In this address, the Masonic leader painted a baleful picture of the barbaric cruelties of slavery, and used the Bible to prove that the institution was not part of God's will. On a more optimistic note, Hall lectured his brother Masons about the nation of Haiti, where six years earlier the slaves had revolted and thrown off the yoke of French government and of slavery itself. Hall saw the revolt in Haiti as a first step

by African Americans in ending the hated system of slavery.

John Marrant, a free African American minister living in Boston, became the chaplain of African Lodge. One of Marrant's sermons to the lodge was delivered and printed in 1789. As was the case with Hall's addresses, Marrant's sermon stressed what later writers would call black pride. Marrant said that African Americans should not be ashamed that their race was enslaved, since nearly every great people had been enslaved at one time or another, and such enslavement had often been the prelude to a great flourishing of that people. Marrant dipped into the Bible and into ancient history to prove that Africa had produced at least as many great civilizations as had any other region on earth.

On at least one occasion, members of the African Lodge put their pride in Africa into action. In 1787, Prince Hall circulated a petition asking the Massachusetts government to aid in returning men and women of color to Africa. Seventy-three persons signed the petition, including most members of African Lodge. The petition is one of the earliest documents in American history associated with a back-to-Africa movement. On most other occasions, however, members of African Lodge preferred to work to improve their standing within the United States.

SPREADING THE WORD

As the free black population in the northern states continued to grow, African Lodge responded to requests to bring Masonry to African Americans in other areas. A number of residents of Providence, Rhode Island, were initiated into African Lodge and later began their own lodge with the blessings of Prince Hall and his followers. African Lodge also helped found new lodges in Philadelphia and New York. Meanwhile, all the Masonic lodges in the United States that were chartered by one of the British Grand Lodges began to have less contact with the Grand Lodges across the ocean. African Lodge was no exception. In 1827, African Lodge declared its independence of the English Grand Lodge and of any other Grand Lodge. It became the Grand Lodge for all chapters of African American Masons it founded in the United States.

The so-called Prince Hall Masonry continued to flourish long after the death of Hall in 1807. In 1995, the order boasted three hundred thousand members in the United States. For more than two hundred years, Prince Hall Masonry has provided moral teachings, aid to members in need, and even business contacts for the millions of African American men who passed through the ranks of the order. For most of that time, white Masons attacked the Prince Hall Masons for claimed irregularities in the latter's organizational history, including the history of the Prince Hall Masons' charters. Yet any alleged irregularities were also part of the history of early white lodges in the United States. While attacks on Prince Hall Masonry are less common today than they were previously, Masonry remains a highly segregated area of American life.

—Stephen Cresswell

See also: Abolition; Black codes; Free African Society; Free blacks; Pennsylvania Society for the Abolition of Slavery Freemasons in Boston / 381

THREE-FIFTHS COMPROMISE

1787

The Event: Agreement reached in the convention that drafted the U.S. Constitution on the apportionment of congressional representation to slaveholding states
Place: Philadelphia, Pennsylvania

Northern delegates to the Constitutional Convention did not want nonvoting slave populations to be counted when congressional representation was apportioned, while southern delegates wanted slaves to be counted equally with nonslaves. The disagreement was resolved in the three-fifths compromise.

The Constitutional Convention in 1787 adopted the three-fifths compromise, whereby five slaves were counted as three people for purposes of taxation and representation. The idea originated as part of a 1783 congressional plan to base taxation on population. Congress rejected the three-fifths idea, but delegate James Wilson of Pennsylvania resurrected it as an amendment to the Virginia plan at the Constitutional Convention.

The Wilson amendment provoked heated debate over the counting of slaves. Most northern delegates regarded slaves as property and not deserving representation, while southern delegates insisted that African Americans be counted equally with whites for purposes of representation. Northern delegates wanted slaves counted for taxation, while southern delegates disagreed.

Delegates also debated whether the Congress or a census every ten years should determine the apportionment of representatives in the national legislature. Several northern delegates wanted Congress to control apportionment because the West was developing rapidly. They considered the three-fifths idea pro-South and opposed its adoption. Southern delegates, meanwhile, threatened to reject the three-fifths idea if Congress controlled representation. Northern delegates eventually agreed to accept a census every ten years and count slaves as people rather than property, demonstrating the numerical strength of the proslavery interests. Until the Civil War, therefore, slaves were counted as three-fifths of nonslaves for purposes of taxation and representation.

—David L. Porter

See also: Politics and government; Slavery

FREE AFRICAN SOCIETY IS FOUNDED

April 12, 1787

The Free African Society, the first major secular institution with a mission to aid African Americans, paved the way for later institutions such as the National Association for the Advancement of Colored People (NAACP). The society existed for less than a decade, however, before its membership merged with African American churches and other religious organizations with similar agendas.

Locale: Philadelphia, Pennsylvania
Categories: Organizations and institutions; social issues and reform

KEY FIGURES

Richard Allen (1760-1831), African American former slave, religious leader, and social reformer
Absalom Jones (1746-1818), leader of the Free African Society
Benjamin Rush (1746-1813), American physician and member of the Continental Congress

SUMMARY OF EVENT

Both the origins of the Free African Society and the long-term repercussions of its founding form an essential part of the religious history of African Americans. The original organization itself was of short duration: About seven years after it was organized, it disappeared as a formal body. In its immediate wake, however, closely related institutions emerged that tried to take over its proclaimed mission.

Generally speaking, prior to the 1790's, people of African slave origins who managed to obtain their individual freedom had only one option if they wished to practice Christianity: association, as subordinate parishioners, in an existing white-run church. Several churches in the American colonies before independence, including the Quakers and Methodists, had tried to identify their religious cause with that of the black victims of slavery.

Richard Allen, born in 1760 as a slave whose family belonged to Pennsylvania's then attorney general, Benjamin Chew, was destined to become one of the earliest religious leaders of the black segment of the American Methodist Church. As a youth, Allen gained extensive experience with Methodist teachings after his family was separated on the auction block in Dover, Delaware.

Allen was encouraged by his second owner, Master Stokeley, to espouse the religious teachings of the itinerant American Methodist preacher Freeborn Garrettson. Allen's conversion to Methodism was rewarded when Stokeley freed him at age twenty to follow the calling of religion. His freedom came just as the Revolutionary War ended.

For six years, Allen worked under the influence of Methodist evangelist Benjamin Abbott and the Reverend (later Bishop) Richard Whatcoat, with whom he traveled on an extensive preaching circuit. Allen's writings refer to Whatcoat as his "father in Israel." With Whatcoat's encouragement, Allen accepted an invitation from the Methodist elder in Philadelphia to return to his birthplace to become a preacher.

At that time, Philadelphia's religious environment seemed to be dominated by the Episcopal Church. This church had been active since 1758 in extending its ministry to African Americans. It was St. George's Methodist Episcopal Church, however, that, in the 1780's, had drawn the largest number of former slaves to its rolls.

Once the circumstances of blacks' second-class status became clear to Allen, he decided that his leadership mission should be specifically dedicated to the needs of his people. Within a short time, he joined another African American, Absalom Jones, in founding what was originally intended to be more of a secular movement than a formal denominational movement: the Free African Society.

Absalom Jones was older than Allen and had had a different set of life experiences. Born a slave in Delaware in 1746, Jones served for more than twenty years in his master's store in Philadelphia. He earned enough money to purchase his wife's freedom, to build his own home, and finally, in 1784, to purchase his own freedom. He continued to work for his former master for wages and bought and managed two houses for additional income. His success earned him great respect among other free blacks and opened the way for him to serve as lay leader representing the African American membership of St. George's Methodist Episcopal Church.

Traditional accounts of Jones's role in the founding of the Free African Society assert that, when Jones refused to comply with the announcement of St. George's sexton that African American parishioners should give up their usual seats among the white congregation and move to the upper gallery, he was supported by Richard Allen, in particular. The two then agreed that the only way African Americans could worship in an environment that responded to their social, as well as religious, needs would be to found an all-black congregation. Some sources suggest that Jones's reaction to the reseating order was the crowning blow, and that Allen previously had tried to organize several fellow black parishioners, including Doras Giddings, William White, and Jones, to support his idea of a separate congregation, only to have the idea rejected by the church elders.

Whatever the specific stimulus for Allen's and Jones's actions in 1787, they announced publicly that their newly declared movement would not only serve the black community's religious needs as a nondenominational congregation but also function as a benevolent mutual aid organization. The latter goal involved plans to collect funds (through membership fees) to assist the sick, orphans, and widows in the African American community.

Other secular social assistance aims included enforcement of a code of temperance, propriety, and fidelity in marriage. It is significant that a number of the early members of the Free African Society came to it from the rolls of other Protestant churches, not only St. George's Methodist Episcopal congregation.

The dual nature of the organization's goals soon led to divisions in the politics of leadership. Apparently, it was Allen who wanted to use the breakaway from St. George's as a first step in founding a specifically black Methodist Church. Others wished to emphasize the Free African Society's nondenominational character and pursue mainly social and moral aid services. Within two years, therefore, Allen resigned his membership, going on to found, in July, 1794, the Bethel African Methodist Episcopal Church. Although this move clearly marked the beginnings of a specifically African American church with a defined denominational status, Allen's efforts for many years continued to be directed at social and economic self-help projects for African Americans, irrespective of their formal religious orientation.

By 1804, Allen was involved in founding a group whose name reflected its basic social reform goals: the Society of Free People of Color for Promoting the Instruction and School Education of Children of African Descent. Another of Allen's efforts came in 1830, when Allen, then seventy years of age, involved his church in the Free Produce Society in Philadelphia. This group raised money to buy goods grown only by nonslave labor to redistribute to poor African Americans. It also tried to organize active boycotts against the marketing and purchase of goods produced by slave-owning farmers, thus providing an early model for the grassroots organizations aimed at social and political goals that would become familiar to African Americans in the mid-twentieth century.

SIGNIFICANCE
The Free African Society passed through several short but key stages both before and after

Richard Allen's decision to remove himself from active membership. One focal point was the group's early association with the prominent medical doctor and philanthropist Benjamin Rush. Rush helped the Free African Society to draft a document involving articles of faith that were meant to be general enough to include the essential religious principles of any Christian church. When the organization adopted these tenets, in 1791, its status as a religious congregation generally was recognized by members and outsiders alike.

More and more, its close relationship with the Episcopal church (first demonstrated by its "friendly adoption" by the Reverend Joseph Pilmore and the white membership of St. Paul's Church in Philadelphia) determined the society's future denominational status. After 1795, the Free African Society per se had receded before a new church built by a committee sparked by Absalom Jones: the African Methodist Episcopal Church. This fact did not, however, prevent those who had been associated with the Free African Society's origins from integrating its strong social and moral reform program with the religious principles that marked the emergence of the first all-black Christian congregations in the United States by the end of the 1790's.

—*Byron D. Cannon*

See also: New York City Slave Revolt; Stono Rebellion; African American Baptist Church Is Founded; Pennsylvania Society for the Abolition of Slavery Is Founded; Northeast States Abolish Slavery; First Fugitive Slave Law.

Related articles in *Great Lives from History: The Eighteenth Century, 1701-1800*: Benjamin Banneker; Benjamin Rush.

NORTHWEST ORDINANCE

July 13, 1787

The last major legislation passed under the Articles of Confederation, the Northwest Ordinance laid out rules for organization of the Northwest Territory and was the first sectional compromise over the extension of slavery.

The Law: National legislation concerning the organization and administration of the North West Territory

In March, 1784, the Congress of the Confederation accepted the cession of lands Virginia had claimed west of the Appalachian Mountains. A congressional committee headed by Thomas Jefferson, delegate from Virginia, then took steps to provide for the political organization of the vast area south of the Great Lakes, west of the Appalachians, and east of the Mississippi River. The committee's task was to draft legislation for the disposal of the land and the government of its settlers. The proposal of Jefferson's committee met the approval of Congress as the Ordinance of 1784.

The Ordinance of 1784 divided the West into eighteen districts. Each district would be admitted to the Union as a state when its population equaled that of the least populous of the original states. In the meantime, when the population of a district reached twenty thousand, it might write a constitution and send a delegate to Congress. As Jefferson envisaged it, as many as ten new states might be carved from the new lands, many of them provided with mellifluous classical names. In Jefferson's original version, slavery was to be excluded after 1800, but this was stricken from the ordinance when it was adopted in 1784. The Ordinance of 1784 was to become effective once all western lands claimed by the states had been ceded to the government. Before the states ceded their lands, however, a new ordinance was adopted that superseded that of 1784.

THE ORDINANCE OF 1787

The Ordinance of 1787, known as the Northwest Ordinance, was passed, according to some historians, at the insistence of land speculators who opposed the liberality of the Ordinance of 1784. The new ordinance did indeed slow down the process by which a territory might become a state, but it also added certain important features and provided for the more orderly creation of new states. While the Northwest Ordinance may have been less liberal than its predecessor, it was not undemocratic.

The Northwest Ordinance established government in the territory north of the Ohio River. The plan provided for the eventual establishment of a bicameral assembly, the creation of three to five states equal to the original thirteen states, freedom of religion, the right to a jury trial, public education, and a ban on the expansion of slavery. To accomplish these goals, legislation provided that the whole Northwest region should be governed temporarily as a single territory and administered by a governor, a secretary, and three judges appointed by Congress. When the population of the territory reached five thousand free, adult, male inhabitants, the citizens might elect representatives to a territorial assembly. Property qualifications for voting were established, but they were small. The general assembly

was to choose ten men, all of whom owned at least five hundred acres, from whom Congress would choose five men to serve as the upper house of the legislature. The governor would continue to be selected by Congress and have an absolute veto over all legislation.

The territory was to be divided into not fewer than three nor more than five districts. Whenever the population of one of the districts reached sixty thousand free inhabitants, it would be allowed to draft a constitution and submit it to Congress. If the constitution guaranteed a republican form of government, Congress would pass an enabling act admitting the district into the Union as a state on an equal basis with those states already in the Union.

The ordinance guaranteed certain basic rights to citizens who moved into the new lands. A bill of rights provided for freedom of religion and guaranteed the benefits of writs of *habeas corpus*, the right of trial by jury, bail, and the general process of law. The third article read: "Religion, morality and knowledge being necessary to good government and the happiness of mankind, Schools and the means of education shall forever be encouraged. The utmost good faith shall always be observed towards the Indi ans." The first of these moral injunctions was implemented as the inhabitants obtained the means to do so. The second, regarding the American Indians, has still to be achieved. The fourth article established the basis for relations between the general government and the territories and states that might be formed from them.

PROHIBITION ON SLAVERY

The fifth article provided for equitable taxation and the free navigation of the waters leading into the Mississippi and St. Lawrence Rivers. The sixth article was epoch-making. It read: "There shall be neither Slavery nor involuntary Servitude in the said territory otherwise than in the punishment of crimes, whereof the party shall have been duly convicted." This provision determined that the society that developed north of the Ohio River would eventually be free. Influenced by the French slaveholders inhabiting the region, the interpretation of Article VI forbade the further introduction of slavery but did not abolish slavery or affect the rights of those holding slaves prior to 1787. No such provision was written into the act establishing the Southwest Territory, in 1790.

The pattern established by the Northwest Ordinance was more or less followed in the later admission of states into the Union. Some, such as Texas and California, came in without a territorial period. Others, such as Michigan, caused trouble because of boundary disputes with neighboring states. As for the Ohio country, Arthur St. Clair, president of the Confederation Congress in 1787, was appointed first governor of the territory. Indiana Territory was organized in 1803, the same year in which Ohio entered the Union. Indiana entered as a state in 1816, Illinois in 1818, Michigan in 1837, and Wisconsin in 1848. Statehood was delayed for Indiana and Illinois territories as a result of their repeated petitions seeking repeal of the restrictions in the ordinance against the expansion of further slavery in the territory. Congress refused to repeal or revise the section, making slaveholders reluctant to move into the area. The predominant settlement by nonslaveholders eventually led to strengthening of the antislavery movement in the region.

The Northwest Ordinance proved to be a crowning legislative achievement of the otherwise lackluster confederation government. However, while Congress was debating the Northwest Ordinance, the constitutional convention was occurring in Philadelphia. It has been argued that the antislavery provisions influenced the debates of the constitutional convention over congressional representation. Since each state won two seats in the Senate, southern states acceded freedom to the Northwest Territory by limiting the number of free states formed from the region. In turn, the southern states hoped for dominance in the House of Representatives through the three-fifths clause counting slaves for congressional representation. Under the new Constitution, Congress reenacted the Ordinance of 1787 as a model of territorial government.

—John G. Clark, updated by Dorothy C. Salem

See also: Compromise of 1850; Fugitive Slave Law of 1793; Missouri Compromise; Slavery

SECOND GREAT AWAKENING

1790's-1830's

Beginning in the 1790's, the United States witnessed a spiritual reawakening that gave expression to the new social, political, and economic realities of the late eighteenth century. The Second Great Awakening, coinciding with the first decades of the new nation's existence, established a long-standing American tradition of charity and humanitarianism.

Locale: United States, particularly the Western frontier
Categories: Religion and theology; social issues and reform

KEY FIGURES

Francis Asbury (1745-1816), English-born American Methodist bishop
Peter Cartwright (1785-1872), American Methodist circuit rider
Timothy Dwight (1752-1817), president of Yale College
Charles Grandison Finney (1792-1875), American evangelist
James McGready (1758?-1817), American Presbyterian minister and religious leader
Nathaniel William Taylor (1786-1858), member of the Yale Divinity School

Theodore Dwight Weld (1803-1895), a leader of the American Anti-Slavery Society

SUMMARY OF EVENT

The upsurge of religious feeling that began at the end of the eighteenth century constituted one of several major revivals in U.S. history. Designated the "Second Awakening" in reference to the First Great Awakening of the 1730's and 1740's, the revival of the 1790's and beyond followed a period of relative religious laxity. The Protestant clergy complained of the decay of morality, particularly in the West, where access to organized religion was difficult. The spread of Deism, not entirely an elite doctrine in the United States, was viewed as a dangerous threat by orthodox believers.

By the late 1790's, stirrings of revived religious consciousness were apparent in all regions of the United States. Revival among the Congregationalists (Puritan denominations) of New England was precipitated in 1802 by a series of chapel sermons by Yale's president, Timothy Dwight, who sought to arrest "freethinking" among the students at his college. The results were impressive, and revival soon spread to other colleges in New England and then to villages and towns. Lyman Beecher, Nathaniel William Taylor, and others soon were enlisted in the cause of revival of faith. To the south, in Virginia, the Presbyterian colleges of Hampden-Sidney and Washington had already experienced renewed religious concern and would provide a significant part of the Congregationalists' evangelical leadership during the Second Awakening. Western New York, which became one of the most fertile areas of spiritual zeal, knew the winter of 1799-1800 as the time of the Great Revival.

The most spectacular of the early manifestations came on the Western frontier. James McGready, a Presbyterian minister, played the leading role in bringing about the Logan County, or Cumberland, revival in Kentucky, which culminated in 1800, and helped spark revivalism throughout the West. The Cane Ridge, Kentucky, camp meeting that attracted between ten thousand and twenty-five thousand people in the following year has been described as the largest and most emotional revival of early U.S. history.

The Second Awakening affected all the major Protestant denominations, although the more evangelical among them gained the most in strength. The Congregationalists and Presbyterians contributed some of the outstanding revivalists, but their participation in the more emotional phases of the revival was inhibited by their more staid Calvinist traditions. Working together in their Western endeavors, the two sects sanctioned "rational" revivalism, a stand that was rejected by such schismatic groups as the Stonite, or New Light Presbyterian, church. Frontier awakening also saw the birth of new churches such as the Disciples of Christ, a church that advocated Christian unity, a radical doctrine of free grace, and a restoration of New Testament Christianity. Mormonism and Adventism also arose in connection with the Great Revival.

Quantitatively, Baptists and Methodists dominated the Second Awakening, being the leaders of frontier revivalism.

The Methodists, however, were most successful in the West, and by the 1830's constituted the largest religious group in the United States. The Methodists saw notable growth among African Americans and Native Americans, whose membership in the church by the 1930's numbered fifteen thousand and two thousand, respectively. Like the Baptists, whose numbers also swelled dramatically during the Second Awakening, Methodists were advocates of a free-will theology that complemented the frontier's independent and optimistic character.

Emphasis on a simple gospel and comfort with an uneducated clergy also contributed to this remarkable

growth. However, the circuit rider, a familiar frontier figure adapted to the American scene by the United States' first Methodist bishop, Francis Asbury, and by charismatic preachers such as Peter Cartwright of Illinois, may have equipped Methodism best to minister to a population at once widely scattered and in motion. The Methodists also enthusiastically adopted the system of protracted outdoor revival service known as camp meetings. By 1825, the camp meeting had become almost exclusively a Methodist institution.

Methodist acceptance of the doctrine that individuals have free will to attain salvation was in accord with a general shift of theological emphasis within American Protestantism in the early nineteenth century. Calvinist sects, including Congregationalists, Presbyterians, and certain Baptists, had traditionally adhered to the doctrine of predestination. In the early phase of the Second Awakening, predestinarian Calvinism and free-will Arminianism were preached side by side.

After 1810, Calvinism was modified by such theologians as Timothy Dwight and Nathaniel William Taylor; later, the revivalist Charles Grandison Finney took the lead in establishing what was clearly an Arminian brand of evangelism within the traditionally Calvinist sector of U.S. Protestantism. The ascendancy of Arminianism appears to have reflected the social and political climate of the country. Although historians have found affinities between Calvinist revivalism and political radicalism in the eighteenth century, by the Jacksonian period the message of free will seemed to many the spiritual counterpart of suffrage and laissez-faire.

Perhaps more significant for the future of revivalism in the United States was the conviction that revivals could be provoked and that methods for creating religious conviction could be cultivated by revivalist preachers, whose ministry shifted from that of a pastor to a winner of souls. Unlike the revivalists of the First Great Awakening—who believed that revivalism was the consequence of a gracious outpouring of God's Spirit, patiently to be awaited—the new revivalists tended to regard revivalism instrumentally as a means or a technique for precipitating religious conviction, inculcating moral principles, or even the restitution of civic life.

At their most successful, these soul-winners became professional mass evangelists, such as Finney, who did much to create the style of modern revivalism represented subsequently by Dwight L. Moody, Billy Sunday, and Billy Graham. With Finney, the preoccupation with theology (exemplified in the Great Awakening by Jonathan Edwards) began to yield to a more one-sided concern with religious experience; revivalism increasingly purveyed a simple religion of the heart.

Another consequence of this emphasis on method and experience was its empowerment of women. Women at revival meetings were encouraged to testify and pray in public. They were emboldened to speak openly of the preacher's opinions and to quote scripture. They formed themselves into voluntary societies that organized and promoted the work of revivalism. In short, revivalism created a psychological and social space for women, within which they could validate their own experience, give voice to their own views, become practiced in organizational ability, and exercise leadership.

SIGNIFICANCE

The tide of religious feeling had begun to ebb by the early 1830's, but the social effects of the Second Awakening were pervasive and lasting. Voluntary societies had been formed to promote religious education and

Sunday schools, distribute Bibles, and advance charitable efforts. Moral and humanitarian crusades were launched. A crusade for the abolition of slavery was entered upon by revivalists such as Theodore Dwight Weld, who employed Finney's revival techniques in opposing slavery.

Colleges and seminaries were founded which, like Oberlin in Ohio, were dedicated to "universal reform"

and the education of women and African Americans. Thus, despite the inherent revivalist concern with individual salvation and the reluctance with which evangelists such as Finney embraced social causes, Finney's own "postmillennialism" involved the belief that the world could be made better in preparation for the Second Coming of Christ.

—*Michael D. Clark, updated by Thomas E. Helm*

See also: First Great Awakening; African American Baptist Church Is Founded;

Related articles in *Great Lives from History: The Eighteenth Century, 1701-1800*: Francis Asbury; Jonathan Edwards; Cotton Mather; Increase Mather;

FUGITIVE SLAVE LAW OF 1793

February 12, 1793

The Fugitive Slave Law aggravated sectional conflict between free and slave states.

The Law: Federal law requiring the return of slaves fleeing across state lines

In colonial America, the return of fugitives within and between jurisdictions was a common practice. These fugitives were usually felons escaping from jails; persons charged with crimes; apprentices and indentured servants fleeing from their employers; or black, white, or Native American slaves running away from their masters. Their rendition between jurisdictions depended on comity among colonial authorities. The articles of the New England Confederation of 1643 included a provision for the return of fugitive slaves and servants. Like all subsequent American legislation on the topic, it did not provide for a trial by jury.

RISING SECTIONAL CONFLICT

In the late eighteenth century, with the growth of antislavery sentiment in the North and the settlement of territory west of the Appalachian Mountains, a uniform method for the return of fugitive slaves became necessary. Article VI of the Northwest Ordinance of 1787 excluding chattel slavery provided that persons escaping into the territory from whom labor or service was lawfully claimed in any one of the original states might be returned to the person claiming their labor or service. The provision did not distinguish between slaves and indentured servants.

The United States Constitution of the same year incorporated the provision, without limiting the claimants to residents of the original states of the union. One of several concessions intended to win support from the slaveholding states, Article IV, Section 2, states that "no person held to service or labor in one state, under the laws thereof, escaping into another, shall, in consequence of any law or regulation therein, be discharged from such service or labor, but shall be delivered up on claim of the party to whom such service or labor may be due."

In 1793, Congress decided to set federal rules for the rendition of alleged fugitives. This action was prompted by Pennsylvania's attempt to recover from Virginia several men accused of having kidnapped John Davis, a free black man. Unable to receive satisfaction, the governor of Pennsylvania brought the matter to the attention of President George Washington, who referred it to the Congress.

A committee of the House of Representatives, led by Theodore Sedgwick of Massachusetts, reported a rendition bill on November 15, 1791, but no action was taken. A special Senate committee, consisting of George Cabot of Massachusetts, Samuel Johnston of North Carolina, and George Read of Delaware, submitted a bill on December 20, 1792, establishing a ministerial procedure for the extradition of judicial fugitives. It also provided a system for the recovery of fugitives from labor or service. A claimant had to present a written deposition from one or more credible persons to a local magistrate who would order officers of the court to seize the fugitive and turn him or her over to the claimant. The bill set penalties for harboring a fugitive, neglecting a duty, or obstructing an arrest. After debate, the bill was recommitted with instructions to amend, and John Taylor of Virginia and Roger Sherman of Connecticut were added to the committee.

A REVISED BILL

January 3, 1793, a revised bill was reported to the Senate by Johnston, allowing the claimant or his agent to seize a fugitive and bring that person to a federal court or a local magistrate. Oral testimony or an affidavit certified by a magistrate of the master's state sufficed to establish a claim. To guard against the kidnapping of free African Americans, residents of the territory or state in which they were seized, the new bill included a proviso assuring them their rights under the laws of that territory or state. This meant they were entitled to a judicial inquiry or a jury trial to determine their status. They were also to be presumed free, until proven otherwise, and allowed to testify on their own behalf.

After two debates, during which the proviso was dropped, the bill passed the Senate on January 18. It was entitled "An act respecting fugitives from justice and persons escaping from their masters." The House passed it with little discussion, February 5, by a vote of forty-eight to seven. Seven days later, President Washington signed the bill into law.

The first two sections of the act, known popularly as the Fugitive Slave Act of 1793, dealt with the interstate rendition of fugitives from justice. The third section provided that when a person held to labor escaped into any state or territory of the United States, the master or a designated agent could seize that individual and bring him or her before a judge of the federal courts in the state or before any magistrate of a county, city, or incorporated town. Title was proven by the testimony of the master or the affidavit of a magistrate in the state from which the escapee came, certifying that the person had escaped. The judge or magistrate then had to provide a certificate entitling the petitioner to remove the fugitives.

The act applied to fugitive apprentices or indentured servants as well as to slaves, a provision important at that time to representatives of the northern states. The act did not admit a trial by jury, and it contained no provisions for the alleged fugitives to offer evidence on their own behalf, although they were not prevented from doing so if the presiding judge or magistrate agreed. Section 4 provided criminal penalties, a fine of five hundred dollars, in addition to any civil action the owner might have under state law, for obstructing the capture and for rescuing, harboring, aiding, or hiding fugitives. Although many attempts were made to amend the act, it remained the law of the land until the abolition of slavery, its constitutionality repeatedly upheld by the Supreme Court. It was amended and supplemented, not replaced, by the Second Fugitive Slave Law of 1850, part of the Compromise of 1850.

IMPACT OF THE LAW

The statute contributed significantly to acerbating the growth of sectional conflict within the United States. Efforts to enforce its provisions encountered immediate resistance in northern states, isolated and scattered at first but increasingly well-organized and vigorous (for example, the Underground Railroad), as slavery prospered in the Old South and spread to western lands. Many northern states passed personal liberty laws (Indiana in 1824, Connecticut in 1828, New York and Vermont in 1840). Designed to prevent the kidnapping of free African Americans, these laws provided for trial by jury to determine their true status. The effectiveness of the statute was further diminished by the Supreme Court's decision in *Prigg v. Commonwealth of Pennsylvania* (1842) that state authorities could not be forced by the national government to act in fugitive slave cases.

Subsequently, Massachusetts (1843), Vermont (1843), Pennsylvania (1847), and Rhode Island (1848) forbade their officials to help enforce the law and refused the use of their jails for fugitive slaves. Because the Fugitive Slave Act of 1793 provided no federal means of apprehending fugitive slaves, owners had to rely on the often ineffectual and costly services of slave catchers. With the outbreak of the Civil War, the law ceased to apply to the Confederate States. It was considered valid in the loyal border states until it was repealed June 28, 1864.

—Charles H. O'Brien

See also: Black codes; Bleeding Kansas; Compromise of 1850; Fugitive Slave Law of 1850; Kansas-Nebraska Act; Missouri Compromise; Northwest Ordinance; Proslavery argument; Slave codes; Slavery and the justice system; Underground Railroad

WHITNEY INVENTS THE COTTON GIN

1793

Eli Whitney invented a machine to separate the useful portion of the cotton plant from its seeds and other extraneous materials. The gin revolutionized methods of agricultural production and increased the demand for slave labor in the American South.

Locale: Georgia, United States
Categories: Inventions; manufacturing; agriculture; science and technology

KEY FIGURES

Eli Whitney (1765-1825), American inventor
Catherine Greene (1753-1814), friend of Whitney
Phineas Miller (1764-1803), Whitney's business partner
Sir Richard Arkwright (1732-1792), English inventor of the water frame for spinning cotton
Edmund Cartwright (1743-1823), English inventor of the power loom
Samuel Crompton (1753-1827), English inventor of the spinning mule
J. D. B. De Bow (1820-1867), editor of *De Bow's Review* in New Orleans and apostle of southern diversification
James Hargreaves (1720-1778), English inventor of the spinning jenny
Edmund Ruffin (1794-1865), American advocate of scientific farming
James Watt (1736-1819), English developer of the steam engine

SUMMARY OF EVENT

Eli Whitney was born December 8, 1765, in Westborough, Massachusetts. The eldest of four children in a middle-class farming family, he had exceptional manual dexterity and a very inquisitive mind. The young Whitney particularly enjoyed dismantling mechanical devices and putting them back together. He also liked to build things in his father's workshop. This early curiosity continued to manifest itself throughout his teenage years and led to a degree from Yale College in 1792.

Following his graduation from Yale, Whitney decided to take a position in South Carolina as a tutor. On his journey south, he became acquainted with Catherine Greene, who persuaded him to visit her home near Savannah, Georgia. Whitney decided to stay at the Mulberry Grove plantation. It was there that Greene first suggested to Whitney that he invent a machine to clean the seeds from cotton. According to Whitney's personal account, he built that first small-scale model of the cotton gin in about ten days. He showed it to Greene and her plantation manager, Phineas Miller, who encouraged Whitney and financed the gin's development. Whitney made several adaptations to the already existing machines (which he had never seen), and the completed model of the cotton gin took months to finish.

Whitney's genius did not bring him the financial rewards he expected. The gin was of such great general utility that the South refused to allow anyone a monopoly on production of the machine and, as a result, there was much pirating. Whitney's problems with the gin and the patent struggles in which he engaged affected his approach to the rest of his industrial career. He was willing to improve the efficiency of his shop only if it did not threaten his security. He designed a musket-barrel-turning machine, for example, but did not build it for fear that competitors would use it to lure away his trained workmen.

Whitney's business abilities were not outstanding.

He was primarily interested in the mechanics and efficiency of production, but in those early days an entrepreneur had to be his own chief engineer, foreman, salesperson, and public relations expert. Only in the latter part of the nineteenth century did industrial specialization become common.

The invention of the cotton gin by Whitney was one of several important technological advances during the eighteenth century that revolutionized methods of production and habits of consumption throughout Europe and the United States. Whitney did for the cotton planter what Sir Richard Arkwright, James Hargreaves, Edmund Cartwright, and Samuel Crompton had done for the cotton manufacturer in Great Britain. The cumulative result of the water frame, the spinning jenny, the power loom, and the spinning mule was to increase the demand in England for raw cotton, and the cotton gin made it possible for U.S. planters to meet that demand. The application of steam to these machines greatly increased the output of yarn and cloth, thus serving to intensify the demands made upon cotton plants in the United States.

SIGNIFICANCE

The growth of the cotton industry in the United States was a major force in the rapid economic development of the nation, and much credit for this fact must go to the invention of the cotton gin. The period of the industry's greatest growth followed hard upon the end of the War of 1812, in 1815. Cotton production in the United States rose from 364,000 bales in 1815, of which 82 percent was exported, to 4,861,000 bales in 1860, of which 77 percent was exported. By 1860, Great Britain was consuming one quarter of the entire U.S. crop. Cotton was the United States' leading domestic export. In 1860, the total value of U.S. exports reached $334 million, 57 percent of which was from cotton. If the value of exports of other southern staples, notably tobacco, sugar, and rice, is added to this figure, the contribution of the South to the nation's export trade approached 65 percent. In spite of these impressive statistics, southerners complained that the fruits of their labor were gathered by other sections of the country.

To a large degree, this charge was accurate. Southern planters sold their crops abroad or to the northeastern states. The market was erratic, varying according to demand and supply; it was sensitive to international incidents and almost impossible to predict. Communications were slow. Planters shipped according to one set of prices, only to find a different set of prices operative when their cargoes arrived in port. Risks at sea were great. The costs of shipment were large and paid in the form of commissions to agents of the planters. These men, called factors, handled every detail of the shipment, in addition to making purchases for, and offering credits to, the planters.

These problems were common to all the participants of the staple trade, but they fell with greater impact, especially after 1830, on the older cotton-producing regions along the South Atlantic coast. There, constant plantings without attention to soil conservation reduced yields per acre while increasing costs of production per unit of crop. South Carolina planters found it extremely difficult to compete with planters on Mississippi's lush and virgin lands. Economic stagnation and nullification inevitably followed. Another result was an effort on the part of some farsighted southerners to stimulate economic diversification in the region. J. D. B. De Bow of New Orleans and Edmund Ruffin of Virginia were among those who preached the virtues of scientific agriculture, industrialization, and transportation improvements.

The dramatic growth of the cotton plantation was more than a matter of production statistics and marketing problems. It was the story of great movements of population into the lush lands of the lower Mississippi River Valley. It was also the story of the master and the slave. To some historians, particularly those from the South, it was the story of the evolution of a culture distinct from that of other regions. Most historians, including those who deny the concept of cultural distinctiveness, agree that by the 1850's—according to most economic indices—the South was in a manifestly inferior position, perhaps in a colonial position, relative to the North. Most also would agree that the institution of slavery was a major cause of this inferiority.

The North was not an industrial area in 1860, although strong beginnings had been made in some parts. The North was basically agrarian but was more industrialized than the South. This meant that the North offered more nonagricultural opportunities for economic advancement. The agricultural sector in the North was based on the small farm. In the South, by contrast, small farmers found it increasingly difficult to compete with the plantation. The size of individual landholdings increased markedly in the South after 1840, while farms became smaller in the North. The population of the North was compact; the plantation system dispersed population in the South, retarding southern town and city development. Fewer urban areas meant there were fewer commercial and banking facilities in the South, which, in turn, meant a slow rate of capital formation and presented difficulties to those wishing to diversify or undertake transportation improvement. Fewer inducements were available to attract skilled labor, and the fear of competing with slaves was also an obstacle. At the same time, the need for unskilled labor—specifically African American slave labor—was increasing as the South struggled to meet the growing demand for cotton made possible by the new technology.

The effect of all these factors was to make the South economically weaker than the North, although the South was integrated in the budding national economy. The South was neither distinct nor unique, but as pressures on, and criticism (particularly abolitionist criticism) of, the South accumulated, southerners created the myth of their cultural uniqueness. Whitney's invention had done much to make this myth—and a growing North-South schism—possible.

—*John G. Clark, updated by Liesel Ashley Miller*

See also: Whitney Invents the Cotton Gin.

Related articles in *Great Lives from History: The Eighteenth Century, 1701-1800*: Sir Richard Arkwright; James Hargreaves; John Kay; James Watt; Eli Whitney.

NEGRO CONVENTIONS

m1817-1880's

The six national Negro Conventions held during the early 1830's addressed a variety of issues, including the organization of economic boycotts and mass protests. The conventions exerted a considerable influence upon local black communities.

The Events: Series of national gatherings to discuss economic, social, and political issues of concern to African Americans

Mass conventions were a popular means of protest among African Americans during the nineteenth century. Rooted in constitutional principles of free assembly and petition, these conventions were a product of the group consciousness that emerged among free blacks in northern urban areas following the American Revolution and were a reaction to a burgeoning institutional racism that legitimized slavery and stripped free African Americans of basic civil rights during the post-revolutionary period.

The first great national Negro convention, held at Philadelphia in August, 1817, produced resolutions opposing slavery and denouncing a plan proposed by the U.S. Congress to colonize black Americans in Africa. Although largely symbolic, the convention of 1817 inspired the Negro Convention movement of the 1830's, which was to provide a forum for expressions of militancy and nationalism among the growing population of free northern blacks.

The Negro Convention movement of the 1830's was aided by the emergence of black leaders with national status and varied agendas. Although dominated by antislavery societies, the six national Negro Conventions held between 1830 and 1835 addressed a variety of issues, including the organization of economic boycotts and mass protests, the observance of national days of prayer and fasting, and the establishment of temperance societies and African missionary groups. The conventions exerted a considerable influence upon local black communities, chiefly through the encouragement of verbal agitation; yet the movement was cut short in mid-decade by white abolitionists who, fearing that the black separatism often advocated by convention delegates would damage the antislavery movement, infiltrated the conventions and split their leadership.

REVIVAL OF THE MOVEMENT

The Negro Convention movement was briefly revived in the early 1840's, when young black militants in New York and Philadelphia called a convention of black leaders to protest slavery and racial inequality. However, this convention, which failed by one vote to endorse slave insurrection, proved a militant exception to a new spirit of gradualism among black abolitionists. The last notable antebellum Negro Convention, held in Cleveland, Ohio, in 1854, yielded compromise proposals for the repatriation of African Americans that early conventions had so vehemently opposed.

The end of the Civil War and the beginning of Reconstruction sparked a revival of Negro Conventions in the 1870's and 1880's, as southern freedmen and northern agitators sought vehicles to petition the government for civil rights and protection from mob violence. These conventions were chiefly local and regional in nature, designed to facilitate political organization and to appeal directly to legislators and state governors. Nevertheless, national conventions continued, the most notable being the National Colored Convention held in Louisville, Kentucky, in 1883, in which the delegates called for an end to economic peonage in the South, equal rights and suffrage for African Americans, and integration of schools and the military.

The convention movement died out in the 1890's as Jim Crow laws and mob violence swept the South and accommodationism replaced agitation and protest as a political strategy for black leaders. However, the tradition of assembly and militancy brought about by the

convention movement survived in the black conferences of the early twentieth century (for example, the Niagara conference of 1909, which spawned the National Association for the Advancement of Colored People), in the mass protest marches of the Civil Rights movement during the 1960's, and in the Million Man and Million Woman Marches of the 1990's.

—Michael H. Burchett

See also: Abolition; Civil War; Jim Crow laws; National Council of Colored People; Niagara Movement; Reconstruction

SOCIAL REFORM MOVEMENT

1820's-1850's

A wave of religious and philanthropic movements, collectively known as the social reform movement, worked for humanitarian and democratic reforms that included abolition, temperance, woman suffrage, and wider access to education.

Locale: Northeastern and western United States Categories: Social issues and reform; organizations and institutions; education

KEY FIGURES

Ralph Waldo Emerson (1803-1882), former Unitarian minister who was a central figure in the Transcendental movement

Lyman Beecher (1775-1863), pastor of Boston's Park Street Church

Elihu Burritt (1810-1879), pacifist editor of the *Advocate of Peace and Universal Brotherhood*

Dorothea Dix (1802-1887), reformer concerned especially with the treatment of the mentally ill

Charles Fourier (1772-1837), French social theorist whose doctrine of communitarian living was embraced by many American reformers

Thomas Hopkins Gallaudet (1787-1851), founder of the first free American school for the hearing impaired

William Lloyd Garrison (1805-1879), abolitionist editor of *The Liberator*

Samuel Gridley Howe (1801-1876), educator who founded the Perkins School for the Blind

Horace Mann (1796-1859), champion of free public education

Theodore Dwight Weld (1803-1895), founder of the American Anti-Slavery Society and organizer of the group "Seventy"

SUMMARY OF EVENT

In 1841, Ralph Waldo Emerson declared, "In the history of the world the doctrine of Reform had never such scope as at the present hour." The wave of reform that swept over much of the United States from the 1820's to the 1850's seemed to prove Emerson's theory that the human being is "born . . . to be a Reformer, a Remaker of what man has made; a renouncer of lies; a restorer of truth and good, imitating that great Nature which embosoms us all, and which sleeps no moment on an old past, but every hour repairs herself." In those decades, people enlisted in a variety of causes and crusades, some of which were of a conservative nature, while others challenged basic institutions and beliefs.

The antebellum reform movement was partly a response to economic, social, and political changes following the War of 1812. Such changes provoked feelings of anxiety in the United States, generating anti-Mason, anti-Roman Catholic, and anti-Mormon crusades. However, change also generated a feeling of optimism and confirmed the almost universal faith in progress that characterized early nineteenth century Americans. Reformers came from two groups:

religious reformers and the wealthy who felt obligated to help the less fortunate.

Evangelical religion played an important role in the origins of the reform movement. The shift from the Calvinistic doctrine of predestination to more democratic teachings that emphasized humankind's efforts in achieving salvation nourished ideas of perfectionism and millenarianism. Not only could individuals achieve "perfect holiness" but the world itself, as evidenced by the movements of reform, was improving and moving toward the long-awaited thousand-year reign of the Kingdom of God on Earth.

In addition to evangelicalism, the legacy of the Enlightenment and the American Revolution—the natural rights philosophy and the faith in humanity's ability to shape society in accordance with the laws of God and nature—was a stimulus to reform. So was the nineteenth century's romantic conception of the individual. "The power which is at once spring and regulator in all efforts of reform," Emerson wrote, "is the conviction that there is an infinite worthiness in man, which will appear at the call of worth, and that all particular reforms are the removing of some impediment."

Antebellum reformers attacked a variety of evils. Dorothea Dix urged humane treatment for the mentally ill; Thomas Gallaudet and Samuel Gridley Howe founded schools for the hearing impaired and the blind. Prison reform engaged the efforts of some, and a campaign to abolish imprisonment for debt made slow but sure progress in the pre-Civil War period. Horace Mann championed common schools, and free public schooling gradually spread from New England to other parts of the United States. Elihu Burritt, the "learned blacksmith," urged the abolition of war and related evils. Communitarians, inspired by religious or secular principles, withdrew from society to found utopian experiments such as Oneida, Amana, Hopedale, Ephrata Cloister, and New Harmony. The communitarian teachings of French social theorist Charles Fourier inspired such experiments as Brook Farm, the North American Phalanx of Red Bank, New Jersey, and the Sylvani Phalanx of northeastern Pennsylvania. Lucretia Mott, Elizabeth Cady Stanton, Lucy Stone, and others championed higher education, the suffrage, and legal and property rights for women.

Temperance and abolition were the two most prominent secular crusades of the period. Both of them passed through several phases, moving from

gradualism to immediatism and from persuasion to legal coercion. The temperance movement began with an appeal for moderation in the consumption of alcoholic beverages and shifted by the late 1820's to a demand for total abstinence.

The Reverend Lyman Beecher's *Six Sermons*, published in 1826, were instrumental in effecting this shift to total abstinence; the "teetotal" position was further popularized during the 1840's by the Washington Temperance Society of reformed "drunkards" (alcoholics) and the children's Cold Water Army. Similar to the temperance movement, the abolition, or antislavery, movement moved from a position favoring gradual emancipation and colonization during the 1820's, to a demand for immediate abolition of the sin of slavery.

William Lloyd Garrison's *Liberator* and Theodore Dwight Weld's "Seventy" preached the immediatist doctrine, and it was adopted by the American Anti-Slavery Society, which had been founded in 1833. During the 1840's, some temperance and antislavery reformers, disillusioned by the lack of results from education and moral suasion, turned to politics as a means of achieving their goals. Some abolitionists supported the Liberty and Free-Soil Parties, and later the Republicans, and sought legislation preventing the extension of slavery into the territories. Temperance advocates succeeded in getting statewide prohibition and local option laws passed in a number of states during the early 1850's.

In most cases, the vehicle of reform was the voluntary association. Virtually every movement had a national organization, with state and local auxiliaries, which sponsored speakers, published pamphlets, and generally coordinated efforts in behalf of its cause. Although such societies were often rent by factionalism, they proved remarkably effective in arousing the popular conscience on the moral issues of the day. By 1850, for example, there were almost two thousand antislavery societies with a membership close to 200,000, compared to about five hundred such societies in 1826.

SIGNIFICANCE

Although most of the reform movements had their largest following in the northeastern and western parts of the United States, their impact was not confined to those sections. Southerners, although hostile to abolitionism and other radical causes, were receptive to pleas for educational and prison reform and for better treatment of the insane and the blind. The temperance crusade made considerable headway in the South. Thus, to a greater or lesser degree, depending on the particular cause, the antebellum social reform movement was a truly national phenomenon.

—Anne C. Loveland, updated by Geralyn Strecker

See also: Congress Bans Importation of African Slaves; Southerners Advance Proslavery Arguments;

American Anti-Slavery Society Is Founded; Seneca Falls Convention; National Council of Colored People Is Founded; Civil Rights Act of 1866.

Related articles in *Great Lives from History: The Nineteenth Century, 1801-1900:* Bronson Alcott; Dorothea Dix; Ralph Waldo Emerson; Charles Fourier; William Lloyd Garrison; Octavia Hill; Samuel Gridley Howe; Horace Mann; Lucretia Mott; Robert Owen.

MISSOURI COMPROMISE

March 3, 1820

By allowing Missouri to enter the union as a slave state, while Maine entered as a free state, this congressional measure helped preserve the delicate balance between northern and southern sectional interests for more than three decades.

Locale: Washington, D.C.

Categories: Laws, acts, and legal history; civil rights and liberties

KEY FIGURES

Henry Clay (1777-1852), Speaker of the U.S. House of Representatives

James Tallmadge (1778-1853), representative from New York

Jesse Burgess Thomas (1777-1853), senator from Illinois

James Monroe (1758-1831), president of the United States, 1817-1825

SUMMARY OF EVENT

Between 1818 and 1819, representatives from both Missouri and Maine petitioned the U.S. Congress to admit their territories to the union as states. The Missouri Territory had been created from the Louisiana Purchase (1803) and was promised constitutional protection. However, Congress could not decide if the right of property applied to the institution of slavery. The question at issues was whether slavery should be allowed in Missouri and the rest of the Louisiana Purchase, or did Congress have the moral responsibility to rectify the issue of slavery that had been avoided since the Constitutional Convention of 1787. It would

take three sessions of Congress between 1818 and 1821 before Missouri was fully admitted as a state. The issue of slavery sparked by the ensuing debate spread throughout the country and threatened to cause disunion between the northern and southern regions of the United States.

At the time Missouri and Maine applied for statehood, the union had exactly eleven free states and eleven slave states. This political balance had been achieved since 1789 by alternately admitting slave and free states, whose status was determined by each state's geographical location and its region's past history with regard to slavery. This arrangement ensued that each section of the country had an equal number of senators, and it attempted to equalize representation in the House of Representatives through the three-fifths clause.

The three-fifths clause, added to the final draft of the Constitution in 1789, allowed slave states to count each slave as three-fifths of a person to balance their representative power against that of the more densely populated North. Nevertheless, the North had a majority of representatives in Congress (105 to 81). Missouri's admission as a free or slave state therefore became an important issue in the very body that would resolve it. Missouri threatened either to extend the influence of the industrial free North in the Senate or to provide the majority to the agrarian slaveholding South.

In 1818, the boundaries of Missouri Territory were approximately the same as those of the modern state, and the territory was estimated to contain two thousand to three thousand slaves. Slavery in Missouri was a historical by-product of prior French and Spanish colonial policies. Representatives from Missouri reasoned that slavery should be allowed to continue there as it had in other territories that had been granted statehood since 1789.

In February, 1819, the House of Representatives responded to this debate by adopting an amendment that Representative James Tallmadge of New York proposed to attach to the bill allowing Missouri to frame a state constitution. The two clauses in the Tallmadge amendment would restrict the expansion of slavery in Missouri and provide that all children born to slaves would become free at the age of twenty-five. Both clauses of his amendment passed the House. Southern senators were shocked by the bitterness of the debate in the House and the ability of the North to muster votes. They saw the Tallmadge amendment as the first step in eliminating the expansion of slavery in the nation as a whole. Voting along sectional lines, the Senate rejected both clauses. Congress then adjourned until December 6, 1819.

During the interim period, Maine framed a constitution and applied for admission to the union as a free state. Maine had originally been incorporated into the Massachusetts Bay Colony in 1691 but had started to agitate for separate statehood during the War of 1812. Its application for statehood as a free state seemed to provide a possible solution to the Missouri debate that threatened the stability of the young nation.

On February 18, 1820, the Senate Judiciary Committee joined the Missouri and Maine measures and the Senate passed both Maine's and Missouri's applications for statehood but without mentioning slavery. This infuriated Maine, which had, as part of Massachusetts, outlawed slavery in 1780. What should have been a routine confirmation of new states became part of the most explosive issue to face the country. Maine was to be allowed to separate from Massachusetts and gain statehood, so long as Congress approved its application by March 4, 1820, or its nine counties would revert to Massachusetts. Even so, many of Maine's constituency urged that Maine's application fail so that slavery would not spread into Missouri.

Senator Jesse Burgess Thomas of Illinois offered a compromise amendment to the Senate bill that would admit Missouri as a slave state with the proviso that the remaining territories in the Louisiana Purchase above 36° 30′ north latitude, Missouri's southern border, would be free of slavery. The northern-controlled House responded by rejecting Thomas's amendment and instead passed a proviso prohibiting the further introduction of slavery anywhere in the United States. The result was polarization along sectional lines. In turn, the Senate struck out the antislavery provision and added the Thomas amendment. Thus began the final debate over whether slavery would be allowed to expand.

Senator Rufus King of New York continued the debate by stating that Congress, under Article IV, section 3 of the Constitution, was empowered to exclude slavery from the territory and to make slavery an issue for statehood. "New states *may be* admitted by the Congress into this Union." A precedent had been established under in the Northwest Ordinance of 1787, which forbade slavery in lands above the Ohio River. Therefore, in the minds of many of the northern congressmen, they should take this opportunity to eliminate slavery from any point west of the Mississippi. In response, Senator William Pickering of Maryland argued that because the United States was made up of equal numbers of slave and free states, Missouri should be allowed to determine its own fate.

Missouri responded with anger and frustration, asserting that the issue was not about slavery but rather the issue of state sovereignty. Congress had delayed Missouri's admission for several years. Missouri, like other states, had the right to choose its own property laws. In Missouri, as well as the rest of the South, the issue swung from one dealing with slavery to one dealing with property rights and the equality of states within the United States. These issues captured the attention of citizens throughout the country and led to heated debates on all levels. For the first time, slavery was being justified and defended as a good way of life not only by southern politicians but also by the southern clergy. Would the country be influenced by restrictionists who sought to control this institution, or would states' rights be preserved?

A compromise was eventually reached, between the two houses, in a conference formed to break the deadlock. Speaker of the House Henry Clay of Kentucky stated that he would not support Maine's admission unless Missouri was admitted without restrictions. The Senate took the House bill and inserted the Thomas amendment. On March 3, 1820, the House under Clay's leadership voted to admit Maine as a free state and Missouri as a slave state and restricted slavery north of 36° 30′. It is interesting to note that seven of Maine's nine representatives in the Massachusetts state delegation voted against Maine's admission so that their state would not be used to provide a solution to the slavery issue.

Missouri continued to be an issue when it presented a state constitution in November, 1820. As if to get the final word, the Missouri constitutional convention had incorporated into its constitution a provision excluding free blacks and mulattoes from the state. This provision incited the antislavery factions in the Senate and House and threatened to destroy the fragile compromise. A "Second Missouri Compromise" was needed that would state that Missouri would not gain admission as a state unless its legislature assured Congress that it would not seek to abridge the rights of citizens. The Missouri legislature agreed to this in June, 1821. On August 10, 1821, President James Monroe admitted Missouri as the twenty-fourth state. After waiting a short time, Missouri's state legislature sought to have the last say when it approved statutes forbidding free blacks from entering the state.

SIGNIFICANCE

The Missouri Compromise would stand until Congress's passage of the Kansas-Nebraska Act in 1854. Until that time, the Missouri Compromise served to mark a clear delineation between the growing regional and sectional problems of the North and South and made states' rights the rallying cry for the South until the Civil War (1861-1865). In 1857, Missouri would again become the focus of a national debate on slavery when the Dred Scott case reached the U.S. Supreme Court, whose ruling nullified the principles of the Missouri Compromise.

—*Vincent Michael Thur*

The Constitution and the Admission of New States

The U.S. Constitution's rules for the admission of new states to the Union are outlined in these two brief paragraphs, which make up the whole of Article IV, section 3.

New States may be admitted by the Congress into this Union; but no new State shall be formed or erected within the Jurisdiction of any other State; nor any State be formed by the Junction of two or more States, or Parts of States, without the Consent of the Legislatures of the States concerned as well as of the Congress.

The Congress shall have Power to dispose of and make all needful Rules and Regulations respecting the Territory or other Property belonging to the United States; and nothing in this Constitution shall be so construed as to Prejudice any Claims of the United States, or of any particular State.

See also: Congress Bans Importation of African Slaves; Webster and Hayne Debate Slavery and Westward Expansion; Compromise of 1850; Congress Passes the Kansas-Nebraska Act; May, Bleeding Kansas; *Dred Scott v. Sandford*; Lincoln-Douglas Debates.

Related articles in *Great Lives from History: The Nineteenth Century, 1801-1900:* Henry Clay; James Monroe; Roger Brooke Taney.

DENMARK VESEY REVOLT

July 14, 1822

Vesey, a former slave who became a carpenter, is credited with leading one of the most significant slave rebellions in the United States. The 1822 South Carolina revolt that bears his name became the largest slave uprising in North America since the 1739 Stono Rebellion, although it quickly failed.

Born: c. 1767; St. Thomas, Virgin Islands
Died: July 2, 1822; Charleston, South Carolina
Also known as: Telemaque Vesey
Area of achievement: Social issues

EARLY LIFE

Denmark Vesey (VEE-see) is a shadowy figure. Not much is known about his early life, and the events of his adult life are disputed by historians. Vesey was probably born into slavery on the Danish Caribbean sugar island of St. Thomas around 1767. In 1781, he was purchased by Captain Joseph Vesey, a slave trader, who trained him as cabin boy. Vesey renamed the boy Telemaque, after the mythical son of Odysseus. In time, he became known as Denmark after the island of his birth.

In 1783, Joseph Vesey settled in Charleston, South Carolina. Denmark, literate and multilingual, lived with the Vesey family and worked in the family's imported goods business as an office clerk and trader. He married a slave woman, Beck, who gave birth to at least three of his children. Any children born to a slave mother were legally slaves from birth, so Vesey had very limited control over his own children, whose names and fates are unknown. Since whites did not recognize the marriages of slaves, Vesey and Beck never lived together and were separated when Vesey's owner moved his household to an Ashley River plantation. The children remained with their mother. When Vesey won fifteen hundred dollars in a lottery, he purchased his freedom and returned to Charleston, possibly to be closer to his children and Beck. He became a carpenter.

LIFE'S WORK

After his relationship with Beck ended, Vesey married Susan and became one of the first members of the African Methodist Episcopal (AME) Church, commonly known as the African Church, in Charleston. Embittered by the continuing enslavement of Beck and their children, Vesey eventually turned his back on the New Testament and what he regarded as Christianity's false promise of universal brotherhood. Vesey began to plan to lead his children and friends to freedom in Haiti. This small Caribbean island nation stood as a beacon of liberty to enslaved African Americans because Haitian slaves had overthrown their French masters in a bloody revolution that concluded in 1804.

What made Vesey's conspiracy unique was both his advanced age of fifty-four and that he planned a mass exodus of black families out of Charleston. The plot called for slaves in the vicinity of the Ashley and Cooper rivers to slay their masters on the morning of Sunday, July 14, 1822, and fight their way toward the city docks. Although Vesey employed several black men to make weapons, the leading conspirators, including Gullah Jack in Pritchard, decided that they would not risk stockpiling weapons or recruiting soldiers before

July. Vesey believed that once the revolt began, men would flock to his side.

Despite efforts to maintain secrecy, conspirator William Paul told of the planned revolt to Peter, a slave, on May 22. At about the same time, another slave, George Wilson, gave information about the plan to his master. Exactly one month later, Vesey was arrested. Found guilty, he was hanged on July 2, 1822, along with five other conspirators as an immense crowd of African Americans and whites watched. Charleston courts eventually arrested 131 slaves and free African Americans, executing 35 and transporting 37 to Spanish Cuba. A total of 23 African Americans were acquitted, 2 died in custody, 3 were found not guilty but whipped, and 1 free black was released on condition that he permanently leave the state. The African Church was razed, possibly as an attack by whites on black independence and autonomy. It was rebuilt in 1865 at the end of the Civil War.

SIGNIFICANCE

In 2001, Michael Johnson, professor of history at Johns Hopkins University, presented evidence that Vesey did not organize the rebellion that bears his name. Johnson argued that Vesey was simply one of many black victims of a conspiracy engineered by the white power structure of 1822 Charleston. The passage of time has made it impossible to know what really happened. However, it is clear that slaves and former slaves did fight back against oppression; they did not passively accept their fate. Whether or not Vesey led the rebellion, he is significant as a symbol of fierce black resistance to slavery.

—*Caryn E. Neumann*

See also: William Craft and Ellen Craft; Frederick Douglass; James Forten; Sally Hemings; Absalom Jones; John Brown Russwurm; Dred Scott; Robert Smalls; Nat Turner; David Walker.

JOHN BROWN RUSSWURM PUBLISHES *FREEDOM'S JOURNAL*

March 1827

Russwurm was the coeditor of the first African American newspaper in America. The abolitionist publication provided one of the first forums in which African American writers were allowed to express

their perspective on black life and culture. It also was revolutionary for African Americans to see members of their race represented in their own words in mass media.

Born: October 1, 1799; Port Antonio, Jamaica
Died: June 17, 1851; Cape Palmas, Maryland in Africa
(now in Liberia)
Also known as: John Brown
Areas of achievement: Abolitionism; Journalism and
publishing; Social issues

EARLY LIFE

John Brown Russwurm was born in Port Antonio, Jamaica, to a white man and his black servant. Historical records do not make it clear whether Russwurm was born a slave or free. He originally was only given his mother's name and known as John Brown. His father later married Susan Blanchard, a white woman who was very supportive of the child and insisted that he take his father's surname, Russwurm. Russwurm remained very close to his stepmother even after his father's death. In 1812, Russwurm moved to Maine with his father. He was educated at Hebron Academy and later taught at a school for African American children in Boston. Russwurm attended Bowdoin College, where he became its first African American graduate in 1826 and one of the first African Americans to graduate from any American college. He also was the first African American to be accepted into a college fraternity. He went on to earn a master's degree from Bowdoin. Russwurm's work took him from America to Africa, and on that journey he met his wife, Sarah McGill. Her father was the lieutenant governor of Monrovia, the capital of Liberia. The couple had three sons and a daughter. Russwurm's stepmother also cared for his sons while they were educated in America.

LIFE'S WORK

After graduating from college, Russwurm moved to New York to work as a teacher. He also became very involved in the abolitionist movement. He was well respected among free African Americans in New York. He and a fellow abolitionist, a minister named Samuel Cornish, decided to dedicate a print publication to their cause. In March of 1827, the first issue of *Freedom's Journal* was published in New York. On July 4 of the same year, slavery was abolished in the state.

Freedom's Journal is an important part of journalism history and the history of the ethnic press. Russwurm—a teacher, scholar, and gifted orator—served as the junior editor and reported the concerns of African Americans in the New York area. The newspaper was filled with stories about prominent members of the African American community. The publishers made a

special effort to keep people abreast of important issues and current events, especially those related to the abolitionist movement and the fate of the slaves even after they were freed.

Freedom's Journal was circulated in the United States, England, Canada, and Haiti. At the time, the American Colonization Society (ACS) was encouraging black Americans to move to Liberia and live a life in which race would not be a factor. Originally, the publication opposed that movement and instead encouraged African Americans to make America their home.

By 1828, Cornish had turned the publication over to Russwurm. Around that time, Russwurm was becoming disenchanted with life in America and began to support the ACS's ideals. He wanted African Americans to no longer be oppressed by whites. His new beliefs were reflected in *Freedom's Journal* and, as a result, Russwurm and the publication became quite unpopular with some readers. He stepped down from his role as editor, and *Freedom's Journal* folded in 1829. It had published a total of 103 issues from 1827 to 1829. Cornish later attempted to revive the publication under a new name, *The Rights of All*. That publication was short-lived. Russwurm moved to Liberia and founded a new publication, *The Liberia Herald*, which had a special focus on education. In 1836, he became governor of the Maryland colony in Liberia. He recruited many former slaves living in America to come to the colony. After his death, the colony eventually became part of the independent Republic of Liberia. A memorial was erected there in Russwurm's honor.

SIGNIFICANCE

Russwurm played a major role in two major movements of the nineteenth century: abolitionism and the first back-to-Africa movement. His change of heart on Liberian colonization reflected many African Americans' frustrations with the state of race relations in America, even in states where slavery had been outlawed. A pioneer in American journalism, he was one of the first to create a national publication by and for African Americans. *Freedom's Journal* is often credited with helping lead the way to the abolition of slavery.

—*Kim M. LeDuff*

See also: Robert S. Abbott; Charlotta Spears Bass; John E. Bruce; Paul Cuffe; Martin Robison Delany; Marcus Garvey.

TURNER'S SLAVE INSURRECTION

1831

The 1831 slave revolt led by Nat Turner sent fear through the southern white community and prompted legislation prohibiting the assembly, education, and movement of plantation slaves.

The Event: Short-lived but bloody slave revolt led by Nat Turner
Place: Southampton County, Virginia

Although neither the first attempted slave rebellion nor the last during the more than two centuries of African American slavery, Nat Turner's assault against the whites in southeastern Virginia marked the only time a group of black slaves banded together to strike successfully against their white masters.

NAT TURNER

So far as is known, Turner spent his entire life as a slave in his native Southampton County, where he had been born on October 2, 1800, on the plantation of Benjamin Turner. His mother was probably a native African, who taught him at an early age to believe that he possessed supernatural powers. He was both a mystic and oriented toward religion. In addition to possessing those traits, he could read, and historians have surmised that he learned this skill from the Turner family. Nat became a Christian through the instruction of his grandmother, Bridget, and mostly read the Bible. Perhaps because of his knowledge of the Bible, he became a Baptist preacher. Because of his mysticism, his ability to read, and his activities as a minister, Turner gained considerable influence over his fellow slaves.

Samuel Turner, Benjamin's son, inherited Nat during times of economic depression in Virginia. A newly hired overseer drove the slaves to work harder, and as a consequence, Nat ran away. Although Nat eluded capture for thirty days, he turned himself in to his owner. His return went unpunished, but in the days that followed, Nat saw that his own freedom could not be realized without his people's freedom.

Nat married a slave named Cherry in the early 1820's, and they had three children. Cherry would later conceal coded maps and lists that Turner used in his revolt, which experts have never been able to decode. When Samuel Turner died in 1822, Nat's family was broken up and sold to different families. Nat went to a neighboring farm owner, Thomas Moore. He was sold again to Joseph Travis in 1831.

Nat Turner thought of himself as an instrument of God. Between 1825 and 1830, Turner gained respect as a traveling neighborhood preacher. He became deeply religious, fasting and praying in solitude. In his own mind he had been ordained—like the prophets of old—to perform a special mission. He professed that God communicated with him through voices and signs in the heavens. On May 12, 1828, Turner heard a "great noise" and saw "white spirits" and "black spirits" battling.

THE REVOLT

In February, 1831, a certain blueness in the atmosphere—a solar eclipse—persuaded him that God was announcing that the time had come for the slaves to attack their white masters. Turner communicated this message to his band of followers; the rebellion ensued on August 21, when Turner and seven fellow slaves murdered the Travis family. Within twenty-four hours after the rebellion began, the band of rebels numbered seventy-five slaves. In the next two days, an additional fifty-one whites were killed. No evidence exists to indicate that Turner's movement was a part of any larger scheme. One slave, Nat Turner, used the power at his command to attempt to break his shackles and those of his followers.

Turner directed his attack toward the county seat, Jerusalem, and the weapons in its armory; he never made it. The white community responded promptly, and with an overpowering force of armed owners and militia, it routed the poorly armed slaves during the second day of the rebellion. Although he eluded capture for six weeks, Turner and all the rebels were either killed or captured and executed. Hundreds of other nonparticipating and innocent slaves were slain as a result of fright in the white community. Turner's court-appointed attorney, Thomas Gray, recorded Turner's "confessions" on November 1, and on November 11, 1831, Turner was hanged. Gray later remarked on Turner's intelligence and knowledge of military tactics.

AFTERMATH

Although Turner's revolt took place in a relatively isolated section of Virginia, the uprising caused the entire South to tremble. Many white southerners called for more stringent laws regulating slaves' behavior, such as making it a crime to teach a slave to read or write. Turner's revolt coincided with the blossoming of the abolition movement in the North, for the rebellion occurred in the same year that William Lloyd Garrison began his unremitting assault on the South's "peculiar institution." Although no one has been able to demonstrate that abolitionist activity had any influence at all on Turner, white southerners were horrified at the seeming coincidence. They described abolitionists as persons who wanted not only to end slavery but also to sponsor a massacre of southern whites. The white South stood as one against any outside interference with its system.

Although white people throughout the South looked anew at slavery, in no place did they look more closely than in Virginia. During the legislative session of 1831-1832, there occurred the most thorough public discussion of slavery in southern history prior to 1861. Only four months after Turner's revolt, the legislature appointed a committee to recommend to the state a course of action in dealing with slavery.

Those Virginians opposed to slavery made their case. They argued that slavery was a prime cause of Virginia's economic backwardness; that it injured white manners and morals; and that, as witnessed by Turner's revolt, it was basically dangerous. While they did talk about abolition as benefiting the slaves, they primarily maintained that white Virginians would reap the greatest rewards, for the African Americans, after a gradual and possibly compensated emancipation, would be removed from the state. These abolitionists, most of whom were from western Virginia (modern West Virginia), an area

of few slaves, could not agree on a specific plan to accomplish their purpose. Slavery's defenders countered by boasting of Virginia's economic well-being and the good treatment and contentment of the slaves. Referring to the well-established belief in the sanctity of private property, they denied that the legislature had any right to meddle with slave property.

The Virginia legislature decided not to tamper with slavery. It rebuffed those who wanted to put Virginia on the road to emancipation. After these debates, white southerners no longer seriously considered any alternative to slavery. In the aftermath of Turner's revolt and Virginia's debate, the South erected a massive defense of its peculiar institution. That defense permeated southern politics, religion, literature, and science. Nat Turner's revolt—the only successful slave uprising in the South—heralded and confirmed the total southern commitment to black slavery. However, Turner left a profound legacy: Slaves would fight for their freedom. Turner's rebellion has inspired black activists since, including Marcus Garvey and Malcolm X.

—*William J. Cooper, Jr., updated by Marilyn Elizabeth Perry*

See also: Abolition; *Amistad* slave revolt; Harpers Ferry raid; *Liberator, The*; New York City slave revolt; Proslavery argument; Stono Rebellion

GARRISON BEGINS PUBLISHING *THE LIBERATOR*

January 1, 1831

During an era when abolitionist newspapers proliferated in northern states, William Lloyd Garrison's The Liberator stood out as the most radical and uncompromising advocate of immediate abolition of slavery.

Locale: Boston, Massachusetts
Categories: Journalism; social issues and reform

KEY FIGURES
William Lloyd Garrison (1805-1879), abolitionist leader and editor of *The Liberator*
Arthur Tappan (1786-1865), first president of the American Anti-Slavery Society
Lewis Tappan (1788-1873), leader of church-oriented abolitionists

Maria Weston Chapman (1806-1885), journalist and associate of Garrison
James Forten (1766-1842), African American abolitionist and financial backer of *The Liberator*
Benjamin Lundy (1789-1839), Quaker abolitionist
Wendell Phillips (1811-1884), orator and Garrison's associate

SUMMARY OF EVENT
William Lloyd Garrison and his newspaper were products of the era of religious revival known as the Second Great Awakening, which transformed Protestant theology in the United States. The Awakening engendered moral reform movements in New England and other parts of the North during the early decades of the nineteenth century. Unlike

William Lloyd Garrison by Jocelyn, c. 1833

their Calvinist predecessors, those who engaged in moral reform assumed that human beings, by their actions, could create a perfect society and bring about the millennial return of Jesus Christ. In his perception of the sinfulness and criminality of slaveholding, which he believed deprived both slaves and masters of a chance for salvation, Garrison went beyond most reformers of his time.

Garrison was born in Newburyport, Massachusetts, in 1805. Deserted by his seafaring father at the age of three, he was raised in poverty by his devout Baptist mother, who instilled in him her own strict moral code. At thirteen years of age, he apprenticed as a printer at the *Newburyport Herald*, where he learned the newspaper business. By 1828, he was in Boston, working as the editor of *The National Philanthropist*, which supported the temperance movement. Garrison also supported what he and others perceived to be the antislavery efforts of the American Colonization Society (ACS), which had been founded in 1817. As the dominant antislavery organization of the 1820's, the ACS advocated the gradual abolition of slavery, combined with the transportation of free black Americans to Africa.

In 1828, Garrison's decision to join Quaker abolitionist Benjamin Lundy in Baltimore as coeditor of Lundy's weekly, *The Genius of Universal Emancipation*, led to *The Liberator* and a more radical antislavery

movement. In Baltimore, Garrison observed slavery in practice. Influenced by members of Baltimore's African American community, he came to believe that gradualism would never end the "peculiar institution." African American influences also led Garrison to conclude that the ACS perpetuated a racist assumption that black and white people could not live together as equals in the United States, and he came to oppose the society's "colonization" goals. Garrison's increasing militancy made cooperation with the more conservative Lundy difficult. Garrison's radicalism also led to his imprisonment for libel in Baltimore and to his decision to return to New England to begin his own antislavery newspaper.

On January 1, 1831, he published the first issue of *The Liberator* in Boston. In that inaugural issue, Garrison proclaimed his conversion to immediate, not gradual, abolition of slavery. Harshly condemning slaveholders as sinners and thieves, he pointed out that one did not ask sinners to stop sinning gradually or require that thieves gradually stop committing crimes. Christian morality and justice, he insisted, required that slaveholders immediately and unconditionally free their bondspeople.

Garrison was not the first to advocate immediate emancipation. What was different about him was his rejection of moderation and his linkage of immediatism with a demand that the rights of the formerly enslaved be recognized in the United States. In his most famous statement, Garrison proclaimed, "I am in earnest—I will not equivocate—I will not excuse—I will not retreat a single inch—AND I WILL BE HEARD."

Garrison's launching of *The Liberator* is also significant for its reflection of biracial cooperation in the antislavery movement. Although Garrison, like other white abolitionists, never entirely escaped the racial prejudices of his time, he and his newspaper enjoyed the strong support of African Americans. Wealthy black abolitionist James Forten of Philadelphia provided crucial financial support to *The Liberator* in its early years. During the same period, Garrison employed black subscription agents, and three-quarters of the newspaper's subscribers were black. In Boston, where white anti-abolition sentiment could produce violent confrontations, Garrison enjoyed the physical protection of African Americans.

Meanwhile, Garrison and *The Liberator* played an essential role in the formation of the American Anti-Slavery Society (AASS). Founded in December, 1833, under the leadership of Garrison and New York City businessmen Arthur and Lewis Tappan, the AASS united immediate abolitionists in the United States through most of the 1830's. Reflecting the pacifistic views of Garrison, the Tappans, and others, the society pledged in its Declaration of Sentiments—modeled on the Declaration of Independence—to use peaceful means to bring about the immediate, uncompensated emancipation of all U.S. slaves, without colonization.

Promoted by *The Liberator*, dozens of other antislavery newspapers, and thousands of antislavery pamphlets, the AASS grew rapidly. By 1838, it claimed a membership in the North of approximately 250,000 people in 1,350 local affiliates. At the same time, however, internal tensions were tearing the AASS apart. The essential problem was that Garrison and his closest New England associates, including Maria Weston Chapman, Wendell Phillips, and Henry C. Wright, had concluded that the spirit of slavery had so permeated the nation that the North, as well as the South, had to be fundamentally changed.

Although other abolitionists were reaching similar conclusions during the late 1830's, many of them objected to the specific policies advocated in the columns of *The Liberator* to effect those changes. In particular, an increasingly unorthodox Garrison antagonized church-oriented abolitionists by his wholesale condemnation of organized religion. He also seemed to threaten traditional concepts of patriarchy by his championing of women's rights and, specifically, female equality within the AASS. He appeared to threaten government through his advocacy of nonresistance, the pacifist doctrine that physical force is never justified, even in self-defense or on behalf of law and order. He frustrated those who desired a separate abolitionist political party by condemning political parties as inherently corrupt.

As a result of these tensions, the abolitionist movement splintered in 1840. Garrison, his New England associates, and a few others throughout the North retained control of the AASS, but the great majority of abolitionists left the organization. Lewis Tappan began the American and Foreign Anti-Slavery Society, which, until 1855, maintained a church-oriented antislavery campaign. Politically inclined abolitionists organized the Liberty Party. By the 1850's, a majority of non-Garrisonian abolitionists had come to support the Republican Party, which advocated neither immediate abolition nor equal rights for African Americans.

During the 1840's and 1850's, Garrison used *The Liberator* and other forums to promote anticlericalism, women's rights, and nonresistance, as well as immediate

Garrison's Declaration of Sentiments

The Declaration of Sentiments, excerpted below, represented the manifesto of the American Anti-Slavery Society. Modeled on the Declaration of Independence, it put forward both the rationale and the objectives of the society.

More than fifty-seven years have elapsed, since a band of patriots convened in this place [Philadelphia], to devise measures for the deliverance of this country from a foreign yoke. The corner-stone upon which they founded the Temple of Freedom was broadly this—'that all men are created equal; that they are endowed by their Creator with certain inalienable rights; that among these are life, LIBERTY, and the pursuit of happiness.' At the sound of their trumpet call, three millions of people rose up as from the sleep of death, and rushed to the strife of blood; deeming it more glorious to die instantly as freemen, than desirable to live one hour as slaves. They were few in number—poor in resources; but the honest conviction that Truth, Justice and Right were on their side, made them invincible.

We have met together for the achievement of an enterprise, without which that of our fathers is incomplete; and which, for its magnitude, solemnity, and probable results upon the destiny of the world, as far transcends theirs as moral truth does physical force.

In purity of motive, in earnestness of zeal, in decision of purpose, in intrepidity of action, in steadfastness of faith, in sincerity of spirit, we would not be inferior to them.

Their principles led them to wage war against their oppressors, and to spill human blood like water, in order to be free.

Ours forbid the doing of evil that good may come, and lead us to reject, and to entreat the oppressed to reject, the use of all carnal weapons for deliverance from bondage; relying solely upon those which are spiritual, and mighty through God to the pulling down of strong holds.

Their measures were physical resistance—the marshalling in arms—the hostile array—the mortal encounter. Ours shall be such only as the opposition of moral purity to moral corruption—the destruction of error by the potency of truth—the overthrow of prejudice by the power of love—and the abolition of slavery by the spirit of repentance.

emancipation and equal rights for African Americans. Although he and his former AASS colleagues remained in agreement on many points, there was also considerable mutual antagonism. Chances for reconciliation among them diminished in 1842, when Garrison began to call on the people of the North to dissolve the union. He argued that it was northern support that kept slavery in existence in the South, implying that, when the North withdrew its support through disunion, the slaves could free themselves. His abolitionist critics responded that disunion was tantamount to the North's divorcing itself from the slavery issue.

When the South, rather than the North, initiated disunion in 1860 and 1861, however, changing circumstances caused Garrison to draw back from some of his more radical positions. He compromised his pacifism and his opposition to party politics by supporting Republican president Abraham Lincoln's war to preserve the union and free the slaves. After the war ended successfully for the North and slavery was formally abolished by the Thirteenth Amendment on December 18, 1865, Garrison, old, tired, and seeking vindication, announced that his work was done—although it was clear that black equality had not been achieved with the end of slavery. The last issue of *The Liberator* rolled off its press on December 29, 1865.

SIGNIFICANCE

Publication of abolitionist William Lloyd Garrison's weekly newspaper, *The Liberator*, helped to transform the antislavery movement in the United States. It symbolized the beginning of a radical effort to abolish slavery and secure equal rights for African Americans throughout the country. Garrison stood out as one of the most uncompromising advocates of emancipation. Early in his career, he was often vilified and sometimes even physically attacked. However, with the achievement of emancipation in 1865, Garrison was seen as a prophetic hero, and he is now regarded as one of the most influential antislavery voices of the nineteenth century.

—*Stanley Harrold*

See also: Social Reform Movement; c. 1830-1865: Southerners Advance Proslavery Arguments; Turner Launches Slave Insurrection; American Anti-Slavery Society Is Founded; Douglass Launches *The North Star*; Underground Railroad Flourishes; Stowe Publishes *Uncle Tom's Cabin*; Thirteenth Amendment Is Ratified.

Related articles in *Great Lives from History: The Nineteenth Century, 1801-1900:* Mary Ann Shadd Cary; Frederick Douglass; Charlotte Forten; William Lloyd Garrison; Sarah and Angelina Grimké.

AMERICAN ANTI-SLAVERY SOCIETY IS FOUNDED

December, 1833

The foundation of the American Anti-Slavery Society reflected a new and more militant trend in the abolitionist movement, away from nonviolent gradualism and toward radical immediatism.

Locale: Philadelphia, Pennsylvania
Categories: Human rights; civil rights and liberties; organizations and institutions

KEY FIGURES

Elizur Wright (1804-1885), one of the founders of the American Anti-Slavery Society
Arthur Tappan (1786-1865), first president of the American Anti-Slavery Society
Lewis Tappan (1788-1873), leader of church-oriented abolitionists
William Lloyd Garrison (1805-1879), abolitionist leader and editor of *The Liberator*

Frederick Douglass (1817?-1895), former slave and the editor of *The North Star*, an abolitionist paper
Sojourner Truth (c. 1797-1883), former slave, abolitionist, and a compelling orator
Harriet Tubman (c. 1820-1913), fugitive slave and leading black abolitionist
James Gillespie Birney (1792-1857), American antislavery leader and presidential candidate for the Liberty Party
Theodore Dwight Weld (1803-1895), American Anti-Slavery Society agent

SUMMARY OF EVENT

The tumult of reform and revivalism that swept over the northern and western areas of the United States during the 1830's and 1840's produced a number of voluntary associations and auxiliaries. Perhaps the most important of these was the American Anti-Slavery Society (AASS), which was founded by Elizur Wright and others in December, 1833. Sixty delegates gathered in Philadelphia to form the national organization, electing Arthur Tappan, a wealthy New York businessman, as president.

They also approved a Declaration of Sentiments, drawn up by William Lloyd Garrison, Samuel May, and John Greenleaf Whittier, that called for immediate, total, and uncompensated abolition of slavery through moral and political action. In signing the declaration, the delegates pledged themselves to do all that in us lies, consisting with this declaration of our principles, to overthrow the most execrable system of slavery that has ever been witnessed upon earth . . .and to secure to the colored population of the United States, all the rights and privileges which belong to them as men and Americans.

Like other reform societies of the day, the AASS organized a system of state and local auxiliaries, sent out agents to convert people to its views, and published pamphlets and journals supporting its position. The society grew rapidly. By 1838, it claimed 250,000 members and 1,350 auxiliaries.

Before the 1830's, most opponents of slavery advocated moderate methods such as gradual and "compensated" emancipation—which would have granted remunerations to former slave owners.

Some abolitionists favored resettlement of free African Americans to Liberia in West Africa by the American Colonization Society, which had been founded in 1817. The formation of a national organization based on the principle of immediatism, or immediate and total emancipation, symbolized the new phase that antislavery agitation entered during the early 1830's—radical, uncompromising, and intensely moralistic.

The shift to immediatism had several causes, including the failure of moderate methods; the example of the British, who abolished slavery in their empire in 1833; and, probably most important, evangelical religion. Abolitionists of the 1830's inherited from earlier antislavery reformers the notion that slavery was a sin. This notion, coupled with the contemporaneous evangelical doctrine of immediate repentance, shaped the abolitionist doctrine of immediate emancipation. Given the influence of evangelical doctrines and methods, it is not surprising that abolitionists emphasized moral suasion over political methods.

The demand for immediate emancipation was a purely moral demand: Abolitionists were calling for immediate repentance of the sin of slavery, an action that they believed would necessarily lead to emancipation itself. They hoped to persuade people to emancipate the slaves voluntarily and to form a conviction of guilt as participants in the national sin of slavery. In effect, abolitionists were working for nothing less than a total moral reformation.

The AASS represented the union of two centers of radical abolitionism, one in Boston, the other based around Cincinnati. William Lloyd Garrison, the key figure among New England abolitionists, began publishing *The Liberator* in 1831 and soon organized the New England Anti-Slavery Society, based on the principle of immediate abolition. Garrisonian abolitionists galvanized antislavery sentiment in the Northeast, where they were later aided by the New York Anti-Slavery Society, which was founded by William Jay, William Goodell, and brothers Lewis and Arthur Tappan in 1834. Meanwhile, the West also was shifting from gradualism and colonization to radical abolitionism. In the West, Western Reserve College and Lane Seminary were seedbeds for the doctrine of immediate emancipation. Theodore Dwight Weld, a young man who had been converted to evangelical Christianity by Charles Grandison Finney, organized a group of antislavery agents known as the Seventy, who preached the gospel of immediatism throughout the Midwest.

Although leadership in the antislavery movement remained predominantly white, free African Americans were a significant vital force in the movement as well. Prior to 1800, the Free African Society of Philadelphia and black spokespersons such as astronomer Benjamin Banneker and church leader Richard Allen had denounced slavery in the harshest terms. By 1830, fifty black-organized antislavery societies existed, and African Americans contributed to the formation of the AASS in 1833. Black orators, especially escaped slaves such as Frederick Douglass and Sojourner Truth, moved large audiences with their impassioned and electrifying oratory.

African Americans also helped run the Underground Railroad, through which Harriet Tubman alone led more than three hundred slaves to freedom. Generally, African American abolitionists shared the nonviolent philosophy of the Garrisonians, but black anger often flared because of the racism they found within the antislavery ranks. Influenced by tactical and race considerations, white abolitionist leaders such as Garrison and Weld limited their African American counterparts to peripheral roles or excluded them from local organizations. Discriminatory policies within the AASS glaringly contradicted the organization's egalitarian rhetoric.

Declaration of the National Anti-Slavery Convention

In addition to a manifesto, the American Anti-Slavery Society, founded by abolitionists in December, 1833, in Philadelphia, articulated its political position with its Declaration of Sentiments, excerpted here.

We have met together for the achievement of an enterprise, without which, that of our fathers is incomplete, and which, for its magnitude, solemnity, and probable results upon the destiny of the world, as far transcends theirs, as moral truth does physical force.

In purity of motive, in earnestness of zeal, in decision of purpose, in intrepidity of action, in steadfastness of faith, in sincerity of spirit, we would not be inferior to them. . . .

Their grievances, great as they were, were trifling in comparison with the wrongs and sufferings of those for whom we plead. Our [founding] fathers were never slaves—never bought and sold like cattle—never shut out from the light of knowledge and religion—never subjected to the lash of brutal taskmasters.

But those, for whose emancipation we are striving,—constituting at the present time at least one-sixth part of our countrymen,—are recognized by the laws, and treated by their fellow beings, as marketable commodities—as goods and chattels—as brute beasts;—are plundered daily of the fruits of their toil without redress;—really enjoy no constitutional nor legal protection from licentious and murderous outrages upon their persons;—are ruthlessly torn asunder—the tender babe from the arms of its frantic mother—the heart-broken wife from her weeping husband—at the caprice or pleasure of irresponsible tyrants;—and, for the crime of having a dark complexion, suffer the pangs of hunger, the infliction of stripes, and the ignominy of brutal servitude. They are kept in heathenish darkness by laws expressly enacted to make their instruction a criminal offence.

These are the prominent circumstances in the condition of more than two millions of our people, the proof of which may be found in thousands of indisputable facts, and in the laws of the slaveholding States.

Hence we maintain—That, in view of the civil and religious privileges of this nation, the guilt of its oppression is unequalled by any other on the face of the earth;—and, therefore, That it is bound to repent instantly, to undo the heavy burden, to break every yoke, and to let the oppressed go free.

. . .

Source: William Lloyd Garrison, "Declaration of Sentiments" (December 14, 1833).

SIGNIFICANCE

The late 1830's marked the high point of the movement for immediate abolition through moral suasion. Abolitionism, like other crusades of the time, was hard hit by the Panic of 1837, which reduced funds and distracted attention away from reform.

At the same time, abolitionists faced an internal challenge as the AASS divided into radicals and moderates. One issue causing the split was women's rights. Moderate abolitionists tolerated and even welcomed women in the society, so long as their activities were confined to forming auxiliary societies, raising money, and circulating petitions.

They refused, however, the request that women be allowed to speak in public on behalf of abolitionism or to help shape the AASS's policies. They also wanted to prevent abolitionism from being distracted or diluted by involvement with any other secondary reform. At the Anti-Slavery Convention of 1840, Garrison and a group of radical followers used the issue of women's rights to capture the organization for themselves. When they succeeded in appointing a woman to the society's business committee, moderates and conservatives seceded and formed another organization, the American and Foreign Anti-Slavery Society.

Another issue that divided abolitionist ranks was that of political action. Some abolitionists, convinced that political action, not merely moral suasion, was necessary to effect emancipation, formed the Liberty Party in 1840 and nominated James Gillespie Birney for president of the United States. During the 1840's and 1850's, a small group of abolitionists, some of them militant "come-outers" such as Garrison and Wendell Phillips, continued to rely on moral suasion. The majority of abolitionists, however, moved gradually into the political arena, where they became involved in the Free-Soil movement and other aspects of the sectional conflict leading to the Civil War (1861-1865).

—Anne C. Loveland, updated by Sudipta Das

See also: Congress Bans Importation of African Slaves; African Methodist Episcopal Church Is Founded; Social Reform Movement; Southerners Advance Proslavery Arguments; Garrison Begins

Publishing *The Liberator*; Turner Launches Slave Insurrection; *Amistad* Slave Revolt; Douglass Launches *The North Star*; Underground Railroad Flourishes; Stowe Publishes *Uncle Tom's Cabin*; National Council of Colored People Is Founded; Last Slave Ship Docks at Mobile; Thirteenth Amendment Is Ratified.

Related articles in *Great Lives from History: The Nineteenth Century, 1801-1900:* Frederick Douglass; William Lloyd Garrison; Sojourner Truth; Harriet Tubman.

TEXAS REVOLUTION

October 2, 1835-April 21, 1836

American settlers in Texas fought a revolutionary war against newly independent Mexico, partly in order to preserve slavery, which was illegal under Mexican law. After winning their independence from Mexico, the Texans maintained their autonomy for only a decade before they sought annexation by the United States.

Locale: Texas

Categories: Wars, uprisings, and civil unrest; government and politics; expansion and land acquisition; colonization

KEY FIGURES

Stephen Fuller Austin (1793-1836), American military leader, *empresario*, and politician

Sam Houston (1793-1863), first president of the Republic of Texas, 1836-1838 and 1841-1844, and later U.S. senator, 1846-1859, and governor of Texas, 1859-1861

Antonio López de Santa Anna (1794-1876), Mexican general, president of Mexico, 1833-1836, 1847-1848, and 1853-1855, and dictator of Mexico, 1844-1845

Manuel de Mier y Teran (1789-1832), Mexican general who recommended limiting U.S. influence in Texas

José Antonio Navarro (1795-1871), Tejano leader jailed by Santa Anna for treason

William Barret Travis (1809-1836), Texan commander of the Alamo

Haden Edwards (fl. early nineteenth century) and *Benjamin Edwards* (fl. early nineteenth century), leaders of the abortive Fredonian Republic

SUMMARY OF EVENT

The movement of Euro-Americans into Texas is usually dated from 1821, when Spanish authorities granted Moses Austin permission to colonize a large tract of largely unpopulated land. Austin's plea for the grant was based in part upon his claim to Spanish citizenship by reason of his previous residence in Louisiana. Moses Austin's death in Missouri the same year and the creation of an independent Mexico failed to stop the colonization project. Austin's son, Stephen Fuller Austin, took over and spent a year in Mexico City persuading the new authorities that his claim should be accepted. When additional grants were made by the provincial government, Austin's colonization scheme prospered, as did those of other *empresarios*, or land contractors, who had received grants. Euro-American settlers from the United States, sometimes accompanied by their slaves, soon represented a large majority of the people of Texas.

Austin worked in harmony with officials of the province of Texas-Coahuila for several years. Slavery was opposed by Mexican officials, but the province of Texas-Coahuila recognized labor contracts that made indentured servants of the slaves. All settlers were required to be Roman Catholics, but they were not required to attend church services. The *empresario* settlers were given such generous terms for acquiring land that they usually sided with the government against people from the United States who were settling illegally in the eastern part of the province. It was with Austin's backing, for example, that the Fredonian Rebellion of 1826, led by the brothers Haden Edwards and Benjamin Edwards, was put down.

The rapid growth of the Euro-American population in Texas created uneasiness among many Mexican officials.

The frequent incidents between Texan and Mexican officials, especially in eastern Texas, were viewed with alarm; the attempts of Presidents John Quincy Adams and Andrew Jackson to acquire all or part of Texas were greeted with hostility. General Manuel de Mier y Teran proposed a plan to save Texas from being overrun by Euro-Americans. Mier y Teran called for placing more Mexican troops in the northern provinces, settling more

Mexicans and Europeans in the area, and increasing coastal trade between Texas and the rest of Mexico.

The Colonization Law of April 6, 1830, adopted Mier y Teran's suggestions and forbade further immigration from the United States. The plan to attract more Mexicans and increase commerce with Texas failed to materialize, however, and the limiting of legal immigration from the United States served only to restrict immigration to illegal settlers who had no vested interest in supporting the Mexican government.

The military occupation of Texas was the only part of Mier y Teran's plan to be realized, and it only increased the friction between the government and the settlers. The Texans looked to the presumably liberal revolutionary forces of Antonio López de Santa Anna for relief, and when he came to power, they held a convention at San Felipe in April, 1833, to make plans to petition the new government for the redress of their grievances. Austin was commissioned to present the new government with their requests, including the separation of Texas from Coahuila and the liberalization of the laws governing immigration and import controls. Austin journeyed to Mexico City, where the Mexican congress agreed to repeal the North American immigration exclusion. Austin, however, was arrested during his return trip on the strength of a letter he had written that appeared to advise the Texans to establish a separate state. He was jailed for two years and could not return to Texas until September 1, 1835.

During Austin's absence, the provincial government of Texas-Coahuila made a number of concessions to the Texans, but Santa Anna's federal government was moving to centralize its authority. Although most Texans disapproved of the seizure of the Anahuac Garrison on June 30, 1835, by a group led by William Barret Travis, they were concerned about the apparent intention of the Mexican government to send a greater number of troops to Texas. The Texans responded by calling conventions on August 15 at Columbia and on October 15 at San Felipe. Meanwhile, the federal government issued an order for the Texans to return cannons that had been given to them by Mexico for defense against Native Americans.

One such cannon was located at Gonzales, and a small detachment of Mexican soldiers was sent to retrieve it. The Texans refused the soldiers, who were temporarily trapped on the other side of a rain-swollen river from Gonzales, and they buried their cannon rather than ceding it. Both sides summoned reinforcements, and in

the early morning hours of October 2, 1835, the Texans attacked the Mexican position, firing the first shots of the Texas Revolution. Later in that same month, Austin helped create a provisional government and issued a call to the Texans for war against Mexico.

Not all Texans were committed to the call to arms, however, and opposition increased during the nearly seven-month war. The mainly Irish settlers in the San Patricio region joined forces with the Mexican army and fought against the rebels at Fort Lipantitlán on November 5. Tejanos, or native-born Texans of Hispanic descent, were divided in their loyalties: Some were centralists; others supported the rebel forces; and still others tried, largely without success, to remain neutral. This split in allegiances made the Texas revolution a civil war in the truest sense, pitting family member against family member. José Antonio Navarro, a hero to many latterday Texans, supported the rebels, while his brother Ángel maintained his support for Mexico.

Many Euro-Americans also attempted to remain neutral during the spring of 1836. Although they did not support the centralists, many did avoid recruitment into the armed forces. Personal and family protection was their motivating force. Of the few Euro-Americans who supported the centralist cause, most were older and had resided in Texas for more than ten years. There is little evidence that they were very active during the war.

The vast majority of Tejanos who supported the rebel cause were from San Antonio. Their knowledge of the area proved beneficial to the rebels. The effects of the war on Tejanos, however, were devastating. After their homes and farms were ransacked and their supplies used to feed and equip the Texas armies, their initial support for the rebellion faded. Most received no compensation for their sacrifices during the war.

On February 23, 1836, Santa Anna and four thousand troops laid siege to the Alamo. The 187 men inside, mainly newcomers from the United States, held out until March 6, when the garrison, commanded by Travis and including David Crockett and James Bowie, was assaulted and wiped out. At Goliad, three hundred defenders under James Fannin surrendered and were massacred by the Mexican army on March 27.

The delegates who met on March 1, 1836, in Washington, Texas, knew of the siege of the Alamo. Continuing their pattern of following the revolutionary example of the United States, they issued a declaration of independence on March 2 and subsequently adopted a constitution. The siege at the Alamo gave Commander in

Chief Sam Houston time to assemble an army. Houston avoided a fight for weeks before surprising Santa Anna's divided army on the west bank of the San Jacinto River near Galveston Bay on April 21, 1836. The Texans defeated twelve hundred Mexicans with their force of eight hundred. Santa Anna initially escaped but was captured the next day. The Texas Revolution was over.

Significance

Before he was released, Santa Anna signed the Treaties of Velasco on May 14, 1836. He pledged to lobby Mexico to secure the independence of Texas, but the Mexican congress disavowed his actions. The Mexican army, however, quickly left Texas and made no serious attempt to regain control. Texas was allowed to become an independent republic by default. Sam Houston was elected president of the Republic of Texas on October 22, 1836. Houston and most Texans were interested in joining the United States, but for diplomatic and domestic reasons, annexation was not accomplished for almost a decade.

—*Mark A. Plummer, updated by Pamela Hayes-Bohanan*

Related articles in *Great Lives from History: The Nineteenth Century, 1801-1900:* John Quincy Adams; Stephen Fuller Austin; David Crockett; Sam Houston; Andrew Jackson; Antonio López de Santa Anna.

AMISTAD Slave Revolt

July 2, 1839

After seizing control of a Spanish ship that was illegally transporting them as slaves, a group of Africans found refuge in New England, only to be prosecuted by the federal government as mutineers.

With the support of abolitionists and John Quincy Adams, they were eventually vindicated by the U.S. Supreme Court, by which time their case had become a national cause célèbre.

Also known as: *Amistad* Mutiny; Case of the African Captives
Locale: Off Cuban coast
Categories: Diplomacy and international relations; wars, uprisings, and civil unrest; civil rights and liberties

Key Figures

Joseph Cinqué (c. 1811-c. 1879), charismatic leader of the captive Africans
Roger Sherman Baldwin (1793-1863), American chief counsel for the Africans
John Quincy Adams (1767-1848), former U.S. president, 1825-1829, who argued the Africans' case before the Supreme Court
José Ruiz (fl. nineteenth century), Cuban who purchased Africans who had been illegally processed as slaves

Death of Capt. Ferrer, the Captain of the Amistad, July, 1839.

Amistad revolt

Lewis Tappan (1788-1873), American abolitionist leader who rallied support for the captured Africans
Martin Van Buren (1782-1862), president of the United States, 1837-1841
Joseph Story (1779-1845), associate justice of the U.S. Supreme Court, 1812-1845

Summary of Event

Under the terms of an 1817 treaty between Great Britain and Spain, all African slave trading was to end by 1820. However, enforcement of the treaty was not adequate to deter many fortune seekers, and a highly lucrative covert slave trade continued to operate, most notably between Africa and Cuba.

In April, 1839, a Portuguese slave ship left West Africa bound for Havana filled with more than five hundred illegally purchased Africans, mostly members of the Mendi society. After Middle Passage voyages that lasted two months and killed approximately one-third of the captive Africans, the ship anchored offshore of Havana and the surviving human cargo was brought to land after dark. Cuban colonial officials receiving kickbacks provided paperwork declaring these Africans to be *ladinos*—the term for slaves who had resided in Cuba before 1820. Slaves with designation could be legally sold.

Within a few days, a trader named José Ruiz purchased forty-nine of the African men, and Pedro Montes bought three girls and one boy. The illegally sold captives were then loaded onto the Spanish schooner *Amistad*, which set sail for Puerto Príncipe, Cuba, a few days' sailing away. Unable to communicate with the ships Spanish-speaking owners and crew, the captives became convinced that they were to be eaten.

On July 2, the third night out, one of the Africans, Joseph Cinqué, picked the lock on his iron collar and broke into the ship's cargo hold, where he and others found cane knives. The Africans then took control of the ship, killing the captain and the cook. Two other crew members disappeared; they may have jumped overboard. Ruiz, Montes, and Antonio, the captain's slave cabin boy, were spared. The Africans demanded to be taken to Sierra Leone, the West African colony that Great Britain had created expressly for the purpose of repatriating recaptured West African slaves. Over the next two months, Ruiz and Montes pretended to comply with the Africans' demand. During the day, they sailed southeast, occasionally landing to scavenge for food and water, but at night they headed north and northeast, in the hope of finding help. Knowing nothing about oceanic navigation, the Africans did not realize they were being duped.

Meanwhile, the schooner slowly tacked up the eastern seaboard of the United States. It was often sighted, and its increasingly decrepit condition and the presence of many black on its decks aroused suspicion. During one of its stops to obtain food off the coast of Long Island, the *Amistad* came to the attention of the U.S. naval brig *Washington*, whose captain, Thomas Gedney, ordered the schooner boarded. The thirty-nine surviving slaves, by then almost starved and unable to resist, were taken into custody.

The Africans were rescued from their physical ordeal, only to begin a nightmarish legal ordeal. After being taken ashore in the United States, Ruiz and Montes filed suits to have their slave property returned to them.

Captain Gedney claimed salvage rights to the *Amistad* and its cargo, including the slaves. The Spanish government demanded the fugitives be handed over to it, and U.S. abolitionists clamored for the Africans to be set free.

The case was a complicated one. Although the United States and Great Britain had outlawed the African slave trade, slavery was legal in Cuba, and Ruiz and Montes had paperwork documenting their ownership of their ship's African passengers. Moreover, the federal government had to consider its treaty obligations with the government of Spain, which owned Cuba, to determine whether it should recognize Spanish property rights to the Africans. Precedents from an 1825 incident with the Spanish slave ship *Antelope* also had to be analyzed. Most important, perhaps, the *Amistad* affair carried grave implications for the slavery issue in the United States—and President Martin Van Buren hoped to avoid that issue in the reelection contest that he would face the following year, as he knew that his success depended on maintaining his coalition of northern and southern supporters.

Newspapers across the land kept an interested public informed of the status of the *Amistad* case. For the most part, northerners were sympathetic toward the Africans, while southerners believed they should be returned to the Spanish government to be tried for piracy and murder.

The affair probably would have been handled quietly and quickly had not the abolitionists recognized in it the potential to raise the public's awareness of the moral and legal issues at stake in the slavery question. They saw in this case an opportunity to argue the principle of natural law, which they felt entitled every person, regardless of color, to liberty. The case also provided them a chance to test the degree to which people of color were protected by the law. Abolitionists and other opponents of slavery quickly formed the *Amistad* Committee, made up of Simeon Jocelyn, Joshua Leavitt, and Lewis Tappan, to raise money for legal counsel and to appeal to President Van Buren to allow the case to be decided by the U.S. court system, rather than turning the prisoners over to the Spanish government. The committee acquired the legal services of Roger Sherman Baldwin, Seth Staples, and Theodore Sedgwick. They also sought native Africans who could communicate with the *Amistad* captives, as depositions had been given only by the Spaniards and the ship's cabin boy. Eventually they engaged the services of James Covey, a West African serving aboard a British naval vessel who could speak the Mendi language. Covey was allowed to leave his naval duties indefinitely in order to serve as interpreter for the Africans.

The legal proceedings began in mid-September, 1839, in the U.S. Circuit Court convened in Hartford, Connecticut. Amid a complex maze of issues dealing with salvage rights, international law, jurisdiction disputes, and legal definitions of property and personhood, the case worked its way over the next eighteen months from circuit court to district court, back to the circuit court and finally to the U.S. Supreme Court. The abolitionists made sure that the case stayed before the public and even filed assault-and-battery and illegal-imprisonment suits against Montes and Ruiz on behalf of several of the Africans to generate further attention. Although ambivalent in its responses to the legal and moral questions, the public stayed interested. People even paid admission to see the Africans, who were eventually allowed to receive visitors, enjoy outdoor exercise, and take English lessons and religious instruction.

The case also excited international interest, and the cause of the abolitionists was substantially aided when Dr. Richard Robert Madden, a British official living in Havana, traveled more than one thousand miles to give a moving and informed deposition concerning the state of the slave trade in Cuba. He spelled out the means and extent of illegal activities and clarified the status of *ladinos*. He also stated that the children on board the *Amistad* were without doubt too young to be pre-1820 Cuban residents, and that he strongly believed that all the *Amistad* captives were in fact *bozales*—newly imported Africans, not *ladinos*.

In January, 1840, Judge Andrew T. Judson of the U.S. District Court of Connecticut ruled that the Africans could not be counted as property in the calculation of salvage value and that they could not legally be held as slaves because their initial purchase had been

illegal. The government then appealed the case, but a few months later, Judge Smith Thompson of the U.S. Circuit Court concurred in Judson's decision.

The government again appealed, and the case came before the U.S. Supreme Court in early 1841. Former U.S. president John Quincy Adams argued passionately on behalf of the defendants. On March 9, 1841, the Supreme Court ruled in the Africans' favor. In an opinion written by Associate Justice Joseph Story, the Court ruled that Africans brought to Cuba illegally were not property, that as illegally held free men they had a right to mutiny, and that they should therefore be released. The Africans, who by now could speak English, spent the next months continuing their religious instruction and going to exhibitions arranged by abolitionists to raise money for their return voyage to Africa. In November, 1841, they sailed to Sierra Leone, accompanied by a small group of New England missionaries.

SIGNIFICANCE

The *Amistad* decision was a great victory for abolitionists and raised the public's awareness of the slavery issue. The case fed secessionist sentiments in the southern states but helped opponents of slavery focus on legal attacks against the institution.

—*Grace McEntee*

See also: Congress Bans Importation of African Slaves; Turner Launches Slave Insurrection; American Anti-Slavery Society Is Founded; Last Slave Ship Docks at Mobile.

Related articles in *Great Lives from History: The Nineteenth Century, 1801-1900:* John Quincy Adams; William Cullen Bryant; Joseph Story; Martin Van Buren.

GROVES V. SLAUGHTER

March 10, 1841

The Supreme Court held that an amendment to the Mississippi state constitution that banned bringing slaves into the state for sale was not valid in the absence of legislation to enforce it, but the majority could not agree on the constitutional issues of the case.

The Case: U.S. Supreme Court ruling on slavery and interstate commerce

The state of Mississippi added a constitutional prohibition against the importing of slaves into the state for sale in 1832 but did not enact any legislation to enforce the amendment. A seller of slaves argued that the prohibition was void because it conflicted with federal authority over interstate commerce. The Supreme Court, in a 5-2 majority decision, held that the amendment to the Mississippi constitution was not binding because it was not implemented by legislation. By ruling that the amendment was not self-executing, the Court did not resolve the explosive issue of whether the federal government or the states had control over the slave trade. In concurring opinions, Justice John McLean of Ohio wrote that the federal government had jurisdiction over slaves transported in interstate commerce, and Chief Justice Roger Brooke Taney insisted that states had control of all questions relating to slavery and African Americans. The deep divisions on the Court reflected the growing sectional controversy in the country.

—*Thomas Tandy Lewis*

See also: Slavery; Slavery and race relations; Slavery and the justice system

LOMBARD STREET RACE RIOT OF 1842

August 1-3, 1842

The Lombard Street race riot of 1842 was one of a series of racially-motivated riots, marches, and demonstrations that occurred in Pennsylvania in the 1830s and 40s due to a number of coinciding factors that resulted in rapid changes to the city's demographics in many urban neighborhoods.

Identification: Race riot that occurred in Philadelphia, Pennsylvania in 1842

The Lombard Street race riot of 1842 was one of numerous violent clashes between African Americans and white residents of Philadelphia, Pennsylvania during the 1930s and 40s due to a number of interrelated factors including the rapid growth of the city's African American population, the local growth of the city's abolitionist movement, and competition between Irish and African Americans (both marginalized minorities at the time) for jobs. The riot occurred when a largely Irish mob attacked a parade commemorating the anniversary of the abolition of slavery in the West Indies. The Irish mob attacked the parade at Lombard and 4th Street, physically attacking marchers and reportedly looting black-owned homes in the area. Over the course of the day, other white residents of the community joined in the attack, decimating African American property along the street and injuring hundreds of residents. The riot continued for three days during which time the mob burned down the Second African Presbyterian Church and the Smith's Hall building on Lombard, both of which were known for hosting abolitionist meetings. The riot culminated when the mob reached the home of prominent African American abolitionist Robert Purvis, at 9th Street and Lombard, and a white Catholic priest intervened, stopping the mob before they attacked Purvis. In 2005, the Pennsylvania Historical Commission erected a sign on the corner of Sixth and Lombard Street to commemorate the event.

—*Micah Issitt*

MUNCY ABOLITIONIST RIOT OF 1842

April 1842

White residents of Muncy, Pennsylvania attack a school house where a local speaker had been invited to deliver an abolitionist lecture. Though 13 men were charged for participating in the attack, Pennsylvania governor David Rittenhouse Porter pardoned the participants.

Identification: Race riot that occurred in Muncy, Pennsylvania in 1842 with white-pro-slavery rioters attacking the home of an abolitionist Quaker.

The town of Muncy, Pennsylvania, was a gathering place for abolitionists in the mid 1800s, largely due to the region's large Quaker population, as the Quakers were early supporters of abolition and women's rights. However, the white majority in surrounding communities and the local Pennsylvania Dutch were largely opposed to abolition. Quaker Enos Hawley, a local tanner and prominent citizen, invited an unidentified abolitionist speaker to give a speech at the local schoolhouse.

During the speech, a group of at least 18 white men attacked the schoolhouse, pelting the building with rocks and other objects. Hawley and the speaker were reportedly injured and fled to Hawley's house where the rioters continued to attack, damaging Hawley's home until police arrived and arrested the rioters.

During the ensuing trial, local abolitionist Abraham Updegraff argued with fellow jurors until the group agreed to formally convict 13 of the 18 men arrested for participating in the attack. However, days after the jury voted to convict, Pennsylvania Governor David Rittenhouse Porter pardoned the men convicted in the case, releasing a statement asserting that the men had been convicted because of political reasons rather than on the merits of their crimes and that the speaker had incited the incident by delivering a speech that offended the morality of the citizens of the community.

—*Micah Issitt*

First Minstrel Shows

February 6, 1843

A form of musical theater, minstrelsy is one of the earliest examples of authentic American popular culture. It mirrored that culture's conflicting attitudes toward race, social class, and gender.

Locale: New York, New York
Categories: Theater; music

Key Figures

Thomas Dartmouth Rice (1808-1860), an original Virginia Minstrel who created the "Jim Crow" character
Dan Emmett (1815-1904), composer and violinist
Edwin Pearce Christy (1815-1862), leader of the Christy Minstrels
George Washington Dixon (1801?-1861), traveling actor associated with the blackface character Zip Coon
Frank Brower (1823-1874), *William Whitlock* (1813-1878), and *Richard Ward Pelham* (1815-1856), members of the original Virginia Minstrels

Summary of Event

"Blacking up" was a theatrical practice in which a white actor painted his face black (usually using burnt cork mixed with water or oil) to masquerade as an African American on stage. This was common American theatrical practice long before the minstrel shows. In legitimate theater productions of *Othello, the Moor of Venice* (pr. 1604, rev. 1623), for example, the title role was usually played by a white actor in so-called blackface. In mid-nineteenth century America, actors who had blacked up as individual entertainers joined forces to create a new form of entertainment. These early "minstrel shows" became immensely popular, appealing to all segments of the public as family entertainment.

The United States at mid-century had yet to produce authentic American entertainment, relying on British and European plays and operas to fill its theaters. Social class was rigidly defined by seating spaces in the theater, with the educated, upper-class audience in the more expensive tiers and the commoners in the cheaper seats in the pit or the upper gallery. Rowdiness, even at times rioting, was not unusual. The gallery audience might yell and throw garbage at the actors to express disapproval. Theater was a profitable business, however, and theater owners, managers, and actors had a strong incentive to give the audience what it wanted. White performers who blacked up billed themselves as "Ethiopian Delineators."

One of themes then popular with audiences was the mythical representation of the lives of "happy darkies" on a southern plantation. Individual entertainers presented their routines in variety shows, circuses, or between acts of both comedies and serious dramas, performing songs and dances representing stereotypes of southern African Americans. Parodies of other ethnic groups, especially German and Irish immigrants, were also common. Demeaning characterizations of women were also presented by the male entertainers. Characterizations of African Americans were the most frequently performed. Some of these routines were probably authentic imitations of the speech and physical characteristics of African Americans by actors who had studied their material. Others were grotesque caricatures of popular stereotypes with no direct basis in reality. Still others were a mixture of songs or dances of European origin with black folk material.

The first minstrel show was performed in New York City in February, 1843. Four performers calling themselves the Virginia Minstrels—Frank Brower, Dan Emmett, Richard Ward Pelham, and William

Whitlock—originated this popular form of entertainment that would create an insatiable demand for minstrel shows. The choice of the term "minstrel" was meant to indicate that the show was respectable family entertainment, with an emphasis on the musical quality of the performance. Although the Virginia Minstrels disbanded after a tour of Europe later that year, other actors were quick to pick up on the public's interest in the new form, and they organized themselves into minstrel troupes. The Christy Minstrels, founded by Edwin Pearce Christy, were originally from Buffalo, New York. They later became one of the most popular minstrel troupes and owned their own theater in New York City.

The format of these early shows was a loose compilation of variety acts including sentimental ballads and love songs, sometimes in whiteface; instrumental selections on violin and banjo; parodies of operas, lectures, and sermons; and rapid-fire comic dialogues. All performers were male. There was constant motion on stage, with quick changes between acts, and audiences responded enthusiastically to the spontaneity and variety of the performances. Although the minstrel show would become standardized in a three-act formula later in the century, these early shows were highly improvisational One of the most popular performers during the late 1820's, Thomas Dartmouth Rice, originated the "Ethiopian Opera," a series of farcical scripts that featured imitations of "Negro" songs. He created the character of Jim Crow, claiming to have observed an elderly, physically deformed black man dancing in a peculiar jumping motion while singing a song. After his "Jump Jim Crow" was first performed in New York City at the Bowery Theater in 1832, Rice enjoyed a long career performing this routine. "Jim Crow" was widely imitated and became a popular inclusion in many minstrel shows. This song-and-dance routine was probably the source of the name later given to southern segregation laws.

Another character, Zip Coon, the sly, deceptive, urban black man, was popularized by George Washington Dixon, who himself had a long criminal record. In another, more common form, the character of Dandy Jim lampooned the urban African American male, with his dandified clothing and his pretensions to social class and education beyond his means. It is possible that Dandy Jim satirized both black and white men who made a ridiculous spectacle of themselves with their foppish clothes and foolish speeches.

The origin and interpretation of the minstrel material is controversial. Social critics of the early twentieth century, especially African Americans, condemned minstrel shows as grossly prejudiced caricatures of black people. In this view, the popularity of blackface represented the psychological need of white people to reinforce racist stereotypes that supported their feelings of superiority. Late twentieth century historians, while acknowledging the racism embedded in minstrelsy, offered more complex theories as to the source and meaning of that racism and of other elements of minstrelsy.

Playbills, newspapers, and other public records from contemporary sources suggest the beginnings of a popular culture that united working-class Americans against the wealthy elite. The satire of upper-class lectures and sermons given by prominent public figures, as well as the homegrown parodies of European operas that could only be enjoyed by those who could afford expensive theater seats, appealed to working-class audiences, both black and white. In a related interpretation, blacking up could be seen to represent the folk ritual of masquerading as a figure different from one's usual self, a fact that did not eliminate but certainly complicated the racism of the practice.

The popularity of minstrel shows declined toward the end of the nineteenth century. Some critics find a significant difference between the early and later shows. Midcentury minstrelsy showed some sympathy for the evils of slavery, particularly in dramatizing its cruel destruction of family life. However, as the nation moved toward civil war, African Americans, considered a threat to the stability of the white society, were less favorably depicted.

After the U.S. Civil War, black performers began to appear on stage in their own minstrel shows, some, strangely enough, in blackface. Arguably demeaning to the performer, this practice nevertheless offered employment for African American entertainers who had until then been barred from white theaters.

SIGNIFICANCE

The story of American minstrelsy is riddled with controversy. The white entertainers who blacked up to masquerade as African Americans undeniably presented exaggerated physical and mental caricatures of "darkies" that appealed to the lowest instincts of white audiences.

Paradoxically, however, since some authentic elements of black culture reached the stage, the minstrel shows marked the beginnings of what would continue to be the immense contribution of African Americans to the popular culture of the nation. These entertainments may also have represented class distinctions

"Jim Crack Corn: Or, The Blue Tail Fly"

Minstrel shows often featured songs portraying the point of view of happy slaves, portrayed by white men in blackface singing for white audiences. One of the most famous of these songs was "Jim Crack Corn" or "Jimmy Crack Corn," sung by a performer portraying a slave who could eat cracked corn because his master was no longer around to stop him. The following version of this song has been attributed to Dan Emmett and was sung by the Virginia Minstrels in 1846.

When I was young a us'd to wait On Massa and hand him de plate; Pass down the bottle when he git dry, And bresh away de blue tail fly.

CHORUS Jim crack corn I don't care, Jim crack corn I don't care, Jim crack corn I don't care, Old Massa gone away.

Den arter dinner massa sleep, He bid dis nigger vigil keep; An' when he gwine to shut his eye, He tell me watch de blue tail fly.

(CHORUS)

An' when he ride in de arternoon, I foiler wid a hickory broom; De poney being berry shy, When bitten by de blue tail fly.

(CHORUS)

One day he rode aroun' de farm, De flies so numerous dey did swarm; One chance to bite 'im on the thigh, De debble take dat blu tail fly.

(CHORUS)

De poney run, he jump an' pitch, An' tumble massa in de ditch; He died, an' de jury wonder'd why De verdic was de blue tail fly.

(CHORUS)

Dey laid 'im under a 'simmon tree, His epitaph am dar to see: 'Beneath dis stone I'm forced to lie, All by means ob de blue tail fly.' (CHORUS)

Ole massa gone, now let 'im rest, Dey say all tings am for the best; I nebber forget till de day I die, Ole massa an' dat blue tail fly.

Source: Minstrel Songs, Old and New (Boston: Oliver Ditson, 1883).

that complicated the meanings of their racial stereotypes, beginning another tradition in American popular culture that continues into the present: the confusion of race with class.

Minstrel shows, with their controversial content, represented the first uniquely American musical theater to break away from European-dominated culture. If, as the evidence suggests, both black and white audiences enjoyed minstrel shows, they might have found a common bond in mocking the pretensions of wealthy and powerful Americans, creating the beginnings of a distinctive popular culture.

—Marjorie J. Podolsky

Related articles in *Great Lives from History: The Nineteenth Century, 1801-1900:* Paul Laurence Dunbar; Stephen Collins Foster; Adah Isaacs Menken.

DOUGLASS LAUNCHES *THE NORTH STAR*

December 3, 1847

Although Frederick Douglass's first newspaper struggled, it contributed a forceful African American voice to the abolition movement and helped to raise Douglass's stature as a public figure.

Locale: Rochester, New York
Categories: Journalism; civil rights and liberties

KEY FIGURES
Frederick Douglass (1817?-1895), orator, abolitionist, and publisher of *The North Star*
Anna Murray Douglass (1813?-1882), Douglass's first wife
Martin Robison Delaney (1812-1885), coeditor of *The North Star*

Frederick Douglass, c. 1879

William Lloyd Garrison (1805-1879), abolitionist and early mentor to Douglass

Gerrit Smith (1797-1874), financial backer of several of Douglass's newspapers

Elizabeth Cady Stanton (1815-1902), feminist and social reformer

SUMMARY OF EVENT

When the first issue of *The North Star* appeared on December 3, 1847, critics and readers discovered a newspaper that blended sardonic humor with moral urgency, written in a polished style. Some readers, however, were skeptical of editor Frederick Douglass's sophistication.

Fathered by a white man and born to the slave Harriet Bailey in Talbot County, Maryland, Douglass had begun his life as a slave. He had witnessed the full horrors of slavery, the brutal beatings, and even murder. In his teens, he had taught himself to read and write from a discarded speller and copybook and had learned public speaking by imitating orations appearing in *The Columbian Orator*, an abolitionist publication. Indeed, *The Columbian Orator* led to his awareness of the abolitionist movement and influenced his writing style when he later published *The North Star*. After clashing with his master in 1838, Douglass had escaped from Baltimore to New York with Anna Murray, a free black domestic servant. After they were married, they settled in New Bedford, Massachusetts, which offered sanctuary. To prevent recapture, Frederick changed his surname from Bailey to Douglass, in honor of a character in Sir Walter Scott's 1810 poem *The Lady of the Lake*.

Douglass then became active in local abolitionist gatherings and discovered his gift as a compelling speaker who provided firsthand examples of barbaric slavery. He became a favorite on the lecture circuit during the early 1840's. His autobiography, *Narrative of the Life of Frederick Douglass* (1845), sold more than thirty thousand copies over the next five years. Meanwhile, Douglass came under the tutelage of the leading abolitionist of the times, William Lloyd Garrison. From Garrison's abolitionist newspaper, *The Liberator*, Douglass no doubt learned much about newspaper operations.

As Douglass's fame increased, so did his risk of capture as an escaped slave. In 1845, he sailed for England and then went to Scotland and Ireland, where he lectured passionately on the inhumane treatment of slaves in the United States. Moved by his personal plight, his newfound friends arranged to purchase his freedom from his former owner for $711.66. Before returning to the United States in 1847, he also received $2,175 in contributions to finance his own antislavery newspaper.

When Garrison objected to Douglass's starting his own newspaper, the two close friends became estranged; eventually, they became bitter enemies. Douglass sensed that white abolitionists regarded him as a child who needed to be led, and he believed that African Americans must lead to gain respect. He held that his newspaper could create that leadership and help increase self-respect among African Americans. Douglass knew of the hazards in starting an African American newspaper, because about one hundred such papers then existed in the United States, the first having been started in 1827. He located in Rochester, New York, because it had strong antislavery sentiments. Also, by publishing his paper there reduced its competition with Garrison's *Liberator* in Boston and the *National Anti-Slavery Standard* in New York City.

On December 3, 1847, the first issue of *The North Star* appeared. It was a four-page weekly with a subscription cost of two dollars per year. It had a circulation of between two and three thousand copies, and its publishing costs were about eighty dollars per week. It was printed in the first print shop owned by an African American. Douglass chose journalist Martin Robison Delaney as his coeditor, but the two soon clashed over the issue of "colonization."

Colonization was a scheme promoted by the American Colonization Society to resettle former slaves in Africa, rather than integrate them within American society. Delaney supported colonization, and Douglass vigorously opposed it. When a disgusted Delaney left in 1848 to found a colony along West Africa's Niger River, Douglass became sole editor of his paper. He vigorously espoused the principle of integration throughout the rest of his life.

In the first issue of *The North Star*, Douglass urged African Americans to become politically active and pledged that his newspaper would aggressively attack slavery, work to free southern slaves, and promote African American morality and progress. The paper's lead article recounted the convention of "colored people" of 1847, with its primary objectives of abolishing slavery and elevating free African Americans. In subsequent years, *The North Star* dealt with such burning issues as social injustice, inequality, racism, the dangers of drink and dissipation, the benefits of integrated school systems, the elimination of segregated hotels and railroads, the folly of war and capital punishment, the worth of laborers, the imperative need for racial unity among African Americans, and the unfair voting practices designed to handicap African Americans in northern states. *The North Star* came to the defense not only of persecuted African Americans but also of Native Americans, the Irish, and members of other immigrant groups. From its beginnings, *The North Star* lived up to its masthead: Right Is of No Sex—Truth Is of No Color—God Is the Father of Us All, and All We Are Brethren.

Douglass vigorously supported the women's rights movement, linking enslaved women to the abolition movement itself. At the Seneca Falls Convention in 1848, Douglass, one of thirty-two men who attended, spoke and voted in favor of Elizabeth Cady Stanton's Declaration of Sentiments, which demanded equality for women. He effectively used *The North Star* to promote Stanton's feminist cause.

Despite its strong editorial start, *The North Star* foundered financially after six months. Douglass mortgaged his house and used his lecture fees to keep the paper going.

From time to time, he received financial gifts from Gerrit Smith, a philanthropist, reformer, and wealthy New York landowner. In 1851, the two men agreed to merge the financially troubled *North Star* with Smith's struggling *Liberty Party Paper*. Douglass maintained editorial control over the paper while including political news of the Liberty Party. The merger allowed him to broaden his audience to four thousand readers, and he accepted a comfortable subsidy from Smith.

The new effort, *Frederick Douglass' Paper*, appeared in June, 1851, and lasted until 1859. Douglass used the paper to continue his crusades in favor of abolition, racial equality, and women's rights. He also dabbled in the Liberty Party campaigns, endorsing Smith and helping him win a seat in Congress. In 1852, Douglass himself became the first African American nominated for vice president on the Equal Rights Party ticket of 1852.

Recurring financial problems forced Douglass to reduce the size of his paper and to publish it less frequently in 1859. His third effort, *Douglass' Monthly*, which circulated in England as well as in the United States, lasted until 1863—the middle of the Civil War. Like Douglass's first two papers, *Douglass' Monthly* remained a magnet for African American writers and reformers and framed Douglass's own inimitable style and wit as well.

Meanwhile, Douglass actively recruited African American soldiers for the Union during the war. He viewed Abraham Lincoln as the best hope for his race and pressed for the Emancipation Proclamation that Lincoln delivered in 1863. He proposed land reform, federally financed education, and a national association for African Americans. He believed that interracial marriages would someday eliminate racial hatred.

SIGNIFICANCE

After the Civil War, Douglass moved to Washington, D.C. There he published the *New National Era*, focusing on the interests of the newly freed African Americans. During that paper's existence (1870-1873), Douglass editorialized on Reconstruction, the rise of mob lynchings in the South, race relations, politics, labor, and education. From 1873 until his death in 1895, Douglass continued to be heard on the lecture circuit and in leading newspapers.

A self-made man, who rose against great odds from slavery to publisher, race leader, prominent abolitionist, social reformer, and political activist, Douglass is one of the most important African Americans of the nineteenth century and became a powerful symbol in the Civil Rights movement throughout the twentieth century.

—Richard Whitworth

See also: Southerners Advance Proslavery Arguments; Garrison Begins Publishing *The Liberator*; American Anti-Slavery Society Is Founded; Seneca Falls Convention; Underground Railroad Flourishes; Stowe Publishes *Uncle Tom's Cabin*; National Council of Colored People Is Founded; Lincoln Issues the Emancipation Proclamation; Thirteenth Amendment Is Ratified.

Related articles in *Great Lives from History: The Nineteenth Century, 1801-1900:* Mary Ann Shadd Cary; Frederick Douglass; William Lloyd Garrison.

HARRIET TUBMAN ESCAPES TO FREEDOM

1849

Abolitionist

Tubman escaped slavery and then dedicated her life to helping others do the same. Her commitment to freedom fueled an intense passion for the abolitionist movement and led her to serve as a Union Army nurse and spy during the Civil War. She also forged ties with the women's suffrage movement and spoke eloquently in support of women's and African Americans' rights.

Born: c. 1820; Bucktown, Dorchester County, Maryland

Died: March, 10, 1913; Auburn, New York

Also known as: Harriet Ross Tubman; Araminta Ross (birth name); Minty; Moses

Areas of achievement: Abolitionism; Social issues; Women's rights

EARLY LIFE

Harriet Ross Tubman was born Araminta Ross around 1820 to Harriet and Benjamin Ross in Bucktown, Dorchester County, Maryland. She decided to take her mother's name when she was older. Tubman and her eight siblings were born on the plantation of Edward Brodess. She began work as a domestic servant at the age of about six years and also was rented out to other households for the same purpose. She often was severely beaten and poorly treated. As a teenager, she preferred to work in the field, where it was easier to escape the brutality of overbearing mistresses and the unwanted sexual advances of her masters.

Ultimately, field work did not provide Tubman with enough protection from the cruelty of slavery. Between the years of 1834 and 1836, she suffered trauma to her head as a result of being struck by a metal weight. The weight was thrown at an escaping slave by the overseer, and Tubman jumped in the way, attempting to prevent the escapee's capture. The impact of the two-pound metal weight against her head nearly killed her. Her skull was badly crushed, resulting in sleeping spells, headaches, and dizziness that she endured for the rest of her life. However, Tubman claimed that the injury also left her with heightened dreams and prophecies. She said that these visions showed her the future and led her on journeys in which she liberated slaves from the South. Her visions were nurtured by her exposure to evangelical teachings and African-influenced cultural traditions.

After Tubman's injury, no buyer was interested in purchasing or renting her services because she was considered damaged property. Tubman's fear that she might one day be sold to a more abusive master because of her injury fueled her desire to escape. Her first flight took place in 1849. At the time, she was being rented from her master by a man called Doctor Thompson. She had lived on his property for two years with her husband, John Tubman, whom she married in 1844. Although John was a free man, he lived with Tubman in the slave quarters. Even though Tubman did her best to convince her husband to accompany her on the journey, he refused.

LIFE'S WORK

In 1849, Tubman escaped to freedom. She traveled by night, guided only by the North Star, until she reached Philadelphia, a free state. She was aided by abolitionists on the Underground Railroad, who helped her evade capture and identify who would help along the journey. Upon arriving in Philadelphia, however, Tubman found herself confused and saddened. The success of reaching the so-called Promised Land was complicated by a painful realization. She was alone in a strange land without family, friends, or community. While she understood that most of the people she knew did not possess the courage to attempt what she had done, her loneliness prompted her to return and secure the freedom of her family members. She constructed a plan that led her to being called the Moses of her people.

First, Tubman secured employment as a domestic laborer, cooking and cleaning house for northern white women. The money she earned cleaning houses was equally divided between her living expenses and a return trip to Baltimore, Maryland, where she rescued her enslaved sister and her two children. In December of 1850, Tubman, her sister Mary Ann Bowley, and Mary Ann's husband and two children arrived in Philadelphia. Tubman's success in her first venture set the stage for a return a few months later in which she safely delivered her brother and two other men to safety. It was not until the fall of 1851 that she returned to free her husband, John. However, John had remarried and still refused to travel with her. Eager to continue her mission, Tubman abandoned thoughts of helping him and quickly identified a group of slaves who were willing to flee. She also brought this group safely to Philadelphia. Almost from the beginning, Tubman's mission to free slaves reached beyond her own family. From 1851 to 1857, she made at least eleven trips into slave country, and she eventually freed all of her brothers and sisters and her parents during the ten years that she conducted the Underground Railroad.

Tubman viewed the problems facing African Americans, women, and humanity as indelibly intertwined, and her life's work began to reflect this belief. Tubman set about developing relationships with women involved in the suffrage movement, such as Susan B. Anthony, and intensified her relationships with staunch abolitionists such as William Grant Still and John Brown. She believed that the nation could take its greatest strides toward liberation and equality when people—no matter their creed, color, or gender—worked in concert. It was this belief that led to Tubman's decision to assist the Union

Army in the Civil War. She worked for the Army for four years as a nurse and spy, without any recognition or financial compensation. She was deployed by the governor of Massachusetts to the South at the beginning of the Civil War in the position of spy and scout and under the direction of Colonel James Montgomery. Tubman organized a group of black men to scout the inland waterways of South Carolina for Union raids. She also nursed wounded soldiers back to health and taught newly freed African Americans strategies for survival and sustenance. Although efforts were made by Secretary of State William H. Seward to secure a pension for her years of service, she was unsuccessful.

After a period of about four years, Tubman left the Army to continue her work, giving speeches on slavery, abolition, and suffrage. Through her powerful oratory, Tubman urged many slaves to find their way to freedom by educating them about the abolition movement. In December of 1860, Tubman was invited to Boston by Gerrit Smith to speak at a large antislavery meeting. Although Tubman was illiterate, people in attendance were startled by her eloquence at the podium. However, her oratory was merely an outgrowth of the shrewd critical thinking faculties upon

Tubman and the Underground Railroad

The Underground Railroad was the name given to the loose network of abolitionists who helped slaves escape to freedom in the North. The Underground Railroad provided protection and guidance for fugitives from the South. "Conducting" the railroad was a dangerous feat that required strength, endurance, and ingenuity; Harriet Tubman possessed all these qualities, and as a result, she enjoyed great success. Frequently, the journey was so treacherous that fugitives would tire and plead to turn back. In cases such as these, Tubman would reveal a shotgun tied to her waist and say, "You gon' be free or you gon' die." She never lost a single passenger.

Song was an important tool in Tubman's work. She used spirituals to communicate danger or safety to her followers while she scouted surroundings or secured supplies and rations. It was a useful form of subterfuge, because many slave owners believed that singing was an indication of a happy slave. Each person who traveled the Underground Railroad was prepared to risk his or her life for freedom, and no conductor was as eagerly hunted by slave catchers as Tubman. At times, the price on her head reached forty thousand dollars. Despite the danger, she made some nineteen trips into slave territory, and some historians estimate that she led as many as three hundred slaves to freedom.

which she had to rely greatly as the most successful conductor of the Underground Railroad. Near the end of her life, Tubman transformed her New York home into a boardinghouse to providing care for old and disabled African Americans. Tubman died of pneumonia on March 10, 1913, after a two-year residence in the Harriet Tubman Home for Aged and Indigent Colored People. Booker T. Washington was a featured speaker at her funeral service.

SIGNIFICANCE

During her lifetime Tubman was internationally renowned as a conductor on the Underground Railroad,

abolitionist, Civil War spy, nurse, suffragist, and humanitarian. Tubman accomplished a great deal during a time of intense racial, social, political, and economic upheaval. Her primary goal was to secure the freedom of enslaved people and to end the institution of slavery. Her deep commitment to this goal led her to associate with all types of people regardless of race, gender, or class. As the debate over slavery intensified, Tubman was a respected spokesperson for the abolitionist movement.

—*Kidogo A. Kennedy*

COMPROMISE OF 1850

January 29-September 20, 1850

A last national attempt to resolve the divisive issue of permitting slavery in U.S. territories, the Compromise of 1850 achieved a temporary settlement but ultimately contributed to leading the United States into civil war.

Locale: Washington, D.C.
Categories: Laws, acts, and legal history; expansion and land acquisition

KEY FIGURES

John C. Calhoun (1782-1850), senator from South Carolina
Henry Clay (1777-1852), senator from Kentucky
Millard Fillmore (1800-1874), president of the United States, 1850-1853
William H. Seward (1801-1872), congressman from New York
Zachary Taylor (1784-1850), president of the United States, 1849-1850
Daniel Webster (1782-1852), senator from Massachusetts
David Wilmot (1814-1868), congressman from Pennsylvania
Stephen A. Douglas (1813-1861), Democratic senator from Illinois

SUMMARY OF EVENT

The acquisition of large land areas by the United States following the annexation of Texas in 1845 and Mexico's cession of land that followed the Mexican War reopened the issue of slavery in U.S. territories as a national issue.

During the same period, most citizens embraced the idea of manifest destiny and its call for expansion of the United States and eventual control of the North American continent.

During the 1830's, thousands of settlers left the United States when they crossed the Mississippi River, intent on harvesting the western lands' potential and earning statehood for their new homes. However, the U.S. Constitution, while creating a mechanism for the addition of states and implicitly acknowledging the right of each state to permit and even encourage slavery within its boundaries, made no mention of slavery's status in future states. Because the power to admit new states lay exclusively with Congress, Congress could impose any condition it wished, conceivably requiring either the guarantee or abolition of slavery as a condition for admission.

The national government had first addressed the issue when the Confederation Congress passed the Northwest Ordinance of 1787. This excluded slavery from the unsettled area north of the Ohio River to the Mississippi River's eastern bank, then the edge of U.S. holdings, as a favor to the Chesapeake's tobacco planters, who feared that competition from western tobacco plantations would drive down the value of their crops.

The issue reemerged in 1817, when Missouri applied to join the United States as a slave state. The question came before the Congress in 1819, and sectional tensions erupted. A balance between slave and free states existed in the U.S. Senate, which had eleven states each from the free North and the slave-owning South. The North's growing population gave it a decisive advantage in the House of Representatives, so proslave forces committed themselves, at the minimum, to maintaining a balance between the regions in the Senate. At the time, between two and three thousand slaves lived in the Missouri Territory, yet some northern leaders, such as Rufus King of New York, argued that Congress should require the restriction of slavery before Missouri received statehood.

A temporary solution emerged in 1820, when Senator Henry Clay of Kentucky brokered a solution to the crisis. The resulting Missouri Compromise stipulated that Missouri would be admitted to the union as a slave state, while Maine, which had petitioned for statehood in late 1819, was admitted as a free state. The compromise also prohibited slavery from the remainder of the Louisiana Territory in the area north of 36°30′ north latitude, while permitting it south of that line. Between 1820 and 1848, this solution maintained the national peace, as the Senate remained balanced with thirty members representing the free states and an equal number representing the slave states.

The Mexican War of 1846-1848 disrupted the American political balance. As a consequence of its victory, the United States received millions of acres of land spanning the area from the Continental Divide west to the Pacific Ocean and south from the forty-ninth parallel to Mexico.

However, the problems flared even before the war ended, when David Wilmot, a member of the House of Representatives from Pennsylvania, attached an amendment to an appropriations bill. As he conceived it, any territory acquired from Mexico must exclude slavery in perpetuity. Although the so-called Wilmot Proviso failed to win passage, it fueled the smoldering fires of sectionalism, as many Americans assumed that any additional western lands would be governed by the Missouri Compromise.

The principle laid down by the Missouri Compromise vanished in 1850. The discovery of gold in California in 1848 attracted thousands of prospectors to Northern California, and less than a year later, the young California Republic petitioned the U.S. Senate for admission to the union.

Besides disrupting the balance between slave and free states, California straddled the 1820 compromise's line of latitude and threw the prior agreements into chaos.

In both houses of Congress, the question of slavery became paramount: Southerners rejected any attempt to exclude the practice from the West by nearly unanimous margins, while Free-Soilers from the North rejected the possibility of losing equal economic competition by similar percentages. Left in the middle were some elements of the national Whig Party, which struggled to preserve the union while remaining a national party itself.

The idea of disunion grew, and the failure to achieve a national solution likely may have triggered a civil war in 1850. Senator John C. Calhoun of South Carolina, long a firebrand for states' rights, proposed the formation of a sectional party to guarantee the practice of slavery. William H. Seward, an abolitionist representative from New York, also rejected the possibility of a compromise, citing the immorality of slavery. President Zachary Taylor, the hero of the Mexican War and himself a southerner, was also an ardent unionist and supported California's admission as a free state while rejecting the extreme position of persons such as Calhoun.

The first concrete proposal for compromise came from Senator Henry Clay of Kentucky, on January 29, 1850. He introduced a series of five resolutions designed to allow "amicable agreement of all questions in controversy, between the free and slave states, growing out of the subject of slavery." Clay proposed that the California Republic join the United States as a free state, that the rest of the territory acquired in the Mexican Cession be organized without any broader decision on slavery, that Texas receive monetary compensation in exchange for giving up its claims to parts of what is now New Mexico, that the slave trade within the District of Columbia be abolished (although the actual practice of slavery would not be affected), and that a more rigorous fugitive slave law be enacted.

Reactions to Clay's proposals reflected the sectional divisions of the day. On February 5 and 6, Clay presented his resolutions and spoke for the union's preservation.

One week later, Mississippi senator Jefferson Davis rejected Clay's proposals, using bitter language that also attacked northern intentions. Calhoun's last Senate appearance before he died on March 31 came on March 4, when he was carried into the chamber as Virginia's James Mason delivered his last speech for him. Calhoun's text rejected compromise on the principle of slavery in the territories and declared that the only way to preserve the union was for the North to concede the South's equal rights in the territories and for the abolitionists to stop agitating on the slavery question.

On March 7, Massachusetts senator Daniel Webster gave one of his most famous speeches, in which he declared that he spoke "not as a northern man, but as an American." He acknowledged that both sides had just grievances and urged support for Clay's whole plan, calming some tensions with his eloquent plea that the union be preserved. The abolitionists' position was explained on March 11 by William H. Seward, who opposed the compromise and cited a higher law than the Constitution, one that rejected the practice of slavery.

In April, the Senate referred Clay's resolutions to a select committee, which Clay chaired. The committee reported back to the full Senate an omnibus bill that contained the substance of the five original resolutions and sparked another four months of debate. Calhoun's death was a blow to the southern position. A second major stumbling block to the compromise disappeared in July, when President Taylor died. Vice President Millard Fillmore, who supported the compromise's ideas, replaced the Taylor, who had bitterly opposed the omnibus bill and had threatened to veto it. While Clay was vacationing away from Washington, D.C., Stephen A. Douglas broke the omnibus bill into five parts and steered them through the Senate, and the House of Representatives followed suit. By September 20, Congress had adopted the five bills that made up the Compromise of 1850.

SIGNIFICANCE

The efforts of various members of Congress to resolve the crisis of slavery in the territories effectively ended with the Compromise of 1850. In 1854, attempts at balancing the competing interests of the Free-Soil North with the proslave South ended when Senator Douglas proposed that the Kansas and Nebraska areas be organized using the concept of popular sovereignty, such as was used for the areas obtained from Mexico. Congress adopted the Kansas-Nebraska Act that year, triggering a number of serious reactions. Among these was the formation of a

---

The Compromise of 1850

Mississippi senator Jefferson Davis was among the many southern politicians who were unhappy with the congressional Compromise of 1850, also known as the Fugitive Slave Act. In this May 8, 1850, speech before the U.S. Senate, he hinted at the secessionist movement that was to come ten years later and make him the president of the Confederate States of America.

It is my opinion that justice will not be done to the South, unless from other promptings than are about us here—that we shall have no substantial consideration offered to us for the surrender of an equal claim to California.

No security against future harassment by Congress will probably be given. The rain-bow which some have seen, I fear was set before the termination of the storm. If this be so, those who have been first to hope, to relax their energies, to trust in compromise promises, will often be the first to sound the alarm when danger again approaches. Therefore I say, if a reckless and self-sustaining majority shall trample upon her rights, if the Constitutional equality of the States is to be overthrown by force, private and political rights to be borne down by force of numbers, then, sir, when that victory over Constitutional rights is achieved, the shout of triumph which announces it, before it is half uttered, will be checked by the united, the determined action of the South, and every breeze will bring to the marauding destroyers of those rights, the warning: woe, woe to the riders who trample them down! I submit the report and resolutions, and ask that they may be read and printed for the use of the Senate.

---

national political party dedicated to the idea of an exclusively free-soil policy in the West. The new Republican Party immediately became a force on the national political landscape, and its candidate, John C. Frémont, came within four states of being elected president in 1856. Ultimately, the 1860 election of Abraham Lincoln, a man committed to both the preservation of the union and the free-soil doctrine, drove the South to secession.

—John G. Clark, updated by E. A. Reed

See also: Missouri Compromise; Second Fugitive Slave Law; Stowe Publishes *Uncle Tom's Cabin*; Congress Passes the Kansas-Nebraska Act; Birth of the Republican Party; Bleeding Kansas; Lincoln-Douglas Debates; U.S. Civil War.

Related articles in *Great Lives from History: The Nineteenth Century, 1801-1900:* John C. Calhoun; Henry Clay; Stephen A. Douglas; Millard Fillmore; Zachary Taylor; Daniel Webster.

FUGITIVE SLAVE LAW OF 1850

September 18, 1850

This law further exacerbated tensions between the North and the South and helped lead the nation into the Civil War.

The Law: Federal law designed to facilitate the return of slaves who fled to northern states from from the South

The U.S. Congress passed the Second Fugitive Slave Law in September, 1850, as part of the Compromise of 1850. This compromise, its supporters hoped, would provide a permanent settlement of the long-standing dispute between the North and the South over slavery. The dispute had reached crisis proportions in 1848, after the United States forcefully acquired from Mexico huge territories in the Southwest, which raised the issue of the status of slavery in those territories. Most of the provisions of the Compromise of 1850 dealt with that issue. Southern white spokespersons also insisted that the government do something to prevent slave escapes into the North and to make it easier for masters to reclaim fugitive slaves from there.

BACKGROUND

Slave escapes had been common long before the United States became an independent country. It was the decision of the northern states following the Revolutionary War to abolish slavery within their bounds that created a sectional issue. As a result, in 1787, southern influence brought about the insertion in the U.S. Constitution of a clause providing that slaves escaping from one state to another were not to be freed but returned to their masters.

This clause established the constitutional basis for fugitive slave laws. The first such law, passed by Congress in 1793, allowed masters, on their own, to apprehend escaped slaves in the free states. Although this law provided no legal protection for persons accused of being fugitive slaves, neither did it authorize state or federal assistance for masters attempting to reclaim slaves.

Several events in the 1840's prompted white southerners to intensify demands for a stronger fugitive slave law. First, the number of slave escapes increased as the slave labor system in the border slave states weakened. Second, a few black and white abolitionists became active in helping slaves escape. Third, northern states began passing "personal liberty laws" requiring jury trials to determine the status of African Americans accused of being fugitive slaves. Such trials provided protection to

those falsely accused and also made it more difficult for masters to reclaim actual escapees.

The Supreme Court addressed this last issue in the case of *Prigg v. Commonwealth of Pennsylvania* (1842). In *Prigg*, the Court ruled that a state could not interfere with the right of a master to recapture slaves. The Court also ruled, however, that, because the power to legislate on the fugitive slave issue was purely national, states were not required to assist in the enforcement of the First Fugitive Slave Law. This ruling allowed for a new series of personal liberty laws that denied masters the support they needed to apprehend alleged slaves. For many southern whites, who feared that slave escapes were a major threat to the existence of slavery in the border slave states, the fugitive slave law issue loomed as large as the issue of slavery in the territories in the late 1840's. In response to these concerns, Senator James Mason of Virginia proposed the passage of a new and stronger fugitive slave law, on January 3, 1850.

THE LAW IS PASSED

When Mason's much-amended bill became law nine months later, it appeared to be all that southern whites demanded. It provided that United States marshals had to assist masters in arresting fugitive slaves and that the marshals could, in turn, summon northern citizens to help. It provided that United States circuit courts appoint numerous commissioners who were empowered to evaluate the truth of a master's claim and authorize the return of fugitives to a master's state. Accused fugitives were not permitted to testify before the commissioners. The commissioners would receive a fee of ten dollars if they accepted a master's claim and only five dollars if they did not. Anyone who interfered with the apprehension of alleged fugitive slaves or who helped such persons escape was subject to a fine of up to one thousand dollars and imprisonment for up to six months.

To many northerners, the new law seemed to be excessively harsh and corrupting. Even northerners who expressed no opposition to slavery in the South had little enthusiasm for assisting in the rendition of fugitive slaves. The denial to the accused of the right to testify, of the writ of habeas corpus, and of a jury trial appeared to be invitations for the unscrupulous to use the new law to facilitate kidnapping of free African American northerners. That commissioners were paid more to remand to the South persons accused of being fugitive slaves than to exonerate such persons seemed to be a bribe in behalf of the putative masters. The official explanation of the different fees—that to send the accused back to the South required more paperwork than to reject a master's claim—seemed a disingenuous excuse to many northerners. Finally, because the law was retroactive, fugitive slaves who had lived safely in the North for many years were now subject to recapture.

To abolitionists, who opposed the very existence of slavery and encouraged slaves to escape, and to antislavery politicians, who contended that the South was seeking to expand its slave system into the North, the new law was anathema. The law's harshness and its apparent invasion of northern states' rights led less committed northerners to oppose it as well. Even as the bill that became the Second Fugitive Slave Law made its way through Congress, antislavery senators Salmon P. Chase of Ohio and William H. Seward of New York attempted, without success, to defeat it or to include in it provisions for jury trials. Antislavery northerners denounced Senator Daniel Webster of Massachusetts for his March 7, 1850, endorsement of the bill. When it became law on September 18, there were protests throughout the North, although most northerners acquiesced in its enforcement.

ENFORCEMENT

In many instances, however, enforcement was very difficult. As soon as the law went into effect, African Americans escaping from the South went to Canada, beyond the reach of the law. Others who had lived in the North for years took refuge across the Canadian border in times of danger. New personal liberty laws in a number of northern states—several of which required jury trials—not only protected those falsely charged with being fugitive slaves but, by adding expenses, discouraged masters from pressing claims. Harriet Beecher Stowe's best-selling novel, *Uncle Tom's Cabin*, first published in serial form in 1851-1852, both reflected and encouraged northern antipathy to the Second Fugitive Slave Law. By portraying slavery as a brutal system and depicting fugitive slaves sympathetically, Stowe aroused an emotional northern reaction against the law.

Most striking, black and white people physically resisted enforcement of the law throughout the 1850's. Shortly after the law went into effect, former slave Harriet Tubman, with the help of black and white abolitionists, began her career of leading bands of slaves out of the South. Meanwhile, in Boston, Massachusetts; Christiana, Pennsylvania; Syracuse, New York; Wellington, Ohio; Milwaukee, Wisconsin; and elsewhere in the North, armed biracial mobs obstructed the enforcement of the act.

While the law was peacefully enforced in large regions of the North, its most important effect was to widen the gulf between the North and South. Many northerners considered the law to be unconstitutional and an immoral southern aggression, in behalf of an oppressive institution, upon not only African Americans but also the rights and values of northern whites. White southerners, many of whom had predicted that the new Fugitive Slave Law would be ineffective, regarded northern resistance to it as another sign of antipathy toward the South and its institutions. What had been designed as part of a compromise to quiet sectional animosities, instead increased those animosities and helped lead the nation into civil war in 1861.

—*Stanley Harrold*

See also: Bleeding Kansas; Compromise of 1850; Fugitive Slave Law of 1793; Kansas-Nebraska Act; Missouri Compromise; Proslavery argument; *Scott v. Sandford*; Slave codes; Slavery and the justice system; Thirteenth Amendment; Underground Railroad

SOJURNER TRUTH SPEAKS AT AKRON WOMAN'S RIGHTS CONVENTION

May 28-29, 1851

This second major women's rights convention highlighted the connections between the women's and abolitionist movements and exposed the internal contradictions that would increasingly emerge in the growing women's movement.

Also known as: Second National Woman's Rights Convention; Second Statewide Convention

Locale: Akron, Ohio
Categories: Women's issues; social issues and reform

KEY FIGURES

Frances Dana Gage (1808-1884), writer and lecturer who presided over the convention
Betsey Mix Cowles (1810-1876), teacher, school founder, and reformer

Sojourner Truth (c. 1797-1883), evangelist who spoke on abolition and women's rights

Summary of Event

By the late 1840's, the accelerated growth of the United States affected all aspects of American life. Territorial expansion to the West and industrial development changed the social fabric as immigrant labor created urban areas and modified gender and class roles. The women's rights movement emerged from this dynamic context. Most of the movement's founders had gained experience in organizing from their participation in the temperance, antislavery, moral purity, and health reform movements through their churches and benevolent societies.

On July 19, 1848, they came from the surrounding areas to assemble in a Wesleyan chapel in Seneca Falls, New York, to begin the organized women's rights movement.

By the end of that first meeting, sixty-eight women and thirty-two men had signed the Declaration of Sentiments, a compilation of gender inequities ending with a series of resolutions to shape the agenda for the coming years.

The movement had able leaders in Susan B. Anthony, a pragmatic, yet intense organizer; theorist Elizabeth Cady Stanton, who had limited mobility because of her large family; Quaker reformer Lucretia Mott; orators Lucy Stone and Ernestine Rose; and many others. Male reformers also participated during these early years.

However, when men joined the women at their next meeting in the Quaker community of Salem, Ohio, the women barred them from vocal participation to raise their awareness of women's plight and won a resolution to secure equal rights for all persons.

The first National Woman's Rights Convention was organized by wealthy reformer Paulina Wright Davis and held on October 26 and 27, 1850, in Worcester, Massachusetts.

New leaders attending this meeting included Antoinette Brown, who became the first ordained female minister; Harriot Hunt, a medical pioneer; and Sojourner Truth, an evangelist and abolitionist.

The connection between women's rights and abolitionism was strong during these early years. Arguments against the moral, legal, and social conditions of slavery raised women's awareness of their own restrictions. Societies, newspapers, lyceums, lecture circuits, fairs, and support networks began to include other reforms, including women's right to speak in public on behalf of slaves.

Gradually, women broke down barriers and developed skills that would help them develop their own movement for women's rights.

These connections appeared at what is generally called the Second National Woman's Rights Convention, on May 28-29, 1851, at Akron, Ohio.

Because of the loose organization through steering committees during the early years of the women's movement, confusion about titles of conventions abounds. Akron's meeting is also known as both the Second Statewide Convention and as the Akron Convention.

However, the Worcester, Massachusetts, Convention of October, 1851, is also sometimes called the Second National Woman's Rights Convention.

Ohio had the most antislavery societies of any state in the union in 1840. It had recently adopted a new constitution, which had mobilized both antislavery and women's rights supporters working to shape the new laws.

Although the Ohio constitution remained unchanged regarding women's rights, agitation for women's rights continued throughout the state.

Akron was a central location in Ohio, drawing leaders from the East and from various pockets of reform in Ohio. The strongest center of support came from Salem, Ohio, the Quaker community in Columbiana County that was the home of the *Anti-Slavery Bugle*, the newspaper of the Garrisonian Western Anti-Slavery Society. Salem was also the home of many male and female supporters of women's rights and equality. These included Jane Elisabeth (Lizzie) Hitchcock and her husband Benjamin Jones, who were co-editors of the *Anti-Slavery Bugle*; Mary Ann and Oliver Johnson, who succeeded Lizzie and Ben Jones as the paper's editors; Emily Robinson; and Lot and Eliza Holmes. The abolitionist and temperance supporter Martha J. Tilden, who was the wife of a congressman, represented Akron. Teacher and school founder Betsey Mix Cowles came from Austinburg, representing Canton. Josephine Sophia White Griffing came from Medina as one of the Western Anti-Slavery Society's most active and effective lecturers. From the southern part of the state came Sarah Ernst, a Cincinnati Garrisonian.

The Akron Woman's Rights Convention tapped Ohio leadership. Frances Dana Gage of McConnelsville, Ohio, a married woman with four young children, was elected president of this convention. Gage's skills as a writer for abolition and temperance had brought her into the reform network that supported women's rights. Although she admitted to having never attended a regular business meeting and to feeling entirely inexperienced in organizational procedures, her natural organizational and intellectual skills provided the basis for her leadership.

Unlike the other Ohio reformers, who had come from New England to settle in the West, Gage was born in Ohio and had married an Ohioan. In her opening speech to the convention, she related how women had struggled alongside men in adapting to the environment.

These experiences demonstrated the common needs of women and their shared humanity with men. She traced the false basis in religion and custom that gave men predominance over women. She sought with "a loving spirit" to bring men into the movement for women's rights to create "a revolution without armies, without bloodshed" to improve the conditions of society by granting women their rights.

Ohio leaders read letters of support from Paulina W. Davis of Rhode Island, Elizabeth Cady Stanton and Amelia Bloomer of New York, former Oberlin student Lucy Stone, and Gerrit Smith. The current status of women was presented in reports. L. Maria Giddings spoke on the common law. Betsey Mix Cowles detailed labor conditions and wages. Pittsburgh's Jane G. Swisshelm related women's sphere to education, a topic also addressed by Emily Robinson.

The reports provided a stage for commentaries and debate, with ministers quoting Scripture assigning women a

secondary role. They pointed out that, according to the Bible, Jesus had chosen no female apostles, that Eve was responsible for all the sin in the world, and that John had instructed women to be silent. As the meeting degenerated in this debate, a tall figure emerged from the back of the church hall and asked to speak. Many in the crowd responded in the negative, saying that women's rights and "nigger's rights" did not mix. Gage, however, had been a strong supporter of the antislavery movement and had great respect for the proposed speaker, Sojourner Truth. Gage assented to the request.

The speech then delivered by Sojourner Truth turned the tide in favor of women's rights. This former New York slave, originally named Isabella Van Wegener, had experienced a religious conversion and had renamed herself Sojourner Truth as she entered a career as an itinerant preacher and antislavery lecturer. Dubbed the "Lybian Sybil" by Lydia Maria Child, Truth stood more than six feet tall and had very dark skin, which gave her a commanding physical presence in any gathering. Although illiterate, she was an eloquent orator and had addressed similar crowds in the antislavery lecture circuit and spoken to earlier women's rights conventions at Worcester, Massachusetts, in 1850.

Truth's speech at the Akron Convention was called "Ain't I a Woman?" by Gage and by the *Anti-Slavery Bugle*.

Truth argued that she had worked as hard as a man, had physical needs similar to those of a man, and thus deserved the same rights in return. She asked the ministry about the origin of Christ—from God and a woman, with man having no part. When challenged on the matter of Christ's having no female apostles, she countered with women's roles attending Christ at the crucifixion and mentioned the women to whom he appeared after resurrection.

In defense of Eve, she argued that if one woman could turn the world upside down, then women together

---

"Ain't I a Woman?"

The abolitionist, evangelist, and women's rights advocate Sojourner Truth delivered a speech that roused women's rights conventiongoers in Akron in 1851. "Ain't I a Woman?" is one of the founding documents of the nineteenth century American women's movement and remains part of the curriculum of many secondary schools, colleges, and universities.

That man over there says that women need to be helped into carriages, and lifted over ditches, and to have the best place everywhere.

Nobody ever helps me into carriages, or over mud puddles, or gives me any best place! And ain't I a woman? Look at me! Look at my arm!

I have plowed, and planted, and gathered into barns, and no man could head me! And ain't I a woman? I could work as much and eat as much as a man—when I could get it—and bear the lash as well! And ain't I a woman? I have borne thirteen children, and seen them most all sold off to slavery, and when I cried out with my mother's grief, none but Jesus heard me! And ain't I a woman? . . .

Then that little man in black there, he says women can't have as much rights as men, 'cause Christ wasn't a woman! Where did your Christ come from? Where did your Christ come from? From God and a woman!! Man had nothing to do with him.

could correct the world's problems, if given rights. Accounts of the magical influence of her speech were in agreement that she had provoked respect and admiration and turned the event into a successful women's rights convention.

SIGNIFICANCE

The convention resolved to use the periodical press to shape public sentiments, to use teachers and mothers to shape young minds, to form labor partnerships, and to repeal laws that created different privileges. Caroline Severance reported on the event in the Cleveland newspapers; in May, 1853, she presided over the first annual meeting of the Ohio Woman's Rights Association, which had been founded May 27, 1852, in Ravenna. The Akron Convention reflected the internal contradictions that would increasingly emerge in the growing women's rights movement.

—Dorothy C. Salem

Related articles in *Great Lives from History: The Nineteenth Century, 1801-1900:* Susan B. Anthony; Amelia Bloomer; Matilda Joslyn Gage; Lucretia Mott; Elizabeth Cady Stanton; Lucy Stone; Sojourner Truth.

SOJOURNER TRUTH

Truth, born a slave, walked to freedom to become an example of courage and survival. Although she was an illiterate woman, she was able to reach white and black audiences through her speeches and her biography. She challenged white supremacy, claiming her rights through legal action and civil disobedience, and proposed ideas to alleviate the suffering of her people.

Born: c. 1797; Hurley, Ulster County, New York
Died: November 26, 1883; Battle Creek, Michigan
Also known as: Isabella Baumfree (birth name); Isabella Van Wagenen
Areas of achievement: Abolitionism; Social issues; Women's rights

EARLY LIFE

Sojourner Truth (soh-JUHRN-uhr) was born a slave around 1797 in Hurley, Ulster County, New York, near the Hudson River. She was the second youngest of ten or twelve children of James and Elizabeth, but as a child she knew only one sibling. Her birth name was Isabella Baumfree. Truth and her family were the property of Colonel Johannes Hardenbergh, who owned nearly two million acres between the Hudson and Delaware rivers in Ulster County. Hardenbergh died when Truth was an infant, and she and her family became the property of his son, Charles. In 1807, after the death of Charles Hardenbergh, Truth was sold to John Neely, a merchant from Twaalfskill, New York (near present-day Kingston). She was about nine years old. After one or two years, the Neelys sold her to Martinus Shryver, a fisherman and

Sojourner Truth, c. 1870

tavern keeper. Shryver, in turn, sold Truth in 1810 to John J. Dumont of New Paltz Landing, where she remained until 1826.

With the Dumont family, Truth did farm work and household chores. In 1814, she married another slave named Thomas, whom Dumont seems to have selected for her, and they lived together for about ten years. They had five children, four of whom—Diana, Peter, Elizabeth, and Sophia—lived past infancy. The fifth may have died in infancy or early childhood. In 1817, the New York state legislature passed a law decreeing that all New York slaves born before July 4, 1799, would be freed on July 4, 1827. Dumont promised Truth and Thomas that he would free them on July 4, 1826, a year earlier than the law required. However, Truth subsequently injured her hand and lost her ability to work quickly; Dumont, arguing that she owed him additional work because of her inefficiency, broke his promise. In the fall of 1826, Truth walked off the Dumonts' property carrying her infant daughter, Sophia. She went to the home of Levi Rowe, a Quaker whom she expected to help her. However, she found him on his deathbed. Rowe sent her to the home of Isaac and Maria Van Wagenen in Wagondale, New York (present-day Bloomington). The Van Wagenens took in Truth and gave her work as a free person. However, when Dumont learned that she was at the Van Wagenen house, he went to claim her as his property. To prevent Truth's reenslavement, the Van Wagenens paid him twenty-five dollars for Truth and Sophia. Truth remained with them for about a year and adopted their last name, becoming Isabella Van Wagenen.

While working for the family, Truth learned that her five-year-old son, Peter, had been sold illegally and taken to Alabama. Determined to rescue her son, she confronted the Dumonts, who did not recognize her claim. With support from Quaker friends, she hired a lawyer who, in 1828, succeeded in having Peter returned to his mother. Truth and Peter moved to New York City in late 1828, leaving Sophia with the Van Wagenens. She joined the Zion African Church and worked as a housekeeper for various families. In 1835, Truth was accused of poisoning her employer but was able to prove that she did not commit the crime. During her fourteen years in New York City, Truth came into contact with employers and other African Americans who were very religious. Several went on to become prominent abolitionists. In this context, Truth had a spiritual experience in which she felt called to become a traveling evangelist. To pursue this calling, she adopted the name "Sojourner Truth." "Sojourner" reflected that she would travel the land, and "Truth"

her determination to speak the truth. Thus, in 1843, she set out from New York on her mission.

LIFE'S WORK

Truth began preaching in Connecticut and Northampton, Massachusetts; there, she found many supporters associated with the Northampton Association, which had been founded by abolitionists, idealists, and workers to pursue equal rights for all. Truth remained with the association until 1846, working as a laundress. During her stay with the Northampton Association, she met prominent abolitionists such as William Lloyd Garrison, editor of The *Boston Liberator* and president of the American Anti-Slavery Society, and Frederick Douglass. In 1846, Truth began dictating her autobiography to Olive Gilbert; in 1850, it was published as *Narrative of Sojourner Truth* and marked her emergence as an abolitionist and women's suffrage advocate.

In 1851, Garrison invited Truth to accompany him and his friend George Thompson, a radical member of the British parliament, on a trip into western New York. Truth made the trip with Thompson, making speeches and selling her book. In Ohio, Truth assisted the Ohio Woman's Rights Convention and delivered a famous speech on equal rights for African American women, which was later published as "Ain't I a Woman?" In 1853, Truth journeyed to Andover, Massachusetts, and asked Harriet Beecher Stowe, the author of *Uncle Tom's Cabin* (1852), to help promote her autobiography. Stowe wrote a short article about the book. Ten years later, based on this brief encounter, Stowe wrote "Sojourner Truth, the Libyan Sibyl" for *Atlantic Monthly*.

In 1857, Truth joined the community of Harmonia, a racially mixed settlement of progressive abolitionists and spiritualists, located six miles west of Battle Creek, Michigan. She was joined there by her daughters, Diana, Elizabeth, and Sophia, who had been legally freed. Her grandsons, James Caldwell and Samuel Banks, became her traveling companions. In 1860, Truth moved to the town of Battle Creek.

With the outbreak of the Civil War in 1861, Truth became deeply involved in politics. She openly challenged slavery and championed the Union cause. In 1862, Truth accompanied Josephine Griffing, a radical feminist, to Indiana, violating a state law prohibiting the entry of black people. She was chased by a mob and arrested. In 1863, when President Abraham Lincoln signed the Emancipation Proclamation and gave orders to recruit African American troops to fight for the Union, Truth went door to door to collect Thanksgiving food for the soldiers of the First Michigan Colored Regiment, stationed at Camp-Ward in Detroit. In 1864, Truth collected more food and clothing from the people of Battle Creek for the Camp Ward troops. Around this time, she addressed the troops and sang a song that she had composed in honor of the regiment.

The Civil War and social struggles of the 1860's moved Truth to make her first trip to Washington, D.C., in 1864, accompanied by her grandson, Banks. She carried a new edition of her autobiography and her portrait printed on postcards. Under her picture was printed the message "The Shadow Supports the Substance." In Washington, Truth and her white companion Lucy Colman met Lincoln; he signed her autograph book, "For Auntie Sojourner Truth, October 29, 1864." In later years, Truth would also visit presidents Andrew Johnson and Ulysses S. Grant. Truth stayed in Washington from 1864 to 1867. During her stay, she saw and experienced the racial discrimination that pervaded everyday life. Although streetcars had been desegregated by federal law in 1865, conductors did not want to stop for black passengers. Truth insisted on riding in the streetcars, even when she was humiliated and assaulted, forcing conductors to respect the law.

In Washington, D.C., Truth worked for the National Freedmen's Relief Association and the Freedmen's Bureau, aiding black refugees from the southern states. The poor conditions in which freed African Americans lived—characterized by cramped housing, crime, and joblessness—led her to argue that her people needed work, not government money. Truth proposed that the government provide land for free African Americans. Massachusetts senator Charles Sumner advised her to collect signatures to pressure Congress to authorize land grants. From 1870 to 1871, Truth and Banks toured New England and the mid-Atlantic region collecting signatures.

Truth and the Abolitionist Movement

Throughout her life, Sojourner Truth was illiterate, and most accounts of her life and accomplishments as an abolitionist and activist have been relayed by third parties who evaluated her based on their own agendas and priorities. Thus, Truth's fame has been attributed to the publication of Harriet Beecher Stowe's 1863 article "Sojourner Truth, the Libyan Sibyl" and Frances Gage's "Reminiscence," which described Truth's "Ain't I a Woman?" speech at the Ohio Woman's Rights Convention of 1851. However, Truth had started her abolitionist activism well before these articles introduced her to wider audiences.

Truth had given speeches telling her story and sold copies of her memoir as a way of supporting herself. She had toured with the British radical George Thompson and met Frederick Douglass. During her journeys she was able to build her network of abolitionist, feminist, and spiritualist supporters; indeed, she bridged many of these disparate movements, connecting the plights of women and slaves and championing all people's equality under God. Her impressive figure—almost six feet tall and gaunt—her natural eloquence, and her courage to speak to white audiences gave her the power to move white abolitionists, women's suffragists, and other important figures to appropriate her as a symbol of struggle against injustice.

Her tour was cut short when Banks fell ill, and they returned to Battle Creek, where he died in 1875. Subsequently, the exodus of many freed African Americans to Kansas in 1879 upstaged Truth's plan, but she supported it enthusiastically. In Battle Creek, at the urging of her friend Frances Titus, Truth updated her *Narrative of Sojourner Truth*, adding her speeches and scrapbook. During the fall of 1883, Truth fell gravely ill. She died before dawn on November 26.

SIGNIFICANCE

Truth was born a slave and became a nationally known advocate for the abolition of slavery and equal rights for women. Truth viewed her advocacy as a religious calling to put her faith into practice. Her escape from slavery and her adherence to her principles in the face of personal hardship and tragedy made her a powerful symbol of the abolitionist and women's rights causes.

—*F. Sonia Arellano-Lopez*

STOWE PUBLISHES UNCLE TOM'S CABIN

1852

Selling more than 300,000 copies in its first year of publication, Harriet Beecher Stowe's antislavery novel Uncle Tom's Cabin *immediately garnered both praise and condemnation. The novel's portrayal of the cruelties of slavery and its memorable characters proved effective tools in mobilizing support for abolitionism and helped to inflame the tensions that led to the U.S. Civil War.*

Locale: Boston, Massachusetts
Categories: Literature; civil rights and liberties; social issues and reform

KEY FIGURES

Harriet Beecher Stowe (1811-1896), American novelist
Gamaliel Bailey (1807-1859), American editor
John Punchard Jewett (1814-1884), American publisher

SUMMARY OF EVENT

The Fugitive Slave Law of 1850, which strengthened procedures for the return of runaway slaves, reaffirmed the commitment of the United States to maintain the institution of slavery despite the presence of an outspoken abolitionist movement. The measure angered opponents of slavery throughout the United States. One of these opponents was Harriet Beecher Stowe, a fiction writer living in Brunswick, Maine. She wrote *Uncle Tom's Cabin: Or, Life Among the Lowly* as a response to the Fugitive Slave Law. With the book she hoped to win new supporters to the antislavery cause by exposing slavery's brutalities.

Uncle Tom's Cabin began as a series of short stories published in the *National Era* in 1851 and 1852. The *National Era*, published weekly in Washington, D.C., and affiliated with the antislavery Free-Soil Party, proved receptive to Stowe's proposed series. Its abolitionist editor Gamaliel Bailey paid Stowe a fee of three hundred dollars for the stories, which he initially agreed to print in three or four issues of the newspaper. Stowe eventually received an additional one hundred dollars after the series expanded to occupy forty issues of the newspaper.

Uncle Tom's Cabin represented something of a departure for Stowe, the daughter of a Connecticut minister who had been raised with antislavery but not activist principles. Her previous fiction and essays published

in magazines and gift books concentrated on romantic tales or idyllic portraits of New England life.

Uncle Tom's Cabin was also something of a departure for antebellum publishing, for few prior antislavery novels had met with much success.

Despite the positive response that the serial received in the *National Era*, the novel form of *Uncle Tom's Cabin* was rejected by at least one publisher before John Punchard Jewett of Boston agreed to print the work.

Jewett, a relatively small publisher, accepted Stowe's novel at the urging of his wife, another fan of the *National Era* series. The book was released in two volumes on March 20, 1852, the hardcover selling for one and one-half dollars and the paperback for one dollar. Another paperback version of the book combining both volumes appeared before the end of the year and cost thirty-seven and one-half cents. *Uncle Tom's Cabin* was an instant success. It sold 10,000 copies in days and more than 300,000 copies during its first year, a feat then unmatched by any other book except the Bible. The novel was even more popular in England, where more than one million copies were sold in 1852.

Uncle Tom's Cabin features parallel plots involving the fates of two slaves living on the Kentucky plantation of Mr. Shelby. Stowe follows Uncle Tom after he is sold by Shelby through two subsequent masters. The first is Augustine St. Clare, a genteel master in New Orleans. Tom forms a special bond with St. Clare's daughter Eva, and her death scene is one of the most emotional in the novel. Tom is later sold to a rural Louisiana plantation owned by Simon Legree. Legree, a cruel master who eventually beats Tom to death, is made an even more powerful character because he originally hails from Vermont. Stowe thus uses her novel to show her readers both the variety of conditions slaves endure and the moral damage the slave system inflicts even on northerners who become involved. The novel also details the successful escape of Eliza Harris, a mulatto slave, from Shelby's plantation after Shelby agrees to sell her four-year-old son, Harry. In one famous scene, Eliza and Harry cross the frozen Ohio River from Kentucky to the free state of Ohio. They eventually reunite with Harry's father, George Harris, and the family emigrates to Liberia.

Stowe's evocative tale prompted almost immediate praise from Northern and abolitionist circles. Encomiums came from Ralph Waldo Emerson, John Greenleaf Whittier, Henry Wadsworth Longfellow, and William Lloyd Garrison. Southern reviews of *Uncle Tom's Cabin* were largely negative. Critics charged that Stowe had presented an inaccurate portrait of slavery in the South and rebutted that most masters treated their slaves well and that most slaves were content.

Critics also noted that Stowe had never lived in the South; indeed, her only visit to the South occurred in 1834, when she spent a few days in Kentucky. Although Stowe and her husband lived in the border city of Cincinnati, Ohio, for almost two decades, there is little historical evidence that she had much contact with either free or enslaved African Americans. These criticisms prompted Stowe to publish *A Key to Uncle Tom's Cabin* in 1853, which attempted to establish the verity of the depiction of slavery presented in the novel. Nonetheless, southern society threatened reprisal for advocates of *Uncle Tom's Cabin* and its message. Southern newspapers urged their readers not to buy the novel, and those who tried to sell it were subject to vigilante harassment. In Maryland, for example, a free African American named Samuel Green received a prison sentence of ten years for being found in possession of the novel. He was released in 1862 on the condition that he leave the United States, which he did by emigrating to Canada.

Northerners were not without their own reservations about Stowe's novel. Some were doubtful that *Uncle Tom's Cabin*, given its sentimental style, would do much more than evoke emotional responses, leaving the political mobilization of antislavery sentiment unfulfilled.

Abolitionists such as William Lloyd Garrison were also unnerved by Stowe's endorsement of relocating freed African Americans to Africa, as the fate of George and Eliza Harris suggested.

Some northern critics of the novel, like their southern counterparts, argued that Stowe's objections to slavery were unjustified because slavery was the appropriate and biblically determined condition of the African American.

African American abolitionists bristled at the colonization issue and at Stowe's depiction of Uncle Tom as unswervingly pious and obedient, although much of this criticism was muted. Frederick Douglass praised the novel, and the term "Uncle Tom" would not assume its pejorative connotation until after World War II.

Contrary to popular assumptions, *Uncle Tom's Cabin* exerted only limited direct impact on antebellum politics. Many of the responses to the work were literary; a rash of novels appeared in the 1850's that claimed to show the truth of slavery by refuting Stowe's description of its cruelty. Few politicians made public mention of the work. The novel, however, proved most effective in winning converts to the antislavery cause through its adaptation for the stage. Theatrical versions of *Uncle Tom's Cabin* appeared a few months after the novel was published.

The most successful script was written by George Aiken of Boston, whose cousin George Howard managed a theater troupe in Troy, New York. Aiken's version was first performed at the Troy Museum theater in November, 1852; it moved to New York City's National Theater in July, 1853, and was so popular that the theater began offering matinee performances and racially segregated seating.

Perhaps because *Uncle Tom's Cabin* as a play could mediate the novel's antislavery emphasis according to the tastes of the communities in which it was performed, most observers then and now consider the play responsible for promoting popular abolitionism in the North. Versions of the play toured throughout the North through the end of the nineteenth century. "Anti-Uncle Tom" plays were popular in the pre-Civil War South.

SIGNIFICANCE

President Abraham Lincoln is said to have quipped upon meeting Harriet Beecher Stowe in 1862, "So this is the little lady who made this great war." Southerners certainly blamed Stowe for encouraging the Northern aggression they considered at the root of the U.S. Civil War (1861-1865). Most abolitionists did not begin attributing such agency to *Uncle Tom's Cabin* until after the war.

In 1893, James Ford Rhodes became the first historian to elaborate on the social and political consequences of the novel. Even in the early twenty-first century, it is difficult to deny that *Uncle Tom's Cabin* and its stage version influenced Northern sympathy for the plight of the slave and also southern hostility. While it would be perhaps overgenerous to describe Stowe as having "made" the Civil War, her novel drew from and intensified extant sentiments in the ongoing debate over slavery and likely convinced those who were otherwise unaffiliated that African Americans were owed their freedom.

—*Francesca Gamber*

See also: Southerners Advance Proslavery Arguments; Garrison Begins Publishing *The Liberator*; American

---

Slavery Sanitized

In "The Slave Warehouse," chapter 30 of Uncle Tom's Cabin, *Stowe writes of the "art of sinning expertly and genteely," that is, of making oneself look good, regardless of the circumstances, in the eyes of others, including those with whom one wants to do business. In this excerpt, Stowe shows how slaves are made presentable by "genteel" slave traders who market slaves as well-maintained commodities, as "shiny" and "clean" things.*

A slave warehouse! Perhaps some of my readers conjure up horrible visions of such a place. They fancy some foul, obscure den, some horrible *Tartarus "informis, ingens, cui lumen ademptum"* [Hell misshapen, monstrous, devoid of light]. But no, innocent friend; in these days men have learned the art of sinning expertly and genteelly, so as not to shock the eyes and senses of respectable society. Human property is high in the market; and is, therefore, well fed, well cleaned, tended, and looked after, that it may come to sale sleek, and strong, and shining. A slave-warehouse in New Orleans is a house externally not much unlike many others, kept with neatness; and where every day you may see arranged, under a sort of shed along the outside, rows of men and women, who stand there as a sign of the property sold within.

Then you shall be courteously entreated to call and examine, and shall find an abundance of husbands, wives, brothers, sisters, fathers, mothers, and young children, to be "sold separately, or in lots to suit the convenience of the purchaser"; and that soul immortal, once bought with blood and anguish by the Son of God, when the earth shook, and the rocks rent, and the graves were opened, can be sold, leased, mortagaged, exchanged for groceries or dry goods, to suit the phases of trade, or the fancy of the purchaser.

Anti-Slavery Society Is Founded; Douglass Launches *The North Star*; Underground Railroad Flourishes; Compromise of 1850; Second Fugitive Slave Law; National Council of Colored People Is Founded; Last Slave Ship Docks at Mobile; U.S. Civil War; Lincoln Issues the Emancipation Proclamation.

Related articles in *Great Lives from History: The Nineteenth Century, 1801-1900:* Susan B. Anthony; Henry Ward Beecher; John Brown; Frederick Douglass; Paul Laurence Dunbar; William Lloyd Garrison; Sarah and Angelina Grimké; Sarah Orne Jewett; AbrahamLincoln; Wendell Phillips; Dred Scott; Elizabeth Cady Stanton; Harriet Beecher Stowe; Bertha von Suttner; Harriet Tubman; Nat Turner; John Greenleaf Whittier.

NATIONAL COUNCIL OF COLORED PEOPLE IS FOUNDED

July 6, 1853

The National Council of Colored People was short-lived and ineffective but remains significant because it was one of the earliest efforts to improve the lives of African Americans on a national level.

Locale: Rochester, New York
Categories: Civil rights and liberties; social issues and reform; organizations and institutions

KEY FIGURES

Richard Allen (1760-1831), African American leader and founder of the first Negro Convention
Frederick Douglass (1817?-1895), former slave and publisher of *The North Star*

SUMMARY OF EVENT

On Wednesday, July 6, 1853, more than one hundred delegates from around the United States assembled in Rochester, New York, for a three-day convention to form the National Council of Colored People. This organization was an outgrowth of the Negro Convention movement that had begun almost twenty-three years earlier.

Philadelphia had been the host of the first meeting for the Negro Convention movement in late September of 1830. Richard Allen organized the convention with the intention of improving the lives of African Americans by raising their social status through education and, possibly, emigration. The convention met many times in many cities, discussing plans for improvement, and the group thrived on the increasing solidarity among its members.

At a convention meeting in Rochester, New York, the plan for the National Council of Colored People was adopted. The Rochester meeting drew many prominent black leaders, including Frederick Douglass, James McCune Smith, and James Pennington. A constitution was drawn up for the new organization, and a president and several vice presidents were chosen.

The twenty-two founding members were divided among four committees. One committee was in charge of public relations and also was responsible for creating a library and museum of African American people. Another committee was instructed to help develop and direct a manual-labor school. A third committee supervised the protective unions. The last committee was the business committee, which dealt with the greatest share of the workload. Its role was to assist in the selling of African American products and the employment of

African American people, and to act as a resource center for the advancement of African Americans.

At the 1853 meeting, the council members also discussed the rampant racial oppression of the African American people, even as they were discussing signs of improvement in society. Members of both the convention and the newly formed National Council of Colored People believed that to accelerate the rate of improvement of the social status of African Americans, it was necessary to create a new institution for the education of African American youth. That new institution would be an industrial school that concentrated on agriculture and the mechanical arts. Convention members believed that the education of African American youth would enable them to acquire wealth, intelligence, virtue, and, eventually, happiness. However, on the second day of the convention, the council elected to withdraw from the proposed school plan because of the exclusive nature of the school.

Discussion on the last day of the meeting of the National Council of Colored People focused on the term "colored" in the name of the organization. After much discussion, the organization determined to retain its original name. In the final hours of the last day of the convention, the council endorsed two seminaries as places for the education of African Americans—McGrawville College and Allegheny City College.

On November 15, 1853, elections were held in several cities to elect delegates for the formation of new state councils that would act in accordance with the National Council of Colored People. The leading delegates would attend the national council meetings as well as their own state council meetings. The first national meeting was held on November 23, 1853, in New York. At least one council member each from the states of New York, Connecticut, Rhode Island, and Ohio was missing, but because of the great distance the other council members had traveled, the meeting continued. After proceeding with the meeting, one delegate from Ohio appeared and demanded that all prior proceedings be nullified. This caused great distress among the council members; eventually, the minutes of the meeting were lost, never to be found again. The controversy resulting from the Ohio delegate's demands created a somewhat hostile working environment, which contributed to the short life of the council. Despite the bleak beginnings of the national council, the state councils were operating much more smoothly and with enthusiasm.

In both the national and state councils, the idea of creating an African American school was revisited. Frederick Douglass defended the school plan unsuccessfully for two years. The country was experiencing an economic depression, which made it hard to fund the school. There also was still concern over the exclusive nature of an African American school. In many ways, the country itself was split on the issue of a separate African American nation, which many emigrationists had proposed.

The idea of a separate African American school brought many emotions to the forefront. Integrationists were wary of accepting such a school plan because of the isolation of the school and its students, yet even they saw benefits in an all-black school. Emigrationists considered the proposal and were much more willing to begin work on construction. Amid much opposition, the convention elected to discontinue plans for the proposed school in October, 1855. The other committees set up by the first national convention and their ambitious plans to assist African Americans in business pursuits and the creation of a library and museum seemed to have stopped on paper. However, there are no records of any progress toward the goals being made or of any meetings of the committees being held.

The second meeting of the National Council of Colored People was scheduled for May 24, 1854, in Cleveland, but it was postponed in order to accommodate more delegates. Eventually, only a few delegates were able to attend. Among the members attending, a debate developed over the recognition of Ohio at the national level, creating a deadlock. A suggestion to dissolve the organization was narrowly defeated in a close vote. However, the Ohio delegates withdrew from the council.

At the meeting of May 8, 1855, nearly all the delegates were from New York, as most others had declined to participate. The issue of an African American school again was discussed and once again defeated. Another issue was discussed for the first time—emigration to Canada.

Although most delegates at the convention were willing to remain in the United States, they expressed trepidation on the matter of the U.S. Constitution and the issue of slavery. The issue of emigration was the last to be discussed before the close of the final meeting of the National Council of Colored People. The state councils continued to operate and pursue social equality for African Americans for a few years longer, with councils in some states surviving longer than others.

SIGNIFICANCE

Although the National Council of Colored People lasted for only a few years, its attempts at social reform—tackling such important topics as the education and emigration of African Americans—were significant because they occurred on a national level, bringing recognition to the need for improvement of African American lives.

—*Jeri Kurtzleben*

See also: African Methodist Episcopal Church Is Founded; American Anti-Slavery Society Is Founded; Douglass Launches *The North Star*; Second Fugitive Slave Law; Stowe Publishes *Uncle Tom's Cabin*; First African American University Opens; Washington's Atlanta Compromise Speech.

Related article in *Great Lives from History: The Nineteenth Century, 1801-1900:* Frederick Douglass.

BIRTH OF THE REPUBLICAN PARTY

July 6, 1854

This new American political party welded together fragments of Whigs, Know-Nothings, and free-soil interests and presaged the sectionalization that eventually brought the U.S. Civil War.

Locale: Ripon, Wisconsin

Categories: Government and politics; organizations and institutions

KEY FIGURES

Alvan E. Bovay (1830-1890), Whig politician generally regarded as founder of the Republican Party

John C. Frémont (1813-1890), Republican presidential candidate in 1856

Horace Greeley (1811-1872), *New York Tribune* editor who joined the party in 1855

William H. Seward (1801-1872), New York senator who joined the party in 1855

Thurlow Weed (1797-1882), New York political boss who joined the party in 1855

SUMMARY OF EVENT

The development of the American political parties went through several stages during the period leading up to the U.S. Civil War (1861-1865). During the Washington administration, domestic and foreign issues combined to produce the Federalists, led by Alexander Hamilton, and the Democratic-Republicans, under the leadership of Thomas Jefferson. Federalism had its day during the 1790's but lost control of the government in 1800. By the 1820's, the Federalist Party had disintegrated, leaving the field to the Jeffersonians.

Over the next two decades, almost every politician claimed to be a Republican, that is, the heir of Jefferson, and political organizations revolved around powerful personalities such as John Quincy Adams, Henry Clay, and Andrew Jackson. After Jackson narrowly lost his bid for the presidency in 1824, the Republican Party split into two rival camps. President John Quincy Adams and Secretary of State Henry Clay provided the leadership of the National-Republicans, while Andrew Jackson, taking the name of the old Jeffersonians, began organization of the Democratic-Republicans, later called the Democratic Party.

Jackson's election in 1828 signaled another development in the evolution of political parties, as opposition to Jackson congealed into the Whig Party. The Democratic-Republican and Whig Parties dominated the political stage until the 1850's. During this period of a growing electorate, issues arising out of reformist impulses, expansion, and slavery stimulated the rise of various third parties, such as the Anti-Masons, the Liberty Party, the Free-Soil Party, and the Know-Nothings. The tensions engendered by the sectional controversy ensured the dominance, among the third parties, of the antislavery groups. The Whig Party suffered the most from the presence of these minor parties, because its major strength lay in the North, the center of antislavery and free-soil sentiment. The Compromise of 1850 seriously weakened the Whig Party, as did the deaths of Henry Clay and Daniel Webster in 1852. The Kansas-Nebraska Act of 1854 dealt the Whigs a fatal blow and helped cause the formation of an entirely new political organization—the Republican Party.

The national uproar over the Kansas-Nebraska Act damaged the unity of both the Whigs and the Democrats.

By repealing the old Missouri Compromise, which had made 36°30′ north latitude (except for Missouri) the dividing line between slave and free-soil territories in the Louisiana Purchase Territory, the Kansas-Nebraska Act split both the Democrats and the Whigs into groups that either endorsed or condemned the extension of slavery into the territories, thus giving encouragement to the Free-Soilers.

Both of the major parties possessed strong free-soil cores. These groups, in opposing the Kansas-Nebraska Act and the efforts of the administrations of Franklin Pierce and James Buchanan to force the admission of Kansas as a slave state, gradually drifted away from their original alignments into loosely knit parties held together by a common opposition to the Democratic policy in Kansas. Protest meetings occurred throughout the country in February and March of 1854. These meetings, encouraged by Free-Soilers, proved to be the first stirrings of a new political party, but the activities of the opponents of the Kansas-Nebraska Act in Ripon, Wisconsin, are generally considered to have launched that party, the Republican Party, into existence.

The events in Ripon came at a meeting held by several Whigs, Free-Soilers, and Democrats in the Congregational Church on February 28, 1854. The meeting had been called by Major Alvan E. Bovay, a prominent Whig who had, in 1852, met with Horace Greeley and discussed the formation of a new party. The group in Ripon passed a resolution stating that if the Kansas-Nebraska bill passed, they would form a new party, to be called the Republican Party. After the passage of the Kansas-Nebraska bill, Major Bovay went from house to house to announce a meeting on March 20, 1854. Of approximately one hundred voters in the village, fifty-three turned out and voted to dissolve the local Whig and Free-Soil organizations. A committee of five was appointed to form the new party.

The birth of the Republican Party may be said to have occurred on July 6, 1854, when a formal convention was held in Jackson, Michigan. Held outdoors under the oaks, this convention attracted hundreds of citizens from throughout the state. The convention adopted a platform and nominated a full slate of candidates for state offices.

This first Republican convention has given Jackson, Michigan, its claim as the birthplace of the Republican Party. Both Michigan and Wisconsin, forging coalitions, elected their candidates on the state ticket that year. In 1855, the Republicans took control and elected Nathaniel P. Banks of Massachusetts as Speaker of the Thirty-fourth Congress. The Republicans were not an immediate success.

Many Democrats and Whigs who did not favor the Kansas-Nebraska Act were reluctant to break with their established parties. In addition, while Republican popularity was damaged by its association with abolitionism, the Temperance and Know-Nothing parties competed with the Republican Party for public support. The political campaigns of 1854 and 1855 were inordinately confused by the numerous groups entering the fray. Republicans were most successful when they arranged fusion tickets with these other groups.

The obvious weakness of the Republicans made their organization less attractive to Whigs, who found themselves politically homeless. The struggle between proslavery and antislavery elements in Kansas again came to the aid of the Republicans, who, of all the anti-Kansas-Nebraska groups, were most persistent in their assaults on the proslavery Democratic policy in Kansas. In 1855, the Republicans won a political victory in Ohio and also gained the support of political boss Thurlow Weed and Senator William H. Seward, former Whigs from New York. With their strength growing rapidly, the Republicans planned to enter a slate in the presidential election of 1856. By that time, the original Free-Soil founders of the party had been reinforced by former Whigs, antislavery Democrats, and former Know-Nothings. All united on the basis of their opposition to the extension of slavery in the territories.

Appreciable support and sympathy for the Republicans were brought about by several factors: a disappointing convention of Republicans and other anti-Nebraskans at Pittsburgh in February, 1856; the sack of Lawrence, Kansas, by a proslavery mob; and the physical assault on Senator Charles Sumner of Massachusetts by Preston Brooks, a representative from South Carolina, in May, 1856. The improvement in Republican hopes guaranteed a lively fight at the Republican National Convention in Philadelphia in June, 1856.

John C. Frémont, the western explorer and adventurer, won the Republican presidential nomination and approached the election with some hope of receiving most of the Whig and some of the Know-Nothing votes. For so young a party, the results of the 1856 election were spectacular. James Buchanan, the victorious Democratic candidate, received 1,838,169 popular votes to Frémont's 1,335,265. Buchanan received 174 electoral votes, Frémont 114. Beneath those figures lay a poignant political fact—of the nineteen states Buchanan carried in the election, only five were free states. The eleven states that voted for Frémont, however, were all free states. The Democratic and Republican parties were sectional parties as no others had been before them. The South believed it had reason to fear a Republican victory in 1860.

SIGNIFICANCE

During the four years following 1856, the new party grew rapidly, capturing the House of Representatives, absorbing most Whigs and Know-Nothings, and acquiring a cadre of experienced political leaders. Comprising diverse elements, the new party emphasized free soil in the territories but successfully disassociated itself from the taint of abolitionism, and attracted support by advocating a homestead bill and old Whig measures such as internal improvements.

The Republicans' remarkable showing in 1856 justified the optimism with which the Republicans faced the future. By the same token, the quick growth of the party testified to the ominous sectionalization of politics in the nation. This sectionalization came to the forefront with the outbreak of the Civil War following the election in 1860 of Republican Abraham Lincoln as president of the United States. In this election, the upstart new political party elected a man whom most historians consider the finest president ever to lead the United States of America.

—John C. Gardner, updated by Kay Hively

See also: Compromise of 1850; Congress Passes the Kansas-Nebraska Act; Bleeding Kansas; Lincoln-Douglas Debates.

Related articles in *Great Lives from History: The Nineteenth Century, 1801-1900:* John C. Frémont; Horace Greeley; Abraham Lincoln; William H. Seward.

Congress Passes the Kansas-Nebraska Act

May 30, 1854

After the Compromise of 1850 proved only a temporary solution to the divisive debate on the extension of slavery into U.S. territories, Stephen A. Douglas's Kansas-Nebraska Act offered another temporary solution. One of the most significant political congressional acts of the nineteenth century, the new law ultimately only accelerated the movement toward civil war.

Locale: Washington, D.C.

Categories: Laws, acts, and legal history; civil rights and liberties

Key Figures

Stephen A. Douglas (1813-1861), Democratic senator from Illinois who introduced the Kansas-Nebraska Act

David Rice Atchison (1807-1886), proslavery Whig senator from Missouri

Archibald Dixon (1802-1876), proslavery Whig senator from Kentucky

Salmon P. Chase (1808-1873), Free-Soil Democrat senator from Ohio

Franklin Pierce (1804-1869), president of the United States, 1853-1857

Alexander H. Stephens (1812-1883), Whig congressman from Georgia who later became vice president of the Confederacy

Charles Sumner (1811-1874), Whig senator from Massachusetts

Summary of Event

When the U.S. Congress passed the Compromise of 1850, it laid aside the argument over the expansion of slavery into the territories only temporarily, even though the compromise seemed to be working successfully during the first two or three years immediately following its enactment. Several events kept the compromise in the public eye, including the seizure in the North of African Americans under the provisions of the Second Fugitive Slave Law (1850), the publication of Harriet Beecher Stowe's antislavery novel *Uncle Tom's Cabin* in 1852, and the last of three filibustering expeditions launched from New Orleans in August, 1851, by Venezuelan Narciso Lopez against Spanish Cuba.

Many people in the United States hoped that the slavery issue would disappear, and the economic pressures of life absorbed the attention of most average citizens. Moreover, no prominent politicians had captured the public's imagination. Noncontroversial and lackluster candidates were nominated in the presidential campaign of 1852—Franklin Pierce of New Hampshire for the Democrats and General Winfield Scott for the Whigs.

The election, which Pierce won, was no more exciting than the candidates. Evidence of the desire of U.S. voters to maintain the status quo was demonstrated further in the poor showing of John P. Hale of New Hampshire, the candidate of the Free-Soil Party. With the Democrats in control and apparently committed to the Compromise of 1850, the United States seemed destined to enjoy at least another four years of relative calm.

In January, 1854, the issue of slavery in the federal territories was reopened when Stephen A. Douglas of Illinois, chairman of the Committee on Territories, reported a bill to organize the Platte country west of Iowa and Missouri as the territory of Nebraska. Douglas's main interest was in opening the West to settlement and to the construction of a transcontinental railroad. He did not wish to reopen the slavery question, and—like his soon-to-be nemesis, Abraham Lincoln—he doubted that slavery could survive on the Great Plains. However, he also realized that he needed southern votes to get his territorial bill through Congress.

In its original form, Douglas's bill included a provision, similar to that found in the acts organizing the territories of Utah and New Mexico, that the territory itself would determine the question of its status as a slave or free state at the time of its admission. The clause dealing with slavery was intentionally ambiguous, but it probably would have left in effect—at least during the territorial stage—the provisions of the Missouri Compromise that barred slavery in the Louisiana Purchase territory north of 36°30′ north latitude. The ambiguity of the bill bothered southern political leaders, particularly the rabidly proslavery David Rice Atchison of Missouri, who was president pro tempore of the Senate and acting vice president.

Yielding to the pressure of Senator Atchison and other southern leaders, Douglas and his committee added a section to the bill that permitted the people of the territory, acting through their representatives, to decide whether the territory should be slave or free. This "popular sovereignty" formula for dealing with the slavery question implied the repeal of the Missouri Compromise's restriction on slavery.

However, proslavery leaders were not satisfied with the implicit abrogation of the Missouri Compromise. As Whig senator Archibald Dixon of Kentucky pointed out, under popular sovereignty, the restriction of slavery would remain in effect until the territorial settlers acted to end it. During the interim, immigration of slaveholders into the territory would be prohibited. Proslavery leadership forced Douglas to amend the bill further so as explicitly to repeal that section of the Missouri Compromise prohibiting slavery north of 36°30′. In addition, the territory was divided at the fortieth parallel into the two territories of Kansas and Nebraska. Most northerners considered the Missouri Compromise to be a sacred pledge, and its repeal was quite enough to destroy the relative political calm that had been prevalent in the nation since 1850.

Much more was at work, however. The Missouri Compromise had led to the creation of the political party system, utilized by the Democrats and finally adopted by the Whigs, under which party loyalty was ensured through the disposition of party and government jobs—a system later known as patronage or the spoils system.

Under that system, the tensions created by the Missouri Compromise were to be kept under control, for anyone could be controlled by the promise of employment, according to the assumptions of the new party system. The effect of the party system was to increase the size and scope of federal government operations in every election, because to get elected, candidates had to promise to award more jobs to their supporters than their opponents did. The result for the slavery interests was that the South, slowly but surely, was being placed in a permanent minority status in the Senate and House. If an antislavery president were elected, the newly powerful federal government could act directly on slavery in the South.

The Kansas-Nebraska Act, especially Douglas's concept of popular sovereignty, offered hope to the South that the dynamic created by the spoils system could be short-circuited. If territories could decide whether or not to permit slavery, then slave interests could flood the new territories with proslavery settlers, who would then vote in favor of slavery, regardless of the attitudes of Congress or the president.

Douglas still had to guide the bill through passage in the face of widespread and violent criticism from the North. The bill was certain of passage in the Senate, although it was the object of impassioned attack by Senators Salmon P. Chase of Ohio and Charles Sumner of Massachusetts. In the House, however, the issue was doubtful, and it was there that Douglas marshaled the power of the Pierce administration to force dissident Democrats into line behind the bill.

By whip and spur, the Kansas-Nebraska Act was driven through the House by a large sectional vote of 113-100 on May 30, 1854. Nearly all southern Democrats supported the measure. All forty-five northern Whigs opposed it, while thirteen of nineteen southern Whigs, led by Alexander H. Stephens of Georgia, favored it. The divisiveness of the issue was represented best by the fact that of eighty-six northern Democrats, forty-two voted against it in spite of patronage and other pressures brought to bear by administration leaders. In doing so, the Democrats showed the utter futility of basing a slavery strategy on the spoils system: Ideology proved stronger than economics, and the idea that the national debate over slavery could be contained with the promise of a few jobs was mortally wounded.

SIGNIFICANCE

The passage of the Kansas-Nebraska Act had momentous consequences. The act touched off the forces that eventually brought war. It reopened sectional issues and embittered sectional relations by arousing the entire North. It destroyed the Whig Party in the Deep South and increased southern unity and influence in the Democratic Party. It contributed greatly to the demise of the Whig Party in the North and divided the northern Democrats, inducing many of them to leave the party. Most important, it led to the formation, beginning in 1854, of the Republican Party. That party was founded in diametric opposition to the operating principles of the Democratic Party. Instead of holding that economic selfinterest took precedence over ideology, the Republicans held that fundamental beliefs mattered more than temporal, material benefits in the long run. The Republicans thus made slavery—the issue that the Democrats and the Whigs refused to touch—the focal point of their campaigns.

On a personal level, Douglas gained little support in the South and lost an important part of his support in the North. Misinterpreting northern sentiment toward this initially innocent piece of legislation, Douglas had opened a political Pandora's box. Nevertheless, the legislation reflected Douglas's personal views accurately.

He sincerely disliked slavery but thought that it should be regarded as an issue of choice by slaveholders. Therefore, the matter of human bondage was not a moral issue but simply a matter of votes. Douglas could say honestly that he opposed slavery personally, but supported the right of slaveholders to own slaves. Thus, the agony of Douglas and the struggle for Kansas had begun.

—John C. Gardner, updated by Larry Schweikart

See also: Missouri Compromise; Jan. Compromise of 1850; Second Fugitive Slave Law; Birth of the

Republican Party; Bleeding Kansas; Lincoln-Douglas Debates; Lincoln Is Elected U.S. President; Establishment of the Confederate States of America; Lincoln Is Inaugurated President.

Related articles in *Great Lives from History: The Nineteenth Century, 1801-1900:* Salmon P. Chase; Stephen A. Douglas; Franklin Pierce; Alexander H. Stephens; Charles Sumner.

EMIGRATION CONVENTION OF 1854
August 24-26, 1854

Cleveland, Ohio meeting arranged by abolitionist Martin Delany to discuss the issue of repatriation of African Americans to Liberia, Africa to establish a new nation for descendants of African slaves. The meeting is considered a foundational event in the formation of the Black Nationalism movement of the 1800s.

Identification: 1854 meeting of African Americans in Cleveland, Ohio to debate the proposal of relocating free African American women and men to Africa.

Martin Delany, a physician, abolitionist, and writer, who became one of the first three African Americans admitted to Harvard University, was one of the first major proponents of the "Back-to-Africa" or "Colonization movements," which promoted the idea of African Americans returning to Africa to help found or develop nations led by members of their race. The American Colonization Society, founded in 1816, was one of the first organizations to advocate for African American

emigration, and influenced numerous later organizations with similar goals. Delaney wrote a manifesto, *Political Destiny of the Colored Race on the American Continent*, which became the literary impetus for a National Emigration Convention held in Cleveland, Ohio, at the Universalist Church on Prospect Street, on August 24-26 of 1854. The emigration movement divided the African American community, with Frederick Douglass openly condemning the idea of repatriation or emigration in favor of remaining in the United States and forming a domestic civil rights movement. Though Douglass's ideas eventually won out, thousands of African Americans emigrated to Liberia and other African nations during the late 1800s and the emigration concept was an important part of the Black Nationalism and the Black Power movements throughout the 1960s and 70s.

—Micah Issitt

BLEEDING KANSAS
May, 1856-August, 1858

The failures of legislative compromises to design a political balance between the North and the South on the issue of slavery in the territories turned the Kansas Territory into a bloody battleground between proslave and free-soil immigrants that presaged the U.S. Civil War.

Locale: Kansas Territory
Categories: Terrorism and political assassination; wars, uprisings, and civil unrest; civil rights and liberties

KEY FIGURES
James Buchanan (1791-1868), president of the United States, 1857-1861
Stephen A. Douglas (1813-1861), senator from Illinois
John White Geary (1819-1873), governor of Kansas Territory, 1856-1857
Franklin Pierce (1804-1869), president of the United States, 1853-1857

Charles Robinson (1818-1894), leader of Free-State Party, which elected him governor of Kansas in 1856

John Brown (1800-1859), militant abolitionist

SUMMARY OF EVENT

Between 1855 and 1858, Kansas was engulfed in chaos that affected all of the United States. While the Whig Party disintegrated under the pressure of the slavery controversy, the Democratic Party split into feuding sectional factions, and the Republican Party was born.

Politicians suddenly found themselves without political homes. Political reputations were made and unmade as prominent national figures paid the price of their inability to resolve the sectional disputes while facing challenges from rising young men. The United States seemed to be drifting off course, and people wondered about the ultimate fate of a nation that apparently had lost control of its own destiny.

With the opening of Kansas Territory to settlement in 1854, a contest began between groups supporting slavery (mainly persons from Missouri) and settlers from the northwestern states who were free-soilers in practice, if not in ideology. Since the Missourians were closest to Kansas, they seized control of the territorial government and immediately enacted proslavery legislation. President Franklin Pierce and his successor, James Buchanan of Pennsylvania, accepted the proslavery Kansas government and committed the Democratic Party to the admission of Kansas as a slave state.

However, the numerical dominance of slavery supporters in Kansas soon dwindled as settlers from free states found their way into the territory. By September, 1855, there were enough Free-Soilers in Kansas to repudiate the territorial legislature, organize a Free State Party, and call for a constitutional convention to meet in Topeka. There, in October and November, 1855, a freestate constitution was written. In January, 1856, Governor Charles Robinson and a legislature were elected.

Kansas thus found itself with two governments— one supporting slavery and considered legal by the Democratic administration in Washington, but resting upon a small minority of the population; and the other representing majority opinion in Kansas but condemned as an act of rebellion by President Pierce and Senator Stephen A. Douglas of Illinois.

Douglas's role in the Kansas dispute was of particular interest, as he had drafted the Kansas-Nebraska Act in 1854 as a way to extend a railroad westward across the territories. Douglas favored the theory of popular sovereignty, to "let the people decide." That doctrine, however, was exposed—eventually by Abraham Lincoln in the Lincoln-Douglas debates—as unconstitutional: The will of the people could not be held above constitutionally protected rights. Douglas's bill, however, created an entirely new concern. The North had started to outdistance the South in population, giving it more seats in Congress, and the Missouri Compromise had ensured that the North would have a permanent advantage in the Senate. Southerners were beginning to realize that if the wrong kind of presidential candidate came to office, their region would find itself excluded from the power.

Although both proslave and free-soil groups moved into Kansas, actual bloodshed remained at a minimum through 1855; nevertheless, the territory quickly came to symbolize the sectional dispute. Anti-Kansas-Nebraska groups made up of former Whigs and dissident Democrats arose and eventually were led by Douglas. At the eleventh hour, Douglas had come to realize the extent of his unpopularity in the North and to recognize the fraud that the proslavery government in Kansas had propagated.

Through the spring and summer of 1856, violence became commonplace in Kansas. Armed free-soil and proslavery parties skirmished along the Wakarusa River south of Lawrence as early as December, 1855; but it was the sack of Lawrence in May, 1856, by a large band of proslavery Border Ruffians from Missouri that ignited the conflict. Retaliation was demanded: John Brown, the abolitionist crusader, his four sons, and three others struck at Pottawatomie, where they executed five settlers who were reputed to be proslavery. That act of terrorism sparked further retaliation.

Early in August, free-soil forces captured the slavery stronghold of Franklin; later that month, Free-Soilers, led by Brown, repelled an attack by a large party of proslavers at Osawatomie. Guerrilla warfare raged throughout the territory until September, when a temporary armistice was achieved by the arrival of federal troops and a new territorial governor, John White Geary. However, a solution to the disorders in Kansas could come only from Washington, D.C., and it would have to overcome the determination of the Democratic administration and its southern supporters to bring Kansas into the union as a slave state. Meeting at Lecompton in January and February, 1857, the proslave territorial legislature called for an election of delegates to a constitutional convention. However, no provision was made to submit what could only be a proslavery constitution to a popular vote. The measure passed over Governor Geary's veto.

The constitutional convention that met in Lecompton in September, 1857, hammered out a document to the electorate; the proslavery leadership would agree only to submit the document to the people with the choice of accepting it with or without the clause explicitly guaranteeing slavery. However, ample protection for slavery was woven into the fabric of the constitution. Even if the "constitution without slavery" clause had won popular approval, thereby causing slavery to exist "no longer," slaves already in Kansas as property would not be affected.

Opponents refused to go to the polls, and the proslavery Lecompton constitution was approved in December, 1857.

Meanwhile, the Free-Soil Party captured control of the territorial legislature and successfully requested the new territorial governor, Frederick P. Stanton, to convene the legislature in order to call for another election.

In the new election, one might vote for or against the entire Lecompton constitution. On January 4, 1858, the Lecompton constitution met overwhelming defeat. Kansas was, by that time, free-soil in sentiment.

The new Buchanan administration, which followed Pierce's, saw the situation in Kansas otherwise. It supported the Lecompton constitution, which became a test of Democratic Party loyalty. Although Douglas came out against the administration's position, the U.S. Senate voted in March, 1858, to admit Kansas under the Lecompton constitution. Public sentiment in the North opposed such a policy, and the House of Representatives voted to admit Kansas as a state only on the condition that the state constitution be submitted in its entirety to the voters at a carefully controlled election. That proviso, called the Crittenden-Montgomery Amendment, was rejected by the Senate.

Out of the deadlock, a House-Senate conference ensued that proposed the English Bill, a compromise measure designed to save the Buchanan administration from utter defeat. The bill stipulated that the Lecompton constitution should be submitted to the people of Kansas again: If approved, the new state would receive a federal land grant; if rejected, statehood would be postponed until the population of the territory reached 93,000 residents, instead of the 60,000 that had been required of all other territories. Although Congress passed the bill on May 21, the voters of Kansas again rejected

the Lecompton constitution, this time by a margin of six to one. In January, 1861, after several southern states announced their secession from the union, Kansas entered the union as a free state under the Wyandotte constitution.

For Kansas, the storm ended with the defeat of the Lecompton constitution in August, 1858; but for Douglas, condemned as a traitor to his party, and for the Democrats, it had just started. Douglas soon met Abraham Lincoln, the Republican nominee for the Senate seat in Illinois, at Ottawa, Illinois, in the first of their historic debates.

In another debate, at Freeport, Lincoln cited the Supreme Court's 1857 ruling in the Dred Scott case—that Congress could make no law prohibiting slavery—to ask Douglas how he would keep slavery out of a territory using popular sovereignty. Douglas replied that the population could vote to install antislave judges and sheriffs who would not enforce slavery restrictions. That answer was ridiculed as the "Freeport Doctrine" by southerners, and destroyed any chance Douglas had of carrying the South in the 1860 election. Lincoln lost the Senate race to Douglas but captured the presidency in 1860 without winning a single electoral vote in the South.

SIGNIFICANCE

The role of the territories in offering the South a means to continue slavery has been subject to considerable analysis.

An important factor in the weakened position of the South was the Democratic Party, which had been created specifically to exclude slavery from the national political debate. The Albany-Richmond axis provided the base of Democratic Party support that tacitly agreed that the party offer presidential candidates who were "northern men of southern principles"—in other words, men who could draw the large electoral states of the North but who would not use the power of the federal government to attack slavery. The irony of the Democratic Party was that it acquired party allegiance by granting government jobs—patronage—which, in turn, caused the government to grow larger and more powerful with each election.

As a result, by the time the Republicans became a national force, the federal government stood to pose a threat to slavery in the "wrong" hands. Since the Republicans' first principle was the elimination of slavery in the territories, their election posed the threat of placing federal power—by then, far greater than anyone had

---

President Buchanan on Kansas Statehood

Excerpt from James Buchanan's inaugural address regarding statehood for Kansas, March 4, 1857: We have recently passed through a Presidential contest in which the passions of our fellow-citizens were excited to the highest degree by questions of deep and vital importance; but when the people proclaimed their will the tempest at once subsided and all was calm. The voice of the majority, speaking in the manner prescribed by the Constitution, was heard, and instant submission followed. Our own country could alone have exhibited so grand and striking a spectacle of the capacity of man for self-government. What a happy conception, then, was it for Congress to apply this simple rule, that the will of the majority shall govern, to the settlement of the question of domestic slavery in the Territories. Congress is neither "to legislate slavery into any Territory or State nor to exclude it therefrom, but to leave the people thereof perfectly free to form and regulate their domestic institutions in their own way, subject only to the Constitution of the United States."

As a natural consequence, Congress has also prescribed that when the Territory of Kansas shall be admitted as a State it shall be received into the Union with or without slavery, as their constitution may prescribe at the time of their admission. A difference of opinion has arisen in regard to the point of time when the people of a Territory shall decide this question for themselves.

This is, happily, a matter of but little practical importance. Besides, it is a judicial question, which legitimately belongs to the Supreme Court of the United States, before whom it is now pending, and will, it is understood, be speedily and finally settled. To their decision, in common with all good citizens, I shall cheerfully submit, whatever it may be, though it has ever been my individual opinion that under the Nebraska-Kansas act the appropriate period will be when the number of actual residents in the Territory shall justify the formation of a constitution with a view to its admission as a State into the Union.

---

dreamed it might be during the 1820's—into the hands of a party determined (in southerners' eyes) to destroy slavery.

Finally, the apparent victory of the Free-Soil elections in Kansas had the immediate effect of convincing railroads that the state would remain free. The Dred Scott ruling made that outcome completely uncertain; as a result, the railroad stocks crashed, bringing on the Panic of 1857, which, ironically, advanced the Republican Party's fortunes in the North.

—*John G. Clark,*
updated by Larry Schweikart

See also: Missouri Compromise; Compromise of 1850; Congress Passes the Kansas-Nebraska Act; Birth of the Republican Party; *Dred Scott v. Sandford*; Lincoln-Douglas Debates; Brown's Raid on Harpers Ferry; Lincoln Is Elected U.S. President.

Related articles in *Great Lives from History: The Nineteenth Century, 1801-1900*: John Brown; James Buchanan; Stephen A. Douglas; Abraham Lincoln; Franklin Pierce.

FIRST AFRICAN AMERICAN UNIVERSITY OPENS

January 1, 1857

The creation of the Ashmun Institute—which later became Lincoln University—provided the first major institution of higher education for African Americans.

Also known as: Ashmun Institute; Lincoln University
Locale: Chester County, Oxford, Pennsylvania
Categories: Education; organizations and institutions

KEY FIGURES

Jehudi Ashmun (1794-1828), editor who worked for the repatriation of African Americans, and for whom Ashmun Institute was named

John Miller Dickey (1806-1878), Presbyterian minister who founded Ashmun Institute
Sarah Emlen Cresson Dickey (fl. mid-nineteenth century), Dickey's wife, who helped found the school
John Pym Carter (fl. mid-nineteenth century), first president of Ashmun Institute

SUMMARY OF EVENT

The institution of higher learning now known as Lincoln University first opened its doors as Ashmun Institute, on January 1, 1857, in Chester County, Oxford, Pennsylvania.

173

Its original purpose was to give African American youths an opportunity to receive sound, well-balanced educations. Although many people through many decades helped to create the idea of a school devoted to the higher education of African Americans, John Miller Dickey was the man who put the idea to work.

The son of a minister and of Scotch-Irish descent, Dickey attended Dickinson College in Milton, Pennsylvania, where he graduated in 1824. He then entered the Princeton Theological Seminary to become a Presbyterian minister, following in the footsteps of his many relatives who also were ministers. In 1827, he graduated from the seminary and received his first assignment, at the Presbytery of New Castle in Newark, Delaware. Two years later, he received a new assignment in Georgia from the Board of Missions. Finding that the slaves in that area listened ardently to his sermons, he was impressed by their desire to learn.

In 1834, Dickey married Sarah Emlen Cresson, the daughter of a wealthy Quaker family. The marriage was frowned upon by the Quakers because Dickey was a Presbyterian, a religion whose beliefs clashed with theirs. Although Sarah was rejected from Quaker meetings, the Quaker religion had helped her to develop and continue her support and concern for African Americans, which she took with her into her marriage to John Dickey.

Many circumstances led to the founding of Ashmun Institute, including the past experiences of both Dickey and his wife. John Miller, Dickey's grandfather, had given money for the education of African American youth in earlier years, and Miller's acquaintance, Benjamin Franklin, also saw the need for an African American school. Both Dickey and his wife had many relatives who were ardently opposed to slavery. Another reason that Dickey himself cited for his interest in African American education was the kidnapping of two young African American girls, Rachel and Elizabeth Parker.

Although both girls were returned to their home, the incident helped Dickey to realize the inherent inequalities in the lives of the African American youths and the difficulties they experienced because they were not given the same opportunities that other young people enjoyed. The death of Dickey's own child was another factor in his decision to create the institute.

Sometime in 1853, Sarah selected the land on which they would establish an educational institute for black youths that would teach science, the arts, and theology. During the same year, John Miller Dickey announced his plans for an African American university, which would be called Ashmun Institute. In order to bring the institute into being, a committee was set up to gather funds and secure the Ashmun Institute's charter through the Pennsylvania legislature. By April 29, 1854, the Ashmun Institute Bill was signed by Governor William Bigler, allowing for the construction of the new school. Because the project had insufficient funds to construct buildings, Dickey used his own money (for which he would later be reimbursed) to finance construction of the president's house and a schoolroom with attached dormitories. By the fall of 1856, the school was nearly ready to open, and the Reverend John Pym Carter was selected as its first president.

The institute was named after Jehudi Ashmun, who had been born in Champlain, New York, in 1794. In 1820, four years after graduating from the University of Vermont, he took the editorship of *The African Intelligencer*, a magazine devoted to the movement to send freed slaves to Liberia promoted by the American Colonization Society. Through his involvement in the magazine, Ashmun learned that a conductor was needed for a trip to Liberia to help take slaves back to their ancestral homeland. After working for repatriation of African Americans, he died in 1828 from the effects of a long illness.

In naming their school after Ashmun, the Dickeys memorialized the man for his work in behalf of freed slaves. The first building of Ashmun Institute was dedicated on December 31, 1856, the fifth anniversary of the kidnapping of Rachel Parker.

Classes at Ashmun Institute began on January 1, 1857, with only two students, James Ralston Amos and his brother Thomas. The first decades of the institution's operation proved difficult—funding continued to be a challenge, and the outbreak of the Civil War (1861-1865) emptied the institute's classroom for a short time.

Moreover, there was some concern that the institute would be raided after the war began, but no such instances were reported. After the war ended and the Thirteen Amendment to the U.S. Constitution abolished slavery, Ashmun Institute experienced a surge in enrollment, and the school began to expand.

Students at the four-year institute received instruction in geography, history, grammar, composition, elocution, and mathematics. They also received instruction in Greek, Hebrew, and Latin. In addition, they studied church theology and history, as well as prayer and pulpit exercises. Although scholarship was important, each term the students were also evaluated on their other qualities, including piety, talents, diligence, eloquence, prudence, economy, zeal, health, and influence. Over time, the curriculum evolved and became more diversified as the school became more firmly established.

On February 7, 1866, the board of the institute began the process to change the name of the institute to Lincoln University in honor of Abraham Lincoln, who was credited with championing emancipation of the slaves. The Pennsylvania legislature approved the change of name, and after April 4, 1866, Ashmun Institute was known as Lincoln University.

SIGNIFICANCE

There were many notable presidents of the university as it continued to grow and become a respected institution. Isaac Norton Rendall, who was among the great contributors, served as president from 1865 until 1905. In 1945, Horace Mann Bond became the first alumnus of Lincoln University to become its president, as well as the first African American to hold the position. He held the position until 1957.

Lincoln University has remained a predominantly African American school and is proudly recognized as the oldest institution of higher learning dedicated to educating African American youths. Among its graduates are such notable persons as the poet Langston Hughes; Thurgood Marshall, the first African American Supreme Court justice; Nnamdi Azikiwe, the first president of Nigeria; and Kwame Nkrumah, the first prime minister and president of Ghana. During the first century of its existence, it graduated more than 20 percent the African American doctors in the United States and more than 10 percent of the country's black lawyers.

—Jeri Kurtzleben

See also: National Council of Colored People Is Founded; Congress Creates the Freedmen's Bureau; Washington's Atlanta Compromise Speech.

Related articles in *Great Lives from History: The Nineteenth Century, 1801-1900:* Frederick Douglass; Abraham Lincoln; Booker T. Washington.

Dred Scott v. Sandford

March 6, 1857

In one of the most reviled decisions in its history, the U.S. Supreme Court ruled that Congress could not limit slavery in the territories, nullifying the Missouri Compromise, and also that African Americans could not be U.S. citizens.

Also known as: Dred Scott Case; *Scott v. Sandford*
Locale: Washington, D.C.
Categories: Human rights; laws, acts, and legal history; civil rights and liberties

KEY FIGURES

Dred Scott (c. 1795-1858), Missouri slave who was the plaintiff in the case
John F. A. Sanford (1806/1807-1857), Scott's legal owner and the defendant in the case (his name was misspelled in the official Court records)
Montgomery Blair (1813-1883), Scott's counsel in Missouri

Roger Brooke Taney (1777-1864), chief justice of the United States, 1836-1864
Benjamin R. Curtis (1809-1874) and
John McLean (1785-1861), associate justices
James Buchanan (1791-1868), president of the United States, 1857-1861

SUMMARY OF EVENT

Few decisions of the U.S. Supreme Court have had the political repercussions of *Dred Scott v. Sandford*. The decision supplied the infant Republican Party with new issues to use against the Democrats, who were already divided by the disturbances in Kansas that historians have called Bleeding Kansas. The decision also was an embarrassment to the Republicans, for in denying the authority of Congress to legislate on slavery in the territories, the ruling destroyed the major platform of the Republican Party. The Supreme Court's opinion also damaged, if not destroyed, the practicability of Stephen

A. Douglas's doctrine of popular sovereignty, for if Congress had no authority to regulate slavery in the territories, then territorial legislatures had no authority either, as they were inferior bodies created by Congress. The Court had thus entered completely into the political issues tearing at the union, and the reputation of Chief Justice Roger Brooke Taney was shattered in the North.

Two pertinent questions were raised by the Scott case.

First, could an African American, whose ancestors were imported into the United States and sold as slaves, become a member of the political community created by the U.S. Constitution and thereby enjoy the rights and privileges of a U.S. citizen? Second, did the Constitution regard African Americans as a separate class of persons distinct from the class known as citizens?

Dred Scott, the plaintiff in *Dred Scott v. Sandford*, was a slave of African descent. In 1834, he had been taken by his owner, John Emerson, an army surgeon, to the free state of Illinois and then to Wisconsin Territory, which was free by the provisions of the Missouri Compromise of 1820. Emerson returned to Missouri with Scott in 1838. After Emerson's death in 1846, Scott sued his widow in the Missouri courts for his freedom, on the grounds that his residence in a free state and in a free territory had made him free. Although he won in the lower court, Missouri's supreme court reversed the decision in 1852 and declared that Scott was still a slave because of his voluntary return to Missouri.

While Scott's litigation was progress, Emerson's widow remarried. Under Missouri law, administration of her first husband's estate passed to her brother, John F. A. Sanford. Because Sanford was a citizen of New York, Scott's lawyer, Montgomery Blair, acting on the grounds that the litigants in the case were residents of different states, sued for Scott's freedom in the United States circuit court in Missouri. The verdict there also went against Scott.

As expected, the case was appealed to the U.S. Supreme Court, where it was argued in February, 1856, and reargued in January, 1857. At first, the justices of the Supreme Court agreed to decide against Scott on the grounds that Scott was a slave under Missouri law, as it was interpreted by its supreme court, despite his residence on free soil. However, for a variety of reasons, the justices changed their minds and determined to deal with the controversial questions of African American citizenship and congressional power over slavery in the territories.

One of the justices confidentially informed President-Elect James Buchanan of the Court's intention. Buchanan supported the Court's plan and even persuaded

one justice to concur in the majority opinion. The Supreme Court announced its decision on March 6, 1857, two days after Buchanan's inauguration as president.

Although each of the nine justices issued a separate opinion, a majority of them held that African Americans who were descendants of slaves could not belong to the political community created by the Constitution and enjoy the right of federal citizenship. They also agreed that the Missouri Compromise of 1820, forbidding slavery in the part of the Louisiana Purchase territory north of 36°30′ north latitude, was unconstitutional.

According to the opinion of Chief Justice Taney, African Americans were "beings of an inferior order" who "had no rights which the white man was bound to respect."

The significance of Taney's comments lies in the fact that they established a perception of African Americans that transcended their status as slaves. In considering the issue of equality, Taney did not limit his assessment of African Americans to those who were slaves but also included African Americans who were free. His opinion raises questions about the extent to which his public pronouncement on the alleged inferiority of African Americans helped to establish conditions for the future of race relations in the United States.

Although individual states could grant citizenship to African Americans, state action did not give them U.S. citizenship under the federal Constitution. Therefore, concluded Taney, "Dred Scott was not a citizen of Missouri within the meaning of the Constitution of the United States, and not entitled as such to sue in its courts." There is considerable evidence that African Americans were not considered citizens and guaranteed rights and privileges by the U.S. Constitution. One of these rights, the ability to sue, was critical to the opinion of the Court.

The Constitution granted each of the original thirteen states the authority to continue the importation of slaves until 1808. In so doing, the Constitution supported an enterprise that relegated African Americans to the status of chattel. In effect, extending the trading of slaves by the states for more than twenty years after the signing of the Constitution shows that African Americans were not included as a class granted citizenship. The Constitution also indicated that states were to make a commitment to each other to assist slave owners in retaining their property. Because slaves were defined as chattel, this applied directly to them as a class. Finally, the intent of the Constitution to exclude African Americans as citizens was revealed in the congruence between the stated ideas and the conduct that was prescribed. That is, the authors of the Constitution expected the language and the actual practices and conventions during that time period to be consistent.

On the second point, Taney declared that, since slaves were property, under the Fifth Amendment to the Constitution—which prohibited Congress from taking property without due process of law—Congress had only the power and duty to protect the slaveholders' rights. Therefore, the Missouri Compromise law was unconstitutional. This part of Taney's opinion was unnecessary, an *obiter dictum*, for, having decided that no African American could become a citizen within the meaning of the Constitution, there was no need for the Supreme Court to consider the question of whether Congress could exclude slavery from the territories of the United States. The Court's decision was consistent with earlier decisions regarding slavery. Historically, the Court's opinions had protected slave owners' rights to their property, even when the chattel was slaves.

The two antislavery justices on the Court, John McLean and Benjamin Curtis, wrote dissenting opinions. They stated that before the adoption of the U.S. Constitution, free African Americans were citizens of several states and were, therefore, also citizens of the United States. Consequently, the United States circuit court had jurisdiction in the Scott case. Because the Constitution gave Congress full power to legislate for the federal territories, it could act as it pleased regarding slavery, as on all other subjects.

SIGNIFICANCE

The nation reacted strongly to the Supreme Court's decision. White slaveholders in the South were delighted, for a majority of the justices had supported the extreme southern position. Under the Court's ruling, all federal territories were now legally opened to slavery, and Congress was obliged to protect the slaveholders' possession of their chattel. The free-soil platform of the Republicans

---

SCOTT V. SANDFORD Decision

It becomes necessary, therefore, to determine who were citizens of the several States when the Constitution was adopted. And in order to do this, we must recur to the governments and institutions of the thirteen colonies, when they separated from Great Britain and formed new sovereignties, and took their places in the family of independent nations. We must enquire who, at that time, were recognized as the people or citizens of a State, whose rights and liberties had been outraged by the English Government; and who declared their independence, and assumed the powers of Government to defend their rights by force of arms.

In the opinion of the court, the legislation and histories of the times, and the language used in the Declaration of Independence, show, that neither the class of persons who had been imported as slaves, nor their descendants, whether they had become free or not, were then acknowledged as a part of the people, nor intended to be included in the general words used in that memorable instrument.

. . .

[N]o laws or usages of other nations, or reasoning of statesmen or jurists upon the relations of master and slave, can enlarge the powers of the Government, or take from the citizens the rights they have reserved. And if the Constitution recognizes the right of property of the master in a slave, and makes no distinction between that description of property and other property owned by a citizen, no tribunal, acting under the authority of the United States, whether it be legislative, executive, or judicial, has a right to draft such a distinction, or deny to it the benefit of the provisions and guarantees which have been provided for the protection of private property against the encroachments of the Government.

Now . . . the right of property in a slave is distinctly and expressly affirmed in the Constitution. The right to traffic in it, like an ordinary article of merchandise and property, was guarantied to the citizens of the United States, in every State that might desire it, for twenty years. And the Government in express terms is pledged To protect it in all future time, if the slave escapes from his owner. This is done in plain words—too plain to be misunderstood. And no word can be found in the Constitution which gives Congress a greater power over slave property, or which entitles property of that kind to less protection than property of any other description. The only power conferred is the power coupled with the duty of guarding and protecting the owner in his rights. . . .

---

was unconstitutional. The Republicans denounced the decision in the most violent terms, as the product of an incompetent and partisan body. They declared that when they obtained control of the national government, they would change the membership of the Supreme Court and secure reversal of the decision. Northern Democrats, while not attacking the Supreme

Court, were discouraged by the decision, for if Congress could not prohibit slavery in any territory, neither could a territorial legislature.

Therefore, popular sovereignty also would cease to be a valid way of deciding whether a federal territory should be slave or free. The Supreme Court's decision in this case and many subsequent opinions of the Court would have an adverse impact upon African Americans seeking legal rights as citizens of the United States. Moreover, as the first decision since *Marbury v. Madison* (1803) to reverse an act of Congress as unconstitutional, it generated lower esteem for the Court among

northerners, widening the growing rift between North and South.

—John G. Clark, updated by K. Sue Jewell

See also: Missouri Compromise; Bleeding Kansas; Lincoln-Douglas Debates; Civil Rights Act of 1866; Civil Rights Cases; *Plessy v. Ferguson*; *United States v. Wong Kim Ark*.

Related articles in *Great Lives from History: The Nineteenth Century, 1801-1900:* Dred Scott; Roger Brooke Taney.

LINCOLN-DOUGLAS DEBATES
June 16-October 15, 1858

Among the most brilliant and famous political debates in U.S. history, the campaign debates between Illinois senatorial candidates Abraham Lincoln and Stephen A. Douglas articulated the fundamental national split over the issue of slavery and elevated Lincoln to a national stature that would carry him to the presidency two years later.

Also known as: Illinois Election for U.S. Senate
Locale: Illinois
Category: Government and politics

KEY FIGURES
Abraham Lincoln (1809-1865), Republican candidate for Illinois's Senate seat and later president, 1861-1865
Stephen A. Douglas (1813-1861), incumbent Illinois senator against whom Lincoln ran
James Buchanan (1791-1868), Democratic president of the United States, 1857-1861, who opposed Douglas

SUMMARY OF EVENT
Republican successes in the U.S. national elections of 1856 attested to the strength of the newly formed Republican Party. In the congressional elections of 1858, the Republicans were prepared to capitalize on such major issues as "Bleeding Kansas" and the *Dred Scott* decision of March, 1857, and expected to solidify their position in the U.S. Congress. Many Republicans were willing to cooperate with members of other parties who opposed the Buchanan administration, including

members of the anti-Nebraska Democrats, Know-Nothings, and former Whigs.

Recent disturbances in Kansas were upsetting the Democratic Party. Although many Democrats had opposed the Kansas-Nebraska Act of 1854 from its enactment, others opposed it only after the situation in Kansas had deteriorated badly and the administrations of Presidents Franklin Pierce and James Buchanan continued to demand the admission of Kansas as a slave state. The proslavery Lecompton constitution that had been proposed in Kansas and Buchanan's insistence that Congress admit Kansas under it caused the Democratic Party split. Stephen A. Douglas, the author of the Kansas-Nebraska Act, broke with Buchanan to lead the opposition to the admission of Kansas as a slave state because a majority of the people in Kansas wanted it to be free. At the same time, Douglas faced the task of defending his Senate seat against a challenge from the well-organized Republican Party.

Before the adoption of the Seventeenth Amendment to the U.S. Constitution in 1913, U.S. senators were elected by state legislatures, not by popular vote. Candidates normally did not conduct statewide campaigns for the office, and parties seeking to remove incumbents normally did not designate official party candidates to challenge the incumbents. However, during the late 1850's, the times were not normal, and Republicans in Illinois formally nominated Abraham Lincoln as their candidate for Douglas's Senate seat. Lincoln then challenged Douglas to a series of debates, and Douglas accepted. Douglas was well aware that his political future was at stake but hoped to turn to his advantage the anti-Lecompton stand that he had taken on the admission of Kansas to statehood. By contrast, Lincoln had little to lose in the debates. He had served only one term in the House of Representatives and had already failed in his bid for Illinois's other Senate seat when he opposed Lyman Trumbull in 1856.

Lincoln and Douglas made a thorough canvass of Illinois in 1858. Lincoln traveled more than forty-five hundred miles and Douglas more than five thousand. Each candidate made about sixty speeches and numerous impromptu appearances, mostly from the rear platforms of railroad cars. Their speeches and the seven debates, in which they met face-to-face, attracted tens of thousands of listeners and received wide newspaper coverage. The debates transformed Lincoln into a person of national reputation.

Lincoln received his nomination for the Senate seat at the Republican state convention in Springfield in June, 1858. In his acceptance speech, which he delivered on June 16, he included a phrase from the New Testament that was arguably the most radical of his career: "A house divided against itself cannot stand" (Matt. 12:25). Although that speech was not part of Lincoln's formal debates with Douglas, its "house divided" theme set the tone for his entire campaign. While avoiding any explicit statements that he would formally work to end slavery, Lincoln continued to defend his prophecy throughout his campaign; Douglas argued equally vehemently that the nation had always existed "half slave and half free" and could continue to do so.

On July 9, Douglas replied to Lincoln's statements in Chicago, and Lincoln spoke again the next day. Their first formal debate was in Ottawa, Illinois, on August 21, 1858, when they had an audience of thousand people. Douglas spoke first, hammering Lincoln and accusing him and the Republican Party of being a party of abolition. Caught unaware by Douglas's ferocity, Lincoln stumbled through his own speech. He would be better prepared in the later debates.

On August 27, the candidates met again, at Freeport. This time, Lincoln took the offensive and trapped Douglas into conceding that residents of a U.S. territory had the authority to "exclude slavery prior to the formation of a State Constitution." Douglas's reply on that subject became known as the Freeport Doctrine—a position that placed Douglas at odds with much of the Democratic Party, which had believed the Supreme Court's Dred Scott decision had ruled against popular sovereignty in the territories on the issue of slavery. The debates then moved on to Jonesboro on September 15, Charleston on September 18, Galesburg on October 7, Quincy on October 13, and Alton on October 15.

Both men had set their debate strategies before their first formal meeting. Lincoln concentrated on attacking Douglas for his authorship of the Kansas-Nebraska Act, which repealed the Missouri Compromise. He charged that Douglas was a puppet of the slave-power conspiracy, that popular sovereignty had been buried by the Dred Scott decision, and that there was a national conspiracy to legitimize slavery in the free states. For his part, Douglas assailed Lincoln as an advocate of African American suffrage and charged him with attempted subversion of the Supreme Court. He accused Lincoln of opposing the Dred Scott decision on the grounds that it denied African American citizenship while masking an insidious intention to interfere with the domestic institutions of individual states.

Lincoln was embarrassed by Douglas's effort to associate him with abolitionism. While admitting his opposition to slavery, Lincoln acknowledged his own inability to offer a solution to the problem of slavery, short of abolition. Like Douglas, Lincoln believed that African Americans were basically inferior to Euro-Americans. However, he differed from Douglas in holding that slavery was an immoral system that was inconsistent with the principles and practices of democratic government. Lincoln insisted that the contagion of slavery must be kept out of the new territories. Douglas countered by demanding that the settlers in the new territories decide on the issue of slavery themselves. Lincoln responded by pointing out that because the Dred Scott decision prohibited Congress from legislating on slavery in the territories, territorial legislatures were similarly prohibited from making such legislation because they were creations of the U.S. Congress.

Seeking to salvage the concept of popular sovereignty, Douglas suggested at Freeport that regardless of the Dred Scott decision, the citizens of people of a territory could lawfully exclude slavery prior to forming their new state government, for slavery could not exist without the protection of a slave code, which would need to be enacted by the territorial legislature. At the conclusion of the joint canvass, Lincoln proposed that the principles of equality set forth in the Declaration of Independence should be applied to the new territories. Douglas concluded with the statement that the nation could endure forever half slave and half free.

In November's national elections, the Republicans swept most of the northern states. However, Douglas was reelected in Illinois, even though the Republican state ticket drew 125,000 votes to 121,000 for the Douglas Democrats and 5,000 for the Buchanan Democrats. Democrats won forty-six seats in the Illinois state legislature to forty-one for the Republicans, and the Democratic-controlled legislature—not the popular vote—re-elected Douglas to the Senate.

SIGNIFICANCE

Despite Abraham Lincoln's defeat in the senatorial contest, the campaign debates made him a national figure, one with a reputation for moderation that was attractive to former Whigs. The radical implications of his House Divided prediction had, by then, drifted into the background.

Lincoln had more than held his own during the debates with Douglas, a well-known rival and formidable opponent. Lincoln's words, although edited in contemporary newspapers, grabbed the attention of all who read them. Lincoln was well aware of the importance of public sentiment and would put this knowledge to excellent use the next time he faced Douglas, in the presidential election of 1860.

—John G. Clark, updated by Richard Adler

See also: Missouri Compromise; Southerners Advance Proslavery Arguments; Compromise of 1850; Congress Passes the Kansas-Nebraska Act; Birth of the Republican Party; Bleeding Kansas; *Dred Scott v. Sandford*; Brown's Raid on Harpers Ferry; Lincoln Is Elected U.S. President; Lincoln Is Inaugurated President; Lincoln Issues the Emancipation Proclamation.

Related articles in *Great Lives from History: The Nineteenth Century, 1801-1900:* James Buchanan; Stephen A. Douglas; Abraham Lincoln.

CLOTILDE CAPTURE

July, 1859

The arrest and prosecution of the Clotilde finally ended the illegal slave trade to the United States and brought a symbolic end to slavery.

The Event: Capture of the last ship to deliver slaves to the United States
Place: Mobile Bay, Alabama

There are contradictory reports about slavers—ships especially built to transport slaves—during the period from 1858 to 1861. Historians, however, have managed to piece together an accurate account of the *Clotilde*, the last U.S. slave ship, which smuggled more than a hundred Africans into Alabama.

The slave trade was outlawed by Congress in 1808. This brutal business continued without serious interference, however, until the early 1820's, when federal officials began capturing slavers and freeing their prisoners. Public sentiment, even in the South, did not favor revival of the trade. To annoy northern antislavery and abolitionist advocates, numerous rumors were spread by slave traders and sympathizers about slavers landing on the southeastern coast. For example, the New York Daily Tribune received many letters reporting landings of slavers in Florida and the Carolinas. There were even rumors in the 1860's of a prosperous underground slave-trading company operating in New Orleans. The *Clotilde's* history, however, has been confirmed by eyewitness accounts and careful reconstruction of events by historians.

Congress had revived laws against slave trading and declared that anyone convicted would be hanged. The United States had been later than almost every other civilized nation in the world in abolishing slave trading. Even New York City, bastion of abolitionists, became a refuge for eighty-five slave ships, many of them built and sent to Africa from that city. Much profit could be made in the $17,000,000-per-year business. According to one account, 15,000 Africans were smuggled to the United States in 1859 alone, the last 117 of whom were brought by the *Clotilde*. In contrast, the British government, after issuing its injunction against the slave trade in the eighteenth century, seized and destroyed 625 slave ships and freed their forty thousand prisoners. In the United States, only the abolitionists consistently confronted the government for its apathy toward slave smuggling.

THE MEAGHER BROTHERS' SCHEME

Timothy Meagher, with brothers Jim and Byrns, masterminded the *Clotilde* project. An imposing Irishman known for his adventurous character, Timothy Meagher was a plantation owner and captain of the steamboat Roger B. Taney, which carried passengers, cargo, and mail to and from Montgomery on the Alabama River. Apparently in a lighthearted argument with some passengers on his steamboat, Meagher made a thousand-dollar bet that within a year or two he would bring a ship full of slaves to Mobile Bay without being apprehended by federal officials. Meagher had many years' experience in cruising the Alabama River. He knew his way around every hidden bayou, swamp, canebrake, and sandbar better than anyone else in the South. For his operation, he needed a slave ship. He purchased a lumber schooner called the *Clotilde* for thirty-five thousand dollars in late 1858 and rebuilt it as a 327-ton slaver. He hired his friend Bill Foster, who was experienced in constructing and sailing the old slavers, as skipper.

Foster was to sail to the west coast of Africa and seek the Dahomey kingdom's assistance in procuring two hundred young slaves. The *Clotilde* was equipped with a crew, guns, and cutlasses. To control the prisoners, Meagher supplied the ship with iron manacles, rings, and chains. Foster hired his crew from all over the South, enticing them with liquor, money, and promises of adventure. In the dead of night, massive quantities of food, mainly yams and rice, and drinking water were transported to the ship from Meagher's plantation. To give the ship the look of a lumber schooner, some piles of lumber were placed on the deck. Captain Foster hired the infamous King Dahomey and his drunken thugs to raid villages and capture two hundred young, healthy men and women. The attacks must have taken place early one summer morning in May or early June of 1859. King Dahomey's band raided the two peaceful villages of Whinney and Ataka. They burned huts, injured women and children, and tied up more than 170 young Africans by their necks. The captives were forced into the hold of the *Clotilde*.

The return trip was an awful scene of helpless people, racked with convulsions, crammed into dark, damp quarters, lacking adequate food and water. Foster had as many as thirty-nine bodies thrown overboard before arriving back in the United States. The ship returned in July, 1859, and waited in front of Biloxi in the Mississippi Sound. Foster hired a friend's tugboat and in the dead of night, pulled the *Clotilde*, undetected by government vessels present in Mobile Bay, to a prearranged location in the swamps of the Tombigbee River. Meagher was the best man to maneuver the craft in the treacherous bayous. The sick, exhausted Africans were moved quietly to an out-of-the-way plantation

belonging to Meagher's friend, John M. Dabney, who hid them in the canebrakes. From there, Meagher took charge of his steamer, the *Roger B. Taney*, and kept Foster and the *Clotilde* crew members hidden aboard her until they reached Montgomery, where they were paid off and whisked to New York City for dispersal.

The slaver *Clotilde* was promptly burned at water's edge as soon as its African cargo had been removed. Meagher made elaborate preparations to throw townsfolk and government officials off the track. The Department of Justice was informed, however, and Meagher was arrested at his plantation and placed on trial in short order. Meagher's trial was a sham. He was released on bond for lack of evidence. His efforts to conceal all signs of the ship and its cargo had paid off, but he had to spend close to $100,000 in lawyers' fees and bribes. The prosecution was delayed, and the secessionists came to his rescue. News of the *Clotilde*'s landing and Meagher's trial was drowned by the presidential campaign and widespread talk of civil war.

Government officials finally learned where the Africans were hidden. They commissioned the steamer *Eclipse* for finding and transferring the Africans to Mobile. Meagher, learning of the government's decision, got the *Eclipse* crew and government passengers drunk, giving him and his men time to move the prisoners to a friend's plantation two hundred miles up the Alabama River.

DISASTER AND AFTERMATH

Meagher's slave-smuggling venture was a financial disaster. He bought the Africans from Dahomey for $8,460 in gold plus ninety casks of rum and some cases of yard goods. He was able to sell only twenty-five slaves; it is not clear exactly what happened to the rest. There were reports that Meagher later transferred the others to his plantation near Mobile. Some ended up marrying and living with local black people in the vicinity. Some were reported to have died of disease. Many others settled in cabins behind the Meagher plantation house, which was burned in 1905.

In 1906, a journalistic account of the *Clotilde* episode appeared in *Harper's Monthly* magazine. The author, H. M. Byers, had found several soft-spoken Africans who told of having been smuggled aboard the *Clotilde*. They still maintained some of their own culture and language, along with their African gentleness of demeanor. Most of their children were married to local black residents of Mobile and neighboring areas. Byers conducted extensive interviews with two who had endured the journey from Africa to Alabama: an old man named Gossalow, who had a tribal tattoo on his breast, and an old woman named Abaky, who had intricate tribal tattoos on both cheeks. Gossalow and his wife had been stolen from the village of Whinney, and Abaky from the town of Ataka, near King Dahomey's land. They had kept many of their old traditions in their original form with little modification. For example, they

still buried their dead in graves filled with oak leaves. They spoke nostalgically of their peaceful West African farms, planted with abundant yams and rice.

—Chogollah Maroufi

See also: Abolition; Amistad slave revolt; Slavery

BROWN'S RAID ON HARPERS FERRY

October 16-18, 1859

Although abolitionist John Brown's attempt to liberate and arm Virginia slaves by raiding a federal armory failed, it helped to make civil war almost inevitable and created an enduring legend.

Locale: Harpers Ferry, Virginia (now in West Virginia)
Category: Wars, uprisings, and civil unrest

KEY FIGURES

John Brown (1800-1859), militant abolitionist who led the raid on Harpers Ferry
John H. Kagi (1835-1859), veteran of the antislavery struggle who served as Brown's chief lieutenant
Robert E. Lee (1807-1870), army colonel who led the troops who captured Brown's rebels
Franklin Benjamin Sanborn (1831-1917), Massachusetts abolitionist and secretary of the Massachusetts State Kansas Committee
Henry Alexander Wise (1806-1876), governor of Virginia

SUMMARY OF EVENT

John Brown's abortive raid on the federal arsenal at Harpers Ferry, Virginia (now West Virginia), in October, 1859, stands out as a critical episode in the spiraling sequence of events that led northerners and southerners into the Civil War in 1861. Long a militant abolitionist, Brown emigrated to Kansas Territory in 1855 with five of his sons to participate in the struggle that pitted proslavery against Free State Party forces for control of the territory. Brown's little insurrection was in the same spirit as earlier violence perpetrated by abolitionist, Free State militias such as the Border Ruffians following election of a proslavery, territorial legislature in 1854. With a small band of Free State men, Brown helped initiate

civil war in Kansas by murdering five allegedly proslavery settlers along Pottawatomie Creek, in May, 1856. Historians would later dub this era "Bleeding Kansas."

Brown's experience in the Kansas civil war convinced him that a conspiracy existed to seize U.S. territories for slavery. Having long since lost faith in combating slavery by peaceful means, Brown vowed to strike a violent blow at the heart of the institution. An intense Calvinist, he had come to believe that he was God's personal instrument to eradicate the inhuman institution. As early as 1857, he had decided to seize a mountain fortress in Virginia with a small guerrilla force and incite a bloody slave rebellion that would overthrow the slave powers throughout the South.

To that end, Brown sought funds and arms from abolitionists in the North. Under the guise of seeking money to continue the Free State fight in Kansas, Brown secured the friendship and financial aid of the Massachusetts State Kansas Committee—a body dedicated to helping the free-soil forces in Kansas and elsewhere. The resolute and persuasive Brown won the support of six prominent antislavery figures, who agreed to form a secret committee of six men to advise him and raise money for his still-secret mission. The Secret Six consisted of a well-educated group of dedicated abolitionists and reformers: Franklin Benjamin Sanborn, a young Concord schoolteacher and secretary of the Massachusetts State Kansas Committee; Thomas Wentworth Higginson, a "disunion abolitionist" and outspoken Unitarian minister; Theodore Parker, a controversial theologian-preacher; Samuel Gridley Howe, a prominent physician and educator; George Luther Stearns, a prosperous merchant and chairman of the Massachusetts State Kansas Committee; and Gerrit Smith, a wealthy New York landowner and reformer.

Throughout the remainder of 1857, Brown trained a small group of adventurers and militant abolitionists in preparation for his mission. In May, 1858, he moved on to Chatham, Canada, holding a secret constitutional convention that was attended by thirty-four African Americans and twelve whites. There, he outlined his plans to invade Virginia, liberate and arm the slaves, defeat any military force brought against them, organize the African Americans into a government, and force the southern states to concede emancipation. Under Brown's leadership, the convention approved a constitution for the new state that would be created after the slaves were freed, and elected Brown commander in chief with John Kagi, his chief lieutenant, as secretary of war.

Brown's proposed invasion was delayed in 1858, when a disgruntled follower partially betrayed the plans to several prominent politicians. The exposé so frightened the Secret Six that they urged Brown to return to Kansas and create a diversionary operation until rumors of the Virginia plan dissipated. Brown also agreed not to inform the Secret Six of the details of his plans, so that they could not be held responsible in case his invasion failed. In December, 1858, Brown conducted the diversion as planned, by leading a raid into Missouri, liberating eleven slaves, and escorting them to Canada. He then began final preparations for the invasion of Virginia. Harpers Ferry, situated at the confluence of the Potomac and Shenandoah Rivers in northern Virginia, was the initial target in Brown's plan because he needed weapons from the federal arsenal to arm the liberated slaves. On July 3, 1859, Brown and three of his men arrived there and then set up headquarters at the Kennedy farm, seven miles east of Harpers Ferry in Maryland. The rest of Brown's sixteen white and five black young recruits slowly trickled in. On the night of October 16, 1859, after several months of refining his plans, Brown led eighteen of his followers in a direct assault on the arsenal and rifle works at Harpers Ferry. The raiders quickly captured the arsenal, the armory, and a nearby rifle works, and then seized hostages from the town and surrounding countryside.

Fearing a slave insurrection, the townspeople armed themselves and gathered in the streets, and church bells tolled the alarm over the countryside. Meanwhile, Brown stood his ground, anxiously waiting for the slaves from the countryside to rally to his cause. By the next morning, Brown's men—holed up in the small fire-engine house of the armory—engaged in a pitched battle with the assembled townspeople, farmers, and militia. By dawn the following morning, a company of horse Marines under the command of U.S. Army colonel Robert E. Lee took up positions in front of the armory. When Brown refused Lee's summons to surrender unconditionally, the Marines stormed the armory, wounded Brown, and routed his followers. Seventeen people died in the raid. Ten of the dead, including two of Brown's sons, were raiders. Five raiders were captured, two were taken prisoner several days later, but five escaped without a trace.

Governor Henry Alexander Wise of Virginia decided that Brown and his coconspirators should be tried in Virginia rather than by federal authorities, even though their attack had been against federal property. Brown and the captured raiders stood trial at Charles Town, Virginia; on October 31, the jury found them guilty of inciting a slave rebellion, murder, and treason against the state of Virginia. After the trial, in a final attempt to save his life, Brown's lawyers collected affidavits from many of his friends and relatives alleging that Brown suffered from hereditary insanity and monomania. Brown rejected this defense, however, claiming that he was sane. He knew that he would better serve the abolitionist cause if he were to die as a martyr, a sentiment shared by northern abolitionists. Governor Wise agreed that Brown was sane, and on December 2, 1859, Brown was hanged at Charles Town. Six of his fellow conspirators met similar fates.

SIGNIFICANCE

Brown's raid intensified the sectional bitterness that led to the Civil War. Although the vast majority of northerners condemned the incident as the work of a fanatic, the outraged South, racked by rumors of a slave insurrection, suspected all northerners of abetting Brown's crime. Republican denials of any link with Brown were of little avail. Northern abolitionists, including the Secret Six, who had been cleared of complicity, gathered by the hundreds throughout the North to honor and acclaim Brown's martyrdom. The South was in no mood to distinguish between the northern Republicans who wanted to contain slavery and the small group of abolitionists who sought to destroy the institution. The South withdrew even further into a defense of slavery, stifled internal criticism, and intensified its hatred and suspicion of the "Black Republican" Party. In 1861, northerners marched to war to the tune of "John Brown's Body"— fulfilling Brown's prophecy that "the crimes of this guilty land will never be purged away; but with Blood."

—*Terry L. Seip, updated by Richard Whitworth*

See also: Turner Launches Slave Insurrection; Underground Railroad Flourishes; Bleeding Kansas; Lincoln-Douglas Debates; Last Slave Ship Docks at Mobile;

U.S. Civil War; Lincoln Issues the Emancipation Proclamation; Thirteenth Amendment Is Ratified.

Related articles in *Great Lives from History: The Nineteenth Century, 1801-1900:* John Brown; Frederick Douglass; Thomas Wentworth Higginson; Robert E. Lee; Nat Turner

LINCOLN IS ELECTED U.S. PRESIDENT

November 6, 1860

The election of the first Republican president of the United States prompted the secession of the southern states from the union that in turn launched the U.S. Civil War, but it also gave the United States one of its greatest presidents.

Also known as: Election of 1860
Locale: United States
Category: Government and politics

KEY FIGURES

Abraham Lincoln (1809-1865), president of the United States, 1861-1865
Stephen A. Douglas (1813-1861), Illinois senator who was the Democratic presidential candidate in the North
William H. Seward (1801-1872), New York senator, 1849-1861
John Bell (1797-1869), Constitutional Union presidential candidate
John Cabell Breckinridge (1821-1875), Democratic presidential candidate in the South
James Buchanan (1791-1868), president of the United States, 1857-1861
Hannibal Hamlin (1809-1891), successful Republican candidate for vice president

SUMMARY OF EVENT

Members of the recently created Republican Party approached the 1860 election with great enthusiasm. The outgoing Democratic president, James Buchanan, had accomplished little of significance during his term in office, and he chose not to be a candidate for reelection. Republican candidates had enjoyed success in northern and western states in both the 1856 and 1858 elections, so the Republicans hoped that an attractive Republican presidential candidate would be victorious in the November 6, 1860, general election.

The Democrats were in serious trouble going into the election. Democratic unity had been shattered under pressures engendered by the Kansas-Nebraska Act of 1854, and Democrats could not be certain of victory in any single northern state in 1860. Democratic candidates who opposed allowing the extension of slavery into newly created states alienated southern voters, and those who supported slavery were politically unacceptable in the northern and western states. Only in the South was the Democratic Party holding firm. However, Democrats throughout the nation recognized that their party could not win behind a southern candidate for president. A northerner was necessary, but the southern wing of the Democratic Party insisted that the candidate not take a strong position against slavery.

Meanwhile, no such disunity existed in the Republican Party, which had expressed its opposition to slavery in its 1856 platform. Republicans were jubilant at the impending split of the Democrats and, in order not to throw away a golden opportunity to take the White House, sought a moderate candidate who would appeal to former Whigs, northerners, and residents of border and western states.

Partisan disputes rather than genuine confrontation with national problems had characterized U.S. politics between the end of Andrew Jackson's presidency in 1837 and the election of Abraham Lincoln in 1860. James Buchanan, the incumbent Democratic president from Pennsylvania, had been singularly ineffective in uniting his party, and his animosity toward Illinois senator Stephen A. Douglas was obvious to fellow Democrats.

The country was enjoying a healthy economy in 1860. The economic downturn of the mid-1850's, culminating in the Panic of 1857, was over. By 1860, the United States had achieved a considerable measure of economic integration, and the various regions had grown more interdependent. Domestic trade was far more important to the national economy than foreign trade. Many southerners, however, continued to feel that their economic growth would depend largely on cotton production. They also believed that slavery was essential and should be protected, not only in southern states but also in the territories and recently created states in the Midwest and West. At the same time, the economy of the North and the Northwest, however, was no longer as dependent on cotton and other agricultural products from the South as it had been earlier. Northern manufacturing and northwestern agriculture had achieved sufficient strength to produce adequate capital for further expansion, as was clearly demonstrated during the Civil War (1861-1865). Southern politicians, however, entered the presidential campaign of 1860 as if nothing had changed economically since the 1840's.

During the winter of 1859-1860, Senator William H. Seward of New York appeared to be the leading candidate for the Republican nomination, but several prominent Republicans, including Salmon P. Chase from Ohio, Simon Cameron from Pennsylvania, Edward Bates from Missouri, and the influential newspaper publisher Horace Greeley from New York, argued that Seward, who had a reputation for being a strident orator, might offend too many voters and cost the Republicans such key states as Ohio, Pennsylvania, New York, Missouri, and Massachusetts. Many Republicans therefore mounted a stop-Seward campaign. At the Republican convention in Chicago, in May, 1860, Seward led on the first two ballots. However, after forty-seven delegates from Pennsylvania changed their votes from Cameron to Lincoln, delegates from many other states also changed their minds, and Abraham Lincoln was nominated on the third ballot. The convention selected Hannibal Hamlin from Maine as the Republican vice presidential candidate.

In contrast to the Republicans, the Democrats were sharply divided. At their national nominating convention in Charleston, South Carolina, in April, 1860, southern delegates demanded the acceptance of the Alabama platform that called for the positive protection by Congress of slavery in the territories. The South was willing to accept Stephen Douglas as the Democratic candidate, but only if he accepted the Alabama platform. Realizing that northern and western voters never would tolerate

the spread of slavery into new U.S. territories and states, Douglas refused to support the Alabama platform. The delegations of eight southern states then withdrew from the convention and called for another convention to meet in Richmond, Virginia. Douglas and his followers adjourned to Baltimore, where he was nominated.

The southern Democratic delegates who met in Richmond intensified the split by nominating a separate ticket, headed by John Cabell Breckinridge of Kentucky. The Republicans' chances for victory improved even more when certain former Whigs formed the Constitutional Union Party. This party was especially popular in border states. At its convention in Baltimore, the Constitutional Union Party nominated John Bell of Tennessee. The field was a full one, with four candidates seeking the support of the nation. With the splintering of the Democrats, the creation of the Constitutional Union Party, and the unity of the Republicans, the election of Lincoln was almost a certainty.

Although the other candidates traveled extensively during the 1860 campaign, Abraham Lincoln chose to adhere to the tradition of the day and stayed home in Springfield, Illinois. Until the twentieth century, many presidential candidates believed that it was undignified for a candidate for the nation's highest office to campaign personally. Moreover, because four candidates were running, Lincoln simply needed a plurality, not a majority, to win the electoral votes in northern, midwestern, and eastern states, in which the Republicans had strong support. By remaining in Springfield, Lincoln was able to deliver set speeches affirming his intention of protecting the U.S. Constitution and preserving the union. He did not have to answer unexpected questions from reporters and avoided making blunders during the campaign.

The Republicans nearly swept the North, with Douglas carrying only New Jersey and Missouri. The Bell ticket carried three border states, while Breckinridge received all the electoral votes in the South. Lincoln was a minority president, with less than 40 percent of the popular vote; he received only 1,866,452 popular votes, compared to a total of 2,815,617 for his three opponents. In electoral votes, however, Lincoln received 180, while his opponents received 123. Nearly 70 percent of the voters opposed expansion of slavery into the territories.

SIGNIFICANCE

During the 1860 election, the Republicans gained control of the presidency and the House of Representatives, but the Democrats retained control of the Senate. However, the Republican success was attended by dire consequences. News of Lincoln's election precipitated the secession of South Carolina, followed by the secession of six other southern states by February, 1861. Outgoing President Buchanan did nothing to stop the illegal secessions. The responsibility of preserving the union fell on Abraham Lincoln, who took his oath of office on March 4, 1861. The Civil War would begin just over one month later.

—*John G. Clark, updated by Edmund J. Campion*

See also: Twelfth Amendment Is Ratified; Congress Passes the Kansas-Nebraska Act; Bleeding Kansas; Lincoln-Douglas Debates; Establishment of the Confederate States of America; Lincoln Is Inaugurated President; U.S. Civil War; Lincoln Issues the Emancipation Proclamation.

Related articles in *Great Lives from History: The Nineteenth Century, 1801-1900:* James Buchanan; Stephen A. Douglas; Abraham Lincoln; Mary Todd Lincoln; William H. Seward.

CIVIL WAR

1861–1865

The war's most profound effects on race relations in the United States resulted from its ending of slavery and emancipation of enslaved African Americans.

The Event: War between Northern and Southern states that established the primacy of the federal government over the states in the administration of justice and elevated the ethical system of free-labor capitalism as the national standard

The Civil War redefined relationships both between the U.S. government and the individual and between the federal and state governments. During the course of the conflict, the Union and Confederate governments pursued aggressively nationalistic policies that undermined states' rights, civil liberties, and property rights.

THE SLAVERY ISSUE

By the mid-nineteenth century, the free-labor ideal had taken hold in the states of the North. It was believed that economic opportunity should be open to all. To many in the North, the slave system in the South appeared to be the antithesis of the free-labor ideal. Northerners believed that slavery was inefficient, that it degraded labor as a whole, and that it created economic stagnation. Though most were willing to tolerate slavery where it existed, they wanted the western territories reserved for free white labor. They interpreted the Constitution as a document that made freedom national and slavery local.

Southerners shared a belief in the positive benefits of economic opportunity, but they identified it with the acquisition of land and slaves. Southerners dreamed of extending the slave system into the territories, arguing that the territories were the common property of all Americans; to prohibit slavery within them deprived southern people of their right to share in the nation's bounty.

The Republican victory in 1860 brought to power an administration pledged to restrict slavery in the territories. Fearing that the new administration would undermine slavery, seven southern states asserted their right to secede from the federal union and form a new government. Abraham Lincoln's administration denied the right of secession and refused to relinquish federal property in the South to the new Confederacy. When the state of South Carolina fired on a federal fort in Charleston harbor, President Lincoln called upon the states to supply troops to suppress the rebellion and preserve the federal union. Four additional states believed Lincoln's action to be an unjust usurpation of federal power and joined the Confederacy.

For the Lincoln administration, the highest good was the preservation of the Union. All issues of justice were considered in relation to that objective. The Confederacy was dedicated to the proposition that human property was an unalienable right and must be preserved. For the first year of fighting, the Lincoln administration took no action to destroy slavery. It enforced the provisions of the Fugitive Slave Law, and Lincoln rebuked Union general John C. Frémont when he issued a proclamation freeing the slaves of Confederate sympathizers in Missouri. Lincoln's Emancipation Proclamation did not take effect until January 1, 1863. When he issued the proclamation, Lincoln justified his action in terms of military necessity. The proclamation freed only the slaves behind Confederate lines, but after the Emancipation Proclamation was issued, the Union army became a force for liberation.

CIVIL LIBERTIES

Both the Union and Confederate governments restricted traditional civil liberties during the conflict. In early 1862, the Confederate Congress authorized Confederate president Jefferson Davis to suspend the writ of *habeas corpus* and to declare martial law in areas in danger of attack. That same year, President Davis ordered the first military draft in North America and established a Conscription Bureau to carry it out. Even more striking, the Confederacy never established a Supreme Court and allowed their attorney general to judge the constitutionality of laws. That omission seriously undermined the notion of judicial independence and gave the executive branch unprecedented powers over the administration of justice.

Thousands of civilians were arrested by the Union government during the war, and many were tried by military courts. In response to civil disturbances in Baltimore, Lincoln suspended the privilege of *habeas corpus* on April 27, 1861, along the rail line from Philadelphia to Washington. The suspension was later extended to other areas of the North and gradually became general in certain types of cases.

Most military arrested by the Union government were not political. The vast majority of civilian prisoners were blockade-runners, residents of Confederate states, army deserters, draft dodgers, foreign nationals, people who dealt in contraband goods, or fraudulent war contractors. A loyal opposition continued to function in the North throughout the war and actually won control of several state legislatures.

Among those arrested early in the war was John Merryman. Merryman was a member of a pro-Confederate Maryland cavalry unit that had damaged railroad bridges in April, 1861. Merryman's attorney successfully petitioned a federal circuit court for a writ of *habeas corpus* to show just cause for his arrest. The commander of Fort McHenry, where Merryman was being held, refused to honor the writ on the grounds that President Lincoln had suspended the privilege in Maryland. Judge Roger B. Taney responded by issuing a circuit court ruling stating that only the Congress had the power to exercise such a suspension (*Ex parte Merryman*, 1861). In spite of the ruling, Lincoln continued to maintain his

right to suspend the writ as an essential power necessary to suppress the rebellion.

For purposes of election propaganda, unscrupulous Republican politicians and military officers attempted to exploit fears that traitorous secret organizations existed in the Midwest. Recent scholarship has demonstrated that the major "Copperhead" societies, such as the Knights of the Golden Circle and the Sons of Liberty, were little more than paper tigers. In the wake of Democratic victories in the state elections of 1862, Republican newspaper editors frequently printed tales of treasonable Democratic activities.

When Ohio Democrat Clement L. Vallandigham declared that the war was being fought to free blacks and enslave whites, General Ambrose Burnside ordered his arrest. A military commission convicted Vallandigham of attempting to hamper the government's efforts to suppress the rebellion and recommended imprisonment. President Lincoln altered the sentence to banishment, and Vallandigham was escorted to Confederate lines. Lincoln justified his action by arguing that it made no sense to shoot a simple-minded deserter and do nothing to the man who induced him to desert.

Later in the war, Democratic activist H. H. Dodd of Indiana organized the Sons of Liberty to protect the civil liberties of those opposed to the Republican administration. Acting on rumors that the Sons of Liberty had aided Confederates, Union general Henry Carrington arrested Indiana Democrats linked to the Sons of Liberty, including editor Lambdin Milligan. A military commission sentenced three of the defendants to death. Others received prison terms. The death sentences were never carried out, but it is clear that the men were tried on questionable evidence by military commissions in areas where civil courts were functioning. After the war, the Supreme Court ruled in Ex parte Milligan (1866) that such trials were illegal.

TREATMENT OF BLACK TROOPS

When the conflict began, neither the Union nor Confederate governments would sanction the use of African American soldiers. As the Union government moved toward an acceptance of emancipation, however, it also began to organize African American regiments.

In spite of the large-scale recruitment of black soldiers during the last two years of the war, the Union army discriminated against African Americans in a wide variety of ways including pay, chance of promotion, and the amount of fatigue duty black units were expected to perform. Although a few African Americans did receive commissions, the vast majority of officers in the United States Colored Troops (USCT) were white combat veterans. The men of the USCT proved their courage at the battles of Port Hudson, Milliken's Bend, and Fort Wagner, where they took heavy casualties. Generally, however, the prejudice of many commanding officers led to the use of USCT regiments for fatigue or guard duty while saving white units for combat.

The Confederacy reacted harshly to the use of black troops by the Union army. President Davis approved of the execution of black prisoners of war in South Carolina in November, 1862. Later, Davis ordered that all former slaves captured while serving in the Union army be returned to the states for trial. The massacre of black prisoners by Confederate troops on several occasions forced Union authorities to threaten retaliation in order to stem the injustice.

The use of large numbers of black troops by the Union war effort helped pave the way for universal emancipation. Throughout his political career, Lincoln consistently asserted that slavery was morally wrong. Though emancipation began as a military tactic, it became a war aim. The courage of black soldiers allowed Lincoln to secure passage of the Thirteenth Amendment, providing for an end to slavery throughout the country.

MILITARY JUSTICE

The system of military justice employed within the army was seriously flawed. At least 267 soldiers were executed by the Union army during the Civil War era. More than half of those executed were either foreigners or African Americans. A number of black soldiers were convicted of mutiny for protesting unequal pay in the Union army. Racial tensions accelerated during the final months of the conflict. A high number of black soldiers were executed for alleged sexual offenses against white women. The Confederacy had an incomplete record of military justice. Since many southern officers had received their training in the prewar U.S. Army, the procedural flaws of courts-martial were similar in both armies.

The Civil War moved the United States toward a more perfect application of its ideals of equality and justice. The United States entered the war as a federal union with contrasting standards of justice, one based on free-labor ideals, the other on the slave system of the southern states. Property rights took precedent over human rights, and equal justice was denied African Americans in virtually every section of the country. The Union government, through its policy of emancipation and the enlistment of African Americans into its armed forces, transformed the war from a crusade to preserve the Union into a war of liberation. In doing so, it expanded the nation's concept of justice to include equality for African Americans.

—Thomas D. Matijasic

See also: Bleeding Kansas; Charleston race riots; Civil Rights Acts of 1866-1875; Colfax massacre; Compromise of 1850; Confiscation Acts of 1861 and 1862; Draft riots; Emancipation Proclamation; Fifteenth Amendment; Fourteenth Amendment; Harpers Ferry raid; Kansas-Nebraska Act; Military; Missouri Compromise; Reconstruction; *Scott v. Sandford*; Thirteenth Amendment; Vietnam War

ESTABLISHMENT OF THE CONFEDERATE STATES OF AMERICA

February 8, 1861

The secession of eleven southern states and the formation of the Confederacy set the United States on an irreversible path toward a devastating civil war.

Also known as: The Confederacy
Locale: Mobile, Alabama
Categories: Government and politics; organizations and institutions

KEY FIGURES

Abraham Lincoln (1809-1865), president-elect of the United States

Howell Cobb (1815-1868), president of the convention called to create a southern republic

Jefferson Davis (1808-1889), former U.S. secretary of war who became president of the Confederacy

Robert Barnwell Rhett (1800-1876), leader of South Carolina's secessionist movement

Alexander H. Stephens (1812-1883), former Georgia congressman who became vice president of the Confederacy

Robert A. Toombs (1810-1885), former Georgia senator who became the Confederate secretary of state

SUMMARY OF EVENT

On December 20, 1860, the delegates of the Convention of the People of South Carolina voted 160 to 0 to adopt an ordinance of secession dissolving the "union now subsisting between South Carolina and the other States under the name of 'United States of America.'" Wishing to maintain their radical leadership of the South, the South Carolinians had moved quickly to take the initiative in the secession movement. News of Abraham Lincoln's election to the presidency of the United States had reached South Carolina on November 7, and on November 13, the state legislature authorized the calling of a state convention. Delegates were quickly chosen in special elections, and the convention met on December 17. Three days later, South Carolina announced its secession from the union.

Secession was justified, according to members of the South Carolina convention, under the ancient "compact theory" of states' rights. According to this concept, individual states were sovereign. They had voluntarily entered into the union, and they could leave lawfully whenever they chose or whenever they believed the terms of the compact or agreement under which they were united were violated. This action could be taken by a specially elected state convention representing the sovereign power of a state.

Most white southerners believed that their liberty and their property, particularly their slaves, were threatened by the electoral victory of a political party composed almost exclusively of northerners. The western territories would, southerners assumed, become free states, and the political imbalance in the nation would be perpetuated and increased.

The other states of the Deep South shared South Carolina's view that to remain in the union would be intolerable.

In fact, Mississippi was prepared to take the initiative had South Carolina delayed. Starting on January 9, 1861, Mississippi, Florida, and Alabama seceded on successive days. In Georgia, Alexander H. Stephens, among others, urged a wait-and-see policy, because the newly elected Republican government of the United States had not yet taken office. However, other powerful Georgians, such as Robert A. Toombs and Howell Cobb, called for separation, and the Georgia convention voted for secession on January 19. Louisiana, where there was strong pro-Union sentiment, adopted an ordinance of secession on January 26. In Texas, the secessionists were opposed by Governor Sam Houston, but a state convention voted to secede on February 1, subject to

a popular referendum, which accepted secession three weeks later. Texas became the last of the seven states to secede before Lincoln took office on March 4, 1861.

Although Robert Barnwell Rhett was a "fire-eater" secessionist, he saw the necessity of forming a new national government for the southern states. He introduced a resolution at the South Carolina convention calling for another convention to be held in Montgomery, Alabama, for the purpose of forming a southern republic. Delegates from South Carolina, Mississippi, Florida, Alabama, Louisiana, and Georgia met in the Alabama state capital on February 4, 1861; the Texas delegation arrived later.

Cobb, a former Speaker of the U.S. House of Representatives and secretary of the Treasury, was elected president of the convention. A committee quickly drafted a provisional constitution, which was adopted on February 8, and the Confederate States of America was born.

The provisional constitution provided for the creation of an interim government for one year or until a permanent government should be established. The members of the convention became the provisional congress and elected Jefferson Davis of Mississippi as provisional president and Alexander H. Stephens of Georgia as provisional vice president. On February 18, 1861, Davis and Stephens were inaugurated, and Davis moved quickly to form a cabinet.

On March 11, the convention unanimously adopted a permanent constitution. It was similar to the U.S. Constitution in that it provided for three branches of the central government, further dividing power between the state governments and the central government. However, there also were important differences, reflecting both the states' rights principles and the interests of southern agriculture.

State sovereignty was expressly recognized; the president and vice president were elected for six-year terms, with one-term limitations. The president was allowed to veto individual items in appropriations bills.

Slavery and the interests of the slaveholders were specifically upheld, including the right to transport slaves from state to state. Slavery was established in the territories, but participation in the international slave trade was outlawed, as a concession to Great Britain and France. Protective tariffs were forbidden, in recognition of the South's primary economic role as an exporter of agricultural goods and an importer of manufactured goods.

Confederate expenditures for internal improvements were prohibited, and a two-thirds vote of both houses of the Confederate congress was required to pass important appropriations bills. The new government had hoped that its states would be permitted to depart from the United States in peace. However, after Confederate artillery units fired on Union troops at Fort Sumter, on April 12-13, 1861, all hopes for voluntary recognition by the northern government vanished.

The incident at Fort Sumter was followed by Lincoln's call for troops from the various states, including those of the upper South. Those states were forced to join the Confederacy or participate in the coercion of the states of the Deep South. Although in each state of the upper South there was strong Union sentiment, Virginia, North Carolina, Tennessee, and Arkansas nevertheless joined the Confederacy in April and May. Missouri and Kentucky were divided and were claimed by both the Union and the Confederacy. Maryland and Delaware, the remaining slave states, did not join the Confederacy.

The Confederate congress welcomed Virginia into the Confederacy by moving its capital to Richmond on July 20, 1861. On November 6, 1861, the first general elections were held under the permanent constitution. Davis and Stephens were then elected president and vice president of the "permanent" Confederacy. The fourth and last sessions of the provisional congress closed in February of 1862, when the new senate and house assembled.

On February 22, 1862, Jefferson Davis was inaugurated president for a term of six years. The first congress under the permanent constitution of the Confederacy held four sessions and the second congress held two sessions, with the final adjournment of the body taking place in March, 1865.

SIGNIFICANCE

The formation of the Confederate States of America and the Confederate assault on Fort Sumter made it evident that no peaceful settlement between the North and the South would be possible. Under the strong leadership of President Abraham Lincoln, the North resolved to preserve the union, and the only way that goal could be achieved would be through an armed conquest of the South, and that could only be effected through an all-out civil war. On July 21, 1861—only one day after the capital of the Confederacy was moved to Richmond—the first great battle of the war was fought at Bull Run Creek in Virginia.

—Mark A. Plummer, updated by Susan M. Taylor

See also: Congress Passes the Kansas-Nebraska Act; Lincoln Is Elected U.S. President; Lincoln Is Inaugurated President; U.S. Civil War; First Battle of Bull Run; Mar. 3, 1863: Union Enacts the First National Draft Law; July 1-Nov. 25, 1863: Battles of Gettysburg, Vicksburg, and Chattanooga; Sherman Marches Through Georgia and the Carolinas.

Related articles in *Great Lives from History: The Nineteenth Century, 1801-1900:* Jefferson Davis; Sam Houston; Abraham Lincoln; Alexander H. Stephens.

LINCOLN IS INAUGURATED PRESIDENT
March 4, 1861

As Abraham spent four months waiting for his inauguration, tensions between the North and the South inexorably moved the United States closer to civil war, and Lincoln quietly pledged to uphold the union while refraining from making any public statements that might increase tensions.

Locale: Washington, D.C.
Category: Government and politics

KEY FIGURES
Abraham Lincoln (1809-1865), president of the United States, 1861-1865

Edward Dickinson Baker (1811-1861), senator from Oregon
James Buchanan (1791-1868), president of the United States, 1857-1861
Hannibal Hamlin (1809-1891), vice president of the United States
William H. Seward (1801-1872), secretary of state
Roger Brooke Taney (1777-1864), chief justice of the United States, 1836-1864

SUMMARY OF EVENT
Abraham Lincoln spent the evening of Election Day, November 6, 1860, reading the election returns at the

telegraph office in Springfield, Illinois. The next day, he received congratulations on his election to the presidency at his temporary office in the Illinois state house. After having spent virtually the entire election campaign close to his home, Lincoln remained in Illinois until February 11, 1861, when he began a personal appearance tour en route to the nation's capital. On February 23, he arrived in Washington, D.C., at 6:00 a.m.; he came unannounced because an assassination attempt against him was feared. Lincoln's secretive arrival was symptomatic of the crisis atmosphere that the United States experienced between his November election and his March inauguration.

The constitutional provision that allowed a four-month delay in installing a new president contributed to the crisis. Until he was actually inaugurated, Lincoln was powerless to take any official action that might quiet the fears of the South, whose white residents were alarmed by the election of a northern Republican known to be opposed to slavery, and he was unwilling to commit himself publicly to a future course of action. Meanwhile, the lame-duck president, James Buchanan, stood by helplessly while seven states of the lower South seceded from the union and took possession of most of the federal military installations in their states.

Lincoln believed that it would be wise to remain in Illinois through most of his interim status as president-elect. Remaining at home would shield him to some extent from office-seekers, and it would also enable him to remain silent concerning the building crisis, about which he could do nothing. Meanwhile, he refused to make any statements on the subject, fearing that anything he said would do no good but might do harm.

Knowing that the situation was tense, Lincoln wanted to do nothing that would provoke the remaining slave states to leave the union, but he also knew that Congress was due to adjourn in mid-April. Between his scheduled March 4 inauguration and Congress's departure, he would have little time in which to do what might be necessary. What time there was to act with the full government in session could not be taken up with explaining speeches or clarifying positions.

Lincoln also realized that there were hotheads on both sides of the issue, North and South, who would seize on any remark, any act, no matter how trivial, to fan the flames of sectional conflict. With his hands tied by the four-month wait for his inauguration and with tensions rising, the politically astute Lincoln preferred to wait until he was actually sworn in as president of the United States. Meanwhile, Lincoln devoted the time

to preparing his own inaugural address and to thinking through his coming options, which would be few indeed.

As president-elect, Lincoln also maintained a low profile because he was not certain of his role in the upcoming Republican administration. It would take some time to form a cabinet, which would have to include a number of prominent politicians, such as William H. Seward and Salmon P. Chase, who were skeptical of Lincoln's administrative abilities and leadership qualities.

Coming, as he did, from Illinois, Lincoln was considered to be a man of the West, and many eastern Republicans resented his high position within the party. Although seven states seceded before Lincoln even left Illinois, he remained steadfast in his decision not to become involved in a public discussion concerning the crisis. Privately, however, he urged his Republican friends in Congress to stand firm against any legislative compromises that might allow the extension of slavery.

Compromises over issues pertaining to slavery had become an American political tradition. In the spirit of the famed compromiser Henry Clay, Kentucky senator John Jordan Crittenden introduced a measure that would prohibit the extension of slavery in all territories north of the old Missouri Compromise line of 1820 (36°30′).

South of the line, slavery would be protected. Furthermore, there would, by federal law, be no interference with the domestic slave trade. A constitutional amendment would be introduced to prohibit any interference with slavery in any state.

Southern senators expressed interest in Crittenden's new compromise if the incoming Lincoln administration would openly endorse it. The argument that passage of the compromise promised to bring the South back into union found support among moderates in the Congress.

Lincoln, on the other hand, quietly opposed the compromise because he believed that it would extend slavery into the territories. If the compromise were endorsed by Lincoln and his Republican supporters, the staunch nonextensionists and abolitionists within the Republican Party would be alienated from the new administration even before Lincoln's inauguration.

Lincoln began his journey to the capital on February 11. Along the way, he made polite speeches before many of the state legislatures and in most of the major cities on his circuitous route. Rumors of attempts to assassinate him were widespread, but Lincoln refused to change his itinerary through Indiana, Ohio, New York, New Jersey, and Pennsylvania. However, after repeated warnings from his closest advisers, he did agree to pass unannounced through Baltimore, Maryland, at night, rather than risk an incident in that slave state. During the ten days he spent in Washington, D.C., before his inauguration, he undertook a fatiguing round of conferences and courtesy calls.

March 4, inauguration day, dawned cloudy and raw, but it soon became bright and clear. General Winfield Scott, anticipating the worst, took extreme but unobtrusive measures to protect the president's route to the capitol. Sharpshooters were placed on the roofs of buildings, soldiers were spaced along the route, cannons were placed on the Capitol Building lawn, and the presidential carriage was heavily guarded by an escort detail. Following custom, President-Elect Lincoln and President Buchanan entered the president's carriage together a few minutes after noon for the final ride to the Capitol. There, they entered the building through a boarded tunnel. The Senate was called to order, and Lincoln watched as the oath of office was administered to Vice President-Elect Hannibal Hamlin.

A crowd of more than thirty thousand people was waiting in front of the portico of the unfinished Capitol Building when, at about 1:00 p.m., the presidential party finally arrived on the platform. Lincoln was introduced by his old friend from Oregon, Senator Edward Dickinson Baker. Lincoln then put on his steel-rimmed spectacles and read his speech, which took about thirty minutes to deliver. Chief Justice Roger Brooke Taney then administered the oath of office to him, and the procession to the White House began.

Lincoln's inaugural address dealt exclusively with the secession crisis. Other topics, "about which there is no special anxiety, or excitement," were dismissed. Lincoln began by assuring the southern states that their property, peace, and personal security were in no danger from the Republican administration. At the same

Lincoln's First Inaugural Address

President Abraham Lincoln was well aware when he took office of the extremity of the tensions between the North and the South. His first inaugural address (March 4, 1861), excerpted below, was delivered primarily to Southerners: Lincoln attempted to reassure the southern states that he had no interest in abolishing slavery and to appeal to them to act within the framework of the Constitution to protect their interests while still preserving the Union.

Apprehension seems to exist among the people of the Southern States that by the accession of a Republican Administration their property and their peace and personal security are to be endangered. There has never been any reasonable cause for such apprehension. Indeed, the most ample evidence to the contrary has all the while existed and been open to their inspection.

It is found in nearly all the published speeches of him who now addresses you. I do but quote from one of those speeches when I declare that "I have no purpose, directly or indirectly, to interfere with the institution of slavery in the States where it exists. I believe I have no lawful right to do so, and I have no inclination to do so." ...

This country, with its institutions, belongs to the people who inhabit it.

Whenever they shall grow weary of the existing Government, they can exercise their constitutional right of amending it, or their revolutionary right to dismember or overthrow it. I cannot be ignorant of the fact that many worthy and patriotic citizens are desirous of having the National Constitution amended. While I make no recommendation of amendments, I fully recognize the rightful authority of the people over the whole subject, to be exercised in either of the modes prescribed in the instrument itself; and I should, under existing circumstances, favor rather than oppose, a fair opportunity being afforded the people to act upon it. . . .

In your hands, my dissatisfied fellow-countrymen, and not in mine, is the momentous issue of civil war. The Government will not assail you.

You can have no conflict without being yourselves the aggressors. You have no oath registered in Heaven to destroy the Government, while I shall have the most solemn one to "preserve, protect, and defend it."

I am loth to close. We are not enemies, but friends. We must not be enemies.

Though passion may have strained, it must not break our bonds of affection. The mystic chords of memory, stretching from every battlefield and patriot grave to every living heart and hearthstone all over this broad land, will yet swell the chorus of the Union, when again touched, as surely they will be, by the better angels of our nature.

time, however, he took the position that the union of the states was perpetual. Because he was pledged to uphold the Constitution, he would use "the power confided to me . . . to hold, occupy and possess the property and places belonging to the government and to collect the duties." Lincoln qualified this statement by hinting that he would forgo the enforcement of federal laws "where hostility to the United States, in any interior locality" shall be universal.

Lincoln ended his speech by placing the question of civil war in southern hands. "The government will not assail you. You can have no conflict, without being yourselves the aggressors." He added: "We must not be enemies. Although passion may have strained, it must not break our bonds of affection."

SIGNIFICANCE

The day after his inauguration, Lincoln was confronted with information that threatened the status quo. Major Robert Anderson, in command of Fort Sumter in the harbor off Charleston, South Carolina, reported that he could hold the fort for only a few weeks, unless he received fresh provisions. Lincoln had to decide quickly whether to send provisions and risk hostilities or do nothing and see the fort, one of the few remaining

symbols of federal authority in the South, abandoned. He decided to send provisions. The Confederacy, having been notified of his plans, bombarded the fort before it could be resupplied. The first shot was fired at 4:30 a.m., April 12, 1861. The U.S. Civil War had begun. It would consume Lincoln's time and energy for the next four years.

—Mark A. Plummer, updated by James J. Cooke

See also: Birth of the Republican Party; June 16-Oct. 15, 1858: Lincoln-Douglas Debates; Lincoln Is Elected U.S. President; Establishment of the Confederate States of America; U.S. Civil War; Lincoln Issues the Emancipation Proclamation; Surrender at Appomattox and Assassination of Lincoln.

Related articles in *Great Lives from History: The Nineteenth Century, 1801-1900:* James Buchanan; Jefferson Davis; Abraham Lincoln; Mary Todd Lincoln; William H. Seward.

FIRST BATTLE OF BULL RUN

July 21, 1861

Although this first major battle of the U.S. Civil War resulted in a victory for the South, it had no important consequences for either side, except as a demonstration of the ferocity and scale of bloodshed that was to come in the war.

Also known as: First Battle of Manassas
Locale: Bull Run Creek, near Manassas Junction, Virginia
Category: Wars, uprisings, and civil unrest

KEY FIGURES

P. G. T. Beauregard (1818-1893), commander of Confederate troops near Manassas Junction
Stonewall Jackson (Thomas Jonathan Jackson; 1824-1863), Confederate general
Winfield Scott (1786-1866) U.S. general
Joseph Eggleston Johnston (1807-1891), commander of Confederate troops sent to reinforce Beauregard
Irvin McDowell (1818-1885), commander of Union troops in northern Virginia

Jeb Stuart (1833-1864), Confederate brigadier general

SUMMARY OF EVENT

Through the three months after Confederate forces fired on Fort Sumter at Charleston, South Carolina, to start the U.S. Civil War on April 12, 1861, small fights but no major battles occurred from the Atlantic coast west to Missouri. Then, in July, in the vicinity of a watercourse in northern Virginia called Bull Run, Union and Confederate soldiers met in the largest battle ever fought to that time on the North American continent. That great conflict, the First Battle of Bull Run, which was called the First Battle of Manassas by Southerners, was the first of many bloody engagements that marked the road between Washington and Richmond, the capitals of the old Union and the new Confederacy.

With the decision, in May, 1861, to make Richmond the infant Confederacy's capital, Confederate leaders began to strengthen their forces in northern Virginia. Confederate president Jefferson Davis brought his country's military hero, General P. G. T. Beauregard, the conqueror of Fort Sumter, to help direct those forces. These troops could both threaten Washington, D.C., and protect Richmond, from a suitable distance.

Confederates forces were divided into two main groups: one, under Beauregard, numbering about twenty-four thousand troops, was centered on Manassas Junction, thirty miles southwest of Washington. The other, under General Joseph Eggleston Johnston, numbering about eleven thousand, was situated sixty miles west of Manassas, near Winchester, Virginia.

While the Confederates were establishing themselves in these positions, the North was beginning to build its own military machine. After the battle at Fort Sumter, President Abraham Lincoln had issued an initial call for seventy-five thousand volunteers. Across the Union, armies were being formed. Directing this mobilization from Washington, seventy-five-year-old Winfield Scott, the veteran of a half-century of military service and the U.S. general in chief, tried to make order out of chaos.

Under Scott, Brigadier General Irvin McDowell was placed in command of the Union forces stationed across the Potomac River in Virginia. From his headquarters in Arlington House, which had earlier been the home of Confederate general Robert E. Lee, McDowell strove to weld his raw recruits into an effective fighting force.

General Scott, who had more fighting experience than any other officer in the U.S. Army, developed a plan for the war known as the Anaconda Plan. According to his strategic concepts, the Union naval river fleet would seize the Ohio and Mississippi Rivers, thereby dividing the Confederacy in two. The Navy would then blockade all major Southern ports, stopping the exportation of cotton and the importation of war material. The South then would be strangled slowly in a vise-like grip—hence the name Anaconda Plan, after the great South American constrictor snake.

Under the Anaconda Plan, the North expected that there would be few casualties, and best of all, a wholesale bloodbath involving Americans would be avoided, making reconciliation easier. Scott, who had worked well with the Navy in the Mexican War, knew that it would take time to train the flood of volunteers, and the longer that major combat could be avoided, the better it would be for all concerned. As a soldier, Scott thought primarily in military terms and did not have to face the tremendous political pressures that President Lincoln was experiencing.

Lincoln was determined to bring the conflict to a head more quickly. Except for the proposed naval blockade, Lincoln rejected Scott's plan in favor of the more

direct, immediate attacks demanded by his Northern constituency. Eventually, however, the Union would gain, through bitter experience, a victory by a process that, in most essentials, resembled Scott's original plan. Meanwhile, the recruits pouring into Washington were totally ignorant of war and had not the slightest idea of drill, military discipline, or camp sanitation. At the beginning of the war, different units in the Northern and Southern armies wore both gray and uniforms—a situation that would lead to dangerous confusion on the battlefield.

Moreover, both sides used a bewildering variety of weapons. Some Rebels and Yankees arrived in their camps with antiquated flintlock muskets and obsolete smoothbore muskets. Officers on both sides were still studying their drill manuals as they put their troops through the required formations. With many units bringing cooks from the best restaurants in New York and New Orleans, opposing army camps took on the air of summer outings rather than schools for war. Scott knew that these "green" attitudes would spell disaster when the issue was finally joined on the battlefield.

While Scott and McDowell wanted time to organize and train their troops, Northern public opinion demanded action. A clamor arose for the Union to march an army to Richmond to put down the rebellion in order to teach the Rebels a lesson. President Lincoln also urged offensive movement, for he believed the North had to attack to win. Finally, upon Lincoln's order, McDowell's untried army of about thirty-five thousand men moved south to challenge Beauregard's Confederates. No American had ever before led so large an army into battle. With his army drawn up behind a small stream named Bull Run, Beauregard knew about McDowell's advance.

To reinforce the defending army, the Confederate government ordered General Joseph E. Johnston to come to Beauregard's aid. Johnston began shifting his troops eastward, but before Beauregard could launch his attack, McDowell struck. On the morning of July 21, he ordered his army across Bull Run and hit Beauregard's left flank. His well-planned assault drove the Confederates back in chaos and confusion.

The inexperienced troops on both sides fought well, but the Union soldiers steadily forced the Confederates to retreat toward Henry House Hill, the commanding topographical feature on the battlefield. As the advancing Union regiments approached the hill, they ran into elements of Johnston's army. Johnston had used the railroad to transport his soldiers—a first in warfare— which enabled him to move rapidly to make his junction with Beauregard. Just as the Confederate line on Henry House Hill seemed about to break, General Bernard Bee of South Carolina pointed to a Virginia brigade on the crest and shouted to his beleaguered comrades that it was standing like a stone wall against the Union onslaught.

General Thomas Jonathan Jackson's stand saved the day for the Confederate troops and earned the general the enduring sobriquet Stonewall Jackson. With Johnston's fresh troops, the Confederates began advancing. Initially, the Northern units withdrew in an orderly fashion. Suddenly, however, Union units were attacked with great violence by Colonel Jeb Stuart's First Virginia Cavalry. Heat, weariness, and lack of water and food began to take their toll, and the Northern troops began, often with no orders, to withdraw from the field. Officers tried with varying degrees of success to keep the troops on the field, while some took charge of the withdrawing regiments to ensure some semblance of order.

When Confederate artillery fire caused the blocking of a key bridge, the retreat became a rout. Caught up in the Union rout were dignitaries from Washington, including congressmen, who had come down to enjoy a Sunday picnic in the countryside while watching the gallant Northern boys "whip the Rebels."

SIGNIFICANCE

Although the Confederates had defeated their enemy and possessed the battlefield, they could not press their advantage. They were too exhausted and too disorganized to mount a major pursuit and threaten Washington, D.C. Although the Confederates had administered a smashing defeat to the Union, like most of the battles that were to follow, this one was indecisive, for it produced neither a serious military disadvantage for the North nor any advantage for the South. The First Battle of Bull Run was widely celebrated in the South, but it was Lincoln and the North that began a serious training and supply program for their troops. In this, the Union gained a slight advantage from the battle.

Although it would be dwarfed in size and ferocity in the months ahead, this first great battle clearly demonstrated that the North and the South were faced, not with a romantic adventure, but with a real and brutal war.

—William J. Cooper, Jr., updated by James J. Cooke

CONFISCATION ACTS OF 1861 AND 1862

August, 1861, and July, 1862

The difference between the first and second acts showed the growing resolve in the Union to end slavery and set the stage for the Emancipation Proclamation.

The Laws: The first act confiscated all property, including slaves used in the Confederate war effort, but did not clearly free the slaves. The second act stated that slaves would not be returned and would be set free after a certain period of time

In August, 1861, the U.S. Congress passed a law confiscating all property, including slaves, used in the Confederate war effort. The law required judicial proceedings before any property could be appropriated, and it left unclear whether any confiscated slaves would be freed. The following July, Congress passed the Second Confiscation Act. The 1862 law, which also required a judicial hearing, declared that rebels were traitors whose property could be seized for the lifetime of the owner. The only property that would not be returned to the rebels' heirs was slaves, who were regarded as captives of war and set free after a period of sixty days. President Abraham Lincoln doubted that Congress possessed the constitutional authority to free slaves in the states. When he signed the bill into law, he included a statement of objections to its provisions. Although the power to confiscate rebel property was rarely used during or after the war, the difference between the first and second acts revealed the growing determination in the Union to end slavery and set the stage for the Emancipation Proclamation, which Lincoln issued in January, 1863.

—Thomas Clarkin

See also: Civil War; Emancipation Proclamation; Slavery

LINCOLN ISSUES THE EMANCIPATION PROCLAMATION

January 1, 1863

Although Abraham Lincoln's Emancipation Proclamation actually freed few slaves, it was a powerful symbolic statement of the North's transformation of the U.S. Civil War into a crusade against slavery.

Locale: Washington, D.C.
Categories: Human rights; laws, acts, and legal history; civil rights and liberties

KEY FIGURES

Abraham Lincoln (1809-1865), president of the United States, 1861-1865
Montgomery Blair (1813-1883), U.S. postmaster general
Salmon P. Chase (1808-1873), U.S. secretary of the Treasury
William H. Seward (1801-1872), U.S. secretary of state
Edwin M. Stanton (1814-1869), U.S. secretary of war
Horace Greeley (1811-1872), editor of the *New York Tribune* who supported emancipation
Charles Sumner (1811-1874), Massachusetts senator
Frederick Douglass (1817?-1895), former slave, abolitionist, and publisher

SUMMARY OF EVENT

On September 22, 1862, President Abraham Lincoln opened a cabinet meeting by reading from a book of humorous stories to put everyone at ease, but he soon came to the business at hand. He announced that he intended to issue that day an emancipation proclamation. Since he had consulted the cabinet on this subject before, he desired no comments from them on this occasion. Then he read the proclamation. As of January 1, 1863, all slaves held in states "in rebellion against the United States" would be forever free.

Lincoln had not reached his decision to proclaim emancipation without much thinking and soul-searching. From his youth, he had opposed slavery on both moral and economic grounds. However, he was a practical politician and a pragmatic man. He negotiated the secession crisis always inspired by a desire to preserve the union. It is fair to say that while Lincoln wished to abolish slavery, he would translate that wish into action only if abolition would enhance his efforts to attain peace and save the union.

Because Lincoln was a practical man, he realized that emancipation was only part of the solution to the problem of race relations in the United States. He foresaw the plight of the slaves after they were freed and favored a form of emancipation that would compensate the former slave owners, along with a plan for voluntary colonization of former slaves in Africa to soften racial adjustment.

Because of the priority Lincoln gave to saving the Union, until 1862 he subordinated his convictions and tentative solutions about slavery to that larger goal. In part, Lincoln hedged on the idea of emancipation so as not to risk the secession of the slave states that were still loyal to the Union—Delaware, Kentucky, Maryland, and Missouri.

Lincoln did not find it easy to divorce the ideals of union from those of emancipation. Both abolitionist ideologists and practical men pressed him to expand his administration's war aims to include emancipation and had done so since the Civil War began in 1861.

Senator Charles Sumner of Massachusetts carried on a one-man campaign to move Lincoln to action on the question of slavery. Horace Greeley's influential *New York Tribune* criticized Lincoln's administration for its lack of concern for the moral issue. Delegations of citizens petitioned Lincoln to act against human bondage. Lincoln heard these and other pleas but made no commitment to official action.

Sometime in the late spring of 1862, the president finally made his decision. The war was not going as well as he wished. He judged that emancipation would not hinder the war effort and might even help it. He determined to emancipate the slaves by presidential proclamation. Still pondering the timing of his momentous step, he told no one of his decision. He retreated often from the White House to the telegraph room of the War Department, in search of privacy. Early in June, he began drafting his proclamation in the telegraph room. He worked slowly and kept his own counsel. Between mid-June and mid-July, he spoke with a few members of his administration about the step he contemplated.

On July 22, 1862, Lincoln finally read his draft proclamation to the entire cabinet and asked for their comments. Secretary of War Edwin M. Stanton applauded the document and expressed the opinion that emancipation would assist the war effort. Secretary of the Treasury Salmon P. Chase thought the move too sudden and sweeping. Chase favored emancipation by the military, as areas of the South were occupied by federal troops.

Postmaster General Montgomery Blair feared political repercussions in the fall congressional elections and predicted doom for the Republicans should the president carry out his intentions. Secretary of State William H. Seward's comments impressed Lincoln most of all. Seward favored the issuance of an emancipation proclamation but questioned the president's timing. Union troops were then in retreat from Richmond, and George B. McClellan's peninsular campaign had proved to be abortive. Emancipation must not seem to be the desperate act of a defeated Union. Lincoln concurred with Seward and waited for a significant Union victory on the battlefield. Victory, however, seemed to be a long time in coming.

The Confederates assumed the offensive in the summer of 1862, defeated federal troops in the Second Battle of Bull Run, and marched into Maryland. On September 17, the Union army fought the Battle of Antietam, and the Confederates withdrew back across the Potomac River into Virginia. Lincoln decided that this withdrawal of the enemy was success enough, and called in the cabinet on September 22. Northern newspapers announced the proclamation the next day.

The document the president presented to his cabinet and made public was actually the preliminary Emancipation Proclamation. Although it was intended to affect millions of Southern slaves, Southern plantation owners paid the announcement little heed, declaring that it was a "Yankee trick" that freed slaves outside Northern borders while keeping those in the North enslaved. Although some Southerners worried that the proclamation might create an atmosphere of rebellion among the slaves, the announcement also strengthened their resolve to defeat the Union armies.

The preliminary proclamation differed in minor respects from the Emancipation Proclamation issued on January 1, 1863, which actually effected emancipation. Perhaps the most significant feature of the document was that it limited emancipation to those states—and portions of states, in the final draft—that were in rebellion. Lincoln limited emancipation in this manner because he based his authority to free the slaves on

---

Emancipation Proclamation

Whereas, on the twenty-second day of September, in the year of our Lord one thousand eight hundred and sixty-two, a proclamation was issued by the President of the United States, containing, among other things, the following, to wit: . . . All persons held as slaves within any State, or designated part of a State, the people whereof shall then be in rebellion against the United States, shall be then, thenceforward, and forever free; and the Executive Government of the United States, including the military and naval authority thereof, will recognize and maintain the freedom of such persons, and will do no act or acts to repress such persons, or any of them, in any efforts they may make for their actual freedom. . . .

And by virtue of the power and for the purposes aforesaid, I do order and declare that all persons held as slaves within said designated States and parts of States are, and henceforward shall be, free. . . .

And I [Abraham Lincoln] hereby enjoin upon the people so declared to be free to abstain from all violence, unless in self-defence; and I recommend to them that, in all cases when allowed, they labor faithfully for reasonable wages.

And I further declare and make known, that such persons of suitable condition, will be received into the armed service of the United States to garrison forts, positions, stations, and other places, and to man vessels of all sorts in said service.

And upon this act, sincerely believed to be an act of justice, warranted by the Constitution, upon military necessity, I invoke the considerate judgment of mankind and the gracious favor of Almighty God.

---

acts of Congress that provided for the confiscation of rebel property and forbade the military from returning slaves of rebels to their owners. Such authority did not encompass a general emancipation. Also, Lincoln hoped to persuade Congress to act upon the principles of compensation and voluntary colonization in dealing with slaves and slave owners in loyal areas.

SIGNIFICANCE

Many African American leaders who lived in the North, Frederick Douglass among them, rallied to the cause, urging African Americans to join the Union army. The Confederacy did not recognize Lincoln's proclamation, and its four million slaves remained in bondage until Union armies occupied Confederate territories. However, many Southern slaves heeded the call, threw down their tools, and escaped into the North. Many of them then joined the Union forces. Those slaves already held within Union lines in Tennessee, Louisiana, and Virginia were freed. As the Northern troops marched southward, they liberated African Americans in the towns they defeated.

Doctrinaire abolitionists in the North criticized the president's moderation. However, on September 22, 1862, Lincoln had taken his stand. The war for union widened into a crusade against slavery. Foreign governments paused in their consideration of aiding the South, but the consensus, as Seward had predicted, was dismissal of the proclamation. Generally, European leaders tried to find fault with it. Nevertheless, Lincoln had ensured the survival of the union and given the slaves hope. In the end, slavery was doomed.

—*Emory M. Thomas, updated by Marilyn Elizabeth Perry*

See also: Southerners Advance Proslavery Arguments; Douglass Launches *The North Star*; Underground Railroad Flourishes; Second Fugitive Slave Law; Stowe Publishes *Uncle Tom's Cabin*; Lincoln-Douglas Debates; Brown's Raid on Harpers Ferry; Lincoln Is Elected U.S. President; Lincoln Is Inaugurated President; Civil War; Thirteenth Amendment Is Ratified.

Related articles in *Great Lives from History: The Nineteenth Century, 1801-1900:* Salmon P. Chase; Frederick Douglass; Horace Greeley; Abraham Lincoln; William H. Seward; Edwin M. Stanton; Charles Sumner.

54TH MASSACHUSETTS VOLUNTEER INFANTRY REGIMENT LEADS A MASS ASSAULT AGAINST FORT WAGNER

May 1863

WILLIAM H. CARNEY SOLDIER

The heroism of Carney and other black soldiers in the Civil War helped dispel racial stereotypes and rallied African Americans to the Union cause, symbolized by the abolition of slavery. Of the two million soldiers and sailors who fought and died for the North, nearly 10 percent were men of color.

Born: February 29, 1840; Norfolk, Virginia
Died: December 9, 1908; Boston, Massachusetts
Also known as: William Harvey Carney
Area of achievement: Military

EARLY LIFE

William Harvey Carney was born on February 29, 1840, to a slave named William and a freedwoman named Ann Dean. Ann previously had been the slave of a Major Carney of Norfolk, Virginia; by prior agreement, she was set free upon Carney's death. At the time of their son's birth, William was still a slave. Following the custom of the time, the younger William, like his parents, was given the plantation master's surname.

Because there were no schools for African American children—education of slaves or their offspring was discouraged in the South—Carney was unable to read or write until his early teens. He took lessons in private and in secret at a local black church and contemplated becoming a preacher. In the mid-1850's, Carney's father escaped from slavery through the Underground Railroad and made

his way to Massachusetts. Carney soon took the same route north. He joined his father as a dockworker in the whaling port of New Bedford and worked loading and unloading ships. The Carney men saved their money and pooled resources to purchase the freedom of other family members, with whom they eventually reunited in Massachusetts.

Before the outbreak of the Civil War, Carney became a member and trustee of Salem Baptist Church and worked restocking wholesale and retail stores in the area.

LIFE'S WORK

On January 1, 1863, President Abraham Lincoln issued the Emancipation Proclamation, in which African Americans were encouraged to join the Union Army and Navy.

In response to published recruiting appeals, Carney soon enlisted in C Company of the Fifty-fourth Massachusetts Volunteer Infantry Regiment, an all-black unit under the command of Colonel Robert Gould Shaw, a white abolitionist.

After training near Boston, the company, 600 strong, marched off to do battle in May, 1863. After a few skirmishes with Confederate troops in Georgia and South Carolina, they engaged in their first major battle: leading a mass assault against Fort Wagner, near Charleston (the battle was dramatized in the 1989 film *Glory*). During the nearly suicidal attack, Carney was wounded twice but kept advancing. When he saw the regimental flag bearer fall, fatally shot, he scooped up the flag and rallied the troops forward. Arriving atop the fort's parapets, Carney found he was alone. (Shaw and more than 50 men were mortally wounded in the attack, 15 were captured, more than 50 were missing in action, and some 150 others suffered wounds.) With no support, Carney retreated, sustaining additional wounds in the leg and head as he struggled to return to Union lines. Before relinquishing the rescued flag to a comrade and falling unconscious, he modestly maintained he had been merely doing his duty in keeping the flag from touching the ground. For his heroism—which disproved the prevailing racist notion that African Americans would be cowardly soldiers—Carney was the first African American cited for the Congressional Medal of Honor. However, he was not the first to actually receive his medal: The presentation did not take place until May 23, 1900.

Promoted to color sergeant for his brave deeds and unable to serve in combat because of his injuries, Carney was mustered out of the military in mid-1864. In 1865, he married Susannah Williams and subsequently fathered a daughter, Clara, who became a music teacher.

He afterward served for a time as New Bedford's streetlight superintendent. After a brief stay in California, Carney returned to New Bedford, where he became the community's first African American postal carrier, serving for thirty-two years until his retirement in 1901. For the remaining years of his life, he worked as a messenger, delivering documents to and from the Massachusetts state house. It was there that an old war wound caught up with him: One day in 1908, his weakened leg became caught in elevator machinery. Carney was severely mangled in the accident and died of his injuries.

SIGNIFICANCE

Long a popular speaker at patriotic events, Carney received high honors after his death. The state house flag was lowered to half-staff, a gesture normally reserved for mourning powerful dignitaries, not former slaves, in 1908. Carney also was prominently depicted on the Augustus Saint-Gaudens-designed memorial to Shaw unveiled on the Boston Common in 1897. The lyrics of a rousing turn-of-the-century song, composed soon after the formal Medal of Honor presentation—"Boys the Old Flag Never Touched the Ground"—also celebrated Carney's heroic deeds. His former home in NewBedford is a local landmark listed on the National Register of Historic Places.

—*Jack Ewing*

DRAFT RIOTS

July, 1863

Estimates of the casualties in the violence range up to more than one thousand. In spite of the violence, the federal government was determined to enforce the draft with even more vigor.

The Event: Wide-scale racial disturbances in New York City prompted by the federal government's first conscription act
Place: New York, New York

The firing on Fort Sumter on April 12, 1861, at the beginning of the Civil War, came at a time when the regular U.S. Army numbered only about 16,000 officers and troops. The traditional method of increasing the size of the army was to expand the state militias and to form a volunteer emergency national army recruited through the states. The immediate response of President Abraham

Lincoln to the firing on Fort Sumter was to call for 75,000 militia volunteers for three months' service. This call was exceeded, and some volunteers were turned away because the expectation was that a show of force would be sufficient to defeat the South. Congress and the president subsequently found it necessary, however, to call for more volunteers. Repeated defeats of the Union army and the resultant loss of men caused President Lincoln to call for 300,000 volunteers in the summer of 1862.

The difficulty of obtaining volunteers was soon apparent; bounties were increased, and the threat of the draft was invoked. Congress passed the Militia Act of July, 1862, which allowed the states to draft men into the militia and encouraged enlistments. President Lincoln called for another 300,000 men to be enrolled into the militia. Although the Militia Act of 1862 gave the federal government power to enroll men in situations where the state machinery was inadequate, the short-term (nine-month maximum) nature of the militia draft and the inequities of the system made it less than satisfactory.

CONSCRIPTION BEGINS

Spurred by the loss of 75,000 men, by news of a conscription law passed by the Confederacy, and by the failure of the states to provide men promptly for the various calls, Congress passed its own Conscription Act on March 3, 1863. Henry Wilson, chairman of the Senate Committee on Military Affairs, was responsible for the introduction of a bill that eventually was passed and labeled "An Act for Enrolling and Calling Out the National Forces and for Other Purposes." This act was the first national draft law in the history of the nation. It called for the creation of the "national forces," which were to consist of all able-bodied male citizens and alien declarants between twenty and forty-five years of age, including African Americans. White opposition to African Americans in federal army uniforms noticeably lessened as a result of the draft. In all, more than 168,000 African American recruits were drafted. Certain high officials, medically unfit persons, and hardship cases were exempted. Exemption could also be obtained by paying three hundred dollars or by securing a substitute.

The system was operated by the War Department under the direction of Colonel James B. Fry, provost-marshal-general. Provost-marshals were appointed in districts similar to the congressional districts and enrollments began. Quotas were established, and credit was given for enlistments. If the quotas were not met, drawings were held to determine who should be drafted. Small cards were placed in sealed envelopes in a large trunk, and the names were drawn in public by a trustworthy citizen wearing a blindfold. The system of paying three hundred dollars for exemption from service subsequently was abolished, but the privilege of hiring a substitute was continued. The names of more than three million men were gathered, but only about 170,000 were drafted, and 120,000 of those produced substitutes. The primary intent for passage of the law was to speed up voluntary enlistment, and more than one million men enlisted. The chief motivation for these enlistments was probably the threat of the draft.

OPPOSITION

The draft brought President Lincoln and Secretary of War Edwin McMasters Stanton into conflict with state governors. Those governors who were unenthusiastic about the conduct of the war openly criticized the president and the draft, while governors who favored a more vigorous prosecution of the war often complained that their states had not been given full credit for previous enlistments. Lincoln and Stanton often temporized with the governors by granting postponements or additional credits as the end of the war drew near.

There was considerable resistance to the draft. Pennsylvania, Illinois, Indiana, and Kentucky had problems with enrollment, and draft offices and officers were attacked in those states. The Irish in New York and New Jersey were particularly incensed by the draft, many viewing the conflicts as a rich man's war and a poor man's fight. With fifty-one categories of diseases qualifying men for medical exemption, the system was fraught with medical resistance problems. Surgeons administering medical qualifying exams were confronted by faked hernias (the most widespread cause of exemption), eye problems caused by applying eye irritants, and pretended deafness. Giving incorrect birth dates, claiming false dependents, and even the enrollment of dead people were other methods of noncompliance. Finally, there were the runaways. Given time to settle their affairs before departing for camp, a considerable number of draftees either relocated or fled to Canada.

With the public generally hostile to the draft, the best way for a community to avoid it was to fill the quota with volunteers. Consequently, bounty taxes were implemented to raise revenues to attract foreigners, new immigrants, and the poverty-stricken to enlist. The paying of bounties corrupted the draft system. It produced bounty jumpers who, attracted by lump-sum payments, were willing to jump off trains or boats to escape conscription.

RIOTS

Notorious resistance to the draft instigated the draft riots in New York City. Governor Horatio Seymour's speech of July 4, 1863, attacking the Lincoln administration for violations of individual liberty, did nothing to decrease the hostility of the New York Irish toward African Americans and the abolitionists. Anti-draft rioting, which took place between July 13 and 15, destroyed property and physically harmed many African Americans. Some New York militia units that had been engaged at Gettysburg were hastily ordered back to New York to stop the rioting. Estimates of the casualties in the violence range up to more than one thousand. In spite of the violence, the federal government was determined to enforce the draft with even more fervor.

CONFEDERACY AND CONSCRIPTION

The Confederacy's calls for volunteers and its national conscription law antedated those of the Union. Jefferson Davis's call for 100,000 volunteers came before the firing on Fort Sumter, and the Conscription Act was passed on April 16, 1862, almost a year before similar legislation was passed by the United States. The Confederate act conscripted men from eighteen to thirty-five years of age; later the same year, it was extended to include those between seventeen and fifty years of age. The Confederate law included a substitute system and a controversial list of exempted persons held to be essential at home. The category that caused the most discussion was that which exempted one slave owner or overseer for each twenty slaves. The Confederate draft was also controversial because it was a national levy; it made no concession to the doctrine of states' rights for which most southerners claimed to be fighting.

It appears that the Confederacy's early use of a conscription law enabled General Robert E. Lee's armies to continue their general success in the Civil War well into 1863. It was only after the North also began drafting men that President Lincoln could be confident of victory. The North, with a much larger population, was able to sustain its losses and to continue the war indefinitely; the Confederacy could not. Continuance of the draft underscored Northern determination to continue the war to its conclusion. The result was Lee's surrender at Appomattox and the restoration of the Union.

—Mark A. Plummer Updated by Irwin Halfond

See also: Charleston race riots; Civil War; Emancipation Proclamation; Race riots of 1866

BATTLES OF GETTYSBURG, VICKSBURG, AND CHATTANOOGA

July 1-November 25, 1863

Northern victories in these major campaigns marked the turning point in the U.S. Civil War by ending the South's offensive capabilities.

Locale: Gettysburg, Pennsylvania; Vicksburg, Mississippi; Chattanooga, Tennessee
Category: Wars, uprisings, and civil unrest

KEY FIGURES

Abraham Lincoln (1809-1865), president of the United States, 1861-1865
George G. Meade (1815-1872), commander of the Union Army of the Potomac at Gettysburg
Ulysses S. Grant (1822-1885), commander of the Union forces at Vicksburg and Chattanooga
William Tecumseh Sherman (1820-1891), Grant's principal subordinate at Vicksburg and Chattanooga
George H. Thomas (1816-1870), commander of the Union Army of the Cumberland at Chattanooga
Robert E. Lee (1807-1870), commander of the Confederate Army of Northern Virginia at Gettysburg
Joseph Eggleston Johnston (1807-1891), Confederate commander in Mississippi in 1863
John C. Pemberton (1814-1881), commander of the Confederate forces at Vicksburg

Braxton Bragg (1817-1876), commander of the Confederate forces at Chattanooga

SUMMARY OF EVENT

Through the first two years of the U.S. Civil War, the North and the South were both militarily strong enough to threaten each other's territories. After the First Battle of Bull Run in July, 1861, no further serious campaigning occurred in the eastern theater of the Civil War during that year. In 1862, George B. McClellan, the commander of the Union Army of the Potomac, tried to take the Confederate capital at Richmond by attacking westward on the peninsula between the York and James Rivers. His campaign failed, and Robert E. Lee, the commander of the Confederate Army of Northern Virginia, invaded Maryland. McClellan repulsed Lee's army at the Battle of Antietam on September 17. During that same winter, Ambrose Burnside replaced McClellan and attempted to assault Richmond from the north. Lee stopped Burnside's advance at the Battle of Fredericksburg on December 13. President Abraham Lincoln then put Joseph Hooker in Burnside's place. Early in the spring of 1863, Hooker tried to move around Lee's left flank, but Lee counterattacked and defeated him at Chancellorsville on May 2.

Lee then launched his second invasion of the North, moving in the general direction of Harrisburg, the capital of Pennsylvania. The Army of the Potomac followed, keeping between Lee and the national capital at Washington.

On July 1, 1863, the two armies finally confronted each other directly at Gettysburg, a small college town southwest of Harrisburg. George G. Meade, who had just taken command of the Union forces, rushed his men to the town, as did Lee, for what would become the greatest land battle ever fought in the Western Hemisphere.

On the first day of the battle, there was fierce fighting on the northern end of the line, where, despite heavy losses, which amounted to 80 percent in one brigade, the Union forces held. On July 2, Lee attacked with his right wing, with similar results.

On July 3, Lee ordered a massive assault on Meade's center, which was fixed on Cemetery Hill. After a planned artillery bombardment of one hour, there ensued a Confederate infantry attack of approximately twelve thousand troops under the operational command of Lieutenant General James Longstreet. Longstreet, commanding First Corps and Lee's "Old War Horse," had argued strongly against any fight at Gettysburg and bitterly opposed the attack on July 3. Longstreet had three divisions, the strongest of which was Major General George Pickett's Virginia division. Union artillery and massed infantry fire inflicted casualties of more than 50 percent on the assaulting force and broke up attacking divisions.

After an hour of bitter fighting, shattered and dispirited Confederate troops streamed back from Cemetery Hill.

At the same time, east of Gettysburg, General Jeb Stuart's once seemingly invincible Confederate cavalry was soundly defeated. July 3, 1863, proved to be Lee's worst day as commander of the Army of Northern Virginia.

Lee's force suffered 28,000 casualties; Meade's force suffered 23,000 casualties. With his army sorely depleted, Lee retired to Virginia. He could now do no more than defend Virginia and hope that the North would abandon its effort to conquer the South, for the Army of Northern Virginia would never again be capable of assuming the offensive.

Meanwhile, in the western theater of the war, the Union was on the offensive. Early in 1862, Ulysses S. Grant had captured Confederate positions at Fort Donelson on the lower Cumberland River and Fort Henry on the Tennessee River. The Confederates fell back to Mississippi, but counterattacked at Shiloh on April 6-7 without success. The Union then took control of all points north of Vicksburg on the Mississippi River.

In October, 1862, Grant began an advance down the Mississippi Central Railroad headed for Vicksburg, a fortified port city on the Mississippi River. Vicksburg was important because it was on a high bluff, from which Confederate artillery denied passage of the river to the Union boats. While Grant moved along the railroad line with 40,000 men, William T. Sherman, with 32,000 men, moved along the river. In December, Confederate cavalry moved into Grant's rear flank and burned his supply dumps at Holly Springs, Mississippi. Grant fell back to bases in Tennessee. Sherman, not realizing that he was unsupported, attacked Vicksburg and suffered heavy casualties.

Grant was determined to take Vicksburg by any means. During the winter of 1862-1863 he tried to bypass Vicksburg by digging a canal opposite the city. This scheme failed, but Grant did not give up the idea of taking the heavily fortified city. Preparing for a spring campaign, he built up a vast quantity of supplies, most placed on barges, which would be floated downriver. He had decided on a daring campaign to move south of Vicksburg, cross from Louisiana to Mississippi, and then march his army into the heart of Mississippi, taking the capital city of Jackson, which was forty miles east of Vicksburg. After Jackson was taken and his rear secured, Grant would move on to Vicksburg, attacking from the east. The wellprepared supply barges that would be offloaded south of Vicksburg would keep Grant's highly mobile army well supplied with ammunition and food. It was a daring plan with many dangers, but taking advantage of surprise, mobility, and a unified command, Grant was confident that he could keep the Confederates confused and incapable of massing forces against his smaller army.

On April 30, Grant was on dry ground on the east bank of the Mississippi River. He then began a campaign in which he achieved six victories in seventeen days.

Moving north, he defeated two Confederate brigades at Port Gibson on May 1. Continuing his move inland, he headed toward Mississippi's capital city, Jackson, which was also a major railroad center directly east of Vicksburg.

With Jackson secure, he would not have to worry about his rear flank when he struck out for Vicksburg.

Joseph E. Johnston, the Confederate commander in the area, could not discover Grant's intentions, and John C. Pemberton, in immediate command at Vicksburg, was equally confused over the Union commander's intentions.

Although Grant's force was outnumbered 70,000 to 40,000 in the region as a whole, his army fought each of its successive battles with overwhelming superiority.

On May 12, one of his three corps defeated a Confederate brigade at Raymond, and two days later, his entire army scattered the 6,000 Confederate troops defending Jackson.

Grant burned Jackson, destroyed its railroad facilities, and turned west toward Vicksburg. When Pemberton finally realized where Grant was, he still had most of his force, but he had no help from Johnston when he engaged Grant halfway to Vicksburg at Champion's Hill on May 16. Grant again drove the enemy from the field, as he did the next day, when Pemberton tried to mount a defense a few miles outside Vicksburg at the Big Black River. Once again, Union troops routed the Confederates, forcing a headlong retreat to the earthworks. Pemberton then withdrew inside his defenses at Vicksburg.

Filled with confidence, Grant and his troops assaulted the Vicksburg fortress on May 19. The Confederates remained safely inside their trenches and easily repulsed the attack. Three days later, Grant tried again, with heavy losses. He then realized that he could not take the city by assault and settled into a siege.

Reinforcements arriving from the North increased the size of Grant's force to 70,000 men, and abundant supplies allowed his artillery to fire a constant barrage on the enemy positions. Within Vicksburg, the Confederates were short of supplies. By early July, the citizens were starving, the troops were eating mule meat, and the gunners could fire their artillery guns only three times a day.

On July 3, Pemberton asked Grant for surrender terms.

Grant allowed the 20,000 Confederates to leave Vicksburg upon signing paroles, promising not to fight again until they were properly exchanged for Union prisoners.

Pemberton accepted. On July 4, Grant raised the Union flag over Vicksburg. With the fall of Port Hudson in Louisiana immediately afterward, the entire Mississippi River was in Union hands, and the one-third of the Confederacy west of the river was permanently cut off.

Following his victory, Grant, accompanied by Sherman and his corps, went east to Chattanooga, Tennessee, where a Union army was under siege. Chattanooga was a railroad center and the largest city in eastern Tennessee, an area noted for its pro-Union sentiments. Braxton Bragg, leading the Confederate forces, had won a victory south of the city at Chickamauga on September 20, 1863, forcing the Union army to fall back into Chattanooga.

Grant arrived there in mid-October. After restoring the supply line that Bragg had cut, Grant launched his attack on November 25.

He planned to strike Bragg's flanks, with a feint in the center. The troops under George H. Thomas, the commander of the Union Army of the Cumberland, made the feint up Missionary Ridge, drove out the Confederates who had been facing them in their trenches, and to the amazement of the Union commanders, continued, without orders, up the hill to destroy Bragg's line. Bragg lost 6,700 troops, Grant 5,800. Mainly because of good luck, Grant had won another victory. With Vicksburg and Chattanooga firmly in the hands of the Union, the Confederate position in the West had become tenuous at best.

Lincoln's Gettysburg Address

On November 19, 1863, a little more than four months after the Battle of Gettysburg was fought, President Abraham Lincoln visited the battlefield, along with many other dignitaries, and participated in a ceremony consecrating the graves of the thousands of soldiers who died there. Although Lincoln was not the featured speaker on that occasion, the brief but poignant speech he delivered has become the most famous oration in American history.

Fourscore and seven years ago our fathers brought forth on this continent a new nation, conceived in liberty and dedicated to the proposition that all men are created equal.

Now we are engaged in a great civil war, testing whether that nation or any nation so conceived and so dedicated can long endure. We are met on a great battlefield of that war. We have come to dedicate a portion of it as a final resting place for those who died here that the nation might live. This we may, in all propriety do.

But in a larger sense, we cannot dedicate, we cannot consecrate, we cannot hallow this ground. The brave men, living and dead who struggled here have hallowed it far above our poor power to add or detract.

The world will little note nor long remember what we say here, but it can never forget what they did here. It is rather for us the living, we here be dedicated to the great task remaining before us—that from these honored dead we take increased devotion to that cause for which they here gave the last full measure of devotion—that we here highly resolve that these dead shall not have died in vain, that this nation shall have a new birth of freedom, and that government of the people, by the people, for the people shall not perish from the earth.

SIGNIFICANCE

The union's strategic and operational victories at Vicksburg and Chattanooga marked the emergence of Ulysses S. Grant as the premier general of the war at that time. Chattanooga confirmed that Grant could win campaigns. In Washington, D.C., Abraham Lincoln, who had dismissed a string of generals and was dissatisfied with Meade's performance after Gettysburg, made Grant the overall commander of Union forces.

Leaving Major General William T. Sherman behind in the West, Grant went east to confront and finally defeat Robert E. Lee and the army of Northern Virginia.

—Stephen E. Ambrose, updated by James J. Cooke

See also: Establishment of the Confederate States of America; Civil War; First Battle of Bull Run; Sherman Marches Through Georgia and the Carolinas; Surrender at Appomattox and Assassination of Lincoln.

Related articles in *Great Lives from History: The Nineteenth Century, 1801-1900:* Jefferson Davis; Ulysses S. Grant; Robert E. Lee; Abraham Lincoln; William Tecumseh Sherman.

SURRENDER AT APPOMATTOX AND ASSASSINATION OF LINCOLN

April 9 and 14, 1865

Five days after the South began capitulating to end the fighting of the Civil War, President Abraham Lincoln was shot by a Confederate sympathizer, leaving his successor to direct the course of postwar Reconstruction in the defeated South.

Locale: Appomattox Courthouse, Virginia; Washington, D.C.

Categories: Terrorism and political assassination; wars, uprisings, and civil unrest

KEY FIGURES

Ulysses S. Grant (1822-1885), chief commander of the victorious Union armies

Robert E. Lee (1807-1870), chief commander of the defeated Confederate armies

Abraham Lincoln (1809-1865), president of the United States, 1861-1865

John Wilkes Booth (1838-1865), professional actor and Southern sympathizer

Andrew Johnson (1808-1875), vice president and successor to Lincoln

William H. Seward (1801-1872), secretary of state

Edwin M. Stanton (1814-1869), secretary of war

SUMMARY OF EVENT

President Abraham Lincoln was the chief architect of the Union victory that ended the long U.S. Civil War. In March, 1864, he called General Ulysses S. Grant to the White House and placed him in overall command of the Union armies. Grant then embarked upon a vigorous campaign aimed at the Confederate capital at Richmond, engaging General Robert E. Lee's Army of Northern Virginia in two important battles west of Fredricksburg, Virginia—Wilderness, May 5-7, and Spotsylvania, May 8-9, 1864. Grant suffered heavy casualties but pushed on to Cold Harbor (June 1-3). There, the Confederates repulsed his attack, which, had it been successful, would have led to the fall of Richmond. Grant then attempted to outflank Lee by crossing the James River and driving toward Petersburg, where he intended to cut vital rail connections.

Lee was able to check Grant's advance short of Petersburg, however, and a nine-month stalemate ensued.

Meanwhile, General William T. Sherman had completed his destructive march from Atlanta to the sea at Savannah, Georgia. He then moved northward in a march that was to take him through South Carolina and North Carolina. All signs pointed to a Confederate defeat in 1865: The Union blockade was becoming increasingly effective; Great Britain no longer showed much sympathy for the Confederacy; the economy of the South was breaking down under the impact of the war; and Grant continued to receive troop replacements, whereas Lee's troops were becoming exhausted. A peace conference, which Confederate president Jefferson Davis had suggested, was held on February 3, 1865. Confederate vice president Alexander H. Stephens led the delegation from the South, while Lincoln spoke for the Union. Lincoln insisted upon the disbanding of the

Confederate forces, but the Confederacy was not then willing to surrender.

In April, 1865, Grant was able to extend Lee's lines to the breaking point, and Lee was forced to evacuate the Confederate capital of Richmond as well as Petersburg. Lee's escape route lay to the west and south; he hoped to join forces with General Joe Johnston in North Carolina, but Grant's forces blocked his escape. Now convinced of the futility of continuing the war, Lee met Grant at the McLean house in Appomattox Courthouse, where he surrendered on April 9. Following the spirit of President Lincoln's instructions, Grant agreed to release Lee's officers and men on parole. Lee's troops were allowed to keep their horses, mules, and sidearms and then return home. In short order, the other scattered Confederate armies followed General Lee's lead and began the ordeal of surrender.

The last significant group of men under arms, those under the command of General Joseph Johnston, began surrender negotiations with Sherman on April 17. The war had wrought a death toll far greater than anyone could have imagined four years earlier: 360,000 Union soldiers, 260,000 men from the South, and unknown numbers of civilians. The economic havoc would leave the South devastated for a century.

News of Lee's surrender reached Washington, D.C., on the same day that it took place, and it was received with great rejoicing. Lincoln made several extemporaneous speeches and delivered one prepared address during the course of the next several days in response to the demands of exuberant crowds. It was Lincoln's view that the South should be welcomed back as brothers to enable healing to begin. In this regard, he was strongly opposed by the Radical Republicans within Congress. It was their view that the South had started the war and should be made to pay for it. Whether Lincoln might have curbed their hatred, had he lived, remains an unanswered question for history.

At approximately 8:30 p.m. on April 14, President and Mrs. Lincoln, in company with Clara Harris and Major Henry R. Rathbone, entered Ford's Theater in Washington to see a performance of the play *Our American Cousin*. At about 10:15 p.m., John Wilkes Booth, a twenty-six-year-old actor who sympathized with the South, slipped into the president's box and fired one shot into the back of Lincoln's head. The president was mortally wounded and died the next morning at 7:22 a.m., without ever regaining consciousness. His body was taken back to Springfield, Illinois, on a circuitous seventeen-hundred-mile route that retraced the 1861

journey he made to Washington, D.C., for his first inauguration.

After shooting Lincoln, Booth jumped onto the stage, breaking a small bone in his leg as he landed. From the stage he shouted the motto of Virginia, *Sic semper tyrannis* (thus ever to tyrants). In the confusion, he managed to evade capture in Washington, escaping over the bridge into Virginia. There, his broken leg was set by Dr. Samuel Mudd. It remains unclear whether Mudd was aware of the Significance of his patient. Booth was eventually trapped in a tobacco shed near Port Royal, Virginia, on April 26. There he died, either by his own hand or from a shot fired by one of the soldiers attempting to arrest him.

The assassination of Lincoln was only one part of a major plot to murder the most important Union officials. Secretary of State William H. Seward and his sons, Frederick and Augustus, suffered knife wounds at the hands of Lewis Paine, a former Confederate soldier and devotee of Booth. George A. Atzerodt, an alcoholic, was assigned by Booth to kill Vice President Andrew Johnson, but he failed to make the attempt. Secretary of War Edwin Stanton took charge of the investigation and ordered the arrest of Paine, Atzerodt, David Herold, Edward Spangler, Samuel Arnold, Michael O'Laughlin, Samuel Mudd, and Mary E. Surratt, the owner of the boardinghouse in which the conspirators met. It is likely that Surratt knew nothing of Booth's plot. However, she and Dr. Mudd were caught up in the passion for revenge that followed Lincoln's murder.

The alleged conspirators were tried before a military commission whose jurisdiction in their cases was questionable. The trial lasted from May 10 to June 30, and all the defendants were found guilty. Atzerodt, Paine, Herold, and Surratt were hanged seven days after the trial ended, while Spangler, Arnold, Mudd, and O'Laughlin were sentenced to life imprisonment. Surratt's execution was almost certainly a miscarriage of justice that could not have been carried out if a few weeks or months had been allowed for passions to cool. By contrast, her son John escaped immediate capture and, when tried in 1867, was released after a jury failed to agree on a verdict.

SIGNIFICANCE

Those sentenced to life imprisonment were pardoned in 1869, with the exception of O'Laughlin, who died of yellow fever at the Dry Tortugas prison off Key West. Dr. Mudd was found guilty as an accessory after the fact, and also sentenced to life imprisonment. However, his heroic actions during the yellow fever epidemic resulted in a commutation of his sentence, and he also was freed in 1869. Mudd's descendants have continued to argue for his innocence. Former president of the Confederacy Jefferson Davis was taken prisoner soon after Lee's surrender.

Although he was indicted for treason and imprisoned two years at Fort Monroe, he never came to trial.

The most important, and also the most enigmatic, consequence of Lincoln's assassination was the fact that the task of reconstructing the South after the war was left to his successor, Andrew Johnson. An entirely different kind of politician, Johnson quickly ran afoul of the Radical Republicans in Congress and nearly lost his presidency to impeachment. Meanwhile, Congress took control of Reconstruction and was inclined to punish the South for having caused the Civil War. If Lincoln

had lived through his second term in office, Reconstruction would certainly have taken a different course, but it is impossible to know for certain what that course might have been.

—Mark A. Plummer, updated by Richard Adler

See also: Lincoln Is Elected U.S. President; Lincoln Is Inaugurated President; Civil War; First Battle of Bull Run; Battles of Gettysburg, Vicksburg, and Chattanooga; Reconstruction of the South; Sherman Marches Through Georgia and the Carolinas; Watie Is Last Confederate General to Surrender.

Related articles in *Great Lives from History: The Nineteenth Century, 1801-1900:* Edwin Booth; Ulysses S. Grant; Andrew Johnson; Robert E. Lee; Abraham Lincoln; William H. Seward; Edwin M. Stanton.

SHERMAN MARCHES THROUGH GEORGIA AND THE CAROLINAS
November 15, 1864-April 18, 1865

By employing what later came to be known as the tactics of total war and doing almost everything possible to demoralize the enemy, General William Tecumseh Sherman carved a path of destruction through Georgia and the Carolinas that materially moved the Union closer to victory in the U.S. Civil War.

Locale: Georgia; Carolinas
Categories: Wars, uprisings, and civil unrest; atrocities and war crimes

KEY FIGURES
Ulysses S. Grant (1822-1885), commander of the Union forces at Vicksburg and Chattanooga
William Tecumseh Sherman (1820-1891), commander of the Union's Army of the Tennessee
Oliver O. Howard (1830-1909), commander of Sherman's right wing
Henry Warner Slocum (1827-1894), commander of Sherman's left wing
Joseph Eggleston Johnston (1807-1891), first commander of the Confederate Army of Tennessee
John Bell Hood (1831-1879), Johnston's replacement
Robert E. Lee (1807-1870), commander of the Confederate Army of Northern Virginia

General William Tecumseh Sherman, 1865

SUMMARY OF EVENT

Following his victory at Chattanooga, General Ulysses S. Grant went to Washington, D.C., where he was promoted to commander in chief of the Union army. His successor in the western theater was General William Tecumseh Sherman. In the spring of 1864, both generals launched new offensives. Grant advanced on General Robert E. Lee's Army of Northern Virginia, and Sherman moved against General Joseph E. Johnston's Army of Tennessee. Grant spent the spring and summer fighting Lee in northern Virginia, where his men suffered heavy casualties but forced the Confederates to fall back.

By fall, the Union forces were besieging the Confederate capital at Richmond in overwhelming numbers.

Sherman began his own campaign on May 7, starting from Chattanooga with 100,000 troops and heading toward Atlanta. Johnston, his opponent, had a strength of about 62,000. Johnston used delaying tactics, refusing to fight a major battle and falling back toward Atlanta.

Johnston's tactics—which are called "Fabian," after the ancient Roman general Quintus Fabius Maximus, who defeated Hannibal by avoiding decisive confrontations in the Second Punic War—exasperated Confederate president Jefferson Davis, who replaced him with John Bell Hood.

Despite having inferior numbers, Hood then attacked Sherman twice, at Peachtree Creek on July 20 and in the Battle of Atlanta on July 22. Hood lost 8,500 soldiers to Sherman's loss of 3,700 and had to abandon Atlanta. Hood then slipped around Sherman's flank, heading toward the Union supply dumps at Chattanooga and Nashville, Tennessee.

General Grant, Union chief of staff Henry Halleck, and President Abraham Lincoln all wanted Sherman to follow Hood and to destroy his army. Instead, Sherman left a comparatively small force under George Thomas at Nashville and prepared to march across Georgia to the Atlantic port of Savannah. After burning Atlanta, he began the march on November 15. With Hood moving against Thomas in Nashville—where Hood eventually lost most of his army—the Confederates could oppose Sherman's 60,000 troops with only 13,000 soldiers, mostly cavalry. Sherman advanced in two wings, brush his right wing, and Henry Warner Slocum commanded the left wing.

Sherman's men lived off the land. "Bummers" went out each morning to the flanks, collecting chickens, cows, vegetables, and whatever else they could find. Along the way, they burned down homes and buildings and destroyed the railroad system. Sherman was determined to see to it that Georgia's civilians realized the horrors of war, and he succeeded. He also wished to cut off Lee's food supply and encourage desertion in the Army of Northern Virginia. He hoped that Confederate soldiers would want to return to their homes to protect them from his "bummers." As Sherman expressed his philosophy, Until we can repopulate Georgia, it is useless to occupy it; but the utter destruction of its roads, houses and people will cripple their military resources. . . . I can make the march, and make Georgia howl.

After Sherman reached Savannah on December 10, he sent President Lincoln a telegram stating that he wished to offer Savannah as "a Christmas present" to the commander in chief. After refitting his army with supplies carried from Washington by sea, he marched north into the Carolinas. Again his troops, facing no major opposition, devastated the countryside. The Northern troops were even more ruthless in South Carolina than they had been in Georgia, since they tended to blame South Carolina, the first state to secede, for the war. As Sherman put it,

We can punish South Carolina as she deserves. . . . I do sincerely believe that the whole United States, North and South, would rejoice to have this army turned loose on South Carolina to devastate that State, in the manner we have done in Georgia.

South Carolina's capital city, Columbia, was engulfed in flames in late February. By late March, 1865, Sherman was in the middle of North Carolina, where his old Confederate opponent, Joseph Johnston, had scraped together a small force to resist him. In Virginia, meanwhile, Grant had forced Lee to abandon Richmond and retreat toward western Virginia. By early April, Grant was in close pursuit. Lee, with his army almost gone as a result of starvation and desertion, surrendered on April 9 at Appomattox Courthouse, Virginia. By then, the proud Army of Northern Virginia was reduced to a force of 26,700, while Grant still had nearly 113,000 troops. Johnston, with the major Confederate army gone, decided to follow Lee's example, and on April 18 he signed an armistice with Sherman.

SIGNIFICANCE

With Johnston's surrender to Sherman, the Civil War was effectively over. As Sherman, who earlier in his career had directed a Louisiana military school, explained succinctly, "The South bet on the wrong card and lost."

His fifty-seven-mile-wide path of destruction had demoralized the South's population and, with Grant's military success, helped hasten the war's end. By that time, to many, the Civil War had become a total war, and this fact finally led to the Confederacy's capitulation. Sherman's march to the sea was also an early intimation of the German Blitzkrieg of World War II.

—*Stephen E. Ambrose, updated by Joseph Edward Lee*

See also: Establishment of the Confederate States of America; Civil War; First Battle of Bull Run; Battles of Gettysburg, Vicksburg, and Chattanooga; Reconstruction of the South; Surrender at Appomattox and Assassination of Lincoln; Watie Is Last Confederate General to Surrender.

Related articles in *Great Lives from History: The Nineteenth Century, 1801-1900:* Jefferson Davis; Ulysses S. Grant; Abraham Lincoln; William Tecumseh Sherman.

JUNETEENTH

JUNE 19, 1865
Identification A celebration initiated by former slaves in Texas upon learning some two and a half years after the signing of the Emancipation Proclamation that they were free.
Locale: Galveston, TX
Categories: Emacipation Proclamation; Frederick Douglas, Rosa Parks, Martin Luther King, Jr.

KEY FIGURES
Gordon Grander (1821-1876), general in the Union Army
Abraham Lincoln (1809-1865), president of the United States, 1861-1865
William Tecumseh Sherman (1820-1891), commander of the Union's Army of the Tennessee

Juneteenth is the oldest known celebration that honors the end of U.S. Enslavement of Africans, mulattos, and Negros. Although President Abraham Lincoln signed the Executive Order for the Emancipation Proclamation, which was intended to free the slaves in America, and enacted it on January 1, 1863, slaves in the state of Texas did not receive the news of their freedom status until some two and a half years later, on June 19, 1865. It was brought to them by Union soldiers' General Gordon Granger, who arrived in Galveston, TX to inform the 100,000 slaves that remained in Texas, that the General Robert E. Lee had surrendered on April 9, 1865, that the Civil War had ended, and thus they were all, now, free. This delay was due to the small Union presence within Texas. Without a strong Union presence, the Proclamation had yet to be enforced by Confederate resisters, which included masters slow to announce to their slaves

that they were no longer enslave, but free. Even the arrival of the Freedmen's Bureau was delayed until September 1865. Upon his arrival, General Gordon read the to the people of Texas, General Order No. 3, which informed them of the freedom of those previously enslaved per President Lincoln's Executive Order. This order required total equality of rights, and the right to property for both former masters and former slaves alike. And, that from that moment onward, the relationship between both parties became that of employer and free laborer.

For many of the newly freed slaves there was great jubilation, while for others there was a sense of shock and fear at what lie ahead for them as they made decisions about going forward on their own. Some sought to leave Texas for other states they believed represented true freedom, while others traveled to nearby states seeking our their loved ones, whom, they had been separated from. This was all uncharted territory for the former slaves – one in which they existence they had always, and only, known, was no more, for a new one that did not yet exist. Juneteenth offered former slaves the opportunity to celebrate their legal freedom, and inspire them to seek out and establish their own ideas of being both free and equal. During the Juneteenth celebration—a moniker that is a combination of June and nineteenth—they offered each other prayers of reassurance as they went about the process of gathering up their belongings, their lost and scattered loved ones, and their courage to embark upon, seek out, and establish their own ideas of what being free meant to them, even while knowing that they would be risking their lives. Some former slaves chose to stay on at their former masters plantations and participate in the sharecropping institution.

Representative Al Edwards, of Houston, is known as the Father of the Juneteenth holiday, is recognized as being a "source of strength," in the movement for making Juneteenth a nationally recognized U.S. Holiday. To date, 41 states, including the District of Columbia, recognize it as a state holiday or observed holiday.

In 1997, Clifford Robinson, of New Orleans, founded www.Juneteenth.com and Rev. Ronald Mays founded the National Juneteenth Observance Foundation. Both are committed to Juneteenth becoming a recognized federal holiday. On June 19, 2013, a statue of Frederick Douglas was unveiled on the site of the U.S. Capitol's Visitor Center, right along side Soujourner Truth, Martin Luther King, Jr. and Rosa Parks. This effort was spear-headed by Representative Eleanor Holmes Norton.

The old adage goes, "Lest, We Forget," speaks to the impetus for Opal Lee's determination to walk 1400 of the 2100 miles to DC, at the wise elder age of 90. Ms. Lee began walking 10 miles a day, August of 2016 in order to meet with President Obama, to seek the official recognition of Juneteenth as a national holiday, to inspire Americans, especially our young folks, to remember, so that we may collectively heal. And, til this day, many former slaves, and their descendants, journey back to Galveston, TX, annually, to participate in this freedom celebration.

—Patricia A. McDaniel

WATIE IS LAST CONFEDERATE GENERAL TO SURRENDER
June 23, 1865

Among the thousands of Native Americans who fought in the Civil War, the Cherokee leader Stand Watie stood out—both as the only Native American to achieve the rank of brigadier and as the last Confederate general to surrender his forces after the war was declared over.

Locale: Indian Territory; southwestern Missouri; western Arkansas

Category: Wars, uprisings, and civil unrest

KEY FIGURES
Stand Watie (1806-1871), Cherokee leader who became a Confederate brigadier general
John Drew (1796-1865), Cherokee who commanded a regiment of full-blooded Cherokees
Jefferson Davis (1808-1889), president of the Confederate States of America
Ben McCulloch (1811-1862), Confederate Indian Territory commander
Albert Pike (1809-1891), Confederate commander in the Department of Indian Territory
John Ross (1790-1866), principal chief of the Cherokee Nation

SUMMARY OF EVENT
After the outbreak of the Civil War in April, 1861, both the Union and the Confederate governments looked toward Indian Territory for support from Native Americans. Most of the Indians in the territory were members of the so-called Five Civilized Tribes—Cherokee, Chickasaw, Choctaw, Creek, and Seminole. Many of them had connections with the federal government through various agencies, but many also had southern roots in the Carolinas, Alabama, Kentucky, Georgia, and Tennessee. Hence, their loyalties in the Civil War were divided.

In March, 1861, the new Confederate president, Jefferson Davis, commissioned Albert Pike to visit Indian Territory to seek treaties with the Five Civilized Tribes. Davis hoped that a strong Confederate force in Indian Territory would prevent Union sympathizers in Kansas from raiding Texas. Pike's visit with all the tribes in Indian Territory was largely successful. Shortly afterward, Confederate general Ben McCulloch raised two regiments from among the Indians. One was led by Colonel John Drew, a full-blooded Cherokee, and the other was commanded by Colonel Stand Watie, who was threequarters Cherokee.

Drew and Watie were bitter enemies, and through much of the war, Confederate commanders on the western front had to keep their two Cherokee regiments separated as much as possible. Watie had been born in Georgia and was one of the signers of the New Echota Treaty (1835), by which the Cherokees sold their lands in Georgia to the U.S. government. He was also a prosperous Cherokee landowner and businessman, a brilliant warrior, and a member of an opposition faction within the Cherokee tribe. His signature on the new Echota Treaty put him at odds with the more dominant faction of the Cherokee Nation, led by John Ross.

209

Watie proved to be a great military leader, and even in the face of extreme hardships, especially during the winter months, he kept his regiment together and participated in numerous battles. He would eventually become the last major Confederate commander to surrender at the conclusion of the war.

Although the treaties that the Indians signed with the Confederacy promised that Indian regiments would not be required to fight outside Indian Territory, Watie's troops also were called to duty in Missouri and Arkansas.

Over a four-year span, the old Cherokee warrior and his forces fought at Wilson's Creek, Newtonia, Bird Creek, Pea Ridge, Spavinaw, Fort Wayne, Fort Gibson, Honey Springs, Webber's Falls, Poison Spring, Massard Prairie, and Cabin Creek. Watie's abilities on the battlefield were widely recognized and greatly heralded by both his contemporaries and historians. His greatest skills were gaining and keeping the confidence of his troops and his wily guerrilla tactics. His regiment also fought the Second Battle at Newtonia in Southwest Missouri in 1864 without him.

The first Newtonia battle, fought in 1862, is of major historic Significance, because it was the only Civil War battle in which American Indians fought on both sides. In most battles, Watie's Cherokees fought admirably. In a losing cause at the Battle of Pea Ridge in Arkansas, however, they and Drew's troops were accused of bad conduct because they were too easily routed and because they allegedly scalped some of the Union casualties. This act, when reported to the upper command of the Confederate army, created a great embarrassment among officers, most of whom had been trained at such prestigious military academies as West Point, where cadets were taught to be gentlemen as well as warriors. The loss at Pea Ridge was made even greater by the death of General McCulloch, who had organized and fought with the Cherokees from the beginning.

Despite the overwhelming support that Indians initially gave to the Confederacy in 1861, after the tide of war turned in favor of the Union, and the Confederacy could no long supply its forces on the frontier, disenchantment took hold of the leaders of the various tribes.

In February, 1863, the Cherokee Council met on Cowskin Prairie in Indian Territory and voted to end its alliance with the Confederacy. However, Watie refused to accept the vote and vowed to continue his fight. This created an even deeper split within the Cherokee Nation.

Watie's forces and Cherokee civilians with attachments in the South remained loyal to Watie and even established a government that they claimed was the legitimate government of the Cherokee Nation. These Southern sympathizers elected Watie as the principal chief. The Cherokees who were now aligned with Union forces recognized John Ross as their chief, although he left Indian Territory and returned to his wife's family in Pennsylvania.

At the time of this deepening split, about ten thousand Cherokees had Union sympathies, and about seven thousand supported the Confederacy. This Cherokee split actually created a civil war within a civil war.

On May 10, 1864, Watie was promoted to the rank of brigadier general. He was the only American Indian who attained that rank in the Civil War. During the remaining months of the conflict, Watie fought without reservations for the Confederacy. One of his most spectacular successes was the sinking of the steam-driven ferry *J. R. Williams* on the Arkansas River at Pleasant Bluff and making off with food and clothing for his Cherokee and Creek troopers, while breaking a major supply route for Union forces at Fort Gibson. Successful raids on Union supplies kept Watie's forces busy, well supplied, and inspired to stay in the fight. As the military situation for the Confederacy grew worse, Watie called all the Cherokee units to his camp on June 24, 1864. At that meeting, the Cherokee troops resolved unanimously to reenlist for the duration of the war, regardless of how long it lasted.

During the following September, Watie masterminded a plan to attack and steal a Union supply-wagon train worth one million dollars. This battle was fought at Cabin Creek in Indian Territory and is said to have been Watie's greatest success. His brilliance and bravery were not enough, however, as the Confederacy continued to lose battle after battle. On April 9, 1865, General Robert E. Lee surrendered for the Confederacy at Appomattox Courthouse in Virginia. General Watie fought on, hoping to win the battle for the West, but it was not to be. On June 23, 1865, he surrendered at Doakesville in Indian Territory. He was the last Confederate general to lay down his sword.

SIGNIFICANCE

The contribution made by American Indians in the Civil War was enormous. Of the estimated 3,500 who fought for the Union, 1,018, or more than 28 percent, died while in service to their country. Census figures in the Cherokee Nation showed a population of 21,000 in 1860. By 1867, that number had dropped to 13,566. Approximately one-third of the nation had been lost, either in battle or to hunger and exposure, which were suffered by soldiers and civilians alike. After the war, Stand Watie became more involved in the political activities of the Cherokee Nation and in resettling his people in the aftermath of the conflict. On September 7, 1871, the great general became ill and was taken to his old home at Honey Creek, where he died on September 9.

—Kay Hively

See also: Establishment of the Confederate States of America; Civil War; Sherman Marches Through Georgia and the Carolinas; Surrender at Appomattox and Assassination of Lincoln.

Related articles in *Great Lives from History: The Nineteenth Century, 1801-1900:* Jefferson Davis; John Ross.

THIRTEENTH AMENDMENT IS RATIFIED

December 6, 1865

This first of the three Civil War amendments brought a final and definitive end to slavery in the United States but did not by itself confer civil rights on former slaves.

Locale: Washington, D.C.
Categories: Human rights; laws, acts, and legal history; civil rights and liberties

KEY FIGURES
Frederick Douglass (1817?-1895), abolitionist and orator
William Lloyd Garrison (1805-1879), publisher of *The Liberator* and a founder of the American Anti-Slavery Society
Abraham Lincoln (1809-1865), president, 1861-1865
Andrew Johnson (1808-1875), vice president under Lincoln and president, 1865-1869
Robert Dale Owen (1801-1877), abolitionist whose writings influenced Lincoln

SUMMARY OF EVENT
The antislavery and abolition movements in the United States did not begin with the Civil War (1861-1865). As early as 1652, the state of Rhode Island passed antislavery legislation. In 1773, Benjamin Franklin and Dr.

Benjamin Rush formed the first abolition society in America. In 1832, the New England Anti-Slavery Society was formed by newspaper editor William Lloyd Garrison, who also helped found the American Anti-Slavery Society in 1833. The Society of Friends, or Quakers, a religious group who settled early in the history of the United States, were also active in the antislavery movement.

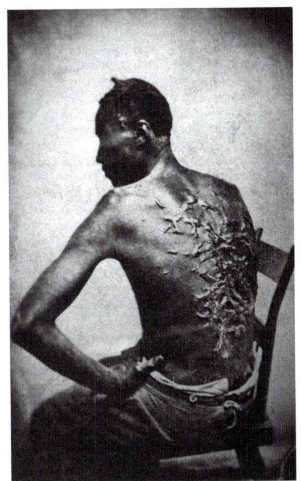

Abolitionist imagery focused on atrocities against slave (1863 photo of Gordon)

Their religion forbade the holding of slaves. Quakers primarily settled in the northern part of the country.

In 1807, federal legislation was passed outlawing the importation of slaves after January 1, 1808. However, that law did not end the use of slaves in the United States.

The writers of the U.S. Constitution had not been able to resolve the issue of slavery in 1787 and had declared that the slave trade could end by 1808 or anytime later. Eventually, the inability of national leaders to resolve this issue would divide the nation.

The Missouri Compromise of 1820 banned slavery in most of the western states and territories. This was overturned by the Supreme Court in 1857, in the infamous *Dred Scott* decision.

By the 1850's, the split between the slave and free states was well entrenched. In an attempt to appease pro and antislavery proponents, Congress adopted five provisions in the Compromise of 1850. The most notable was the Second Fugitive Slave Law, passed in 1850. It provided for slaves who escaped from the South and were found in northern antislavery states to be returned to their owners. A great deal of violence erupted over this legislation, which led to the act's repeal on June 28, 1864. Meanwhile, the split between the North and the South eventually resulted in the Civil War.

The abolitionist movement had fought for decades for an end to slavery. Robert Dale Owen, an abolitionist and legislator, struggled for the emancipation of slaves and is thought to have influenced President Abraham Lincoln with his tract *Policy of Emancipation* (1863). Another radical opponent of slavery was Wendell Phillips, a noted speaker and a graduate of Harvard Law School. He believed that the U.S. Constitution supported slavery and therefore was owed no allegiance by abolitionists. Harriet Tubman was active in the Underground Railroad, which was successful in bringing many slaves into northern states that would not return them to their owners.

John Brown adopted more violent means of expressing his abolitionist sentiment. He raided the federal arsenal at Harpers Ferry, Virginia, and encouraged a slave revolt.

He was eventually hanged for his fanaticism. Frederick Douglass was an important abolitionist who played a significant role in the passage toward freedom for the slaves. A runaway slave, he spoke eloquently about the need to redress the wrongs created by slavery.

After the Civil War began in April, 1861, the abolitionist movement placed greater pressure on President Lincoln to issue an emancipation proclamation. Lincoln had focused a great deal of attention on the issue of slavery during the famous Lincoln-Douglas debates. Lincoln finally issued his Emancipation Proclamation on September 22, 1862, well after the war started. His proclamation announced that in states that had seceded from the union, all slaves would be freed effective January 1, 1863. This proclamation did not actually free many slaves. It did not apply to slave states that were still part of the Union and was unenforceable in those states involved in the Confederacy. The major function of the Emancipation Proclamation was to announce to all that one of the Union's goals in the Civil War was to end slavery.

Also, as Union troops occupied Confederate territories, they freed the slaves in the areas they controlled.

At the time that the war began, the African American population of the United States consisted of approximately 4.5 million people, 4 million of whom were slaves. White supremacy was the general ideology of both southerners and northerners. Slaves were denied such rights as the right to legal marriage, choice of residence, and education, and existed in perpetual servitude.

Without significant changes in institutional structures, there was no hope of freedom.

The Thirteenth Amendment was one of three amendments known as the Civil War amendments. The combined purpose of these three amendments was to free the slaves and promote their participation in their country.

The Thirteenth Amendment states that neither slavery nor involuntary servitude, except as a punishment for crime whereof the party shall have been duly convicted, shall exist within the United States, or any place subject to their jurisdiction.

One of the battles surrounding the Thirteenth Amendment in particular, and all the Civil War amendments in general, concerned the interpretation of the Tenth Amendment to the Constitution. Part of the Bill of Rights that was adopted in 1791, the Tenth Amendment states that no federal legislation can detract from the power of state government. Those who opposed the Thirteenth Amendment claimed that the right to allow slavery was not specifically denied in the Constitution and therefore fell within the authority of the state.

With the passage of the Thirteenth Amendment, the long fight to abolish slavery in the United States was over. The amendment was ratified on December 6, 1865, and officially announced on December 18, 1865. For some abolitionists, such as William Lloyd Garrison, the battle had been won: Slavery was ended. Others, however, saw the Thirteenth Amendment as only a beginning in the struggle for African American rights.

Frederick Douglass did not share Garrison's high hopes. He believed that slavery would not be fully abolished until the former slaves acquired the right to vote.

The passage of the Civil Rights Act of 1866 did not provide this right. It was not until the passage of the Fourteenth Amendment, in 1868, that citizenship and the rights thereof were guaranteed to "all persons born or naturalized in the United States." Finally, in February, 1870, ratification of the Fifteenth Amendment expressly awarded former slaves the right to vote. Within weeks, the first African American in the U.S. Senate, Hiram R. Revels of Mississippi, took his seat.

Thirteenth Amendment to the U.S. Constitution

Section 1. Neither slavery nor involuntary servitude, except as a punishment for crime whereof the party shall have been duly convicted, shall exist within the United States, or any place subject to their jurisdiction.

Section 2. Congress shall have power to enforce this article by appropriate legislation.

SIGNIFICANCE

On April 15, 1865, President Lincoln died from wounds inflicted by an assassin. Vice President Andrew Johnson then became president and prepared to oversee Reconstruction of the nation. Johnson, however, was not highly supportive or sympathetic to the needs of the former slaves. He blocked every attempt to extend rights to former slaves. In fact, Johnson vetoed most of the civil rights legislation passed by Congress, only to have his vetoes overridden by Congress. Impeachment charges eventually ensued, and Johnson was spared by only a one-vote margin. At that point, Johnson withdrew from Reconstruction activities and allowed Congress to control the process.

One interesting note is the relationship between the woman suffrage movement and the abolition and black suffrage process. The decision over whether to support the call for the black vote divided the woman suffrage movement.

Some believed that a gradual transition, in which first black men received the vote and then all women received the vote, would meet with greater success. Two such women were Lucy Stone and Julia Ward Howe. Others believed that suffrage was "all or nothing," and that women should not forsake their own cause in order to gain the vote for others. Susan B. Anthony and Elizabeth Cady Stanton were opposed to legislation that specifically referred to men and neglected suffrage for women. It was not until the passage of the Nineteenth Amendment in 1920 that women gained the long-sought suffrage.

Meanwhile, the major impact of the Thirteenth Amendment was to end American slavery forever. The Supreme Court subsequently ruled that the amendment might also provide grounds for congressional action against the "badges and incidents" of slavery. However, use of the amendment for that purpose has been relatively uncommon.

—*Sharon L. Larson*

See also: Congress Bans Importation of African Slaves; Southerners Advance Proslavery Arguments; American Anti-Slavery Society Is Founded; Douglass Launches *The North Star*; Civil War; Lincoln Issues the Emancipation Proclamation; Reconstruction of the South; Civil Rights Act of 1866; Fourteenth Amendment Is Ratified; Civil Rights Cases; *Plessy v. Ferguson*.

Related articles in *Great Lives from History: The Nineteenth Century, 1801-1900:* Frederick Douglass; William Lloyd Garrison; Andrew Johnson; Abraham Lincoln.

CONGRESS CREATES THE FREEDMEN'S BUREAU

March 3, 1865

the U.S. Congress authorized and created the Freedmen's Bureau to assist recently freed Africans, mulattos, and Negros with adjusting to freedom, since the Civil War was coming to a close; however it never provided it with the resources needed to fulfill its mission properly.

The Freedmen's Bureau

Also known as: U.S. Bureau of Refugees, Freedmen, and Abandoned Lands

Locale: Washington, D.C.

Categories: Civil rights and liberties; organizations and institutions; social issues and reform

KEY FIGURES

Oliver O. Howard (1830-1909), chief commissioner of the Freedmen's Bureau

Andrew Johnson (1808-1875), president of the United States, 1865-1869

Thaddeus Stevens (1792-1868), Pennsylvania congressman

SUMMARY OF EVENT

On March 3, 1865, shortly before the Civil War (1861–1865) ended, the U.S. Congress created the Freedmen's Bureau as a temporary agency within the War Department. Also known as the U.S. Bureau of Refugees, Freedmen, and Abandoned Lands, the new agency was administered by General Oliver O. Howard from 1865 until it was dismantled by Congress in 1872. The primary objective of the bureau was to help newly freed, formerly enslaved, Africans, mulattos, and Negros to function as free men, women, and children. To achieve its goal, the bureau was expected to assume responsibility for all matters related to the newly freed men, women, and children in the southern states. The Bureau faced enormous challenges because of the broad scope of its mission, its limited resources, political conflicts over Reconstruction policies, and a generally hostile environment. The work of The Bureau was performed by General Howard and a network of assistant commissioners in various states, largely in the South.

The Freedmen's Bureau attempted to address many of the needs of the newly freed former slaves, including labor relations, education, landownership, medical care, food distribution, family reunification, legal protection, and legal services within the African, mulatto, and Negro community. The Freedmen's Bureau dealt with such labor-related issues as the transporting and relocating of refugees and newly freed persons for employment, contract and wage disputes, and harsh legislation enacted by some states.

After the Civil War, many southern states passed laws known as The Black Codes that required former slaves to have lawful employment or businesses. Otherwise, they would be subject to fines and could be jailed for vagrancy. Sheriffs could hire them out to anyone who would pay their fines. Because of the desperate scarcity of jobs in the postwar South, state laws allowed former slave owners to maintain rigid control over newly freed former slaves. Another type of discriminatory law gave former owners of orphaned Africans, mulattos, and Negros the right to hire them as apprentices instead of placing them with their relatives.

This law also resulted in the continuation of virtually free labor for many white southerners. The Freedmen's Bureau has been criticized for the failure of its agents to negotiate labor contracts in the interest of the newly freed Africans, mulattos, and Negros. The bureau was frequently accused of protecting the rights of the southern planters instead.

Obtaining education was an important goal for newly freed former slaves. They understood that literacy would enable them to enter into contracts and establish businesses on their own, and would aid them in legal matters. The Freedmen's Bureau provided some support by providing teachers, schools, and books and by coordinating volunteers. The bureau also made a contribution to the founding of Negro colleges and universities. Southern whites generally opposed educating former slaves because of their fear that education would make former slaves too independent and unwilling to work under the terms established by white employers. Southerners therefore sought to control the educational systems in their states. White planters used various methods to exert control: frequent changes in administrative personnel, the use of racial stereotypes regarding the intellectual inferiority of Freedmen, and educational policy making based on paternalism and self-interest. Consequently, educational opportunities were significantly restricted for Negro youth. Eager to acquire property, newly freed former slaves demonstrated their desire to own their own land as individuals and formed associations to purchase large tracts of land.

Their sense of family and community was the basis for their strong desire to own land. The Freedmen's Bureau was initially authorized to distribute land that had been confiscated from southern plantation owners during the Civil War. Specifically, on the sea islands of South Carolina, The Bureau was mandated to lease or sell lands that had been confiscated. This land was to be distributed in parcels of forty acres. The decision of Congress to authorize the distribution of land was based on a proposal made by Thaddeus Stevens, a Republican congressman from Pennsylvania. However, President Andrew Johnson acceded to pressure from the rebellious planters to return their lands.

The plantation owners were pardoned, and their property rights were restored by the president. Consequently, all land that had been distributed to Freedmen was returned to its previous owners. The dispossessed Negro people were then encouraged to sign contracts to work on the land that they had briefly owned. Many refused to comply with this arrangement. Others would not voluntarily leave the property they once owned. Those who refused to vacate were evicted.

A medical department was created within the Freedmen's Bureau to be a temporary service, to ensure that medical services were provided to former slaves until local governments assumed that responsibility. In spite of inadequate resources, The Bureau founded forty five hospitals in fourteen states. Among the common problems of the medical department were inadequately staffed hospitals, medical personnel with little control over health concerns, frequent personnel changes hospital relocations, and a lack of funds to purchase food for patients. Despite these problems, The Bureau experienced some success in providing for the medical needs of freed African, mulatto, and Negero people. Although it could not meet the medical needs of many, it rendered medical services to large numbers of former slaves.

The Freedmen's Bureau also attempted to provide for the social welfare of the freed persons of color. The agency was noted for rationing food to refugees and former slaves; it assisted families in reuniting with members who had been sold or separated in other ways during the era of slavery.

Protecting the civil rights of the former slaves was a major task of the Freedmen's Bureau. Many Republican politicians believed that Freedmen should have the same rights as white Americans. However, The Black Codes of many southern states severely restricted the civil rights of former slaves. Exacting social and economic control over the Freedmen, these laws represented a new form of slavery. In cases in which state laws limited freed Africans, mulattos, and Negros' rights, The Bureau attempted to invoke provisions of the 1866 federal Civil Rights Act, which offered Freedmen the same legal protections and rights as whites to testify in courts, own property, enforce legal contracts, and sue. However, the bureau found it difficult to enforce the Civil Rights Act and to prosecute state officials who enforced discriminatory laws. A shortage of agents and a reluctance among bureau commissioners to challenge local officials contributed to the agency's limited success.

Finally, the Freedmen's Bureau also established tribunals to address minor legal disputes of Freedmen within their own communities. In many instances, freed former slaves were able to resolve their own problems. When they could not, they presented their legal concerns to Bureau agents.

SIGNIFICANCE

The task assigned to the Freedmen's Bureau was monumental. The responsibilities of the bureau significantly exceeded the resources and authority granted to it by Congress. The Bureau's ability to perform its varied tasks also was impeded by personnel shortages. President Johnson's Reconstruction policies represented another major challenge to the bureau, as they were not always supportive of the bureau's mandate and objectives. Myriad problems associated with The Bureau meant that the newly freed men, women, and children were not able to receive the goods and services necessary to gain economic independence. Consequently, they developed extensive self-help networks to address their needs.

—K. Sue Jewell , updated by Patricia A. McDaniel

See also: First African American University Opens; Reconstruction of the South; Mississippi Enacts First Post-Civil War Black Code; Birth of the Ku Klux Klan; Civil Rights Act of 1866; Memphis and New Orleans Race Riots; Fourteenth Amendment Is Ratified; Mississippi Constitution Disfranchises Black Voters; Sept. 18, 1895; Washington's Atlanta Compromise Speech.

Related articles in *Great Lives from History: The Nineteenth Century, 1801-1900:* Samuel Gridley Howe; Andrew Johnson; Thaddeus Stevens.

BIRTH OF THE KU KLUX KLAN

1866

Formed by white southerners who were disaffected by the outcome of the Civil War and the liberation of African Americans, the original Ku Klux Klan was short lived. However, it left a legacy that would grow into an organization of institutionalized race hatred and survive into the twenty-first century.

Locale: Pulaski, Tennessee
Categories: Organizations and institutions; terrorism and political assassination

KEY FIGURES

Nathan Bedford Forrest (1821-1877), grand wizard of the first Klan

Edward Young Clarke (b. 1839), advertising man who promoted the Klan during the 1920's

Samuel Moffett Ralston (1857-1925), senator with Klan connections

Edward L. Jackson (1873-1954), governor of Indiana

William Joseph Simmons (1880-1945), preacher who founded the second Klan in 1915

D. C. Stephenson (1891-1966), grand dragon in Indiana

David E. Duke (b. 1950), klansman who ran for national office

SUMMARY OF EVENT

With the end of the Civil War (1861-1865) in the United States in 1865 and the emancipation of African American slaves in the South, tension arose between old-order southern whites and Radical Republicans of the North who were devoted to a strict plan of Reconstruction that required southern states to repeal their discriminatory laws and guarantee civil and voting rights to African Americans. Federal instruments for ensuring African American rights included the Freedmen's Bureau and the Union Leagues. In reaction to the activities of these organizations, white supremacist organizations sprouted in the years immediately following the Civil War. Such organizations included the Knights of the White Camelia, the White League, the Invisible Circle, the Pale Faces, and the Ku Klux Klan (KKK).

The Ku Klux Klan would eventually lend its name to a confederation of organizations spread throughout the United States, but it began on a small scale in 1866. It was started in Pulaski, Tennessee, as a fraternal order for white male Protestants who were linked by their opposition to Radical Reconstructionism and an agenda to

Mississippi Ku-Klux members in the disguises in which they were captured.

promote white dominance in the South. The early Klan established many of the unusual rituals and violent activities for which the Ku Klux Klan would become notorious throughout its long history.

The early members of the Klan regarded the South as an "invisible empire," with "realms" consisting of the southern states. A "grand dragon" headed each realm, and the entire "empire" was led by Grand Wizard General Nathan Bedford Forrest. Leadership posts had titles such as "giant," "cyclops," "geni," "hydra," and "goblin." The original Klan also established the practice of members wearing white robes and pointed hoods that covered their faces. The practice arose from the belief that black people were so superstitious that they would be easily intimidated by the menacing, ghostlike appearance of their oppressors. The hooded costumes also allowed members to maintain anonymity during nighttime rides, when they harassed African Americans whom they considered to be "uppity Negroes" and anyone who defended them. Such offensive language remains a testament to the bigotry and racism deeply entrenched in white American society and fed upon by the Klan.

The early Klan soon began perpetrating acts of violence, including whippings, house-burnings, kidnappings, and lynchings. In 1869, as Klan violence was escalating, Forrest disbanded the organization. On May 31, 1870, and on April 20, 1871, the U.S. Congress passed the Ku Klux Klan Acts, or Force Acts, designed to break up the white supremacist groups. Speaking in the Senate on March 18, 1871, for the second Force Act, John Sherman said of the Ku Klux Klan: They are secret, oath-bound; they murder, rob, plunder, whip, and scourge; and they commit these crimes, not upon the high and lofty, but upon the lowly, upon the poor, upon the feeble men and women who are utterly defenceless. . . . Where is there an organization against which humanity revolts more than it does against this?

The Ku Klux Klan Acts were passed, but parts of them were later ruled unconstitutional by the U.S. Supreme Court. The original Klan was short lived, but it later resurfaced during times of racial tension, often in conjunction with periods marked by xenophobia and anti-immigrant paranoia. The first major resurgence of the Klan occurred in 1915. In November of that year, the new Ku Klux Klan was founded by preacher William Joseph Simmons on Stone Mountain, Georgia. Simmons proclaimed the new organization to be a "high-class, mystic, social, patriotic" society devoted to defending womanhood, white Protestant values, and "native-born, white, gentile Americans."

The image of the Klan as a protector of white virtue was reinforced by D. W. Griffith's popular 1915 film *Birth of a Nation*, which was based on the novel *The Clansman: An Historical Romance of the Ku Klux Klan* (1906) by Thomas F. Dixon, Jr. Griffith's film depicted lustful blacks assaulting white women, with hooded members of the Klan riding to the rescue. It was probably no coincidence the rise of the new Klan presaged the period of the Red Scare (1919-1920) and the Immigration Act of 1921, the first such legislation in the United States to establish immigration quotas on the basis of national origin.

The new Ku Klux Klan cloaked itself as a patriotic organization devoted to preserving traditional American values against enemies in the nation's midst. An upsurge of nationalist fervor swelled the ranks of the Klan, this time far beyond the borders of the South. White men and women both joined to ensure the survival of the white race. This second Klan adopted the rituals and regalia of its predecessor as well as the same antiblack ideology, to which it added anti-Roman Catholic, anti-Semitic, anti-immigrant, anti-birth-control, anti-Darwinist, and anti-Prohibition stances. Promoted by ad-man Edward Young Clarke, Klan membership reached approximately 100,000 by 1921. By some estimates, membership rose to more than 5 million during the 1920's, and the Klan rolls included some members of Congress.

Some Klan observers have argued that the power of the Klan was actually worse in the North than it was in the South. In 1924, an outspoken opponent of the Klan, journalist William Allen White, lost a bid for the governorship of Kansas to a Klan sympathizer. In Indiana, local grand dragon D. C. Stephenson, who was known to rule the statehouse, helped elect Samuel Moffett Ralston, a Klan member, to the Senate in 1922. Stephenson also influenced voters to elect Edward L. Jackson as governor in 1925. Jackson and Stephenson were later disgraced by investigations into their misuse of funds. Stephenson was also later convicted of second-degree murder after kidnapping and raping his secretary, who took poison to force him to get her to authorities.

Stephenson is only one example of the criminal personalities that typified Klan membership. The Klan has been credited with perpetrating more than five hundred hangings and burnings of African Americans. Klan victims were primarily men who broke the "racist codes" kept in secret by the Klan. In 1924, forty thousand Klansmen marched down Pennsylvania Avenue in Washington, D.C., sending a message to the federal government that there should be a white, Protestant United States. Eventually, however, the Klan's growing identification with brutal violence alienated many of its members, whose numbers are believed to have dropped to about thirty thousand by 1930.

Klan activities again increased shortly before U.S. entry into World War II in 1941, and membership rose toward the 100,000 mark. However, when the U.S. Congress assessed the organization more than one-half million dollars in back taxes in 1944, the Klan again dissolved itself to escape payment. Two years later, however, Atlanta physician Samuel Green united smaller Klan groups into the Association of Georgia Klans and was soon joined by other reincarnations, such as the Federated Ku Klux Klans, the Original Southern Klans, and the Knights of the Ku Klux Klan. These groups revived the old racist agenda and violent methods of previous Klans and during this period were responsible for hundreds of criminal acts. Of equal concern was the Klan's political influence: A governor of Texas was elected with the support of the Klan, and a senator from Maine was similarly elected. Even a Supreme Court justice, Hugo Black, revealed in 1937 that he had once been a member of the Ku Klux Klan.

During the 1940's, many states passed laws that revoked Klan charters, and many southern communities issued regulations against the wearing of Klan masks. The U.S. Justice Department placed the Klan on its list of subversive elements, and in 1952 the Federal Bureau of Investigation used the Lindbergh law (one of the 1934 Crime Control Acts) against the Klan. Another direct challenge to the principles of the Klan came during the 1960's with the rise of the Civil Rights movement and new federal civil rights legislation. Martin Luther King, Jr., prophesied early in the decade that it would be a "season of suffering." On September 15, 1963, a Klan bomb tore apart the Sixteenth Street Baptist Church in Birmingham, Alabama, killing four young children. Despite the outrage of much of the nation, the violence continued, led by members of the Klan who made a mockery of the courts and the laws that they had broken.

Less than a year after the Birmingham bombing, three civil rights workers were killed in Mississippi, including one African American and two whites from the North involved in voter registration drives. This infamous event was later documented in the 1988 motion picture *Mississippi Burning*. Such acts prompted President Lyndon B. Johnson, in a televised speech in March, 1965, to denounce the Klan as he announced the arrest of four Klansmen for murder. After the convictions of many of its members in the 1960's, the Ku Klux Klan became comparatively dormant, and its roster of members reflected low numbers.

However, as it had done in previous periods of dormancy, the Klan refused to die. Busing for integration of public schools during the 1970's provoked Klan opposition in both the South and the North. In 1979, in Greensboro, North Carolina, Klan members killed several members of the Communist Party in a daylight battle on an open street. Since that time, Klan members have been known to patrol the Mexican border, armed with weapons and citizen-band radios, in efforts to drive illegal immigrants back to Mexico. The Klan has even been active in suburban California, at times driving out African Americans who attempted to move there. On the Gulf Coast, many boats fly the infamous AKIA flag, whose acronym stands for "A Klansman I Am," a term that dates back to the 1920's. Klan members try to discourage or run out Vietnamese fishers.

Notable Klan leaders active after 1970 include James Venable, for whom the Klan became little more than a hobby, and Bill Wilkinson, a former disciple of David Duke. Robert Shelton, long a grand dragon, helped elect two Alabama governors. David Duke, a Klan leader until the late 1980's, was elected

a congressman from Louisiana, despite his well-publicized Klan associations. In 1991, Duke ran for governor of Louisiana and almost won. During the 1980's, the Klan stepped up its anti-Semitic activities, planning multiple bombings in Nashville. During the 1990's, Klan leaders trained their members and their children for what they believed was an imminent race war, and taught followers survival skills and weaponry at remote camps throughout the country.

SIGNIFICANCE

Throughout its many generations, the Klan has maintained that it is a patriotic organization, interested in preserving the principles upon which the United States was originally based. However, the Klan's history of violence against African Americans, nonwhites in general, and Jews is the most anti-American sentiment conceivable in a republic founded on the principles of tolerance in service of "life, liberty, and the pursuit of happiness."

A major blow was struck against the Klan by the Klanwatch Project of the Southern Poverty Law Center, in Montgomery, Alabama, when, in 1984, attorney Morris Dees began pressing civil suits against several Klan members, effectively removing their personal assets, funds received from members, and even buildings owned by the Klan. Despite such setbacks, as late as 2005, the Ku Klux Klan continued to solicit new "Aryan" members and even maintained a Web site for this purpose. However, in contrast to the organization's traditional image, it now stressed a different message:

The Imperial Klans of America Knights of the Ku Klux Klan are a legal and law abiding organization that will NOT tolerate illegal acts of any sort. If you take it upon yourself to violate the law, you do so on your own. If you commit an illegal act it will result in your membership with the IKA to be on suspension and you may be banished. We cannot and will not be responsible for any member committing any illegal acts.

—The Editors

See also: Reconstruction of the South; Congress Creates the Freedmen's Bureau; Mississippi Enacts First Post-Civil War Black Code; Civil Rights Act of 1866; Memphis and New Orleans Race Riots; Fourteenth Amendment Is Ratified.

Related article in *Great Lives from History: The Nineteenth Century, 1801-1900:* Thaddeus Stevens.

BLACK CODES
1866 to 1868

The Black Codes served to take away many of the free-doms that former slaves hoped to enjoy.

Definition: Post-Civil War Confederate state laws aimed at restricting the rights of newly freed Africans, Freed-men, mulattos, and Negros, to guarantee a labor force for southern planters, since slavery had been abolished.

The months immediately following the end of the U.S. Civil War were a period of great uncertainty. War-time president Abraham Lincoln had been assassinated, and his successor, Andrew Johnson, was wholly un-tested. No leadership could be expected from Capitol Hill, since Congress had gone into a long recess. In the southern states, a host of questions required immediate answers; foremost among these were questions relat-ing to the place of the recently freed slaves in post-war southern society. Would the freed slaves continue to fur-nish an economical and reliable labor force for southern cotton planters? Would the former slaves exact subtle or blatant revenge upon their former masters? Should lawmakers grant freed Africans, mulattos, and Negros the right to vote in the southern states?

Should the U.S. government give them land? Should the states pay the cost of a basic education for them? What legal rights would these five million Freed-men enjoy in the post-bellum South?

RECONSTRUCTION PLANS
President Johnson developed a lenient plan for Re-construction, one that called on the southern states to quickly reorganize their state governments. His only major demands of these new governments were that they admit that no state had the right to leave the Union, and that they ratify the Thirteenth Amendment, which ended slavery. As the new southern state legislatures began to meet, their exclusively white members were most interested in passing laws that would answer some of the nagging questions about the future place of freed Africans, mulattos, and Negros in southern so-ciety. Many legislators believed the freed slaves would not work unless forced to do so, and they feared the double specter of an economy without a labor supply and a huge mass of people who would live on charity or plunder. In earlier years, laws known as the "slave codes" had controlled the African, mulatto, and Negro population; some lawmakers now called for a renewal of the slave codes to control the freed Africans, mulat-tos, and Negros.

Mississippi's legislature was the first to take up the question of the rights of, or limitations on, freed Africans, mulattos, and Negros. This body met in October, 1865, and quickly fell into arguments over what policies on racial matters should be enacted. Nearly half of the legislators favored laws that would, in almost every way, return the Freedmen to the position they had occupied in the time of slavery. Mississippi's governor, Benjamin G. Humphreys, intervened and urged lawmakers to ensure certain basic rights to the newly freed slaves. After Humphreys' inter-vention, the moderates in the Mississippi legislature had the upper hand and, on November 24, 1865, enacted a bill entitled "An Act to Confer Civil Rights on Freedmen."

As its title promised, Mississippi's new law did confer some basic rights on Freedmen that they had not enjoyed as slaves. These rights included the right to sue and be sued, the right to swear out criminal complaints against others, the right to purchase or inherit land, the right to marry, and the right to draw up labor or other contracts. Although the law's title did speak of conferring civil rights, and a few new rights were indeed granted, this law—the first of The Black Codes of the southern states—was remarkable primarily for the rights it de-nied to freed Africans, mulattos, and Negros. It did give Freedmen the right to own land, but it denied them the right to rent rural land—thus the legislators sought to per-petuate large gangs of landless agricultural workers. The act recognized the right to marry, but it also provided that interracial marriage would be punished by life imprison-ment for both parties. The right to testify in court was eroded by certain provisions that said the right to testify did not apply to cases in which both parties in a lawsuit or criminal case were white, nor to criminal cases in which the defendant was African, mulatto, or Negro.

LABOR PROVISIONS
Most ominous was the provision that every freed Afri-can, mulatto, and Negro citizen in the state must sign a one-year labor contract by January 1 of each year and must honor that contract. Should the employee leave the employer before the end of the year, law enforcement officers were empowered to return the worker forc-ibly to his or her place of employment. In a provision reminiscent of the old laws that forbade giving help to

runaway slaves, this new law made it a crime to give food, clothing, or shelter to any Freedman worker who had left his or her employer while still under contract. The punishment for helping a runaway was up to two months in jail; for those who helped the fugitive find work in a state other than Mississippi, the punishment was up to six months in jail. Once again, securing a stable labor supply for the state was at the forefront of lawmakers' goals.

After Mississippi passed this first black code, a flood of other laws soon followed in Mississippi and the other southern states. South Carolina's black codes forbade freed Africans, mulattos, and Negros from pursuing any occupation other than agricultural work, unless the worker paid a prohibitively expensive fee. African, mulatto, and Negro freedmen farm workers there were required by law to work from sunup to sundown and forbidden from leaving the plantation without the permission of their employer. South Carolina and Mississippi both enacted severe vagrancy laws that called for the arrest of idle persons, drunkards, gamblers, wanderers, fighters, people who wasted their pay, circus hands, actors, and even jugglers. If these persons were African, mulatto, or Negro , they were to be considered vagrants and fined up to one hundred dollars and imprisoned. If unable to pay their fine, their labor would be auctioned off to a white employer, and their wages used to satisfy the fine.

DIFFERENCES AMONG THE STATES

The Black Codes varied from state to state, but their northern opponents said they all had the common goal of returning the freed slaves to a system equivalent to bondage. In some southern states, the Freedmen were prohibited from owning guns. In other states, their assembly in groups was forbidden, or an evening curfew was imposed. President Johnson, himself a southerner, saw little that was objectionable in The Black Codes,

but many northerners did. Occupying generals Daniel E. Sickles in South Carolina and Alfred H. Terry in Virginia overturned all or parts of The Black Codes in their areas, pending action in Congress. In Washington, Senator Lyman Trumbull wrote the Civil Rights Act of 1866, which declared that all persons born in the United States were U.S. citizens, and that all U.S. citizens enjoyed equality before the law. Congress passed this measure over the veto of President Johnson. By 1868, the Fourteenth Amendment brought this same promise of equality before the law and was added into the Constitution itself.

The Black Codes were barely enforced. Overturned by the actions of occupying generals, and later by the U.S. courts, which found them in conflict with the Fourteenth Amendment, they were important chiefly for fueling a conflict in Washington between Johnson's lenient Reconstruction plan and Congress's insistence that the basic rights of freed Africans, mulattos, and Negros be protected. These codes are also important for their role in bringing about the passage of the Fourteenth Amendment. Although Freedmens' rights were generally protected between 1866 and 1876, the southern states found many ways to draft laws that were colorblind on their face, but that could be enforced in a racially biased way. After Reconstruction, few southern elected officials, and few officeholders nationwide, were very interested in championing civil rights for Africans, mulattos, and Negros.

—Stephen Cresswell, updated by Patricia A. McDaniel

See also: Civil Rights Act of 1866; Civil Rights Acts of 1866–1875; Civil Rights cases; Compromise of 1877; Disenfranchisement Laws in Mississippi; Fourteenth Amendment; Freedmen's Bureau; Jim Crow Laws; Ku Klux Klan; *Plessy v. Ferguson*; Reconstruction; Segregation

RECONSTRUCTION

1866-1877

The Reconstruction Acts of 1867 divided the ten states of the Deep South into military districts under martial law. An army general overseeing each district was charged with securing a new electorate, enrolling former slaves, and disenfranchising former rebels for the purpose of providing for more efficient government

in the former rebel states. Thus—over the objections of moderate Republicans and with the aid of sympathetic Democrats—Radical Reconstruction succeeded in disfranchising former Confederate leaders. Radical Reconstruction also required that the Southern states present acceptable state constitutions to Congress and ratify the Fourteenth Amendment before readmission to the Union would be granted.

The Event: Post-Civil War era during which the Republican controlled Union government took control of the defeated South and tried to force southern states to grant Africans, mulattos, and Negros equal rights Reconstruction gave the Supreme Court a unique opportunity to extend full constitutional rights and protections to African Americans. Instead, however, the Court's conservatism merely worked to undermine congressional Reconstruction plans.

After the Civil War ended in early 1865 the U.S. government faced fundamental constitutional questions. That the Union was indestructible and states had no right to secede had been settled on the battlefield. However, the relation of the former Confederate states to the Union was unsettled, and the meaning of freedom for the former slaves remained to be worked out. Wresting control of Reconstruction from President Andrew Johnson, who was overanxious for reconciliation with the unrepentant white South, the Republican-controlled Congress passed a series of measures designed to secure a broad nationalization of civil rights and establish a rule of law strong enough to protect black Americans for the long haul.

THE BEGINNINGS OF RECONSTRUCTION

There is no debate about when Reconstruction ended—with the 1877 inauguration of President Rutherford B. Hayes. However, many dates have been assigned to its beginnings. Many members of Congress initially believed that the Thirteenth Amendment (1865), which abolished slavery and empowered Congress to enforce its provision with appropriate legislation, would provide sufficient constitutional support for the newly freed people. However, it soon became evident that northerners and southerners held fundamentally different assumptions about what freedom meant.

When the southern states enacted discriminatory laws—the notorious Black Codes—designed to keep Africans, mulattos, and Negros in a slave-like condition, Congress imposed further restrictions on the recalcitrant South. In early 1866 Congress passed a Civil Rights Act that guaranteed basic legal rights to former slaves. President Andrew Johnson vetoed the bill, but Congress overrode his veto. In June Republican leaders in Congress proposed the Fourteenth Amendment, which would define Africans, mulattos, and Negros as citizens and mandate that all federal and state laws apply equally to all citizens. President Johnson urged the

states to reject it (which all former Confederate states except Tennessee did), but the Fourteenth Amendment was finally ratified two years later, in 1868. A third "Civil War amendment," the Fifteenth, was proposed in 1869. Ratified the following year, it outlawed denying any citizen the right to vote because of race.

Meanwhile, in 1867, Congress passed a series of laws called the Reconstruction Acts. These laws abolished the South's newly formed state governments and placed every former Confederate state, except Tennessee, in a military district governed by federal troops, under martial law. States wishing to qualify for readmission to the Union were required to write new constitutions that would allow for black suffrage. They also had to ratify the Thirteenth and Fourteenth Amendments and democratically elect new state governments. Black voters participated in every step of this process. By 1870 all southern states were readmitted to the Union under reconstituted state governments. However, white southerners never recognized the legality of their integrated state governments.

Nightriders of the Ku Klux Klan terrorized black voters despite the ratification of the Fifteenth Amendment (1870). Congress responded in 1870, and again in 1871, with enforcement acts designed to stop Klan violence and enforce the Fourteenth and Fifteenth Amendments against private acts of violence, as well as illegal state actions. Responsibility for interpreting these new amendments and the laws that supported them eventually fell on the U.S. Supreme Court.

CONSTITUTIONAL ISSUES

The fact that the three Civil War amendments made some changes in the federal system seemed clear. However, the exact nature of those changes was less clear. For example, the question of precisely which privileges and immunities national citizenship conveyed remained. It was not clear whether the Fourteenth Amendment "nationalized" the Bill of Rights, making its provisions apply to the states as well as to the federal government.

It was also unclear whether the national government was empowered to protect black citizens against private interference with their rights. Other questions included the matter of whether the Fourteenth Amendment's state action provision limited federal intervention to cases in which there was statutory discrimination. Was segregation a remnant of slavery outlawed by the Thirteenth Amendment? Did the Fifteenth Amendment provide a positive right to vote? These constitutional issues found their way into the lower federal courts and made their way to the Supreme Court at a time when most northerners had tired of southern questions. The Court's conservative, formalistic answers to these questions effectively eroded the constitutional rights of African, mulatto, and Negro Americans living in the South. By the end of the nineteenth century their future was firmly under control of white southerners.

FOURTEENTH AMENDMENT CONTROVERSIES

The Supreme Court first articulated its interpretation of the Fourteenth Amendment in the so-called *Slaughterhouse Cases* (1873). Ironically, these cases involved neither African, mulatto, or Negro Americans nor the U.S. government itself as parties. For this reason, the Court was able to construe the Fourteenth Amendment apart from the potentially explosive racial issues of Reconstruction. The cases themselves originated in Louisiana, whose state legislature had granted a meat-slaughtering monopoly in New Orleans that threatened to drive all other butchers out of business. A group of white butchers hurt by this monopoly brought suit, claiming that the monopoly denied them their equal privileges and immunities under the Fourteenth Amendment.

Slaughterhouse presented an opportunity for the Court to recognize that the Fourteenth Amendment had radically altered the federal system, making the U.S. government responsible for protecting the rights of all citizens. However, it was not to be. Justice Samuel F. Miller, speaking for a closely split majority, chose a rigidly narrow interpretation that adhered to a traditional understanding of dual federalism—the notion that state and federal government were sovereign in their separate spheres. National citizenship and state citizenship were separate and distinct, according to *Slaughterhouse*, and only the privileges and immunities of *national* citizenship could be protected by the United States. The states were still responsible for protecting the basic day-to-day rights of their own citizens. The *Slaughterhouse* precedent seriously limited the protections of the Fourteenth Amendment for African, mulatto, and Negro Americans, who had hoped to find a federal shelter under the Fourteenth Amendment when the governments of the southern states refused to protect their rights.

The Court's ruling in *United States v. Cruikshank* in 1876 continued to narrow the scope of rights that federal courts could protect under the Fourteenth Amendment. *Cruikshank* involved a race riot in Louisiana, in which perhaps a hundred black Republicans were killed by white Democrats. Closely following Joseph Bradley's circuit court opinion, Chief Justice Morrison R. Waite—recently appointed by President Ulysses S. Grant—announced that the Bill of Rights protected citizens only against actions of the national government. The due process clause, Waite declared, established protection "against arbitrary and unjust legislation," but did not protect African, mulatto, and Negro Americans from private acts of violence. *United States v. Harris* (1883) made more explicit the state action concept implicit in *Cruikshank* by overturning portions of the Civil Rights Act of 1871 (also known as the Second Enforcement Act) because they punished private wrongs without reference to state law.

FIFTEENTH AMENDMENT ISSUES

United States v. Reese (1876), a companion case to *Cruikshank*, construed the Fifteenth Amendment for the first time. Waite ruled that this amendment did not establish a positive right to vote but did establish a constitutional right not to be discriminated against because of race. *Reese* declared parts of the First Enforcement Act unconstitutional for overbreadth, while leaving standing sections of the law that explicitly prohibited voter discrimination because of race. This ruling enabled lower federal courts to continue to prosecute voter discrimination cases. Within a few years, however, the southern states devised other, allegedly nonracial, ways of disenfranchising African, mulatto, and Negro Americans. These included poll taxes, grandfather clauses, and literacy tests.

CIVIL RIGHTS CASES

The *Civil Rights* cases (1883) tested the constitutionality of the Civil Rights Act of 1875, which made it a misdemeanor to deny equal access to privately owned places of business such as hotels, theaters, and public transportation. The five cases that made their way to the Supreme Court in 1883 originated in New York, California, Kansas, Missouri, and Tennessee, demonstrating that the issue of racial discrimination was not limited to former Confederate states in the South. Grounding his ruling in the state action concept of the Fourteenth Amendment, Joseph Bradley, speaking for an eight-person majority, declared the Civil Rights Act unconstitutional. The national government could not reach private wrongs under the Fourteenth Amendment; it was limited to cases of overtly discriminatory state law. The Court also ruled that the Thirteenth Amendment did not support the Civil Rights Act. Although there was no state-action limitation in the Thirteenth Amendment, segregation was not a "badge of slavery" prohibited by the amendment.

Justice John Marshall Harlan, a Kentuckian, former slave owner, and opponent of the Fourteenth Amendment, was the only voice of dissent in the *Civil Rights* cases. Harlan found ample authority for the Civil Rights Act in both the Thirteenth and Fourteenth Amendments. Segregation was a burden of slavery in Harlan's mind, therefore the Thirteenth Amendment's enabling clause gave Congress authority to legislate against it. Moreover, Harlan read the Fourteenth Amendment broadly, finding authority there for the national government to protect the former slaves in all their rights.

PRO-BLACK DECISIONS

The Reconstruction-era Court clearly did not champion African, mulatto, and Negro Americans rights, but it did occasionally decide cases in their favor. In *Ex parte Yarbrough* (1884), for example, Justice Miller ruled that Congress had authority, under Article 1, section 4 of the Constitution, to protect national elections without benefit of the Fifteenth Amendment. Thus the national government retained broad powers to protect African, mulatto, and Negro Americans in federal elections against both state officials and private individuals. Under this ruling, the federal courts continued a vigorous prosecution of voting rights offenders through the 1880's.

In a series of jury cases, the Supreme Court again supported African, mulatto, and Negro Americans rights in cases of overt state action. *Strauder v. West Virginia* (1880), for example, overturned a state statute requiring all-white juries as a violation of the Fourteenth Amendment's equal protection clause. *Ex parte Virginia*, decided the same term, upheld the prosecution of a state judge who had systematically excluded African, mulatto, and Negro Americans from juries in his court. In *Virginia v. Rives* (1880), however, the Court ruled that the mere absence of African, mulatto, and Negro Americans on juries in situations in which no discriminatory state law existed did not demonstrate deliberate racial exclusion; the burden of proof was on the aggrieved parties. Southern states were quick to discern that this decision left room for exclusion that was implicit in the system rather than explicit.

WOMEN AND THE FOURTEENTH AMENDMENT

The Reconstruction-era court was even more conservative in addressing women's rights issues than it was of the issues of African, mulatto, and Negro men. Women who hoped to use the Fourteenth Amendment to overturn discriminatory state legislation were disappointed. In *Bradwell v. Illinois* (1873), Justice Miller ruled that the amendment's equal protection clause did not remove gender restrictions for admission to the bar. Chief Justice Waite decreed in *Minor v. Happersett* (1875) that the amendment did not extend to women the right to vote.

Joseph Bradley, concurring in *Bradwell*, appears to have summed up the attitude of the Court in his later infamous observation that a woman's "destiny and mission" is to be a wife and mother. While African, mulatto, and Negro Americans had made some progress under the Fourteenth Amendment, the status of women remained unchanged.

CONSERVATISM VS. RACISM

Even though the Reconstruction-era Court was not generous to African, mulatto, and Negro Americans, its rulings were grounded more in conservative adherence to traditional notions of dual federalism than in overt racism. While the Court insisted on a state-action theory of the Fourteenth Amendment, it moved to protect African, mulatto, and Negro American rights in cases of overt state action. Not until two decades after Reconstruction ended did the Court establish a judicial doctrine that explicitly sanctioned racial segregation.

Under Chief Justice Melville W. Fuller, the Court's overtly racist *Plessy v. Ferguson* decision of 1896 upheld a Louisiana statute that outlawed racial mixing on railroad cars. Winking at the differences between Black and white cars, Henry Brown for the Court established the notorious separate but equal doctrine, which the Court did not overturn until 1954. Again, as in the *Civil Rights* cases, Harlan was the Court's only voice of dissent. Harlan decried the "thin disguise of 'equal' accommodations" and prophesied accurately that *Plessy* would eventually prove as damaging to the nation as the Court's 1857 *Scott v. Sandford* decision.

The Supreme Court failed during Reconstruction to establish the constitutional rights of African, mulatto, and Negro Americans. The justices' conservatism, racism, and formalistic readings of the law worked against extending federal protections to African, mulatto, and Negro Americans. However, it should be kept in mind that the justices reflected the racial and legal values of their time. The Court would not fully support African, mulatto, and Negro American rights until the Warren Court instituted what has been called the "Second Reconstruction" era during the 1950's and 1960's.

—Lou Falkner Williams, updated by
Patricia A. McDaniel

BUFFALO SOLDIERS

July 28, 1866

Regiments of buffalo soldiers served on the western frontier from 1866 until 1898. They played instrumental roles in helping the United States defeat the Apaches, as well as Mexican outlaws led by Pancho Villa. In addition to protecting settlers, installing telegraph lines, and building roads, buffalo soldiers escorted wagon trains and stagecoaches, built forts, and found sources of drinkable water. The name was retained by black units in the twentieth century, and many buffalo soldiers earned Medals of Honor for their valiant service in the U.S. military.

Definition: Respectful Indian nickname given to black soldiers in the U.S. Army during the nineteenth century

During early 1866, the first U.S. military units composed solely of African Americans, the Fifty-seventh and 125th United States Colored Infantry Regiments, were organized to provide protection for mainly white settlers in New Mexico. On July 28, 1866, the U.S. Congress approved the formation of six additional regiments of African American troops. The Ninth Cavalry regiment was activated on September 21, 1866 at Greenville, Louisiana. On the same day, the Tenth Cavalry regiment began duty at Fort Leavenworth, Kansas. Later in 1866, the Thirty-eighth, Thirty-ninth, Fortieth, and Forty-first infantry units composed of African Americans were assembled. Enlistment periods were for five years, with salaries of thirteen dollars per month, along with room, board, and clothing.

The members of these regiments fought many engagements against Plains Indians, who came to respect them greatly. Because the exceptional courage, dark skin, and curly hair of the African American soldiers resembled characteristics of the buffalo, the Indians dubbed members of the Ninth and Tenth Cavalry regiments "buffalo soldiers." The soldiers themselves were proud of the respect that the name conveyed. Before long, the title was applied to all African American soldiers. The Ninth Cavalry served in Texas from 1867 until 1875, when they were transferred to the New Mexico District. There they participated in several military campaigns against the Apaches, who were led by such skilled leaders as Victorio, Geronimo, and the Apache Kid.

After serving for over eight years in Kansas and

Non Commissioned Buffalo Soldiers, c. 1900

Buffalo Soldier in the 9th Cavalry, 1890

present-day Oklahoma, the Tenth Cavalry opened more than 300 miles of new roads and strung more than 200 miles of telegraph lines in Texas. In 1879–1880, the Tenth served in a key military campaign against Victorio and the Apaches whom the government regarded as "renegades."

During the Spanish-American War of 1898, buffalo soldiers fought in Cuba, and companies from the Ninth and Tenth Cavalries participated in Theodore Roosevelt's famous charge on San Juan Hill. In 1899, members of the Ninth and Tenth served in the Philippines to help control the Filipino nationalists. Buffalo soldiers also served in later conflicts in Malaysia, China, and Japan.

During World War I, buffalo soldiers patrolled the U.S.-Mexico border, while others served in the Philippines, Hawaii, and Europe. In 1941, the Ninth and Tenth Cavalry regiments were combined into the Fourth Cavalry Brigade, which was deactivated in 1944. During World War II, buffalo soldiers fought in Italy during the fall of Rome in 1944 and in breaking through the Gothic line in France in 1945. In 1948, U.S. armed forces were officially desegregated, and buffalo soldiers were transferred to integrated military units.

—*Alvin K. Benson*

See also: Military; Military desegregation; Tuskegee Airmen; World War II

THE CIVIL RIGHTS ACT OF 1866

April 9, 1866

After President Andrew Johnson vetoed the Civil Rights Act, Congress overrode his veto, and the new law joined the Thirteenth Amendment to the Constitution as the first federal legislation to enhance the rights of former enslaved Africans, mulattos, and Negros.

Locale: Washington, D.C.
Categories: Laws, acts, and legal history; civil rights and liberties; social issues and reform; government and politics

KEY FIGURES

Andrew Johnson (1808-1875), president of the United States, 1865-1869
Thaddeus Stevens (1792-1868), antislavery Republican congressman
Charles Sumner (1811-1874), Republican senator opposed to slavery

SUMMARY OF EVENT

At the end of the U.S. Civil War (1861-1865) lay the long road of Reconstruction. As early as 1863, President Abraham Lincoln had expressed a plan for Reconstruction after the Civil War. These plans required a loyalty oath and acceptance of emancipation from southern states desiring readmission to the union. It was not until after Lincoln's assassination that Reconstruction began in earnest.

Andrew Johnson, the seventeenth president of the United States, was vice president at the time of Lincoln's death in 1865. He inherited the problems of rebuilding the country after a lengthy civil war, which had ended in April, 1865. Johnson believed that the responsibility for developing Reconstruction policy should be handled by the president. Johnson's Reconstruction policy provided for a loyalty oath by citizens of states seeking re-admission, revocation of the act of secession, abolition of slavery, and repudiation of the Confederate war debt.

Several states—including Arkansas, Louisiana, and Tennessee—were readmitted in early 1865 without congressional approval. By the end of 1865, all states had been readmitted except Texas. This Reconstruction plan, however, failed to address the issues associated with the former slaves and their rights.

Congress believed that a debt was owed to the former slaves. In 1865, it created the Freedmen's Bureau as a temporary assistance program to address some of this debt. Food, medicine, schools, and land were made available to freedmen. Early in 1866, Congress passed a new Freedmen's Bureau Act and the first federal Civil Rights Act. Both were vetoed by President Johnson, because he feared that the legislation would extend to people of other races. He asked, "Was it sound to make all these colored peoples citizens?" Congress succeeded in quickly overturning these vetoes. J. W. Forney reported that the Senate, prodded by the abolitionist senator Charles Sumner, agreed to pass the vetoed legislation with a two thirds majority on April 6, 1866. The House of Representatives, similarly led by Thaddeus Stevens, followed suit on April 9, 1866, the anniversary of the Confederacy's surrender.

During this same time, less positive events were affecting the free blacks. The year 1866 brought the founding of the Ku Klux Klan. African Americans were subjected to killings, beatings, and torture. This often occurred to keep them out of the political arena, which offered opportunities for power. Perhaps more detrimental to African Americans was the institutionalized racism of the black codes. Also known as black laws, black codes were legal enactments developed to regulate the actions and behaviors of freedmen in the South. These codes allowed legal marriage between African Americans, limited rights to testify in court, and limited rights to sue others.

The black codes also supervised the movements of African Americans in the South, restricted the assembly of unsupervised groups of black people, forbade intermarriage between people of color and whites, banned African Americans from carrying weapons, restricted African American children to apprenticeships that were nearly slavery, and forced black people into employment contracts that carried criminal penalties if abandoned.

Violation of these codes often resulted in stiffer criminal punishment for African Americans than similar violations did for whites. Southern politicians reinstated by Andrew Johnson's Reconstruction policy were responsible for passage of these codes. It was in this environment that Congress found it necessary to develop legislation to combat the antiblack sentiment.

The Civil Rights Act of 1866 was the first federal law to protect the civil rights of African Americans. Section 1 of this provision established the right of citizenship to all persons born in the United States, without regard to previous servitude. As citizens, African Americans were granted the right to enter into and enforce contracts; inherit, lease, sell, hold, and convey property;

give evidence in courts; benefit equally from all laws and ordinances; and be subject to punishments that were the same as given to whites for similar crimes.

Section 2 provided for misdemeanor penalties for anyone who deprived another of the rights afforded in section 1. Additional sections dealt with those who were granted the authority to prosecute and enforce this legislation. In order to ensure that this legislation would be enforced, Congress further established acts that were referred to as enforcement acts. Additionally, Congress drafted the Fourteenth Amendment to the Constitution of the United States to protect the freedmen's status.

Historically, the U.S. Constitution had been the source of civil liberties for citizens of the United States. The first eight amendments to the Constitution provided for a variety of freedoms. The First Amendment granted the freedoms of speech, religion, and assembly, as well as the right to petition the government for the redress of grievances. The Second, Third, and Fourth Amendments provided for a federal militia, the right to own private property, and the right to be protected from unreasonable seizures and searches of private property. The Fifth Amendment provided for the right of due process, ensured that one need not present evidence against oneself, and prevented double jeopardy in court (that is, one cannot be tried for the same offense twice). The Sixth through Eighth Amendments provide for further fair and equitable treatment by the judicial system. The purpose of various civil rights acts has been to extend these rights to all people, particularly those groups for whom these rights were originally withheld, and provide for their enforcement.

SIGNIFICANCE

In addition to its role in Reconstruction, the Civil Rights Act of 1866 set an important precedent for the enactment and protection of civil rights by statute rather than through the Constitution. Several civil rights acts have been passed in the United States since 1866. The Civil Rights Act of 1871 made it a crime to deny equal protection under the law through duress or force. Civil rights legislation passed in 1875, which guaranteed black people the right to use public accommodations, was ruled unconstitutional eight years after it was passed. This continued a downhill turn in the rights of African Americans, eventually leading to the Supreme Court's "separate but equal" decision in *Plessy v. Ferguson* (1896).

This was the rule until 1954, when the Supreme Court determined that separate but equal was inherently unequal, in *Brown v. Board of Education of Topeka,*

Kansas. It was not until 1964, and again in 1968, that any additional civil rights legislation was enacted at the national level. The 1964 and 1968 acts prohibited discrimination in employment, in use of public accommodations such as hotels, and in housing and real estate.

When President Andrew Johnson vetoed civil rights legislation aimed at granting rights to freed blacks, he began a twoyear campaign that would end with an impeachment trial. Congressmen became increasingly concerned with Johnson's apparent plan to subvert and sabotage Reconstruction. His appointment of former Confederate leaders who had not vowed allegiance to the union, his lack of tact in dealing with those with whom he disagreed, his efforts to circumvent Congress and extend presidential powers, and his veto of important civil rights legislation resulted in a special meeting of the House of Representatives on March 2, 1867. Two measures were passed at this special session.

One deprived Johnson of his responsibilities as commander in chief of the military; the second deprived him of the right to remove those with whom he disagreed from their cabinet positions. Finally, a resolution was passed to impeach Johnson for alleged violations of these measures. The senate failed to convict Johnson by one vote. However, Johnson was more compliant in the Reconstruction process after this trial.

—*Sharon L. Larson updated by Patricia A. McDaniel*

Civil Rights Act of 1866

The first section of the Civil Rights Act of 1866, reproduced below, established the civil rights due every United States citizen. The other nine sections of the law defined crimes against civil rights, designated punishments for those crimes, and established the jurisdiction of federal officers and federal courts to enforce the law. An Act to protect all Persons in the United States in their Civil Rights, and furnish the Means of their Vindication.

Be it enacted by the Senate and House of Representatives of the United States of America in Congress assembled, That all persons born in the United States and not subject to any foreign power, excluding Indians not taxed, are hereby declared to be citizens of the United States; and such citizens, of every race and color, without regard to any previous condition of slavery or involuntary servitude, except as a punishment for crime whereof the party shall have been duly convicted, shall have the same right, in every State and Territory in the United States, to make and enforce contracts, to sue, be parties, and give evidence, to inherit, purchase, lease, sell, hold, and convey real and personal property, and to full and equal benefit of all laws and proceedings for the security of person and property, as is enjoyed by white citizens, and shall be subject to like punishment, pains, and penalties, and to none other, any law, statute, ordinance, regulation, or custom, to the contrary notwithstanding.

See also: Black Codes; *Dred Scott v. Sandford*; Civil War; Lincoln Issues the Emancipation Proclamation; Reconstruction of the South; Congress Creates the Freedmen's Bureau; Thirteenth Amendment Is Ratified; 1866: Birth of the Ku Klux Klan; Fourteenth Amendment Is Ratified; Civil Rights Cases; Mississippi Constitution Disfranchises Black Voters; *Plessy v. Ferguson.*

Related articles in *Great Lives from History: The Nineteenth Century, 1801-1900:* Andrew Johnson; Abraham Lincoln; Thaddeus Stevens; Charles Sumner.

CIVIL RIGHTS ACTS OF 1866-1875

April 9, 1866 and March 1, 1875

Although the Civil Rights Acts of the Reconstruction era failed to secure any long-lasting equality for freed Africans, mulattos, and Negros, they did provide points of reference for the Civil Rights movement of the 1950's and 1960's.

The Laws: Federal legislation granting citizenship rights to freed Africans, mulattos, and Negros and outlawing racial discrimination in public accommodations

After the Thirteenth Amendment abolished slavery throughout the United States in 1865, almost all freed Africans, mulattos, and Negros were without property or education, and most white southerners bitterly opposed any fundamental improvement in their political and social status. In 1865–1866, southern legislatures enacted the highly discriminatory Black Codes , and proponents of racial equality responded by calling for new federal laws.

Congress, using its new authority under the Thirteenth Amendment, overrode President Andrew Johnson's veto to pass the first Civil Rights Act on April 9, 1866. This law conferred citizenship on African Americans, a measure necessitated by the Supreme Court's *Dred Scott* decision (*Scott v. Sandford*, 1857). The law included a list of enumerated rights, including the right to make and enforce contracts, to sue and give evidence in court, and to purchase and inherit all forms of property. It also punished public officials if they used their legal powers to deny equality to freed Africans, mulattos, and Negros. Since the law's constitutionality was questionable, many of its major provisions were incorporated into the Fourteenth Amendment.

On July 16, 1866, Congress again overrode President Johnson's veto, this time to enlarge the scope of the Freedmen's Bureau. Among other items, this law authorized the bureau to use military commissions to try persons accused of violating the civil rights of freedmen. Again voting to override a presidential veto on March 2, 1867, Congress passed the First Reconstruction Act. Dividing the South into five military districts, the act required southern states to call new constitutional conventions elected by universal manhood suffrage and to ratify the Fourteenth Amendment. Under the act, 703,000 freed Africans, mulattos, and Negros and 627,000 whites were registered as voters, with African, mulatto, and Negro majorities in five states.

As the Ku Klux Klan conducted a wave of terrorism against freed Africans, mulattos, and Negros and Republicans in the South, Congress responded with the Ku Klux Klan Acts of 1870 and 1871, which provided police protection to enforce the rights guaranteed in the Fourteenth and Fifteenth Amendments. In several decisions, such as *United States v. Cruikshank* (1876), the Supreme Court ruled that key parts of the statutes exceeded the constitutional powers of Congress.

Finally, on March 1, 1875, President Ulysses S. Grant signed into law the Civil Rights Act of 1875. This far-reaching act, largely the work of Senator Charles Sumner, outlawed discrimination based on race in public accommodations (inns, businesses, theaters, and the like) and made it illegal to exclude freed Africans, mulattos, and Negros from jury trials. In the Civil Rights cases (1883), however, the Supreme Court struck down most of the 1875 law, holding that the Fourteenth Amendment did not authorize Congress to prohibit discrimination by private individuals. This decision ended almost all federal attempts to protect freed Africans, mulattos, and Negros from private discrimination until the passage of the Civil Rights Act of 1964.

Although the Civil Rights Acts of the Reconstruction era failed to guarantee any long-lasting equality for freed Africans, mulattos, and Negros, they did provide points of reference for The Civil Rights movement of the 1950's and 1960's. The Civil Rights Act of 1866 was resurrected in *Jones v. Alfred H. Mayer Company* (1968), when the Supreme Court upheld its use to outlaw private racial discrimination in economic transactions as a "badge of slavery."

—*Thomas Tandy Lewis, updated by Patricia A. McDaniel*

See also: Black codes; Civil Rights Act of 1957; Civil Rights Act of 1960; Civil Rights Act of 1964; Civil Rights Act of 1968; Civil Rights Act of 1991; Civil Rights cases; Civil War; Disfranchisement laws in Mississippi; Fourteenth Amendment; Freedmen's Bureau; Grandfather clauses; *Jones v. Alfred H. Mayer Company*; Ku Klux Klan; Race riots of 1866; Reconstruction; *Runyon v. McCrary*; *Scott v. Sandford*; Thirteenth Amendment; United States Commission on Civil Rights; *United States v. Cruikshank*

MEMPHIS AND NEW ORLEANS RACE RIOTS OF 1866

1866

Economic and social disparities between the races, along with a continuing military presence, led to violence during Reconstruction.

The Events: Civil disturbances in two southern cities in the aftermath of the Civil War post-reconstruction era.
Places: Memphis, Tennessee; New Orleans, Louisiana

Racial disturbances in Memphis, Tennessee and New Orleans, Louisiana in 1866 were the result of economic, social, and political issues that troubled the nation during Reconstruction. Given the upheaval in the lives of southerners after the Civil War, the racial disturbances are hardly surprising. In the simplest terms, one of the major tasks of Reconstruction was to assimilate the more than four million former slaves into U.S. society. A more complex view must consider the problems faced by the newly freed Africans, Freedmen, mulattos, and Negros who had to achieve a new identity in a society that had allowed them no control over their own lives.

White southerners had to live with the economic, social, and political consequences of defeat. The military occupation of the South by federal troops after the Civil War angered southern whites, who believed in their right to rebuild and rule their own society without interference from the North. The presence of federal troops (many of them freed Africans, mulattos, and Negros), an armed citizenry, and the psychological difficulty of accepting the end of the world they had known created explosive conditions that erupted into violence.

THE BLACK CODES

The Memphis and New Orleans race riots were one result of this upheaval. Soon after the surrender of the Confederate army at Appomattox in April, 1865, legislatures in the South acted to pass a series of black codes. These laws were intended to maintain control over the lives of the newly freed Africans, mulattos, and Negros and, in effect, keep them enslaved. For example, harsh vagrancy laws allowed police to arrest freed Africans, mulattos, and Negros people without cause and force them to work for white employers. President Abraham Lincoln's Emancipation Proclamation, on January 1, 1863, had freed—on paper—the slaves in the Confederate states.

The U.S. Congress, having abolished slavery throughout the nation with the Thirteenth Amendment to the Constitution in 1865, founded the Freedmen's Bureau to assist the former slaves and was in the process of enacting, over the strong opposition of President Andrew Johnson, a series of Reconstruction Acts intended to repeal the South's black codes. President Johnson resisted congressional attempts to admit freed Africans, mulattos, and Negros to full citizenship, but Congress ultimately overrode his veto and took control of the Reconstruction program in the South.

Many former slaves, rejecting the life they had known on the plantation, moved to the cities of the South. Most Freedmen—Africans, Freedmen, mulattos, and Negros—were refugees without any economic resources, competing with Irish and German immigrants for scarce jobs in the war-torn South. Southern white Protestants feared both the immigrants and the freedmen as threats to the social order.

MEMPHIS

Conditions in Memphis were especially volatile in May, 1866. The city was a rowdy river town known for heavy drinking, gambling, prostitution, and fighting. In 1865, the Freedmen population of Memphis had increased to between twenty and twenty-five thousand, many of them living in a run-down district near Fort Pickering. The white citizens were alarmed by incendiary newspaper accounts of crime and disorder.

The Memphis police, mostly Irish immigrants, were corrupt and ill trained and had a record of brutality toward Africans, mulattos, and Negros people. Added to this already explosive mixture was a body of federal troops, four thousand of whom were Africans, mulattos, and Negros soldiers stationed at Fort Pickering waiting to be mustered out of the army. The violence began on April 29, with a street confrontation between Freedmen soldiers and white policemen. On May 1, the violence escalated, with fights breaking out between groups of Africans, mulattos, and Negros soldiers and the city police. By May 2, the mob included a number of people from the surrounding countryside as well as white citizens of Memphis. The mob rampaged through the Africans, Freedmen, mulattos, and Negros district, attacking families, raping women, and burning homes. Civil authorities took no steps to curb the disturbance.

After considerable delay, Major General George Stoneman, commanding the federal troops, brought the city under control. The three days of mob violence resulted in the deaths of forty-six Africans, mulattos, and Negros and the wounding of seventy others, along with the destruction of four schools, ninety homes, and twelve churches. Southern newspapers and civic officials blamed the Freedmen soldiers for the outbreak. A committee appointed by Congress, however, attributed the disturbances to white people's hatred for the "colored race."

NEW ORLEANS

Although the Memphis riots were the result of local conditions, the New Orleans disturbance of July 30 was caused by state politics and had national significance. Louisiana governor James Madison Wells, a Union sympathizer who needed to consolidate his power over the Confederates in New Orleans and the state, supported a plan to reassemble the state constitutional convention that had been disbanded in 1864. This convention, supported by Unionists, planned to gain votes by enfranchising Freedmen. The city, sympathetic to Confederate politics, was armed, and the corrupt police force had a record of false arrests and mistreatment of freed Africans, mulattos, and Negros The local newspapers, using highly emotional language, incited the fear of white citizens that Freedmen, would gain political control.

The commander of the federal troops, General Absalom Baird, should have foreseen the impending violence but apparently ignored the problem. When the delegates to the state convention began to assemble on July 30, outside Mechanics Institute, fighting broke out between the city police and 130 freed Africans, mulattos, and Negros New Orleans residents, marching behind a U.S. Flag . These marchers were supporters of the right to vote. Delegates were dragged from the convention hall and assaulted by people in the street and by the police, who joined in the mob violence. The attacks on the Freedmen were savage; the wounded were dragged to the city jail and beaten, and the bodies of the dead were mistreated. As the violence escalated, fueled by the drunkenness of the mob, Africans, mulattos, and Negros were dragged from their homes and beaten.

The death toll in the one-day riot included 34 Africans, mulattos, and Negros and 3 white people; approximately 136 people were injured. Although General Baird declared martial law, his action was too late. Several observers, including General Philip H. Sheridan, who was called in to restore order, described the mob violence as a "slaughter." As in the case of the Memphis riots, nearly all the dead and injured were Africans, mulattos, and Negros

Although the Memphis riots were caused by local conditions, the disturbances in New Orleans had state and national political consequences. The Republican Party lost power, paving the way for Democratic control of the state. Precedents for the racial violence that would mark the years of Reconstruction and beyond had been established.

—Marjorie Podolsky, updated by Patricia A. McDaniel

See also: Black codes; Civil Rights Acts of 1866-1875; *Civil Rights* cases; Clinton massacre; Draft riots; Emancipation Proclamation; Fourteenth Amendment; Freedmen's Bureau; Gerrymandering; Ku Klux Klan; Race riots of 1943; Race riots of the twentieth century; Reconstruction; Thirteenth Amendment

PULASKI RACE RIOT OF 1867

1867

Race riot that occurred in the town of Pulaski, Tennessee, believed to be the birthplace of the Ku Klux Klan hate group, where a group of armed white men attacked a group of African American patrons in a local grocery store.

Identification: Race riot led by the Ku Klux Klan in Pulaski, Tennessee.

The Pulaski, Tennessee race riot of 1867 began as a personal dispute between a white man, Calvin Lamberth, and an African American man, Calvin Carter concerning Lamberth's African American mistress Lucy Reynolds, who claimed Carter threatened to beat if she continued her affair with the white man. In response, Lamberth and friends went looking for Carter and found Carter's friend Whitlock Fields, who was shot and killed by the group. Immediately after the shooting started, a group of armed white men emerged from houses carrying loaded weapons, approached the grocery store owned by John Carter, and began firing at the store's patrons, eight African American men. Several of the men were armed and began firing back. Reportedly, a ceasefire was arranged, with the eight African Americans agreeing to leave peacefully. However, they were ambushed by the white mob, who killed two of the men, Orange Rhodes and Calvin Carter, and wounded four others before the town marshal intervened. An investigation of the incident by the Assistant Commissioner of Tennessee resulted in the first documented evidence of the Ku Klux Klan, which is believed to have formed in Pulaski or in a nearby area of Tennessee and was connected to dozens of lynchings and attacks on African Americans in the year after the 1867 Pulaski riot. The infamous hate group continues to claim Pulaski, Tennessee as the organization's original home.

—Micah Issitt

IMPEACHMENT OF ANDREW JOHNSON

February 24-May 26, 1868

Motivated primarily by partisan political differences, this first attempt to impeach a U.S. president created a constitutional crisis that crippled Andrew Johnson's presidency and weakened federal Reconstruction policy in the defeated southern states.

Locale: Washington, D.C.

Categories: Government and politics; crime and scandals

KEY FIGURES

Andrew Johnson (1808-1875), president of the United States, 1865-1869

Salmon P. Chase (1808-1873), chief justice of the United States

Ulysses S. Grant (1822-1885), commanding general of the U.S. Army and Johnson's successor as president

Edwin M. Stanton (1814-1869), U.S. secretary of war

Thaddeus Stevens (1792-1868), Republican congressman from Pennsylvania

Charles Sumner (1811-1874), Whig senator from Massachusetts

SUMMARY OF EVENT

On February 24, 1868, when the U.S. House of Representatives passed a resolution declaring that President Andrew Johnson should be impeached, few observers were surprised. Angry Republicans, especially members of the radical faction who saw Johnson as the great enemy of their program, had put through the House a resolution directing the Judiciary Committee to inquire into Johnson's conduct in January, 1867. Among the many charges made against Johnson was the accusation that he had been involved in the Lincoln assassination plot. However, although the committee recommended impeachment at that time, the full House had voted it down.

The impeachment campaign arose over Johnson's alleged violation of the Tenure of Office Act passed by Congress on March 2, 1867, and subsequently passed again over the president's veto. This act made the removal of cabinet officers subject to approval by the Senate. Even supporters of the bill declared that its provisions referred only to cabinet members appointed by a president in office and not to those who had been appointed by his predecessor. Thus, the law should not have applied to cabinet

appointees of Lincoln still serving under Johnson in 1867. The conflict grew out of Johnson's determination to replace Edwin M. Stanton as secretary of war and to test the constitutionality of the Tenure of Office Act in court.

A holdover from Lincoln's cabinet whom Johnson considered disloyal, Stanton supported the Reconstruction program of Congress, not that of the president. In the summer of 1867, Johnson asked Stanton to resign, but Stanton refused to do so. Johnson thereupon suspended Stanton from office pending concurrence by the Senate, the procedure required by the Tenure of Office Act. He then appointed General Ulysses S. Grant as the interim secretary of war. If the Senate did not concur in his action, Johnson planned to challenge the Tenure of Office Act in court in order to test its constitutionality.

Grant accepted the cabinet post but soon became unhappy because he supported the congressional party and knew that he was its choice for the Republican presidential nomination in 1868. As his discomfort increased, his relations with the president worsened. As a consequence, modern historians have debated Grant's integrity, or lack of it, in the episode. When the Senate, as expected, refused to concur in Stanton's ouster, Grant turned the office back to him. Johnson, however, remained determined to rid himself of Stanton. He then invited General William Tecumseh Sherman to take over from Stanton, but Sherman refused. At last, the adjutant general of the Army, garrulous old Lorenzo Thomas, agreed to take Stanton's place. On February 21, 1868, Johnson fired Stanton and appointed Thomas. However, since Stanton refused to give up his office, Thomas would not take it.

At that point, the Radical Republicans in the House saw their chance to strike at Johnson. On February 24, 1868, the House passed, by a large majority, the Covode Resolution, which declared that the president should be impeached. For many, it was a psychological catharsis to bring down the great opponent of Reconstruction and the great sustainer of rebellion. Some powerful legislators, such as Senator Charles Sumner of Massachusetts and Representative Thaddeus Stevens of Pennsylvania, considered Johnson, a Union Democrat originally from North Carolina, to be too closely allied with former Confederates who had only recently laid down their arms.

Another motive of the Republicans in Congress was to deal with the real problem of military Reconstruction. In his capacity as chief executive, Johnson had removed

Union generals in the South who had been enthusiastic about military Reconstruction and replaced them with men of his own temper. Congressional Republicans wanted the secretary of war to be someone who supported their own program of Reconstruction. When Johnson moved against Stanton, they concluded that they had to stop the president. To many, impeachment seemed to be the only solution. The resolution that the House finally passed had eleven articles. The first nine articles dealt with the president's alleged violation of the Tenure of Office Act, and the last two charged Johnson with making speeches designed to denigrate Congress and with failing to enforce the Reconstruction laws.

After the House had done its work by initiating Johnson's impeachment, it was left to the Senate to convict or acquit him. The U.S. Constitution stipulated that a two-thirds majority vote was necessary for conviction. In 1868, that meant that the votes of thirty-six senators were needed. In early March, with Chief Justice Salmon P. Chase presiding, the senators took the oath to try the president. As this was the first impeachment trial ever conducted against a president, there was a long debate about whether the Senate sat as a court or as a political body. To Chase, the Constitution clearly indicated that the Senate sat as a court, so he conducted the proceedings as a formal trial.

On March 30, the trial opened. The prosecution, composed of important Radical Republicans, claimed that Johnson had subverted the will of Congress, the will of the Republican Party, and the will of the people.

As the defense duly noted, the prosecution made no effort to pin any specific crime on the president. Emphasizing that fact, Johnson's defense counsel argued that Johnson had done nothing to warrant impeachment under the Constitution.

Voting took place on May 16; the result was one vote short of the number needed to convict. Two more votes were taken on May 26, with the same result. Thirty-six votes were needed, but each time the outcome was only thirty-five to nineteen. Johnson was saved by seven Republicans who supported Reconstruction in Congress but who did not believe there were legal grounds for conviction in this case. Typical of the Republican senators who reluctantly opposed conviction was Kansas's Edmund G. Ross.

Although Ross was no supporter of Johnson, he opposed the president's removal from office because he believed the office of the presidency itself would be seriously damaged if Thaddeus Stevens and Sumner succeeded in their struggle with Johnson.

SIGNIFICANCE

President Johnson was acquitted by the narrowest of margins. He served the remainder of his term with little further direct influence on Reconstruction policies. The office of the presidency survived this constitutional crisis, but the direction of Reconstruction remained firmly in the hands of the leaders of Congress. There would not be another impeachment trial of a U.S. president until 1998, when the House voted to impeach President Bill Clinton on charges of perjury and obstruction. As with Johnson's trial, Clinton was acquitted by the Senate on all charges.

—William J. Cooper, Jr., updated by
Joseph Edward Lee

See also: Reconstruction of the South; Surrender at Appomattox and Assassination of Lincoln; Thirteenth Amendment Is Ratified; Civil Rights Act of 1866; Fourteenth Amendment Is Ratified.

Related articles in *Great Lives from History: The Nineteenth Century, 1801-1900:* Salmon P. Chase; Ulysses S. Grant; Andrew Johnson; William Tecumseh Sherman; Edwin M. Stanton; Thaddeus Stevens; Charles Sumner.

FOURTEENTH AMENDMENT IS RATIFIED

July 9, 1868

The most important addition to the U.S. Constitution since adoption of the Bill of Rights, the Fourteenth Amendment was prompted by the need to protect the rights of former slaves; it defined citizenship and established a principle that would later be used to apply the protections of the Bill of Rights to actions by state governments.

Locale: Washington, D.C.
Categories: Civil rights and liberties; laws, acts, and legal history

KEY FIGURES

Andrew Johnson (1808-1875), president of the United States, 1865-1869

Thaddeus Stevens (1792-1868), Republican congressman and radical leader who helped draft the Fourteenth Amendment

Charles Sumner (1811-1874), Republican senator and prominent radical

SUMMARY OF EVENT

Ratified on July 9, 1868, the Fourteenth Amendment to the U.S. Constitution was part of the Reconstruction plan formulated by the Republican majority in the Thirty-ninth Congress. Before Congress met in December, 1865, President Andrew Johnson had authorized the restoration of white self-government in the former Confederate states, and congressmen and senators from those states waited in Washington to be seated in Congress.

Meanwhile, southern state legislatures elected under Johnson's program had met to develop a series of laws called black codes, which restricted the rights of the former slaves. Although the Republican majority in Congress had no intention of permitting the Johnson approach to Reconstruction to prevail or allowing the seating of the unrepentant white southern representatives, they had no comprehensive counterproposal. To gain time and to work out a positive approach, Republicans in the House and the Senate created the Joint Committee of Fifteen on Reconstruction. This committee was composed of six senators and nine representatives.

The Republican majority rejected Johnson's plan because, as the black codes demonstrated, the old Confederate politicians could not be trusted to respect the rights of the freedmen. Moreover, the Republicans had no intention of permitting white southerners, whom they regarded as rebels and traitors, to increase the representation in the House of Representatives of the southern Democrats. The abolition of slavery had destroyed the old compromise under which five slaves counted as three free persons in apportioning representation in the House and the electoral college, and the Republicans wanted to make sure that the South did not add to its numbers in the House and thereby profit from rebellion.

Between December, 1865, and May, 1866, Republicans attempted to hammer out a program that would accomplish their purposes in the South, unite members of their party in Congress, and appeal to northern voters.

Given the diversity of opinion within the Republican Party, this undertaking proved to be difficult. The radical wing of the party wanted African American suffrage, permanent political proscription of former Confederate leaders, and confiscation of the property of former Confederates.

Representative John Bingham of Ohio, principal author of the Equal Protection Clause

Some Republicans maintained they were authorized in these actions by the Thirteenth Amendment, which, they believed, gave Congress the power to abolish the "vestiges of slavery." Moderate Republicans, on the other hand, feared political repercussions from African American suffrage, as such a requirement would result in beginning the Reconstruction process over again. Many moderates also believed that an additional amendment to the Constitution was needed to provide precise authority for Congress to enact civil rights legislation.

From deliberations of the joint committee and debate on the floor of the House came the Fourteenth Amendment. Many Republicans believed that the proposal was in the nature of a peace treaty, although this view was not explicitly stated. According to this view, if the South accepted the amendment, the southern states were to be readmitted and their senators and representatives would seated in Congress. In other words, Reconstruction would end. Republicans presented a united front during the final vote as a matter of party policy. Because the amendment was an obvious compromise between radicals and moderates, it was too strong for some and too weak for others.

233

The Fourteenth Amendment became the most important addition to the constitution since the Bill of Rights had been adopted in 1791. It contains five sections.

Section 1, the first constitutional definition of citizenship, states that all persons born or naturalized in the United States are citizens of the United States and of the states in which they reside. It includes limits on the power of states, by providing that no state may abridge the privileges and immunities of citizens, deprive any person of life, liberty, or property without due process of law, or deny to any person within its jurisdiction the equal protection of law. This section was intended to guarantee African Americans the rights of citizenship, although the amendment's framers did not define exactly which rights were included. Nor did they define "state action" to specify whether the term meant only official acts of state government or the actions of individuals functioning privately with state approval.

The courts later interpreted the amendment's due process clause to extend the rights of the accused listed in the Bill of Rights, which had applied only to the federal government, to the states. They would eventually expand the notion of equal protection to include other categories, such as sex and disability, as well as race. They also interpreted the word "person" to include corporations as legal persons; under this interpretation, corporations found protection from much state regulation.

Section 2 gave a new formula of representation in place of the old three-fifths compromise of the Constitution, under which five slaves were counted as equal to three free persons in determining a state's representation in the House of Representatives and the electoral college. All persons in a state were to be counted for representation, but if a state should disfranchise any of its adult male citizens, except for participation in rebellion or any other crime, the basis of its representation would be reduced proportionately. Although not guaranteeing suffrage to African Americans, this provision threatened the South with a loss of representation should black men be denied the vote.

Section 3 declared that no person who had ever taken an oath to support the Constitution (which included all who had been in the military service or held state or national office before 1860) and had then participated in the rebellion against the Union could be a senator or representative or hold any civil or military office, national or state. This disability could be removed only

---

Fourteenth Amendment to the U.S. Constitution

Section 1. All persons born or naturalized in the United States and subject to the jurisdiction thereof, are citizens of the United States and of the State wherein they reside. No State shall make or enforce any law which shall abridge the privileges or immunities of citizens of the United States; nor shall any State deprive any person of life, liberty, or property, without due process of law; nor deny to any person within its jurisdiction the equal protection of the laws.

Section 2. Representatives shall be apportioned among the several States according to their respective numbers, counting the whole number of persons in each State, excluding Indians not taxed. But when the right to vote at any election for the choice of electors for President and Vice President of the United States, Representatives in Congress, the Executive and Judicial officers of a State, or the members of the Legislature thereof, is denied to any of the male inhabitants of such State, being twenty-one years of age, and citizens of the United States, or in any way abridged, except for participation in rebellion, or other crime, the basis of representation therein shall be reduced in the proportion which the number of such male citizens shall bear to the whole number of male citizens twenty-one years of age in such State.

Section 3. No person shall be a Senator or Representative in Congress, or elector of President and Vice President, or hold any office, civil or military, under the United States, or under any State, who, having previously taken an oath, as a member of Congress, or as an officer of the United States, or as a member of any State legislature, or as an executive or judicial officer of any State, to support the Constitution of the United States, shall have engaged in insurrection or rebellion against the same, or given aid or comfort to the enemies thereof. But Congress may by a vote of two-thirds of each House, remove such disability.

Section 4. The validity of the public debt of the United States, authorized by law, including debts incurred for payment of pensions and bounties for services in suppressing insurrection or rebellion, shall not be questioned.

But neither the United States nor any State shall assume or pay any debt or obligation incurred in aid of insurrection or rebellion against the United States, or any claim for the loss or emancipation of any slave; but all such debts, obligations and claims shall be held illegal and void.

Section 5. The Congress shall have power to enforce, by appropriate legislation, the provisions of this article.

by a two-thirds vote of both houses of Congress. This section took away the pardoning power of the president, which congressional Republicans believed Andrew Johnson had used too generously.

Section 4 validated the debt of the United States, voided all debts incurred to support rebellion, and invalidated all claims for compensation for emancipated slaves made by their former owners.

Section 5 gave Congress authority to pass legislation to enforce the provisions of the Fourteenth Amendment.

SIGNIFICANCE

After the Civil War (1861-1865), the framers of the Fourteenth Amendment desired to protect the former slaves and boost Republican Party strength in the South by barring old Confederates from returning to Congress and bolstering the electoral college with increased voting strength. They hoped to do this without threatening the federal system or unduly upsetting the relationship between the central government and the states. At the same time, Republicans wanted to unify their party and project a popular issue for the approaching electoral contest against Andrew Johnson.

Since its passage in 1868, the U.S. Supreme Court has used the due process and equal protection clauses of the Fourteenth Amendment to expand both the number and breadth of rights protecting individuals. More than any other amendment, the Fourteenth has provided the basis for the range of rights that Americans came to take for granted during the twentieth century.

—William J. Cooper, Jr., updated by
Mary Welek Atwell

See also: Reconstruction of the South; Congress Creates the Freedmen's Bureau; Black Codes; Thirteenth Amendment Is Ratified; 1866: Birth of the Ku Klux Klan; Civil Rights Act of 1866; Impeachment of Andrew Johnson; Civil Rights Cases; Mississippi Constitution Disfranchises Black Voters; *Plessy v. Ferguson.*

Related articles in *Great Lives from History: The Nineteenth Century, 1801-1900:* Andrew Johnson; Abraham Lincoln; Thaddeus Stevens; Charles Sumner.

KU KLUX KLAN ACTS

1870-1871

Enacted by the U.S. Congress in response to the terrorist activities of the Ku Klux Klan and other white supremacy groups in the South during Reconstruction, the three Ku Klux Klan Acts were effective in repressing white supremacy organizations.

The Laws: Three federal laws designed to suppress white supremacist terrorism during Reconstruction

Also known as the Enforcement Acts, or Force Acts, these three laws were enacted by the U.S. Congress in response to the terrorist activities of the Ku Klux Klan and other groups committed to white supremacy in the South during the era of Reconstruction, immediately following the Confederate defeat at the end of the Civil War. The first act, passed in May, 1870, made night riding (the practice of riding on horseback at night and committing various acts of intimidation and harassment) a federal felony and reaffirmed the rights of African Americans provided for in the Fourteenth and Fifteenth Amendments.

Congress passed a second act in February, 1871, which provided for election supervisors to ensure against fraud and racial discrimination. Two months later, Congress approved a third statute aimed specifically at the activities of the Ku Klux Klan. This law made it a federal offense to violate anyone's voting rights. In addition, it allowed the president to proclaim areas in which state governments failed to curb domestic violence to be in "rebellion" and authorized the use of military force and the suspension of the writ of *habeas corpus* to end rebellions. In October, 1871, President Ulysses S. Grant used the law to declare nine counties in South Carolina to be in rebellion. These laws proved effective in suppressing white supremacy organizations.

—Thomas Clarkin

See also: Fifteenth Amendment; Fourteenth Amendment; Ku Klux Klan; Reconstruction

FIFTEENTH AMENDMENT

1870

The U.S. Supreme Court has used the Fifteenth Amendment to decide many cases involving discrimination in access to voting, especially after the passage of the Voting Rights Act of 1965. The law and the Court's interpretive decisions ended racially discriminatory voting restrictions in the United States.

The Law: Amendment to the U.S. Constitution forbidding discrimination in voting rights on the basis of race, color, or previous condition of servitude. Section 2 gives enforcement power to Congress

The original U.S. Constitution tied the right of individuals to vote in federal elections to state election laws. A person who was eligible to vote in elections for the lower house of the state legislature was entitled to vote in federal elections. The result was that eligibility to vote was determined by state, not federal, law. If a national decision on voting rights was to be made, a constitutional amendment such as the Twenty-fourth, which ended poll taxes, was required.

In 1868, after the Northern victory in the Civil War, the Fourteenth Amendment established citizenship and civil rights for the newly freed slaves. On February 3, 1870, the Fifteenth Amendment was adopted to prevent state governments from denying freed slaves the right to vote. Its language however, is much broader, because it prohibits denial of the right to vote "on account of race, color, or previous condition of servitude." Section 2 of the amendment gives Congress the power to enforce its terms by remedial legislation.

DISCRIMINATORY LAWS

Immediately after the ratification of the amendment, Congress passed the Enforcement Act of 1870, which made it a crime for public officers and private persons to obstruct the right to vote. Enforcement of this law was spotty and ineffective, and most of its provisions were repealed in 1894. Meanwhile, beginning in 1890, most of the states of the former Confederacy passed laws that were specifically designed to keep African Americans from voting. Literacy tests were a major disqualifier because at that time more than two-thirds of adult African Americans were illiterate. At the same time, white illiterates were allowed to vote under grandfather clauses, property qualifications, and "good character" exceptions, from which African Americans were excluded.

An 1867 drawing depicting African Americans casting ballots

Racially discriminatory enforcement of voting qualifications became the principal means by which African Americans were barred from the polls.

In the absence of a statute, the only remedy for these discriminatory practices was case-by-case litigation. The Supreme Court, in case after case, struck down the discriminatory state practices. Grandfather clauses were invalidated in *Guinn v. United States* (1915). The state-mandated all-white primary was outlawed in *Nixon v. Herndon* (1927); party-operated all-white primaries were forbidden by *Smith v. Allwright* (1944) and *Terry v. Adams* (1953). The Court held in *United States v. Thomas* (1959) that phony polling place challenges to African Americans seeking to vote—by the time the challenges had been resolved, the polls had closed—were improper under the Fifteenth Amendment.

Racial gerrymandering was forbidden by *Gomillion v. Lightfoot* (1960). In that case, Alabama had redefined the shape of the city of Tuskegee so as to exclude all but four or five of its four hundred African American voters, thus denying this group the opportunity to influence city government. The Court also dealt with discriminatory administration of literacy tests in several cases, most important, *Schnell v. Davis* (1949), in which Justice William O. Douglas, writing for the Court, remarked that "the legislative setting and the great discretion it vested in the registrar made it clear that…the literacy requirement was merely a device to make racial discrimination easy."

VOTING RIGHTS ACT OF 1965

The mass disfranchisement of African Americans could not be reached efficiently or fully by means of individually brought cases. Although some of the discriminatory state practices were halted, every voting registration decision could be made on the basis of race if voting registrars wished to do so. Against this background, Congress passed the Voting Rights Act of 1965. Section 2 of the Fifteenth Amendment provided constitutional authority for this law, which was aimed at "ridding the country of racial discrimination in voting," according to the statute's preamble. The law forbade a number of discriminatory practices. Literacy tests were "suspended" for five years in areas where voting discrimination had been most flagrant. To deal with voting discrimination through outright intimidation and violence, the law provided for federal voting registrars and protection by federal marshals.

The first important cases arising under this law came to the Court in 1966. In *South Carolina v. Katzenbach* (1966), the Court held unanimously that the most important provisions of the Voting Rights Act were constitutional. Chief Justice Earl Warren wrote that "the record here showed that in most of the States covered, various tests and devices have been instituted with the purpose of disenfranchising Negroes, have been framed in such a way as to facilitate this aim, and have been administered in a discriminatory fashion for many years. Under these circumstances, the 15th Amendment has clearly been violated." Because Congress's power under the amendment is remedial, this finding of fact was necessary to invoke federal power. The broad construction of Congress's power to deal with discrimination in voting in *South Carolina v. Katzenbach* established an important precedent to which the Court consistently adhered.

VOTING RIGHTS ACT OF 1970

Congress renewed the Voting Rights Act in 1970 and extended the literacy test ban to the entire country. The extension reached New York State's English-language literacy test, which had the practical effect of disfranchising many Puerto Rican voters. The English-language literacy test had been in place long before any substantial Puerto Rican migration to New York City had taken place. The extension was upheld by the Court in *Oregon v. Mitchell* (1970). Although the justices disagreed on some aspects of the new law, they were unanimous in upholding the constitutionality of the literacy test ban, even though there was no showing that New York had attempted to discriminate against Puerto Ricans. However, in *Rome v. United States* (1980), the Court became enmeshed in the question of the extent to which Congress may control state and local government under the Fifteenth Amendment. The question arose as to whether the remedial power reached only deliberate attempts by states and municipalities to deny Fifteenth Amendment voting rights or whether it was the effect of state practices on African American—and by extension, other minority group—voting that authorized federal action. The Court has not fully settled this extraordinarily complex constitutional question. Congress renewed and further extended the requirements of the Voting Rights Act again in 1982, this time for a period of twenty-five years.

The effect of the Court's Fifteenth Amendment decisions coupled with the broader provisions of the Voting Rights Act has been immense. In 1961 only 1.2 million African Americans were registered to vote in the South—one-quarter of voting-age African Americans. By 1964 nearly 2 million were registered. In 1975 between 3.5 and 4 million African Americans were registered to vote in the South. By the end of the century, although electoral turnout among African Americans and other persons of color in the United States is still lower than that of whites, the gap has nearly been closed. Formal legal discriminatory barriers to voting no longer exist.

—*Robert Jacobs*

See also: Civil War; Fourteenth Amendment; Gerrymandering; *Gomillion v. Lightfoot*; Grandfather clauses; *Guinn v. United States*; Ku Klux Klan Acts; *Lassiter v. Northampton County Board of Elections*; Poll taxes; Reconstruction; *Smith v. Allwright*; *Terry v. Adams*; Thirteenth Amendment; Twenty-fourth Amendment; Understanding tests; Voting Rights Act of 1965; White primaries; Yarbrough, Ex parte

GRANDFATHER CLAUSES

1866

Until the Supreme Court struck down grandfather clauses as a violation of the Fifteenth Amendment to the U.S. Constitution, states used this as a method to disenfranchise freed Africans, mulattos, and Negros, yet allow illiterate white men to vote.

Definition: The legal provision enacted in some southern states after the passage of the Fifteenth Amendment that exempted men who could vote before 1866 and their descendants from suffrage restrictions such as literacy tests and poll taxes.

The Fifteenth Amendment, adopted in 1870, guaranteed that citizens of the United States could not be denied their right to vote by the federal or state government on account of race, color, or previous condition of servitude. However, many southern states passed laws, including grandfather clauses, designed to disenfranchise freed Africans, mulattos, and Negros through literacy tests or poll taxes.

Guinn v. United States (1915) involved an Oklahoma law that required all voters to prove that they or a direct ancestor could vote before 1866 or to pass a literacy test. The Supreme Court found The Grandfather Clause to be an unconstitutional evasion of the Fifteenth Amendment. Although the Oklahoma provision did not directly cite race, most white men could prove that an ancestor could vote. Therefore, it was mostly freed people of color who were forced to take the literacy test. In *Lance v. Wilson* (1939), the Court ruled that literacy tests were also unconstitutional.

—Siobhan McCabe Matthew Lindstrom, updated by Patricia A. McDaniel

See also: Civil Rights Acts of 1866-1875; Civil Rights movement; Fifteenth Amendment; *Guinn v. United States*; Politics and government; Poll taxes; Voting Rights Act of 1965; White primaries

COLFAX MASSACRE

April 13, 1873

Fighting for political rights, more than sixty African Americans died in what was the bloodiest single case of racial violence during the Reconstruction. Afterward, President Ulysses S. Grant ignored pleas for justice on behalf of the slain.

The Event: Killing of more than sixty African Americans by a white terrorist organization
  Place: Colfax, Louisiana

The terrorist group known as the White League formed across Louisiana during the Reconstruction (1866–1877) to keep African Americans out of the political arena. The league's activities led to the Colfax massacre, the bloodiest single instance of racial violence in the Reconstruction period in all the United States. Disputes over the 1872 election results had produced dual governments at all levels of politics in Louisiana. Fearful that local Democrats would seize power, former slaves under the command of African American Civil War veterans and militia officers took over Colfax, the seat of Grant Parish, Louisiana.

On Easter Sunday, April 13, 1873, a series of brutal acts were carried out by the White League in Colfax, resulting in the deaths of more than sixty African Americans. After the African American men had laid down their weapons and surrendered, many were flogged, mutilated, and murdered, and African American women were also raped and murdered. A pile of more than twenty bodies was found half-buried in the woods. Monroe Lewis, an elderly black gentleman, was dragged from his bed, forced to say his prayers, and then shot. After being forced to cook food for a party of more than ninety white men, Charles Green was executed. Petitions to President Ulysses S. Grant requesting that justice be rendered were ignored.

—Alvin K. Benson

See also: Charleston race riots; Civil War; Clinton massacre; Lynching; Orangeburg massacre; Reconstruction

SLAUGHTERHOUSE CASES

April 14, 1873

In these cases, the U.S. Supreme Court for the first time interpreted the Thirteenth, Fourteenth, and Fifteenth Amendments and upheld a state statute granting monopoly status to a corporation. Although the case had no direct bearing on African Americans, its interpretation of the Civil War amendments would have important ramifications for later Supreme Court decisions regarding African American civil rights.

The Case: U.S. Supreme Court ruling on the Civil War amendments

In 1869, the state of Louisiana created a corporation and gave it monopoly status to operate a meat-slaughtering facility south of the city of New Orleans. It prohibited all other slaughterhouse operations in the three parishes surrounding the city. The goal of the law was to remove slaughterhouse operations from areas that polluted Mississippi River water traveling through the city and consolidate them at one central location downstream from the city. The law also regulated the prices charged for use of the facility by butchers. Butchers not included in the monopoly claimed the law was unconstitutional under the recently adopted Thirteenth and Fourteenth Amendments to the U.S. Constitution. The Louisiana Supreme Court affirmed the law, and the case was appealed to the U.S. Supreme Court.

Justice Samuel F. Miller, writing for the five-member majority of the Court, upheld the law. He used the case to reflect on the purpose of the three Reconstruction-era amendments to the U.S. Constitution, the Thirteenth, Fourteenth, and Fifteenth Amendments which had been ratified between 1865 and 1870. He wrote that the three taken together were intended to end slavery

and the effects of slavery on African Americans. This portion of the opinion is important, as it reflects contemporaneous thinking on the rationale for the ratification of the three amendments.

Justice Miller rejected the claim that granting a monopoly to the corporation created an "involuntary servitude" in violation of the Thirteenth Amendment, noting that the amendment intended to apply narrowly to the incidents of slavery. He also refused to find that the state of Louisiana had violated the Fourteenth Amendment protection of the "privileges and immunities of citizens of the United States" by awarding the monopoly. He refused to give the Fourteenth Amendment a broad interpretation or permit the concept of due process to be used to challenge state law through the U.S. Constitution.

The four-member minority opinion authored by Justice Stephen J. Field sharply disagreed with the majority. Justice Field wrote that the Fourteenth Amendment protects a broad array of privileges and immunities from state interference. Justice Joseph P. Bradley wrote a second dissenting opinion asserting that the Fourteenth Amendment due process clause requires that persons be protected from state actions and that the clause should be given a broad interpretation. This minority view later gained support by the Court majority in the use of substantive due process to limit state regulation of economic activities. It also has been used as a source to protect fundamental rights such as the right to privacy and in criminal law.

See also: Civil War; Compromise of 1877; Reconstruction

CLINTON MASSACRE

September 4–6, 1875

The Clinton massacre served as the impetus that inspired white Mississippi "redeemers," as they were called, to do whatever was necessary to take control away from the Republicans and force black submission.

The Event: Killing of more than twenty African Americans by angry white mobs
Place: Clinton, Mississippi

In 1875, widespread resentment of congressional Reconstruction (the effort to rebuild and rehabilitate the South after the Civil War) mounted among whites in Mississippi. White Democrats began coordinating efforts to carry the fall statewide elections. The dominant issue for Democrats in the 1875 electoral campaign was the threat or fear of race war. Several race riots had already occurred throughout Mississippi during the summer.

Democratic political solidarity was still in question, however, until the Clinton massacre of September 4–6. Clinton, a town in Hinds County, was the site of a political rally to which both Democratic and Republican speakers were invited. The rally was disrupted by gunfire, and both black and white people were killed and wounded. Confusion followed.

News of the incident quickly spread throughout the state. Bands of armed whites converged on Clinton, and a reign of terror followed. Officials estimated that twenty to fifty African Americans were killed by the angry white mobs. Many African Americans fled to other towns, and some sought refuge in the woods. The Republican governor of Mississippi, unable to convince the president to send troops, watched helplessly as an undeclared race war waged throughout the state. Freedmen were denied access to the polls or were forced to vote for Democratic candidates. The Clinton massacre had served as the spark that inspired white Mississippi "redeemers," as they were called, to do whatever was necessary to take control away from the Republicans and force black submission.

—Donald C. Simmons, Jr.

See also: Colfax massacre; Disfranchisement laws in Mississippi; Dyer antilynching bill; Lynching; Race riots of 1866; Race riots of 1943; Race riots of the twentieth century; Reconstruction

UNITED STATES V. CRUIKSHANK
March 27, 1876

Drawing on narrow interpretations of the Fourteenth and Fifteenth Amendments, the Supreme Court severely limited the authority of the federal government to protect the civil rights of African Americans.

The Case: U.S. Supreme Court ruling on federal enforcement of civil rights and states' rights

In 1875, William Cruikshank and two other men were convicted in a federal court of participating in the lynching of two African Americans. The 1870 Reconstruction statute under which they were convicted was broadly written to make it unlawful to interfere with most rights of citizens. The constitutional authority claimed for this federal statute was the Fourteenth Amendment. Cruikshank and his codefendants, who were charged with interfering with the right and privilege "peaceably to assemble," argued that the Fourteenth Amendment does not authorize the federal government to establish so broad a criminal statute because the amendment was written to limit state governments, not private persons.

In 1876, the U.S. Supreme Court, in an opinion written by Chief Justice Morrison R. Waite, unanimously agreed with Cruikshank. The Fourteenth Amendment, which establishes citizenship and then says, "No State shall make or enforce any law which shall abridge the privileges or immunities of citizens of the United States," applies in the first instance to state, not private, action. Private action such as the lynching in which Cruikshank participated may be punished by the federal government only if it can be shown that the intent was to deprive a specific constitutional right—and even then the indictment must specify the intent very narrowly. The decision effectively sanctioned the lynchings of African Americans for the next few decades.

—Robert Jacobs

See also: Civil Rights Acts of 1866–1875; *Civil Rights cases*; Dyer antilynching bill; Lynching

UNITED STATES V. REESE
March 27, 1876

The Supreme Court voided part of the 1870 Enforcement Act, claiming that voting was a privilege, not a right.

The Case: U.S. Supreme Court ruling on the right to vote and the Fifteenth Amendment

United States v. Reese (1876) marked the first major test of voting rights under the Fifteenth Amendment, which had been passed in 1870 and stated that the right to vote "shall not be denied or abridged by the United States or by any State on account of race, color, or previous condition of servitude." A Kentucky voting official was indicted for refusing to let an African American, who had offered to pay his poll tax, vote in a municipal election. The U.S. Supreme Court, by an 8–1 margin, declared unconstitutional the Enforcement Act of 1870, the law on which the indictment was based. The Enforcement Act provided penalties for obstructing or hindering persons from voting in an election. In the majority decision delivered by Chief Justice Morison R. Waite, the Supreme Court ruled that the U.S. Congress had overreached its powers by seeking to punish the denial of voting rights on any grounds and could only legislate against discrimination based on race.

According to the U.S. Supreme Court, the Fifteenth Amendment did not confer the right of suffrage on anyone but merely prohibited the United States from excluding a person from voting because of race, color, or previous condition of servitude. The ruling made it constitutionally possible for southern states to deny the right to vote on any grounds except race, thus allowing the use of poll taxes, literacy tests, good character tests, understanding clauses, and other devices to disfranchise African Americans.

—*David L. Porter*

See also: Disfranchisement laws in Mississippi; Fifteenth Amendment; Poll taxes

HAMBURG MASSACRE OF 1876

July 8, 1876

The Hamburg Massacre, or Hamburg Riot, was a race riot that occurred in 1876 when a group of armed white farmers and residents of Augusta, Georgia attacked a group consisting of members of an all-African American militia unit in Hamburg, South Carolina.

Identification: Race riot that occurred in the predominantly African American community of Hamburg, South Carolina in 1876.

The Hamburg Massacre was one of numerous race-riots and racially-motivated killings that occurred in the American south during the restoration period, when the United States was rebuilding after the Civil War and the legal freedoms of African Americans were in a state of flux. On July 4th, two white farmers, Thomas Butler and Henry Getzen, were attempting to drive a carriage through the main road of Hamburg, South Carolina, a small, African American community across the Savannah River from Augusta, Georgia. The farmers found

their way blocked by a group of African American members of the South Carolina National Guard performing a military exercise. On July 8th, Butler and Getzen returned with hundreds of white men armed with weapons intending to attack the militia, who took refuge in a stone warehouse. The two groups exchanged fire during the afternoon until the white rioters obtained a cannon and used it to destroy part of the building where the militia members were taking cover. Some of the militia members escaped into the surrounding woods, while four were captured and executed by the mob. In total, six African Americans and one white man were killed in the incident, which was used by conservative Democratic politicians of the era to justify a series of prejudicial laws restricting the freedoms of African Americans living in the state.

—*Micah Issitt*

CHARLESTON RACE RIOTS

September-November, 1876

Political corruption and intimidation characterized both sides in the conflict.

The Event: Fighting between white Republicans and black Democrats during the months leading up to a presidential election

Place: Charleston, South Carolina

After the Civil War ended in 1865, South Carolina was controlled by northern-born whites and black southerners with support from the U.S. federal government. Southern whites who were allied with some black southerners attempted to regain control of the local government. By 1876, a tense atmosphere had developed between the two forces as a gubernatorial election approached between Republican Daniel H. Chamberlain, the incumbent and a Massachusetts-born former Union army officer, and Democrat Wade Hampton, a former slaveowner and Confederate lieutenant general.

Political corruption and intimidation characterized both sides. On September 6, black Democrats rallied in Charleston to support Hampton. A group of black Republicans attacked the black Democrats and their white escorts, and a riot ensued. The riot lasted for several days with black Republicans destroying property and attacking whites. One black man and one white man died, and about one hundred people were injured.

Tensions remained high until the election on November 7, and the next day, as people were awaiting the election results, gunfire erupted in Charleston. Black police officers loyal to the Republicans began firing at the rioters. One black man and one white man were killed, and about a dozen other people were injured. Federal troops intervened and restored order. Both candidates claimed victory in the election, but by 1877, power had returned to white Democrats because of a political deal with the Republican presidential candidate.

—*Abraham D. Lavender*

See also: Civil War; Colfax massacre; Draft riots; Reconstruction

COMPROMISE OF 1877

January, 1877

To get its candidate into the presidency, the price that the Republic Party paid in the Compromise of 1877 was ending Reconstruction in the South.

The Event: Political resolution of the disputed presidential election of 1876 that put Republican Rutherford B. Hayes in office

The Compromise of 1877 represents the attempt toward equality that failed during Reconstruction when newly elected President Rutherford B. Hayes ended efforts to establish a biracial democracy in the South. During his presidential campaign, Hayes favored "home rule" for the South as he campaigned against New York governor Samuel J. Tilden, a Democratic reformer. Although Tilden won the popular vote, Hayes claimed victory in South Carolina, Florida, and Louisiana. Republican Reconstruction governments still controlled these states, and it was doubtful that a former Union general could carry them by any other means than fraud.

Many southern Democrats, particularly scalawags, accepted Hayes's election, particularly if he would leave the South alone after taking office. Ohio Republicans and southern Democrats met in a Washington, D.C., hotel and reached an agreement that if Hayes could assume the presidency, he would remove federal troops from South Carolina and Louisiana so that Democrats could regain control. Hayes consented after being sworn in. Race relations worsened because the Democrats ignored their promises to treat black southerners fairly and Hayes forgot his pledge to ensure the rights of Africans, Freedmen, mulattos, and Negros. Reconstruction had allowed African Americans to reconstitute their families, participate in government, and enjoy equality in dealing with whites, but the 1877 Compromise engendered a hatred of reform throughout the South for nearly one hundred years. African Americans would suffer social restrictions until the 1960's.

—*Douglas W. Richmond, updated by Patricia A. McDaniel*

See also: Black codes; Disfranchisement laws in Mississippi; Gerrymandering; Politics and government; Reconstruction; Slaughterhouse Cases

STRAUDER V. WEST VIRGINIA

March 1, 1880

The Supreme Court declared that exclusion of African Americans from juries was a violation of the equal protection clause of the Fourteenth Amendment.

The Case: U.S. Supreme Court ruling on jury composition

During the late nineteenth century, West Virginia had a statute that explicitly limited jury service to "white male persons."

Strauder, a black man convicted of murder, claimed that he had not received a fair trial because of the statute. The Supreme Court agreed. Writing for a 7–2 majority, Justice William Strong explained that such a law constituted precisely the kind of discrimination that the Fourteenth Amendment was designed to prevent. Also in 1880, the Court decided three other important cases dealing with racial exclusion from juries. In *Neal v. Delaware* and *Ex parte Virginia*, it held that even if the state's laws did not exclude blacks, the actual practice of exclusion was a denial of equal protection. In *Virginia v. Rives*, however, the Court ruled that the mere absence of African Americans from juries was not in itself a violation of the Fourteenth Amendment. In effect, *Rives* allowed local officials to use their discretionary authority to exclude African Americans from juries. Although *Strauder*, *Ex Parte Virginia*, and *Neal* had limited impact during the Jim Crow era, they nevertheless helped prepare a constitutional foundation for the Civil Rights movement of the mid-twentieth century.

—Thomas Tandy Lewis

See also: *Batson v. Kentucky*; *Edmonson v. Leesville Concrete Company*; *Powers v. Ohio*; *Williams v. Mississippi*

CIVIL RIGHTS CASES

October 15, 1883

In a set of five cases consolidated in a single decision, the U.S. Supreme Court found the Civil Rights Act of 1875 unconstitutional. The decision affirmed the premise that the Fourteenth Amendment gave Congress the power to prohibit discrimination only by state governments and not by private individuals or businesses.

Also known as: *United States v. Stanley*; *United States v. Ryan*; *United States v. Nichols*; *United States v. Singleton*; *Robinson and Wife v. Memphis & Charleston Railroad Company*

Locale: Washington, D.C.

Categories: Laws, acts, and legal history; government and politics; civil rights and liberties; social issues and reform

KEY FIGURES

Joseph P. Bradley (1813-1892), associate justice of the U.S. Supreme Court, 1870-1892

John Marshall Harlan (1833-1911), associate justice of the U.S. Supreme Court, 1877-1911

Robert Brown Elliott (1842-1884), African American U.S. representative from South Carolina

John Mercer Langston (1829-1897), head of the Equal Rights League and a civil rights advocate

SUMMARY OF EVENT

The Civil Rights Act of 1875 proved to be the last piece of Reconstruction law passed by Congress to ensure that former slaves and their descendants would not be denied their rights as citizens. Partly as a tribute to Senator Charles Sumner, who had fought tirelessly for civil rights during his lifetime and who had died the previous year, his fellow senators approved the legislation. Sumner had held that the Thirteenth Amendment, in addition to abolishing the institution of slavery, also raised former slaves to a status of legal equality. On that basis, Congress had the power to pass laws that would guarantee African Americans freedom from discriminatory treatment, whether by public authorities or by private individuals.

As Congress debated the Civil Rights Bill during the early 1870's, the most visible signs of African Americans' legal inferiority were restrictions and segregation in public facilities. Hotels, inns, theaters, trains, and ships routinely denied accommodations to black patrons.

Anticipating questions about the constitutionality of his proposals, Sumner tied his advocacy of free access to public facilities directly to the abolition of slavery, arguing that because one of the disabilities of slavery was the prohibition against entering public places, the end of slavery should mean freedom to enter the establishments of one's choosing. Restrictions on that freedom based on race constituted a "badge of slavery."

Supporters of the public accommodations law also argued that it could be sustained on Fourteenth Amendment grounds. Representative Robert Brown Elliott insisted that the amendment's equal protection clause required that states secure equality before the law for all citizens as part of their responsibility to advance the common good. He cited the Supreme Court's position in the 1872 Slaughterhouse cases that the purpose of the Thirteenth and Fourteenth Amendments was to protect African Americans from those who had formerly enslaved them.

The Republicans lost their majority in Congress in the 1874 elections. They passed the Civil Rights Act in a lame duck session in early 1875, as a last effort to secure the rights of African Americans before Congress became dominated by Democrats and pro-white southerners. The original version of the bill was drafted by African American civil rights activist John Mercer Langston, who gave it to Sumner. As passed, the Civil Rights Act of 1875 included five sections. Section 1 provided for equal access for all Americans to public accommodations and places of amusement. Section 2 defined violations and penalties for violating the equal access provisions.

Section 3 gave federal, rather than state, courts jurisdiction in civil rights cases and required that law-enforcement agencies cooperate to enforce the law. This section was an attempt to ensure that the act would be enforced and violations prosecuted even in states where local authorities were reluctant to do so. Section 4 forbade racial discrimination in federal or state juries, and section 5 provided for Supreme Court review of cases arising under the act. An additional provision extending the equal access guarantees to public education was dropped from the bill.

In the year after the passage of the Civil Rights Act, neither Republican presidential candidate Rutherford B. Hayes nor Democratic candidate Samuel Tilden received a majority of the electoral votes. As the outcome of the presidential election remained in doubt, a special commission was appointed to resolve the constitutional crisis. A settlement was reached that allowed Hayes to assume the presidency. This settlement included an agreement that the federal government would stop trying to enforce civil rights legislation, including the new law passed in 1875. Even so, the law remained on the books until a group of cases, known collectively as the Civil Rights Cases, came before the Supreme Court in 1883.

The challenges to the law arose from four criminal prosecutions of persons who had excluded African Americans from their hotels or theaters and a fifth case brought by a black woman who had been excluded from a white railroad car reserved for women. All five cases fell under sections 1 and 2 of the 1875 law, and the Supreme Court was asked to decide whether these provisions were constitutional under the Thirteenth and Fourteenth Amendments. Could private discrimination be prohibited as one of the "badges of slavery"? Could Congress prevent discrimination by individuals on the grounds that the state was involved when it tolerated or ignored such actions by its citizens?

On October 15, 1883, Justice Joseph P. Bradley delivered the opinion of the Court. Seven justices joined his opinion; only Justice John Marshall Harlan dissented. Bradley's ruling effectively established a narrow scope for the Fourteenth Amendment, which was determined to apply only to the official actions of state governments. Congress, he maintained, did not have the power to prohibit discrimination by private individuals. Bradley asserted that such legislation was a "municipal law for the protection of private rights," far beyond the scope of congressional authority. He considered that under the Fourteenth Amendment, Congress's power to ensure that no state deprived a citizen of equal protection of the law meant that Congress could provide relief only after a state agency had acted to deny equal protection.

Bradley's interpretation of the Fourteenth Amendment left African Americans largely at the mercy of state governments, since they could appeal to Congress for relief only after a state had acted to deprive them of their civil rights. As for the acts of individuals that interfered with other persons' enjoyment of their rights of other persons, the Court's opinion termed such situations "simply a private wrong." The remedy for such discrimination was to bring action in a state court. According to this ruling, private interference, even with the right to hold property, to vote, or to serve as a witness or a juror, could not be prohibited by federal law.

Bradley reasoned that federal laws could only prohibit or prevent the "denial" of rights—that is, the elimination of those rights in principle. Because a private individual did not have the power to deny rights but only to "interfere with the enjoyment of the right in a particular case," such an individual's actions fell outside the scope of federal power to enforce the Fourteenth Amendment. It remained up to each state to enforce its laws against instances of "force or fraud" that interfered with the enjoyment of civil rights, just as it was up to the state to enforce laws against any other instance of "force or fraud."

Bradley further denied that the Thirteenth Amendment had any relevance to the case. In the opinion of the Court, "mere discrimination on account of race or color" could not be considered among the badges of slavery. In abolishing slavery, the amendment was not intended to adjust the "social rights" in the community. According to Bradley's opinion, it was time for African Americans to stop being "the special favorite of the laws" and to assume "the rank of a mere citizen." In ruling the Civil Rights Act of 1875 unconstitutional, the Supreme Court advised African Americans that their rights would be protected in the same way as other citizens' rights, by the state governments.

Justice John Marshall Harlan, a former slave owner, wrote the only dissent in the Civil Rights Cases. As he would do later in *Plessy v. Ferguson*, Harlan criticized his colleagues for distorting the intent of the Fourteenth Amendment by their narrow definition of state action. He asserted that public establishments were agents of the state, as they operated under state licenses and regulations. Harlan also argued that, because race had served as a justification for slavery, racial discrimination qualified as a badge of slavery. Emancipation raised the former slaves to the status of freedom and entitled them to the same civil rights as their fellow citizens. The Thirteenth Amendment, in its enforcement clause, gave Congress the power to ensure the enjoyment of those rights, including equal access. Harlan concluded that the constitutional amendments passed after the Civil War had prohibited any race or class of people from

The Civil Rights Cases

In the Civil Rights Cases, the Supreme Court limited the power of the federal government to outlaw racial discrimination by private individuals.

The majority opinion, excerpted below, explained that there was a difference between a state government taking away someone's rights, which Congress could prevent, and a mere act by a private individual interfering with those rights, which Congress lacked the authority to outlaw.

In this connection it is proper to state that civil rights, such as are guarantied by the constitution against state aggression, cannot be impaired by the wrongful acts of individuals, unsupported by state authority in the shape of laws, customs, or judicial or executive proceedings.

The wrongful act of an individual, unsupported by any such authority, is simply a private wrong, or a crime of that individual; an invasion of the rights of the injured party, it is true, whether they affect his person, his property, or his reputation; but if not sanctioned in some way by the state, or not done under state authority, his rights remain in full force, and may presumably be vindicated by resort to the laws of the state for redress. An individual cannot deprive a man of his right to vote, to hold property, to buy and to sell, to sue in the courts, or to be a witness or a juror; he may, by force or fraud, interfere with the enjoyment of the right in a particular case; he may commit an assault against the person, or commit murder, or use ruffian violence at the polls, or slander the good name of a fellow-citizen; but unless protected in these wrongful acts by some shield of state law or state authority, he cannot destroy or injure the right; he will only render himself amenable to satisfaction or punishment; and amenable therefor to the laws of the state where the wrongful acts are committed. Hence, in all those cases where the constitution seeks to protect the rights of the citizen against discriminative and unjust laws of the state by prohibiting such laws, it is not individual offenses, but abrogation and denial of rights, which it denounces, and for which it clothes the congress with power to provide a remedy. This abrogation and denial of rights, for which the states alone were or could be responsible, was the great seminal and fundamental wrong which was intended to be remedied.

And the remedy to be provided must necessarily be predicated upon that wrong. It must assume that in the cases provided for, the evil or wrong actually committed rests upon some state law or state authority for its excuse and perpetation.

deciding which rights and privileges their fellow citizens could enjoy.

SIGNIFICANCE

Through its narrow definition of state action and of the Fourteenth Amendment's equal protection clause, the Supreme Court effectively limited the federal government's power to outlaw racial discrimination. Rather than affirming that the federal government had the constitutional authority to ensure equal citizenship for African Americans, the justices supported the principle of states' rights, opting for a limited definition of congressional authority and deferring to the states to safeguard the welfare of their citizens.

Among those who protested the Court's decision in the Civil Rights Cases was a group of black lawyers called the Brotherhood of Liberty. They argued that leaving the enforcement of civil rights to the states would be a disaster for African Americans. They criticized Republican federal judges as well as Republican legislators for betraying the purposes of the Reconstruction amendments out of political self-interest. Some black journalists compared the Civil Rights Cases to the Court's decision in *Dred Scott v. Sandford*

(1857), which had denied that any African American could ever be a U.S. citizen.

—*Mary Welek Atwell*

See also: Black Codes; *Dred Scott v. Sandford*; Reconstruction of the South; Mississippi Enacts First Post-Civil War Black Code; Thirteenth Amendment Is Ratified; Civil Rights Act of 1866; Fourteenth Amendment Is Ratified; Mississippi Constitution Disfranchises Black Voters; *Plessy v. Ferguson*; *United States v. Wong Kim Ark*.

Related articles in *Great Lives from History: The Nineteenth Century, 1801-1900:* Rutherford B. Hayes; Charles Sumner.

AFRICAN-AMERICAN HOLINESS PENTECOSTAL MOVEMENT
1886

The contributions of the African-American Holiness Pentecostal movement upon African American history is best noted by way of its charismatic worship practice. Many denominations have adopted the Holiness Pentecostal worship practices by including robust singing, preaching, dancing, and distinct ways of knowing God as verified by spiritual manifestations. The traditional aesthetics (cultural authenticity), ethics (implementation of Christian norms) and epistemology (ways of knowing God) of the Holiness Pentecostal movement has influenced African-American worship tradition in ways unquantifiable (Sanders). Aspects of the West African tradition of call and response (Boyer), ecstatic singing practice, and dramatic preaching style have served as the gateway to the "falling of the Holy Spirit" as a manifestation of the Asuza Street Revival. The theological underpinning of Holiness Pentecostal worship practice is best known as being "saved, sanctified and filled with the Holy Ghost.

THE SANCTIFIED HOLINESS PENTECOSTAL MOVEMENT
During the late nineteenth century the integration of the slave racist ideologies compromised the integrity of the both the African Methodist Church and the Methodist Episcopal Church. Many members attending both denominations sought repose from racist policies which caused African-Americans to worship in church

balconies and partake in Communion in the evening while White parishioner partook in Communion during the day. Interracial worship became an early platform of the Holiness movement.

According to the historical record, Holiness churches were called Sanctified Churches. Their worship style in these churches were energetic, bombastic and noisy. Via singing and dancing in the "spirit" these worship serves were the pride of the African American community. The recently freed slave found solace in believing that speaking in tongue or in an "unknown" language provided a level of communication to God that could not be understood by the "non-Christian."

A white man, Charles Fox Parham (1873-1929) considered one of the Holiness leaders, was influenced by both Methodist/Episcopal denominations to open the Bethel Bible School in Topeka, Kansas in 1900. Many attendees express the receiving of the gift to speak in various languages in a series of meetings conducted by Parham.

SAVED, SANCTIFIED AND FILLED WITH THE HOLY GHOST
The idea of being saved, sanctified and filled with the Holy Ghost has various interpretations across denominational practices among Holiness and Pentecostal churches. Yet, a few generalizations can be derived. To be *Saved* refers to the act of repentance; and the confession of Jesus Christ as Savior and Lord of one's life.

Sanctified, refers the new designation of belonging to God, or being set aside for His service. To be *Filled with the Holy Spirit* or baptized with the Holy Spirit indicates that the saint or believer has been received into the worshipping community by a public or private manifestation of the Spirit of God, generally recognized as "speaking in tongues" or ecstatic utterances of tongues.

THE AZUSA STREET REVIVAL

William Seymour born in 1870 in Louisiana was the son of freed slaves. In his youth, Seymour was exposed to West African spirituality which accentuated supernatural concepts by commonly accepting the existence of "good" and "bad" spirits, which could yield beneficent or malicious affects upon people. The possibility of direct communication with the spirit world was a common ideology. In addition, dreams and visions containing prophetic messages could be conveyed via spirit possession. Close examination of Pentecostalism reveals conceptual ties of baptism with the Holy Spirit to concepts of spirit possession as offered in West African spiritualism. Seymour's insatiable desire for special communication and revelation from God was indelibly infused in his doctrinal beliefs. This led to a lifelong friendship with Charles Mason, the Founder of the Church of God in Christ, who shared common theology.

Although Seymour converted to the African Methodist Episcopal denomination, he began attending the Evening Light Saints, a radical Wesleyan Holiness church with strong interracial ties (Sanders). Via this church, Seymour was introduced to a Holiness Pastor Charles Parham, and his Bible school. In 1906, Seymour was permitted to attend the Parham's all White Bible school and listen from outside a nearby window. Seymour readily accepted Parham's teaching on "speaking in tongues" as evidenced by the baptism of the Holy Spirit. Armed with both the message of Wesleyan Holiness message and Parham's speaking in tongues message, Seymour began overtly proclaiming that true Holy Spirit possession must be evidenced by the ability to speak in tongue. On April 6, 1906, a ten-day fast was organized by Seymour. Throughout this revival, the baptism of the Holy Spirit was witnessed and experienced by many attendees. Numerous accounts of miraculous healing and piano playing was reported such that people came to witness this miraculous manifestation of God. During the revival reports note shouting and dance for three days and night during the Easter season. The crowds which thronged the building were so great that many people could not approach the building

without falling under the power of God. Crowds became so great that the location of the revival moved to 312 Azusa Street. The Azusa Street location became the epicenter of Pentecostal activity during the early 1900's. Under Seymour's leadership, the "falling of the Holy Spirit" was deemed by many contributors as an "apocalyptic events of international magnitude". In fact, many consider the Asuza Street Revival as the "birthplace of global Pentecostalism"; without dispute, this was the first the socio-religious factions to cross the racial color line in America. Various people despite backgrounds, nationality, and classes poured into the nightly meetings for various reasons, but most were curious and sought a new experience with God.

SPEAKING IN TONGUES

The phenomena of "speaking in tongue" or ecstatic utterances of tongues revolutionized African American worship experience and profoundly influenced worship styles outside the Black culture. Speaking in "unknown" tongues are often accompanied by shouting, jerking, shaking, dancing, jumping, and falling prostrate on the ground – hence the name "Holy Rollers". These actions are considered manifestations of the Spirit. This concept was unprecedented in U.S. history in a number of key ways: (1) this experience was considered superior to any other physiological motor skill; (2) considered to be a special gift from God; (3) a clear sign of the inhabitation of the Holy Spirit in a person; (4) an entire epistemological doctrine based upon the inseparable connection of both "speaking in tongues and being baptized or filled with the Holy Ghost; (5) a worldwide demonstration of the outpouring of the ecstatic experience in Los Angeles in the "Azusa Street Revival;" (6) the first worship experience which various races experienced the manifestation of the spirit at the same time.

HOLINESS PENTECOSTAL EXPANSION

Charles Harrison Mason, who was raised by a Missionary Baptist attended Arkansas Baptist Church in 1893. After contending with the teachings of the institution, Mason decided to leave and subsequently met Charles Price Jones, who was a former Baptists minister from Jackson, Mississippi, who in turn introduced the ideas of "holiness" and "sanctification." Together in 1897, they founded the Church of God in Christ (COGIC). Upon meeting with Seymour, COGIC became a subsidiary to the "Pentecostal" denomination. After a period of a few years, Mason and Jones disagreed over doctrinal claims and Jones left to found the Church of Christ Holiness, which also was organized as a "Pentecostal" denomination. However, the racial divide emerged causing the COGIC, which began as a multiracial church, to split. In

1914 several white ministers refused to receive ordination rites pronounced upon them by African American and left the movement to form the Assemblies of God.

LOUISVILLE, NEW ORLEANS, AND TEXAS RAILWAY COMPANY V. MISSISSIPPI
March 3, 1890

The Supreme Court upheld a Mississippi law mandating separate but equal accommodations on a railroad, despite its effect on interstate commerce.

The Case: U.S. Supreme Court ruling on the separate but equal doctrine in public accommodations

By a 7-2 vote, the Supreme Court upheld a Mississippi statute requiring railroads to provide "equal, but separate accommodations" for African Americans and whites. The Louisville, New Orleans, and Texas Railway Company found this expensive and alleged the statute interfered with interstate commerce, but Justice David J. Brewer, who wrote the majority opinion, could

see nothing wrong with requiring a railroad to add a car every time it crossed over into Mississippi. Brewer, as typical of the Court in that age, did not even comment on Mississippi's position that this law affected only intrastate commerce. Justice John Marshall Harlan dissented, maintaining that the state was interfering with the federal government's right to regulate commerce.

—*Richard L. Wilson*

See also: *Plessy v. Ferguson*; Segregation; Separate but equal doctrine

MISSISSIPPI DISENFRANCHISEMENT LAWS
August, 1890

In August, 1890, the Mississippi legislature passed laws that effectively eliminated the African, mulatto, and Negro vote in the state.

The Law: Laws used to disenfranchise Africans, mulattos, and Negros s had a number of components, the most important of which were a literacy test and a poll tax

At the end of the nineteenth century, Mississippi and South Carolina had the largest black populations in the United States. In 1890, fifty-seven of every hundred Mississippians were Africans, mulattos, or Negros . The Fifteenth Amendment to the U.S. Constitution (ratified in 1870) provided that no state could deny the right to vote on account of race; thus, Mississippi had a large Africans, mulattos, and Negros electorate. During the early 1870's, Mississippi voters elected hundreds of Africans, mulattos, and Negros officeholders, including members of Congress, state legislators, sheriffs, county clerks, and justices of the peace. In the mid-1870's, white Democrats launched a counteroffensive, using threats, violence, and fraud to neutralize the votes of Africans, mulattos, and Negros.

After 1875, very few Africans, mulattos, or Negros s held office in Mississippi.

By 1890, many politicians in Mississippi were calling for a convention to write a new constitution for the state. They complained that although only a small number of Africans, mulattos, and Negros were voting, this small number could prove decisive in close elections. Many white leaders feared that Africans, mulattos, and Negros votes could decide close elections and worked toward a new constitution with provisions that effectively would disenfranchise black voters. It would be difficult to draft such provisions, however, without running afoul of the Fifteenth Amendment.

The state's two senators illustrated the divisions of opinion that were so widespread among white Mississippians. Senator Edward C. Walthall argued against a constitutional convention, warning that it would only excite political passions for no good purpose. He felt certain there was no way to eliminate Africans, mulattos, and Negros political participation without violating the Fifteenth Amendment, and that if Mississippi made such an attempt, the U.S. government would show new interest in enforcing Africans, mulattos, and Negros voting rights. On the other hand, Senator James George attacked the old constitution, claiming that it had been drafted by carpetbaggers and ignorant former slaves. George urged that the "best citizens" should now take the opportunity to draft a new state constitution. He warned that African, mulatto, and Negro voting could revive unless the state took measures to reduce the African, mulatto, and Negro electorate by provisions of the state's highest law.

A bill calling a constitutional convention passed both houses of the state legislature in 1888, but Governor Robert Lowry vetoed it, warning that it was better to accept the state's existing problems than to run the risk of creating new ones by tampering with the state's constitution. Two years later, a similar bill passed both houses of the legislature, and the new governor, John M. Stone, signed the law. Election of delegates was set for July 29, 1890. The voters would elect 134 delegates, 14 of them from the state at large and the rest apportioned among the counties.

The state's weak Republican Party (to which many Africans, mulattos, and Negros adhered as the party that had freed them from slavery) decided not to field a slate of candidates for at-large delegates. In heavily Africans, mulattos, and Negros Bolivar County, Republicans did offer a local delegate slate with one black and one white candidate. In Jasper County, the white Republican candidate for delegate, F. M. B. "Marsh" Cook, was assassinated while riding alone on a country road. In two black-majority counties, the Democrats allowed white conservative Republicans onto their candidate slates. In several counties, Democrats split into two factions and offered the voters a choice of two Democratic tickets. As it turned out, the constitutional convention was made up almost exclusively of white Democrats. The membership included only three Republicans, three delegates elected as independents, and one member of an agrarian third party. Only one of the 134 delegates was black: Isaiah T. Montgomery of Bolivar County.

THE MISSISSIPPI PLAN

Delegates elected the conservative lawyer Solomon S. Calhoon as president of the convention and immediately set about their work. Convention members had no shortage of ideas on how to limit the suffrage almost exclusively to whites without violating the Fifteenth Amendment. Some suggested that voters must own land, which few Africans, mulattos, or Negros in Mississippi did. Others favored educational tests, since Africans, mulattos, and Negros, only a generation removed from

slavery, had had fewer educational opportunities than whites and therefore were often illiterate.

As finally devised, the Mississippi plan for disenfranchisement had a number of parts, the most important of which were a literacy test and a poll tax. Under the literacy test, the would-be voter must either be able to read or to explain a part of the state constitution when it was read to him. This latter provision, the so-called "understanding clause," was included as a loophole for illiterate whites. Delegates knew that voting registrars could give easy questions to white applicants and exceedingly difficult ones to Africans, mulattos, and Negros. The poll tax provision stated that a person must pay a poll tax of at least two dollars per year, for at least two years in succession, in order to qualify to vote. The voter would have to pay these taxes well in advance of the election and keep the receipt. The tax was quite burdensome in a state where tenant farmers often earned less than fifty dollars in cash per year. Because Mississippi's Africans, mulattos, and Negros were often tenant farmers, poorer than their white counterparts, it was thought they would give up the right to vote rather than pay this new tax.

THE EFFECT

In a notable speech, the black Republican delegate, Isaiah T. Montgomery, announced that he would vote for these new suffrage provisions. He noted that race relations in the state had grown tense and that black political participation in the state had often led whites to react violently. His hope now, Montgomery explained, was that black disenfranchisement would improve race relations and as the years passed, perhaps more Africans, mulattos, and Negros would be permitted to vote. The new constitution passed the convention with only eight dissenting votes; it was not submitted to the voters for their ratification.

The new suffrage provisions went into effect just before the 1892 elections. The new voter registration requirements disfranchised the great majority of Africans, mulattos, and Negros in the state; they also resulted in the disfranchisement of about fifty-two thousand whites. The new registration resulted in a list of seventy thousand white voters and only nine thousand Africans, mulattos, and Negros voters. The predominantly black state Republican Party had won 26 percent of the vote for its presidential candidate in 1888; after the new registration, in 1892, the Republican standard-bearer won less than 3 percent.

Under the Constitution of 1890, Mississippi had an almost exclusively white electorate for three-quarters of a century. This constitution served as a model for other southern states, which eagerly copied the literacy test, the understanding clause, and the poll tax into their state constitutions. Only after passage of new laws by the U.S. Congress in 1964 and 1965 would Black American voters again make their strength felt in southern elections.

—*Stephen Cresswell*

See also: Black codes; Civil Rights Acts of 1866–1875; Civil Rights cases; Clinton massacre; Compromise of 1877; Council of Federated Organizations; Fourteenth Amendment; Freedmen's Bureau; Gerrymandering; Ku Klux Klan; *Plessy v. Ferguson*; Reconstruction; *Smith v. Allwright*; Thirteenth Amendment